CRITICAL THINKING: ARGUMENT AND ARGUMENTATION

SECOND EDITION

CRITICAL THINKING: ARGUMENT AND ARGUMENTATION

SECOND EDITION

JEAN SAINDON
YORK UNIVERSITY

PETER JOHN KREK
RYERSON UNIVERSITY

NELSON / EDUCATION

NELSON / EDUCATION

Critical Thinking: Argument and Argumentation, Second Edition
by Jean Saindon and Peter John Krek

Vice President, Editorial Higher Education:
Anne Williams

Acquisitions Editor:
Maya Castle

Marketing Manager:
Terry Fedorkiw

Developmental Editor:
Toni Chahley

Production Service:
MPS Ltd.

Copy Editor:
Susan James

Proofreader:
MPS Ltd.

Indexer:
Maria Sosnowski

Senior Production Coordinator:
Ferial Suleman

Design Director:
Ken Phipps

Managing Designer:
Franca Amore

Interior Design:
Trinh Truong

Cover Design:
Trin Truong

Compositor:
MPS Ltd.

Printer:
RR Donnelley

Library and Archives Canada Cataloguing in Publication Data

Saindon, Jean Emmett
    Critical thinking : argument and argumentation / Jean Saindon and Peter John Krek. – 2nd ed.

Previous edition published under title: Argument and argumentation.
Includes bibliographical references and index.

ISBN 978-0-17-666100-7

    I. Krek, Peter John, 1972-   II. Title.

BC177.S18 2013 168
C2012-906924-8

ISBN-13: 978-0-17-666100-7
ISBN-10: 0-17-666100-X

BRIEF CONTENTS

CONTENTS

PREFACE

We wrote this text to move beyond traditional approaches to critical thinking and help students develop a broad set of skills that they could integrate into their daily lives. The desire to write such a text also arose because we are disheartened by the level of personal and public discourse we witness within and outside of the classroom, especially in the public arena, and would like to celebrate the role of reasoned discourse as the foundation of personal and public life.

Much of public discourse has abandoned the attempt to be *reasonable*. It relies on sound bites instead of reasoned discussion. Political and social commentators heap invective and abuse on their opponents, distort their ideas, and repeat unexamined platitudes as established truths. Politicians use attack ads instead of reasoned discussion of policy. Scientists use disinformation to discredit the scientific consensus on issues such as climate change. Fanatics of all stripes believe any tactic is justified so long as their side "wins."

On the personal level, individuals tend to believe all opinions are equally true, that tolerance requires that we accept any idea, no matter how absurd or unsupported, and that ethics is just a matter of opinion and one can believe anything one wants. Some even extend this to the acceptance of scientific facts: evolution is just a theory, a view held by several U.S. presidents; climate change is a matter of opinion; and the age of the Earth and the most effective sexual education are dictated by one's religious beliefs, not scientific evidence.

In all of this, the very idea of passionate reasoned discourse has been lost. Much of the public no longer knows what reasoned discourse and critical thinking entails. We wrote this text to help correct this. If we can raise the level of public discourse even slightly for our students and help introduce a more civil, rational basis for discourse in the public and private arenas, then we will have contributed something, however modest, to the creation of a more civil society. While we realize that one text is not sufficient, our hope is that by modelling what reasoned discourse is, demonstrating the skills of critical thinking necessary for such discourse, and encouraging others to see that this enterprise is a valuable one, then we will have made a solid start.

Jean's friend and colleague, Dr. John King, once said that higher education teaches four basic skills: to read critically and analytically, to reason effectively (both critically and synthetically), to research, and to write. Jean would add a fifth basic skill to this list: to reflect. Most critical thinking texts address the critical reasoning dimension. This text addresses the reading, reasoning, and writing dimensions.

We also wrote this text to integrate the recent interest in argumentation with traditional critical thinking. Much of our reasoning is done verbally, yet we still teach students largely based on written materials. While this text retains much of the traditional focus of critical thinking texts on analyzing written arguments, it expands the focus to include the developing of one's own arguments and verbal argumentation. We see all three as central to developing a more reasonable society. While teaching students to critically analyze arguments and texts is central to developing good critical thinking skills, writing and developing one's own arguments is also central to the development of student's reasoning abilities. Too often teaching the written development of arguments is left to composition courses, English courses, or simply not done. If we want students to make and present good arguments, we have to teach them how to identify and construct good arguments.

One can learn the techniques of critical thinking, argument, and fallacy analysis, and use them as weapons to intimidate and coerce others. Our focus on argumentation is meant to counter that by introducing the idea that we are reasoning with others, that reasoning with others has many purposes, including understanding our reasoning partner, being understood, and persuading rationally, that reasoning with others involves a shared commitment to the goal of seeking the truth about an issue and being constrained in that pursuit by high standards, and that reasoning with others involves a set of shared norms. Critical thinking is often taught (or understood by students) as a way of "being critical of," of challenging the ideas of others as a way of dismissing their ideas. That is, we contend, a very limited idea of what critical thinking is about. Critical thinking involves challenge and response to challenges, not to score points, but to understand and seek the truth about an issue. As such, critical thinking and argumentation is as much about our understanding of self and our positions and the positions of others as it is about identifying the weaknesses in the arguments of others. We help others to improve their arguments through rigorous critique. And we learn to improve our own through equally rigorous critique and our response to that critique.

We wrote this text with these ideas in mind. We believe that critical thinking and the rigorous defense and challenge of positions through the arguments we use to support them is essential for understanding who we are and what we believe, for our interactions with others, and for achieving and maintaining a reasonable society, which is the proper foundation of democracy, and more importantly, civil society, in the true sense of the word.

Audience and Uses

This text is designed for introductory courses in informal logic, critical thinking, fallacies, essay writing, and argument and argumentation. It can also be used as a secondary text for upper-level university courses that focus on argumentation, the analysis of arguments, conceptual analysis, essay writing, and areas that use these skills, including philosophy, humanities, social studies, and science studies.

The modular format of *Critical Thinking: Argument and Argumentation* allows instructors the flexibility to use the text in a variety of ways, for a range of audiences and classes. Some modules or parts of modules can be used independently of one another to meet instructors' individual teaching needs. Typical informal logic courses may focus on Modules 1 through 7. Courses devoted to the study of fallacies can concentrate on Modules 1 through 3, and then 5, and then focus heavily on Module 7. Instructors focusing on argumentation may use selective parts of Modules 1 through 3 and then concentrate on Modules 10 and 11. Those who wish to emphasize developing written arguments can focus on Modules 1, 2, 5, 6, 8, and 10. Someone interested in critical thinking, but not having time to devote several weeks to fallacies, could use Modules 1 through 6 and selected parts of 7.

This text is designed to be used in conjunction with the accompanying Premium Website (www.criticalthinking2e.nelson.com), which provides answers to the Quick Quizzes and additional exercises.

New to This Edition

The new second edition of *Critical Thinking: Argument and Argumentation* has been revised and reorganized to empower learners to build effective arguments and to analyze arguments effectively.

Module 1: Getting Started in Argument and Argumentation has been substantially rewritten. It now includes the core elements of issue analysis from the former Module 9. It also integrates argumentation into critical thinking and provides a stronger defence of the role of critical thinking in effective reasoning. *Module 2: Clarifying Meaning* has been refined and edited for flow. *Module 3: Analyzing Arguments* now includes several new tables that have been added for better flow and understanding; we have included, for example, a table on inference indicators. *Module 4: Assessing Deductive Arguments* includes a substantially revised section on necessary and sufficient conditions. *Module 5: Assessing Non-Deductive Arguments* has been rewritten to shift the focus from inductive arguments to the broader category of non-deductive arguments. *Module 6: Assessing Claims* has been rewritten with a stronger emphasis on assessing ethical claims in a non-relativistic way. *Module 7: Fallacies* has been reorganized and rewritten. The module organizes the fallacies in terms of the argumentation model introduced in Module 1 to make it easier for students to understand and remember the fallacies. The basic pedagogical tools of the first edition (including lookalike, not a fallacy, and neutralizing fallacies) have been moved to earlier in the module so that they can be integrated into the teaching of all of the fallacies rather than acting as a stand-alone at the end. *Module 8: Analyzing and Assessing Extended Arguments* has been completely rewritten to simplify both the analytical model and the example used. The example for analysis is integrated with the ongoing dialogue that starts the module. *Module 9: Conceptual Analysis, Module 10: Argumentation* (formerly Module 11), and *Module 11: Written Argumentation* (formerly Module 12) have been revised for clarity.

Pedagogical Features

Boasting a beautiful new four-colour design, the second edition of *Critical Thinking: Argument and Argumentation* also includes pedagogical elements designed to enhance student understanding.

NEW! A Dialogue on Copyright and Piracy boxes appear at the beginning of each module. In these boxes, the authors of the book engage in a dialogue that models some of the skills to be taken up in each module. Using the timely topic of copyright and piracy as a topic of discussion, these boxes provide continuity across all the modules, and provide students with a cumulative application and illustration of the key concepts covered in the text. In some modules these boxes serve as a basis for analysis of the skills from that module. In essence, the A Dialogue on Copyright and Piracy boxes model the dynamics of argumentation.

A DIALOGUE ON COPYRIGHT AND PIRACY— CONTINUED

Peter: I want to go back to a couple of your arguments. In a previous discussion, you claimed that Internet piracy (sorry, downloading of copyright material without authorization) harms no one. What do you base that on?

Jean: Various artists have encouraged downloading of their songs and said it actually helps them.

Peter: How many artists?

Jean: I don't know, a lot.

Quick Quizzes are located at key points within each module and give students the opportunity to test their understanding of the concepts as they are discussed. Answers to the Quick Quiz questions are located on the Premium Website for the text at www.criticalthinking2e.nelson.com.

QUICK QUIZ 7.17

Straw Person

(A) Identify which of the following arguments are straw person fallacies;
(B) For those that are, explain how the criteria for this fallacy apply in this example; and
(C) For those that are not, explain why you do not consider it to be a fallacy of straw person.

1. *Original source - biology text:* Although we have many transition fossils for the large families, we have not yet found such transition fossils for many specific species. And we have none for the soft-body species. Nor are we likely to find any, since these creatures do not produce fossils.
   Argument: Even evolutionists admit that evolution is impossible. If evolution were true, then we should find many fossils for transition species. Yet a noted biology text claims that we don't have fossil remains showing any transition species, nor are we ever likely to.

2. Lara: "Unless we construct a nuclear power plant in this area within the next 10 years, we will not be able to meet the significantly growing demands for electrical power in the province."
   Arkadi: "What you are saying is that you don't care what happens to the plant life and wildlife in the area or even to human lives that might be dislocated by the building of this plant."

3. The core claim in evolution is that species evolve over time. Yet we have no direct evidence of this. The best we have is fossil evidence or DNA evidence. But neither establishes that evolution has occurred. Both are compatible with the hypothesis that species are fixed and do not change.

Answers to the Quick Quizzes are available on the Premium Website at www.criticalthinking2e.nelson.com.

NEW! Running Glossary. Key terms are bolded in the text, with definitions provided in the margin for easy reference.

An *ethical rule* is a rule of behaviour or judgment that identifies a specific kind of action as right or wrong (such as, "stealing is wrong" or "you should not lie"). Ethical rules are concerned with a relatively specific kind of action. If we probe deeper to find out why stealing is or should be wrong, we may come up with a variety of reasons. For example, someone might say stealing is wrong because it violates a basic agreement we have with others in our society to treat them fairly. In this case, there is a basic principle, namely, we have an agreement with others in our society to treat them fairly. Within this framework, taking someone's property without permission is treating them unfairly. The basic value enshrined in this principle is the fair treatment of all members of one's society. Different ethical systems can be based on different fundamental values (such as, obedience to the will of a deity, satisfying the needs and wants of human beings as living creatures, respect for the autonomy of individuals, and human choice, are but a few that have served as the foundations of ethical systems).

> An **ethical rule** is a rule of behaviour or judgment that identifies a specific kind of action as right or wrong.

NEW! Writing and Argumentation Exercises have been added to the end of each module. These exercises build on the specific skills developed in each module. The instructor can assign these to give students additional practice and experience with writing arguments and engaging in verbal argumentation. Suggested answers to these exercises have been provided in the Instructor's Manual.

Argumentation Exercise: Replying to a Challenge

Continue the dialogue between Ramon and Tali (page 157) by developing how Ramon could respond to Tali's challenges by (a) rejecting her counterexamples (or showing they are not a relevant difference); and (b) accepting her counterexample as relevant and limiting the scope of his claim. Develop several further counterexamples Tali could raise and give possible responses for Ramon. Identify the kind of response.

Writing Skills Exercise: Supporting Your Claims

Write a one page argument essay (an essay in which you defend an argument). The essay should contain at least two of conceptual, empirical, and normative claims. For each statement in the essay:

1. identify the kind of claim;
2. whether the claim needs support (i.e., is contentious or could be challenged);
3. whether the claim is supported; and
4. what kind of claim it is.

Unique Approach of This Text

A number of unique features characterize this text:

- **Distinctly Canadian:** This is a Canadian text with the vast majority of examples being Canadian, focusing on issues and using exercises of immediate concern to Canadian students — same-sex rights, euthanasia, gender issues, and issues around social media, for example.

- **Written and Verbal Argumentation:** While treating the traditional elements of argument analysis and assessment and fallacies, the text focuses on argumentation, both written and verbal. Integrated writing and argumentation components are also included in every module. Written argumentation exercises are included in the Writing Skills Exercises at the end of each module. Verbal argumentation is included in the dialogues that start each module and in the Argumentation Exercise at the end of each module.

- **Dynamics of Argumentation:** Includes material on the dynamics of argumentation, including challenging and responding to arguments, and material on developing arguments.

- **Diversity of Coverage:** The text contains not only the traditional critical thinking topics but also materials on writing and argumentation.

- **Current and Relevant:** Throughout the text we have included discussion of contemporary controversial issues, including euthanasia, same-sex marriage, human origins, sexuality, and science and religion.

- **Treatment of Fallacies:** Treatment of fallacies includes the role of context, what is not a fallacy, lookalikes, and neutralizing a fallacy. Its unique treatment of some standard topics (such as methods for neutralizing fallacies, identifying lookalikes, and incorporating challenges and responses as part of argument analysis) distinguishes this text from other works in the field.

Ancillaries

Instructor Ancillaries

Instructor's Manual. The Instructor's Manual to accompany *Critical Thinking: Argument and Argumentation* has been prepared by the textbook authors. This manual contains answers for the Argumentation and Writing Skills Exercises in the book, as well as the Questions for Discussion found on the Premium Website. It also contains additional short answer questions that instructors can use for exams or assignments.

Premium Website

Nelson Education's Premium Website brings course concepts to life with interactive learning and exam preparation tools that integrate with the printed textbook. Students can activate their knowledge through Quick Quiz answers, self-test questions, and questions for discussion that can be used as assignments or in online discussion forums.

The Premium Website provides immediate feedback that enables students to connect results to the work they have just produced, improving their learning curve. It encourages contact between students and instructors. You can select to monitor your students' level of engagement, correlating their efforts to their outcomes. You can even use quizzes to practice "Just in Time" teaching by tracking results in the Engagement Tracker and customizing your lesson plans to address their learning needs.

Watch student comprehension and engagement soar as your class engages with this Premium Website. Ask your Nelson representative for a demo today.

Student Ancillaries

Critical Thinking: Argument and Argumentation includes a Premium Website, which helps you make the grade.

The Premium Website includes:

- Answers to the Quick Quizzes found in the textbook and interactive learning tools, including:

  ○ Self-Test Questions with instant feedback.

  ○ Questions for Discussion.

Acknowledgments

From Jean Saindon

To the scholars who reviewed this text, for your thoughtful, helpful, and stimulating comments, thank you:

Laura Byrne, University of Ottawa
Jonathan Katz, Kwantlen Polytechnic University
Iva Apostolova, Carleton University
Peter Raabe, University of the Fraser Valley
Patrick Walsh, University of Manitoba

To all of my students in Modes of Reasoning, for whom this text is written, for your challenges and inspiring enthusiasm for the material, thank you.

To my students in philosophy and in natural science and science studies who have been exposed to parts of this material and responded enthusiastically, thank you.

To Dr. Peter Krek, for taking on this project, encouraging and supporting me and providing me with key ideas and a close watch to prevent my going too far astray, and for being an exemplary and inspiring teacher, thank you, my friend.

To Dr. John King, an exemplar of good critical thinking, for your challenges, provocations, and conversations over the years, thank you, my friend.

To those who have sustained, nurtured, and encouraged me, and been inspirations in life and critical thinking in so many different areas: Geon van der Wyst and Aleksander Antonijevich, Rob Gentry and Alycia Chambers, Kate Krug, Tali Thompson, Richard Dickinson and Chris Doran, Roy Salole and Shari Salole, Chris Johnston and Kristen Millen-Johnston, Joe Rudyk and Angela Korwan, Anjana Dooling, and many others too numerous to name, thank you, my friends.

Finally, to Kathie Conlin-Saindon, without whom this project would not have been possible, for being an inspired educator, practitioner, and living exemplar of critical thinking, who has sustained, supported, inspired, and challenged me, and been my lifeline to the world for the past fifteen years, thank you for coming into my life, sharing my passions, including critical thinking, and encouraging me to be more than

I thought I ever could be. *Ensemble d'avantage* — "together we are more" — our life vision and inspiration and a fitting axiom for argumentation and for living a good life. Thank you, my love.

From Peter John Krek

To my parents for encouraging me to think and express myself (despite the fact that this often resulted in their ideas and practices being endlessly challenged) and for their understanding of the learning curve involved in such an undertaking; my brother Michael for being himself and his appreciation; and to my grandmother, Amalija Krek, whose erudition and edge was unmatched by anyone else I have ever met since and will likely ever meet again.

To Kenneth Montague, while at University of Guelph, for first introducing to me the subject and skill of philosophy in a way that would change my life path for the better, and for his support and encouragement while at Ryerson University.

To Patricia Huntington, while at American University, for generously offering her tutelage and friendship at the Master's level and beyond, and for demonstrating that academic pursuits can be rigorous without being impractical or inhuman.

To my friends for their endless understanding and support of what was undoubtedly an awkward journey: Julie Gourley, Virginia Butler-Alderman, Charlene Casey, Slobodan Perovic, Ljiljana Radenovic, Burcu Gurkan, Linda Carozza, Kevin Buzinski, Patti Babin, Chrissy Pappas, Alexander Jay Brown, Glen Bazouzi, Charlie Guiang, André Voshart, Fiammetta Yack, Linda Rees-Shaw, Mario DeLucia, Nicola Sutton, Peter Khan, Tara Wilson, Julia Fischer, Logan Adams, Jami Steele and all those too numerous to be named individually.

To Jean Saindon, while at York University and well beyond, for being a beacon of decency and unconditional support at a time when there was no obligation for him doing so. You are a rare and decent human being, and I am truly happy to have continued to develop our friendship through our collaboration on this project.

Finally to all, *pozdravlja, pokriza in poljublja* — greetings, a blessing and a kiss!

ABOUT THE AUTHORS

JEAN SAINDON

Jean Saindon received his honours B.A. (1969; with majors in philosophy, sociology, English literature, and humanities (17th & 18th centuries), and minors in East Asian studies and psychology) from the University of Kansas, his M.A. (1974) in philosophy from York University, and his Ph.D. (1978) in philosophy from York University. His research and teaching have been multi-disciplinary, including critical thinking and argumentation; the philosophy, sociology, and biology of sex and gender; applied ethics; epistemology; and the philosophy and social studies of science, with particular emphasis on biology and evolutionary theory. He has taught philosophy, sociology, anthropology, genetics, natural science, science and technology studies, and, at Osgoode Hall Law School, alternate dispute resolution. He was named a Woodrow Wilson Fellow, and did post-doctoral work at the Institute for the Advanced Study of Human Sexuality in San Francisco with Wardell Pomeroy, co-author of the Kinsey Report. He also worked as a management consultant and Director of Training and Development for over fifteen years at an equity-based consulting firm, focusing on organizational development, policy analysis, communications, organizational and interpersonal negotiation, conflict management, and affirmative action in the areas of disability, gender, and race. He continues some unpaid consulting on implementing critical thinking in organizations and in applied ethics, particularly in nursing. He has been an associate of the Centre for the Support of Teaching at York University, and has twice received university teaching awards. He has held a full-time appointment at York University in the Department of Philosophy and the Faculty of Science since 1999.

PETER JOHN KREK

Peter John Krek received his B.A. (1995) in History and Philosophy from the University of Guelph, his M.A. (1998) in Philosophy and Social Policy from American University in Washington, D.C., and his Ph.D. (2007) in Philosophy from York University. His research and teaching continue to focus on issues of social policy, ethics, psychology, and existentialism, as well as how these factors intersect in the formation and function of community. Between graduate degrees, and while pursuing doctoral studies, he worked in a variety of roles in the financial sector. He continued in this industry as he was starting his teaching career. Most recently, Peter served as a corporate training specialist with a leading insurer. In addition to being a member of Ryerson University's Program Advisory Council for the Continuing Education Certificate in Ethics, Peter teaches at Ryerson University's G. Raymond Chang School of Continuing Education, where he delivers courses including *Human Rights and Justice*, *Existentialism*, *Philosophy of Love and Sex*, *Philosophy of Law*, *Philosophy of Human Nature*, and *Freedom, Equality, Limits of Authority*.

Getting Started in Argument and Argumentation

LEARNING OBJECTIVES

After completing this module you should be able to:

1. Explain and distinguish the key concepts (critical thinking, argument, argumentation, reason, conclusion, and issue) and how they relate to one another;
2. Identify the differences between personal opinion, reasoned opinion, and evidential claims, and identify and distinguish these in a passage or dialogue;
3. Explain the concept of constitutive rules of argumentation, identify how the specific rules function in argumentation, and be able to apply these to various moves in an argumentation dialogue; and
4. Analyze some of the dynamics of argumentation in a dialogue.

 ## A DIALOGUE ON COPYRIGHT AND PIRACY

In the dialogue below, Jean and Peter are doing something people do every day. They are reasoning about an issue, engaging in making claims, giving arguments, challenging those arguments, engaging in argumentation, and getting back on track after having been sidetracked. In short, they are engaged in critical thinking in order to better understand an issue.

Jean: I know you wanted the latest Lady Gaga recording, so I made you a copy.

Peter: Thanks. I didn't know you had it.

Jean: I didn't, but I downloaded it from the Web.

Peter: Great, what do I owe you?

Jean: Nothing, I got it from Pirate's Den.

Peter: You mean it's a pirated copy? Don't you know that's illegal? I can't believe you'd do something so stupid!

Jean: It's not stupid, you jerk!

Peter: Who are you calling a jerk, you unprincipled thief!

Jean: I'm not a thief. I tried to do you a favour and this is how you repay me? See if I ever do anything nice for you again.

Peter: Like you'd ever do anything without your own self-interest at heart (dripping sarcasm).

Jean: Yeah, like you're a Mister Goody-Two-Shoes!

Peter: Wait a minute, we've been friends for too long to let something like this come between us. I'm sorry for calling you a thief. Let's calm down a bit and see if we can understand this better.

Jean: Yeah, I'm sorry for reacting the way I did, I was just surprised.

Peter: Okay, let's start over. Why do you think it's okay to download and use copyright material without paying for it?

Jean: Well, that's just what I think. I guess it's just my opinion.

Peter: Okay, it's your opinion, but does that mean I should think it's okay?

Jean: Well, everybody does it.

Peter: So that's your reason, but is it a good one? I don't think so, and I don't think it's true, nor do most of my friends.

Jean: Well, most of my friends do. So I assumed most people do.

(continued)

Peter: But your friends aren't everyone. They're just the people you know. May be you just know a select bunch of people with flexible morals [smiles].

Jean: We're not going to start that again [smiles]. Well, a lot of people do think it's OK, because fewer CDs are being made and sold and people are still listening to music.

Peter: Okay, let's grant that many people do it. Why does that make it right? A lot of people do things that are not right. Many people cheat on their income taxes, but that doesn't make it right, does it?

Jean: Well, it doesn't hurt anyone.

Peter: So, if something doesn't hurt anyone, then it is okay?

Jean: Yes.

Peter: If I cheat, just a little on my income taxes, no specific person is hurt. Is that okay?

Jean: No. That's not the same.

Peter: Why not?

Jean: Because you have an obligation to pay your taxes, but I don't have any obligation to a record company.

(to be continued)

This text will introduce you to aspects of arguing and help you develop the skills related to being able to think more critically. While most texts focus on understanding and assessing arguments primarily through logic and fallacies, this text includes those within the broader context of critical thinking in verbal and written argumentation. To help achieve this, the Copyright Dialogue above will be continued through the text in order to demonstrate how the skills related to critical thinking are employed in our everyday lives. Join us as we develop our skills.

1.1 Introduction

Reasoning is the process of connecting and assessing ideas.

Virtually every aspect of our lives involves ***reasoning***, which is the process of connecting and assessing ideas. We reason every time we formulate or solve a problem, make a decision, draw an inference, connect or synthesize ideas, analyze, make a prediction, evaluate, make a judgment, explain an event, apply an idea or thought to a new situation, generalize from experience, interpret an event or work of literature, or follow or give directions. We also reason when we consider what program to major in, ask a mechanic why the car keeps stalling, explain how evolution works, or question if it is okay to download copyright materials from the Internet. We use reason when we assess an explanation of why a friend was late, whether a grade given on a paper is fair, and whether we have enough money to get through the month. The purpose of developing our reasoning and argument skills is to help us reason more accurately. This involves addressing questions such as whether our judgments are based simply on opinion, or have a reasoned basis to them, and whether they are based on evidence or simply unexamined beliefs and claims.

We reason often, usually implicitly without reflecting on what we are doing or subjecting our reasoning to critical analysis. Being *critical* in this context involves looking at the details of issues and ideas for the purpose of evaluating them. It is associated with the term "critique" rather than the narrower and more common use that suggests being negative (its opposite is being naïve or general with respect to issues and ideas). *Analysis* involves breaking ideas down into their component parts in order to assess them (its opposite is synthesis, which is bringing or putting things together).

Sometimes we follow patterns of reasoning or use ideas that we have been exposed to in our environments by parents, peers, school, and society. Although many of these patterns may work most of the time, they can also sidetrack us. As people who reason implicitly, we tend to generalize without adequate data, make determinations based on a small number of cases (or from atypical cases if they catch our attention), or simply adopt other people's views without questioning them. But choosing economics as a major because Uncle Fred said it would result in a good income may not be the best choice if you do not like mathematics, have no passion for it, or if there is no employment market for economists (he may have been right twenty years ago, but not today).

Reasoning implicitly is not a fault in the sense that we normally can and do reason correctly and simply fail in some cases. This is because our minds are naturally inclined to identify and follow patterns. While some patterns naturally evolve to help us deal with situations (like avoiding being eaten in a primeval jungle), they do not necessarily lead to the best decisions or the most complete understanding of the world. To develop those reasoning patterns we need to make reasoning explicit, systematic, and disciplined.

Critical reasoning primarily involves thinking systematically and reflecting on our reasons by analyzing and evaluating them according to standards. It also involves assessing the standards we use in that evaluation. In other words, making our reasoning explicit and being critical about it. To help us improve our reasoning skills in this respect we must develop standards and learn how to apply them to how we think.

Critical reasoning can help us make better decisions. To do so, we test our claims against standards of good reasoning and evaluate the adequacy of those reasons. This gives us better knowledge with which to make decisions and act. We can choose to major in a subject because we like it or because a friend has chosen this major. However, if my goal in school is to prepare myself for life, which includes developing job skills, then simply liking the subject or following a friend's lead may not be the best choice. Acting on an uninformed decision can have far-reaching consequences, and critical reasoning skills can help us anticipate and understand them.

It can also help us become autonomous agents. Rather than simply naïvely reflecting the ideas of those around us or those of our culture, we can critically assess the ideas we are exposed to. This means we arrive at our beliefs on the basis of an understanding of what those beliefs mean and commit us to. It also means our choices are *ours* and not simply a reflection of those around us.

We can develop critical reasoning skills in any area in which we reason: in observing the world, problem-solving, interpreting actions, or arguing. This text focuses on the critical reasoning skills involved in doing all those things.

> **Critical reasoning** primarily involves thinking systematically and reflecting on our reasons by analyzing and evaluating them according to standards and assessing the standards we use.

1.2 Why Think Critically?

Critical thinking has been characterized as making our reasoning explicit and then assessing it according to the best available standards and criteria. This involves the careful and reflective examination and assessment of the claims we and others make and the support for those claims, as well as the ability to develop our reasoning into a coherent form.

We often consider critical thinking too narrowly, as simply criticizing another person's reasoning on a position. This can lead us to become mere "flaw catchers" or people who simply look for flaws in positions in order to dismiss them. But critical thinking is far more than that. While the critical examination and identification of errors in reasoning is important, identifying errors is only a first step to effective critical thinking. Critical thinking centrally involves developing arguments to support positions and responding to the challenges to those arguments. Through arguments we develop a better understanding of positions. As we develop arguments and respond to challenges we develop a more accurate understanding of positions and how they are connected to related issues. Knowing the elements of good arguments and the common ways of making errors in judgment can help us create better arguments when we come to construct and present our own.

We rarely engage in critical thinking on our own. We are often hindered by a lack of interest, time, social support for doing so, and the models of good critical thinking. Everywhere in society we are surrounded by sound bites, slogans, clichés, stereotypes, appeals to emotion, and traditions that are often given and taken as a substitute for reasoned assessment. Our naïve and native patterns of reasoning are more geared for general survival than for careful, systematic thought. Some of these barriers to critical reasoning and thinking are illustrated in Figure 1.1.

Figure 1.1 Barriers to Critical Thinking

Although this illustrates why we often do *not* think critically, it does not yet explain why we should. After all, being critical can disrupt existing patterns of thought, lead us to question widely held beliefs, and ultimately lead us to face and make difficult choices. Furthermore, it involves learning new (and often unlearning old) skills and habits of mind. Such learning takes time and practice and can be frustrating, but it can also be rewarding and liberating!

So why be critical? And in what ways is it rewarding? One simple reason is that it is part of a course you need to complete successfully. If it was not required, you probably would not take it. That is an extrinsic reason, not an intrinsic one. An *extrinsic reason* is a reason why something is good for some secondary purpose (like taking a course solely because it is required for a degree or because it might help you in other courses or to get a job). An *intrinsic reason* is a reason why something is good for its own sake (like taking a course because you are interested in and like the subject). Although an extrinsic reason is not a bad reason, it gives us no independent motivation to develop skills in critical reasoning nor any reasons to use those skills beyond a particular course. While extrinsic reasons may help motivate us in the short term, they do not provide a motivation for developing critical thinking skills as an ongoing part of our lives.

So what are the intrinsic reasons for developing critical thinking skills? At the very least, they have practical benefits (such as, critical thinking skills can help us make better decisions, understand the world more clearly, and distinguish between true and false claims). We face many practical decisions in our lives. Thus, we face many practical questions. Should we make decisions about what to do based on our horoscopes, where to invest our money based on the advice of a hedge fund manager, decide which car to buy based on advertising? How do we know if any of these are good reasons for acting? How should we make a decision about who to vote for or even whether to vote in the next election? Is it a good idea to keep taxes down by cutting staff and services and selling publicly owned assets for a one-time financial benefit? Is evolution simply a belief and should it be taught or banned in secular or religious schools? Do vaccines cause autism? Critical thinking can help us answer such questions and make better decisions, sort good from bad claims, and generally understand the world more accurately. Much of society encourages us to accept one answer on each of these questions without examining alternative answers and without assessing the relevant evidence. This can lead us to make important decisions based on little, faulty, or even no evidence. Conversely, critical thinking can give us a deeper understanding of ideas and issues based on a thorough examination of the relevant evidence.

More generally, thinking critically is important for two reasons. First, critical and reflective thought gives us a better understanding of who we are by enhancing our autonomy, what we believe, and who we can become. Rather than simply accepting the prevailing views and ideas of those around us, critical thinking encourages us to examine those views, allows us determine whether or not they are true or merely appear to be, and clarifies whether they apply to us and how. It encourages us to assess those ideas and arguments for their truth and applicability, and this puts us in a better position to make decisions that are more reflective of who we are as individuals rather than decisions dictated by society, the media, parents, friends, and social groups. In short, critical thinking helps make us more *autonomous*, more able to assess situations, make decisions, and act in a way that reflects our reasoned assessment and choices. This gives us more control of our lives by grounding our understanding, decisions, and actions on reason rather than merely on intuition, habit, and social convention.

Second, and perhaps more important, critical thinking is basic to knowing and defending our freedoms and rights, which is the foundation for an informed democratic public. Through critical thinking we can come to understand what our freedoms and rights are, why they are important, and how they apply to us and others. And it can often result in more questions than we had to begin with. For example, some people claim they have a right to free speech that justifies saying anything (including utterances some consider hate speech) and doing anything, regardless of the consequences. They claim whatever they do is justified simply because they have a right and choose to do it. Others claim hate speech is not protected as free speech and so it is not an absolute right. Is the fact that one chooses to do something sufficient grounds in itself for saying it is okay? Which is true? What is freedom of speech and why should it be a basic right? Is it more basic than a right not to be offended? Should we have a right not to be offended? Should we be free to do whatever we want, regardless of the consequences? In order to defend our rights and freedoms we need to understand what they mean and what their functions are. And in order to understand our rights and freedoms we also need to be able to critically understand what their implications and consequences are. We need to consider the arguments for the situations in which they apply and do not apply. Otherwise, we defend our rights and freedoms on the basis of tradition, what others accept, or what the government says; that is, merely on the basis of some external authority, rather than on the basis of our own understanding and rational assessment. To the degree that we fail to base our acceptance of rights and freedoms on a critical and substantial understanding of these considerations we surrender our thinking to an external authority without an adequate understanding, which is tantamount to abandoning of our fundamental autonomy. So, thus far, we have identified three intrinsic ways in which critical thinking can benefit us, namely, by helping us understand (1) what a given right or freedom is, (2) the relationship between our rights and the obligations they entail, and (3) how rights and obligations apply to a given situation.

With these points in mind we can start to understand why critical thinking is basic to freedom and democracy. Democracy is not simply the right of citizens to vote for preferred candidates or issues. The freedom to vote in a democracy is based on the assumption that citizens are in principle capable of making informed and rational decisions (even if in practice we do not always rise to our potential in this regard). The gap between what we are capable of in principle and how we act in practice is what critical thinking aims to bridge. Ideally, individuals (given the correct skills) are able to make rational decisions, rather than ones merely based on sound bites, slogans, and appeals to emotion on one-dimensional issues. If democracy was simply a popularity contest based on who presented the most appealing case, rather than the best arguments or social policies, simply voting for the best "spin-doctor" would be all that was needed. However, history has proven this to have disastrous effects (such as, when we elect politicians who advocate poor policies detrimental to the public interest, favour special interests, or are entirely counter-productive to the general welfare). Critical thinking can help us see through false and misleading claims, identify what is important, and help us make selections based on which individuals and policies will support the general welfare. In doing so, we are supporting the basis of a truly democratic state, that is, one based on the reasoned consensus of critically reflective individuals, rather than on an uninformed and naïve majority. That is the fundamental basis of a properly functioning democracy: an informed and literate citizenry capable of critical thinking.

1.3 Claims: Opinions, Reasoned Opinions, and Evidence

A *claim* is a statement that can be true or false. The sentence "Is downloading copyright material without paying for it ethical?" is not a claim, but a question. However, the answer to a question like this might be a claim. For instance, "Downloading copyright material is unethical" is a claim that may be either true or false. A phrase or sentence fragment (such as, "downloading copyright material") is not a claim, but it can be turned it into a claim by making it into a complete sentence. Only complete sentences can be claims, but not all sentences are necessarily claims. The sentence "Insert Tab 1 into slot B" is a direction rather than a claim, showing that only some sentences make claims. (Kinds of claims are further discussed in Module 6.)

The following are examples of claims:

- AIDS is a serious disease;
- Creationism should not be taught in science courses; and
- Mandatory drug testing violates an individual's rights.

> A **claim** is a statement that can be true or false.

Although the above sentences are claims, we do not have any justification for accepting them. We often accept the claims people make without exploring whether they are true or false. Without knowing whether the support offered for a claim is true we have no basis for accepting it. Although the statement "You should not download copyright material" is a claim, we do not know whether it is true or false because the person making it has not given any justification for whether it should be accepted. Once we give some justification for the claim it becomes a *supported claim,* or a claim for which we provide support, justification, or evidence. Conversely, an *unsupported claim* is a claim for which no support is given. "You should not download copyright material because it harms the person who owns the copyright" is a supported claim. Without examining the support people give for the claims they make we are not being critical. To know whether a claim is true or false we need to know the evidence, justification, or support for the claim.

> A **supported claim** is one for which support, justification, or evidence is given.

Why should we provide support for the claims we make? While some people hold that claims are just opinions, and everyone is entitled to hold an opinion, an *opinion* is merely an unsupported belief. Does the fact that people have different opinions or give different reasons for their beliefs make reasoning subjective in nature? These are common objections to the role that reasons and arguments commonly play in our thinking. However, these objections rest partially on a false understanding about what arguing can do, and also involve poor reasoning.

> An **opinion** is an unsupported belief.

Let us examine these objections further. If the claims we made were just opinions (not in need of support) and reasoning was purely subjective in nature, it would mean that when different people have different beliefs, the truth of a belief would simply be a matter of personal preference. The consequence of this would be that critical reasoning would not have much value in seeking truth and understanding.

Having a *simple opinion,* or a belief for which we have no explicit reasons, is not enough. I may believe the Beatles are better than the Rolling Stones without any reasons other than I prefer the music of one to the other. But that is not enough to convince someone to adopt my opinion. Nor is it sufficient for understanding my own position. If asked why the Beatles are better than the Rolling Stones, I might be able to give reasons (such as, I might claim the Beatles did far more to transform

> A **simple opinion** is a belief for which no explicit reasons are provided.

GETTING STARTED IN ARGUMENT AND ARGUMENTATION

rock 'n' roll than the Rolling Stones did). Whether my reasons are right or wrong, they are nonetheless reasons, and providing them turns my simple opinion into a ***reasoned opinion***, or a belief for which explicit reasons are provided. Reasoned opinions are things we can engage in an argument about it. Most of us (especially initially) have simple opinions about many things, but that does not prevent us from turning them into reasoned opinions. Turning them into reasoned opinions enables us to understand our beliefs better and opens up the possibility of correcting them if they are wrong.

Once we start giving reasons for our opinions, we can start examining whether those reasons actually support the conclusion, and whether the reasons offered are true. In some cases we can discover or identify reasons we can accept and which support one claim over another. For instance, we might agree that the best criterion for determining whether one musician was more important than another is how much the music in question transformed a particular genre. Though we often start out with a difference of opinion, by examining reasons for our beliefs we may discover an underlying basis for agreement.

Matters can quickly become more complicated if a belief involves issues on which agreement is less likely (such as, whether abortion is ever morally justifiable). The differences on these issue often run deep and divide people, but this does not mean arguing about them is futile or that reasons have no function. Rather, it suggests the opposite, namely, that reasons have a more important function. By articulating reasons and evaluating arguments for and against a position involving complex issues, we can discover something about the beliefs we are committed to, and better understand what we believe and why. Understanding our fundamental commitments on such issues can lead to properly affirming or changing them. We may discover underlying common presuppositions and assumptions or false presuppositions and assumptions behind commonly held beliefs, either of which might help in the practical task of determining a reasonable social policy for a society in which there is diversity in beliefs. Thus, examining arguments can teach us something about both sides of a position on all issues, as well as our commitments to our own position. And aside from that, at the very least we can gain a better understanding that might contribute to managing disagreements in a more meaningful and productive manner.

Once we have reasons for our opinions we can examine them critically and see whether we should accept them. We may not always agree, but we will come to a better understanding of our own position and the positions of others, and in some cases we might change our minds for good reason.

The claim that all reasoning and giving of reasons is subjective is not true in all cases. Some claims are not merely ones for which we can give reasons, but also ones for which reasons make claims about the world independent of our beliefs. An ***evidential claim*** is a claim for which we can give reasons that refer to things in the world independent of subjective beliefs. For example, I may believe the world is flat, gravity is an illusion, or gold has an atomic number of 237, while others may believe something different. Our believing these claims does not itself make them true, because these claims have consequences independent of what we believe about them. If I believe gravity does not exist and try to walk off the top floor of the CN Tower I will quickly discover it does exist (albeit, and sadly, too late to revise my belief). Thus, evidential claims are not merely a matter of opinion as they require evidence that exists independently of anyone's belief about the world. In this situation my belief about the non-existence of gravity can be reasoned to be false given the available evidence (and my death). In this way the evidence goes beyond what I simply believe to what the world is actually like independent of my beliefs about it. Not all of the evidence may be available at a given point in time and/or we may disagree about what the evidence is and/or its implications, but that only makes the claim an unresolved evidential claim, rather than merely a matter of personal or subjective opinion.

We do not give reasons only to persuade others or to defend ourselves. We also give reasons because we are interested in seeking the truth about an issue, and want to base our beliefs and actions on the best available evidence and reasons for those beliefs and actions. By probing the reasons behind beliefs we can identify what we and others are really committed to, resolve conflicts between various beliefs and values, understand each other more accurately, make better decisions, and act more intelligibly.

The claim that reasoning is subjective and we all have different reasons for our beliefs (and, therefore, should not challenge them) rests on a confused understanding of tolerance. *Tolerance* is the idea that we recognize and respect others and their rights to hold their own beliefs. However, this does not mean we accept all reasons and beliefs as equally legitimate. This is because, properly understood, tolerance is an attitude about respecting the right of others to make and hold beliefs independent of the content of those beliefs (a point that is often overlooked). We can respect all people equally without necessarily considering all beliefs and practices as equally legitimate (another point that is often overlooked). Not all reasons and reasoning are equally good. All people can make errors in reasoning, use false and irrelevant claims as reasons, and/or become confused, and critical thinking is the method to correct this tendency.

If I choose to study computer science because I believe everyone who graduates with a computer science degree gets a high-paying job, and if in reality the market for people with computer science degrees is poor, I am basing my actions on a false belief about the world. In other words, I have a reason for my decision that is simply not true. Someone who respects me and does not want me to make a costly mistake should, as a gesture of respect for me as a person, point out the error in reasoning rather than tolerate my mistaken belief. Allowing me to persist in maintaining a mistaken belief does me a disservice, plain and simple, and does not show respect for me as a rational and autonomous agent.

Respecting others and their ideas does not mean we should not challenge their ideas and beliefs when we think those ideas are misguided. We show other people the greatest respect when we challenge their mistaken ideas and allow them to correct them. We cannot force others to accept our challenges and change their minds through argumentation, but we can try to show the weakness of the claims and arguments presented and leave it to them to decide what to do about it. We thereby help others to better understand their own ideas and what those ideas commit them to. Some people may change their beliefs, and others may take the critique as a challenge to find better reasons for their positions. We show greater respect for others by engaging in rational argumentation about their ideas than by simply tolerating whatever they think.

Reasoning and using arguments to help examine what we believe and what our beliefs commit us to can help us make better choices about our actions, understand the world, and interact with others more productively. Thus, reasoning matters for individuals specifically and for society in general.

1.4 Arguments

Once we have given reasons to support a claim, we engage in the giving of arguments. An *argument* consists of a set of at least two related claims, one of which is offered as justification, evidence, or support for another. We call the claim for which support is offered the *conclusion*. We call the claim providing the support, evidence, or justification for the conclusion the *reason* (sometimes called premise). The conclusion of an argument is the main claim being supported and is the clam for which reasons are given, while reasons are the claims supporting the conclusion.

In Section 1.3 we identified a number of unsupported claims. By providing reasons we can turn those claims into conclusions and generate the following arguments:

- AIDS is a serious disease because over half of those who contract it die;
- Creationism should not be taught in science courses because it is not a scientific theory; and
- The right to privacy is a basic human right and mandatory drug testing violates that right; therefore, mandatory drug testing violates basic human rights.

Each of the claims in the first list (in Section 1.3) has been transformed into the conclusion of an argument in the list in this section because one or more reasons have been offered in support of each.

However, this does not mean an argument has to be good to be considered an argument. It merely has to have one or more reasons in support of a conclusion. A good argument has reasons that are true and support the conclusion. An argument might be bad because the reasons offered may not be good, and/or may not adequately support the conclusion, and/or might not be the best support possible for the conclusion. In each of the cases listed above, a reason has been offered as a claim in support of a conclusion, making it an argument. Assessing whether an argument is good or bad will depend on applying criteria of assessment.

An **argument** consists of a set of at least two related claims, one of which is offered as justification, evidence, or support for another.

The **conclusion** is the claim that is being supported and for which reasons are given.

A **reason** (sometimes called a premise) is a claim that provides support, evidence, or justification for the conclusion.

We often confuse two different senses of the term "argue" (and "argument"). In the Copyright Dialogue that opens this module, Jean and Peter start off disagreeing in a way that results in a confrontation, with raised voices, name-calling, and escalating emotions. This is the everyday and negative meaning of "argue," namely, to disagree, to engage in a confrontation, to dispute with raised voices and heightened emotions. In this sense *argue* and *argument* are being used pejoratively and mean to disagree in a way that is not obviously productive (which is why there are often no winners in such disputes).

However, to **argue** can also mean providing support for the claims we make by giving reasons for a conclusion. Eventually, Jean and Peter start to engage in giving and exploring reasons for their claims. This is when they start arguing in a second and productive sense of the term, one that aims to expand understanding by allowing issues to be explored through discussion. By providing reasons for their claims they are providing support for their arguments. This is the sense in which the terms "argue" and "argument" will be used in the context of critical thinking. The primary goal of this text is to help you develop the critical skills necessary for developing, analyzing, assessing, challenging, and defending reasoning involving arguments.

> To **argue** is to give reasons for a conclusion.

We use arguments in all kinds of reasoning: to justify, explain, and defend a position; to urge and evaluate a course of action for ourselves and others; and to predict consequences. For example, lawyers marshal arguments to win cases, accountants provide evidence to support financial recommendations, spouses use reasons to convince each other which vacation destination is best, and politicians use persuasion to get elected. We use arguments to negotiate deals, establish social policy, and/or convince a friend where to go on a Saturday night. Using arguments is one of the most basic and practical skills we have.

We can also use arguments for many underlying purposes: to find out the truth about an issue, to persuade, to inquire, to prove something, and/or to examine a line of reasoning. Furthermore, arguments can be used to intimidate, legitimize, justify, or rationalize almost anything. Critical thinking uses arguments and requires developing tools and skills to analyze, evaluate, create, challenge, and respond to challenges.

QUICK QUIZ 1.2

Identifying Arguments

Identify which (if any) of the following are arguments. If they are arguments, state why. If they are not, state why not.

1. Critical thinking is valuable because it helps us think more clearly and make better decisions.
2. Mary lied when she said she had attended the conference.
3. Mary did not attend the conference but submitted an expense claim for the conference.
4. Mary lied because she claimed to have attended the conference, although she had not.
5. Tuition fees are too high. Many students have to take out huge loans to attend university.
6. The government has raised tuition fees for next year. Tuition fees are too high.
7. The Occupy movement ultimately has failed, since none of its proposals were acted on.

Answers to the Quick Quizzes are available on the Premium Website at www.criticalthinking2e.nelson.com.

1.5 From Arguments to Argumentation

Having a good argument and being convinced by that argument are two distinct things. Jean may have a good argument, but Peter may not have been convinced by it. Peter may have a better argument, or require something other than a good argument to sway him, or Jean's argument may not have addressed an important consideration that Peter feels needs to be addressed.

When giving an argument we present reasons for a claim we want to support or justify. The critical analysis and evaluation of arguments involves:

1. Understanding the meaning of the concepts and claims by clarifying meaning and paraphrasing the key claims;
2. Identifying the parts of an argument (reason and conclusion) and portraying the structure of the argument, that is, the manner in which the reasons are related to the conclusion;
3. Evaluating whether the reason supports the conclusion;
4. Evaluating the truth or acceptability of the reason; and
5. Evaluating the argument for errors in reasoning.

These five points are illustrated in Figure 1.2 below.

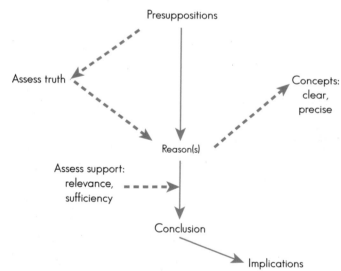

Diagram of an Argument

Figure 1.2 Diagram of an Argument

Generally speaking, good arguments seek to establish the truth of the conclusion by showing that the conclusion logically follows from and is justified by good reasons. The reasons provide us with grounds for accepting the conclusion, which is often in doubt or controversial. The usual study of arguments focuses on the claims made within an argument, the meaning, acceptability or truth of the claims, and the relationship of the claims to one another. Although this is effective for analyzing static and textual arguments, it rarely captures the fluid process by which people construct and defend their positions over the course of an interaction. Nor does it capture the additional rules needed to make sure the argument stays on track. Argumentation does that.

Argumentation is a form of discourse in which we use arguments to understand an issue more accurately. It involves the dynamic process of reasoning with others, that is, of constructing arguments, presenting those arguments, and challenging and responding to the challenges of others. One person makes a claim or takes a position and another person responds to it by asking for elaboration or challenging what is said. The first person then defends the initial argument with further reasons, while the second makes another challenge – a process that continues until a mutual understanding is reached. Thus, argumentation refers to the *dynamic* process of reasoning between people. It allows us to focus on the idea that arguments are given and analyzed in contexts in which we try to create and recreate rational meaning, to persuade and influence, and to engage rationally, not only with an issue, but also with one or more people in the attempt to understand an issue more accurately.

It is important to note that the process of argumentation can occur without another person being present. When we analyze a text, construct our own argument, or write a paper, we can engage in argumentation by considering how other people might respond to our argument, how those with a different point of view might see the issue, and what objections and alternate arguments they might raise. We can even enter into a dialogue with ourselves, taking on the roles of both the presenter and the challenger of the argument.

Argumentation involves three major components illustrated in Figure 1.3 below:

1. The content of the argument;
2. The people or perspectives representing different sides of a position; and
3. The process by which the people relate to each other while arguing.

Argumentation is a form of discourse in which we use arguments to understand an issue more accurately.

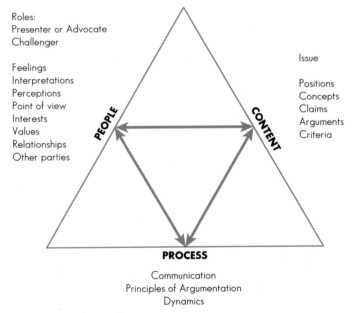

Figure 1.3 Content, Process, People

1. Content

The ***content*** includes the substance of what is being argued: the issues, claims, positions, and conclusions produced through the practice of arguing.

Content includes the substance of what is being argued: the issues, claims, positions, and conclusions produced through the practice of arguing.

2. People

The *people* who engage in the practice of arguing are called ***argument partners***. They provide, critique, and revise arguments. We use the phrase "argument partners" to emphasize that the practice of argumentation is a co-operative process where both roles

An **argument partner** is someone who is either defending or critiquing an argument (or sometimes both).

are involved with mutually promoting understanding and the search for truth. There are minimally two roles taken in argumentation: the advocate of an argument and the challenger. An **advocate** is someone who takes the role of defending a position in an argument. A **challenger** is someone who takes the role of critiquing a position in an argument. Each of these roles has a unique set of functions and expectations; however, a single individual may switch roles in a given interaction or assume both roles in order to represent multiple perspectives in turn when examining an issue. It is important to note that understanding people in this context involves understanding not only their arguments but also their emotions, commitments, interests, and purpose for giving an argument.

3. Process

The **process** is how the people in an argument relate to each other, including both the actual practices and behaviours (or what people are doing), as well as the rules defining the ideal of effective argumentation. The process of engaging in argumentation is often nuanced and complex, and the people do not always follow its rules.

Individuals involved in argumentation engage with various behaviours and practices. Some of these further the aims of argumentation, while others hinder them. People who claim to be engaging in argumentation, but knowingly use false information or force, or employ modes of reasoning they know are misleading, undermine the basic aims and purposes of argumentation. Although such people are often employing tools related to arguing, they are not using them in the pursuit of truth and understanding, and this thwarts the process.

Just as argument critique involves standards for evaluating, so does argumentation. Although argumentation uses the standards for good reasoning found in the analysis and evaluation of arguments, it extends them more broadly and applies them to the dynamic nature of arguments by including principles for such things as listening, challenging and responding, and establishing how to resolve a discussion.

Arguments are used in many kinds of discourse, including advertising, political speeches, policy documents, as well as in everyday life. *Discourse* refers to any form of conversation, discussion, or presentation of ideas, verbal or written, with an audience in mind.

Each form of discourse is defined by its purpose. *Persuasion* is a kind of discourse that aims to convince someone of something. An argument is simply a tool one can use to achieve this aim, but it is not the only tool. We can use appeals to emotion, or common practice, which are often means of non-rational or faulty persuasion that may be useful when the aim of discovering the truth about something is not primary. For example, the goal of defense attorneys is not to seek the truth but to get acquittals for their clients; , while the goal of advertisers is to entice consumers to buy products. In these cases the truth may actually get in the way of convincing people. By contrast, *rational persuasion* is the process of using good arguments to convince someone by illuminating truth and promoting mutual understanding.

The purpose of argumentation is **rational inquiry**, or the rational pursuit of truth about an issue through reasoned discussion using arguments and the rational appreciation of different perspectives. Although related to other forms of communication (such as, negotiation, conflict management or resolution, problem solving, and empathetic communication), argumentation is distinguished by its focus on reasoned discussion using argument and evidence in the pursuit of truth about an issue.

Unlike other forms of persuasive activities (such as, negotiation, where the goal is to arrive at a mutual agreement to resolve conflicting interests; conflict management, where the goal is the resolution or management of conflict; and politics, where the goal is the exercise of power), argumentation is differentiated by its commitment to the aim of rational inquiry and the principle that issues should be resolved solely by an appeal to the evidence and reasoning about those issues as reflected through arguments.

1.6 Reasoning About Issues, Positions, and Reasons

In the dialogue at the start of this module, Peter and Jean are arguing about an issue. Each takes a position and gives reasons, and each tries to convince the other of the truth of his own position and the falsity of the other's position. Yet, at the same time, each is listening to the other, probing the other's position and reasons, and trying to understand what the other is saying. Engaging in argumentation involves providing reasons for conclusions.

Arguments and argumentation focus on issues. An *issue* is a point of contention within a given context and between at least two points of view. It can be either a matter that elicits disagreement about truth and/or a problem that elicits disagreement about the correct or appropriate solution. An issue is a central point on which a debate or inquiry hinges. In the Copyright Dialogue above, one issue might be whether downloading copyright material without paying for it is morally acceptable. Another issue might be whether downloading a specific copyright song is morally acceptable. An important skill in critical thinking is being able to formulate the precise issue in contention. In this example, it may be important to determine whether Peter and Jean are arguing about Jean's specific actions or the general principle governing his behaviour.

Arguments are about issues. We take positions on issues and give reasons for those positions. By focusing on issues we draw attention to the fact that there are alternate positions other than the specific one being argued. The process of argumentation involves identifying the issues, eliciting the positions and reasons on those issues, challenging them, and defending them. This dynamic is illustrated in Figure 1.4 below, using material from the Copyright Dialogue above.

> An **issue** is a point of contention within a given context and between at least two points of view that elicits disagreement about the truth of the issue.

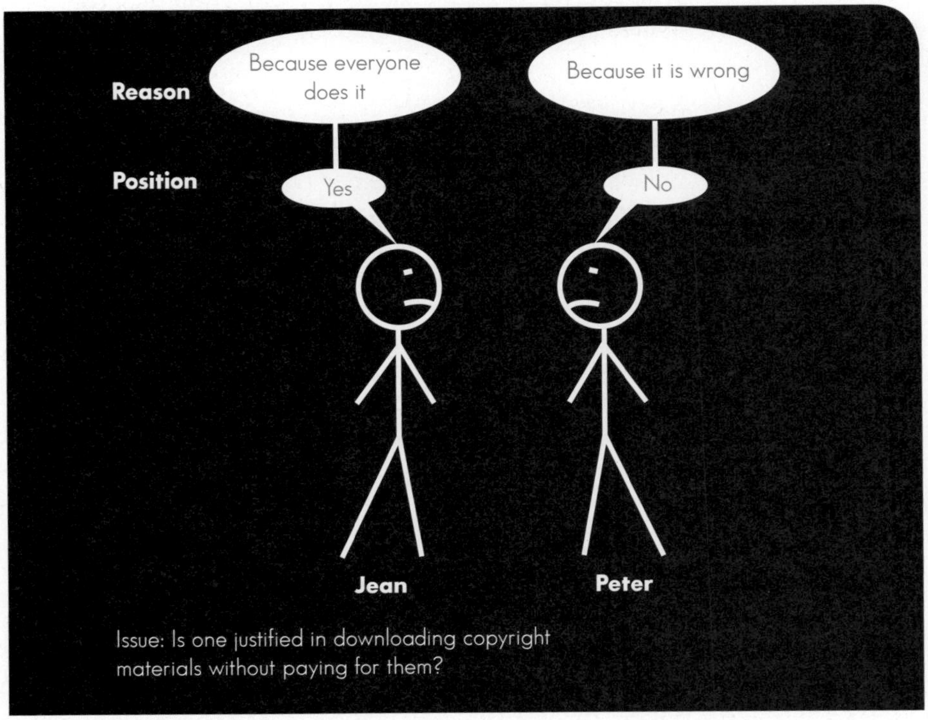

Figure 1.4 Issues, Positions, Reasons

GETTING STARTED IN ARGUMENT AND ARGUMENTATION

Issues are commonly (though not always) phrased as questions, and there are usually differing answers. An issue on the subject of abortion might be "Should there be laws regarding abortion in Canada?" Another issue might be "Should the government accord legal rights to the fetus at any stage of development?" Yet another issue might be "Is abortion immoral?" Any subject may have such multiple issues. By phrasing an issue as a question we can distinguish issues from positions. "Is abortion ever morally justified?" is an issue in the form of a question, whereas "Abortion should be illegal" is a position.

There may be a variety of issues about a subject, dispute, or inquiry. The *main issue* is the one we are trying to resolve or understand. However, other issues may also be central. An issue is central to a dispute or inquiry when its resolution is critical to resolving it. "Is abortion ever morally justified?" may be the main issue in a given context. However, the issue "Is the fetus a moral and legal person?" is central in resolving the dispute over whether abortion is morally justified. If the fetus is not a moral or legal person then it is not entitled to moral or legal protection. An issue is well formed issue if it meets the criteria outlined on Table 1.1.

> The **main issue** is the issue we are trying to resolve or understand.

TABLE 1.1 Criteria for a Well-Formed Issue

Criterion	Explanation	Example
is precise	Precision means being as exact and definite as necessary under the circumstances and clearly distinguishing different relevant possibilities.	"Is one morally justified in downloading material from the Internet?" is not sufficiently precise, whereas "Is one morally justified in downloading copyright material from the Internet?" is more precise and more adequately captures the issue.
is controversial	An issue is controversial if there is or can be reasonable disagreement about it.	"Do people download copyright material from the Internet?" is not particularly controversial, whereas "Does illegal downloading of copyright material cause harm to copyright owners?" is more controversial, as some defenders of such downloading claim it does not.
involves one central idea	Presenting two ideas as a single issue may make it more difficult to resolve the issue. It is better to present a complex or compound issue as separate ones and tackle them separately.	"Do people illegally download copyright material and is it immoral?" involves two distinct issues, whereas restricting the issue to "Is it immoral to download copyright material?" focuses on one central idea.
is stated in neutral terms	Something is stated in neutral terms if does not presuppose a point of view, that is, if it frames the issue in a value neutral way.	"Is one justified in stealing private property?" is value laden because "stealing private property" presupposes an answer and biases the issue, whereas "What is the moral nature of downloading copyright material?" states the issue in a neutral way.

A *position* is a stand taken on an issue. In the Copyright Dialogue, Jean takes the position that downloading copyright material is morally acceptable, while Peter takes a dissenting position that it is not. A third argument partner might take the position that it is morally acceptable under certain conditions but not others.

In the abortion issue discussed above, one position might be "Yes, there should be laws regarding abortion in Canada." This is a relatively ambiguous position since it could mean either we should have laws allowing abortion or laws criminalizing it. This statement or position is *ambiguous* because it has at least two alternative meanings and we are unable to determine which of those meanings is intended (from the context alone).

If no reasons are given for a position, it is *undefended*. In the Copyright Dialogue Peter's position is undefended because he gives no reasons. Once reasons for a position are given, the reasons and the position together become an argument and the position becomes the conclusion of the argument. It is now a *defended position*. Peter, through questioning, elicits reasons from Jean, making his position in the dialogue a defended one. Now the mere fact that it is a defended position does not in itself mean it is a good defense because part of the process of argumentation will be to assess the strength of the defense.

Argumentation typically involves addressing issues on which people take positions, and arguments are provided in support of their positions. However, focusing solely on arguments (claims, reasons, and conclusions) can ignore the fact that arguments function in the larger context of issues. Furthermore, it can ignore the dynamic of the giving and challenging of arguments and claims, the exploring of related issues, sub-issues, and positions.

A **position** is a stand taken on an issue.

Ambiguous refers to a statement or position that can have more than one identifiable meaning in a given context.

QUICK QUIZ 1.3

Identifying Issues

For each of the following topics:

(A) Identify whether or not it is an issue and explain why it is or is not; and

(B) If it is an issue, explain whether it meets the criteria for a proper framing of the issue.

1. The morality of abortion.
2. Abortions have been done illegally by people who are not licensed medical practitioners.
3. Is abortion ever ethical?
4. Should abortion be allowed?
5. Should abortion for the purpose of preventing the spread of defective genes be allowed?
6. Is a woman ever justified in killing her unborn baby?
7. Is a woman ever justified in having an abortion?
8. Is the state ever justified in interfering with a woman's right to choose what to do with her body?

Answers to the Quick Quizzes are available on the Premium Website at www.criticalthinking2e.nelson.com.

GETTING STARTED IN ARGUMENT AND ARGUMENTATION

1.7 The Constitutive Rules of Argumentation[1]

Many human activities are based on a number of ***constitutive rules*** that define the activity. For example, one of the constitutive rules of intimacy is that the parties involved disclose themselves to each other. Another is that the exchange is mutual: each party is expected to disclose to the other. If these rules are violated, it impacts whether intimacy is occurring or not. Argumentation also has constitutive rules; if the constitutive rules are not followed, the two argument partners are not effectively engaging in argumentation.

The following constitutive rules are considered basic principles of argumentation and are ways of making sure arguments are productive and aim to seek truth and understanding (and, conversely, ways to identify and correct for when they are not):

1. The Truth-Seeking Principle

The parties involved in argumentation are committed to searching for the truth or the most rationally defensible position about the issues being discussed. This means the parties should be willing to examine alternative positions, look for the insights in the positions of others, and encourage others to present arguments for alternate positions and/or raise objections to any position with regard to the disputed issue. If we reject the idea that we are searching for truth about an issue, then we are engaged in some other kind of activity (such as, persuasion, negotiation, or conflict management). Violation of this principle subverts the very purpose of argumentation and limits advancing mutual understanding.

2. The Respect Principle

The parties agree to distinguish between the people presenting arguments and the arguments being presented. This principle recognizes that individuals may hold positions for a variety of reasons and may change their positions with arguments. It commits the parties to being "hard" (rigorous) on the arguments, positions, and issues, and "soft" (receptive) on individuals. It demands the respect and recognition of the integrity of those engaged in the argumentation, while at the same time challenging the arguments as strongly as possible. It also recognizes that all parties have an equal right to present their own arguments and challenge the arguments of others.

Many arguments degenerate into name-calling, faulty reasoning, and heated emotions because people fail to heed this principle. They do not distinguish between attacking the position and attacking the person. Much of the language associated with arguing suggests a competition in which people try to destroy each other's positions, act as adversaries in a discourse in which there can only be one correct position, and try to shoot down each other's positions in order to defend their own, rather than engaging in a rational discussion aimed at expanding mutual understanding of each other and the issue.[2]

---

1 This section is based on the ideas of Frans H. van Eemeren and Rob Grootendorst. In *Argumentation, Communication and Fallacies: A Pragma-Dialectical Perspective.* Hillsdale, N.J.: L. Erlbaum, 1994, and T. Edward Damer, *Attacking Faulty Reasoning: A Practical Guide to Fallacy-Free Arguments,* Fifth Edition. Belmont, California: Wadsworth Publishing Company, 2005.

2 The idea of argument as war has been analyzed by George Lakoff with Mark Johnson in *Metaphors We Live By,* University of Chicago Press, 1980. The idea of being tough on the argument and soft on the position comes from Roger Fisher and Richard Ury, *Getting to Yes,* Penguin, 1981.

This has resulted in a tendency to be tough on the positions people take *and* the people taking them, and turns arguments into competitive battles between individuals rather than a co-operative enterprise to find the truth or generate understanding, which is contrary to what the rational tradition purports to facilitate. By considering the people with whom we engage in discussion to be argument partners, we can see argumentation as a joint endeavour to find the truth and/or advance understanding, rather than one that is mutually hostile. Dismissing people's arguments out of hand, attacking them rather than their arguments, and using threats or force to get them to agree, all violate this principle, whereas strenuously challenging an argument partner's arguments is applying this principle.

3. The Argument Principle

Any position a person takes must be established either by agreement of the argument partners or by an argument itself. Establishing a position by argument involves giving reasons that are true and that both argument partners accept as relevant and sufficient to justify the conclusion. Establishing a position by agreement is only tentative. Either person may agree "for the sake of argument" on a given starting position or claim in order to see where the discussion leads them. However, either person can also withdraw the agreement and challenge the claim should the discussion merit it. A challenge to an agreed-upon starting point requires that it be defended. In principle, any claim can be challenged and must be capable of being established by argument even if a given claim in an argument is not. A requirement of the argument principle is that argument partners try to offer the best reason or make the strongest case for their positions and put up the strongest challenges to any *counterarguments* presented. A counterargument is an argument against one's position or the reasons for the position.

> A **counterargument** is an argument against one's position or the reasons for the position.

Committing to the argument principle means the argument partners use the following criteria for developing the best arguments possible:

a. Present positions, claims, and challenges clearly;
b. Give reasons and challenges that are relevant;
c. Give reasons that are true or mutually acceptable; and
d. Give reasons that are sufficient to justify the conclusion.

In short, argument partners should strive to give well supported arguments and should acknowledge that mistakes can be made at different levels of an argument. People who knowingly use false evidence, refuse to provide evidence for their claims, or shift the burden of proof, violate this principle and in doing so create a barrier to advancing understanding.

4. The Fallibility Principle

Argument partners must acknowledge that they could be wrong. Believing certain claims are beyond proof (or disproof) and/or that evidence is irrelevant violates this principle.

5. The Listening Principle

Argument partners have an obligation to listen to and attempt to understand each other's arguments. By extension, they are obliged to present each other's arguments fairly, while: (1) remaining consistent with each other's original claims; (2) remaining consistent with each other's intentions; and (3) giving the strongest possible argument for the position. (These are listed from weakest to strongest.) If there is any doubt about the intention of (or the implicit claims within) the argument, they should be given the benefit of the doubt in any reformulation.

GETTING STARTED IN ARGUMENT AND ARGUMENTATION

6. The Principle of Charity

This is related to the listening principle and requires that argument partners demonstrate a good will effort to engage in discussion honestly. Willfully misrepresenting positions or attributing to them claims that have not been made violates this principle and undermines the aim of expanding understanding and knowledge.

7. The Burden of Proof Principle

Evidence or support required for a claim or position rests on the person who advances the position. If a challenger asks, the defender of a position has an obligation to provide evidence or support (in the form of claims, reasons, or arguments) for the position put forth. Refusing to provide evidence or insisting that one's argument partner disprove them rather than offering proof violates this principle and the aim of argumentation.

8. The Principle of Challenge and Response

Each argument partner has the right and obligation to challenge each other's claims and arguments even if they personally agree with the position the other supports. The challenge must be relevant to the position advanced and defended by the presenter. Anyone whose position is challenged is obligated to respond to the challenge in an appropriate way, present reasons that are directly relevant to the position, and/or concede (even if only temporarily) that more time and thought are required to further develop the position. Dismissing and/or refusing to challenge positions violates this principle and stops any meaningful discussion and the understanding it aims to promote.

9. The Resolution Principle

An issue will be considered resolved if the proponent for one of the positions: (1) successfully defends that position by presenting an argument that uses acceptable and relevant reasons that provide sufficient grounds to support the conclusion; and (2) provides an effective rebuttal to all serious challenges to the argument or position at issue. Unless someone can demonstrate that these conditions have not been met, he or she should accept the conclusion of the successful argument and consider the issue for all practical purposes to be settled. In the absence of a successful argument for any alternative position, the argument partners are obligated to accept the position supported by the best arguments presented (even if it runs counter to one's personal opinion). If someone does not accept the best-supported position he or she is obligated to develop challenges to the position and better arguments for it.

10. The Suspension of Judgment Principle

If no position comes close to being successfully defended, or if two or more positions seem to be defended with equal strength, the argument partners should (in most cases) suspend judgment about the issue. The exception occurs when some action is required, in which case people should consider the relative consequences of the alternate courses of action versus the consequences of not acting.

11. The Reconsideration Principle

If a successful (or at least good) argument for a position is subsequently found to be flawed in any way that raises new doubts about the merit of the conclusion, the issue should be re-opened for further consideration. The principle also applies if a new defense is found for a position that was previously unidentified or rejected.

TABLE 1.2 The Principles of Argumentation

	Name	Main Elements
1.	The Truth-Seeking Principle	The purpose is to seek truth and advance understanding of an issue.
2.	The Respect Principle	By separating the people from their positions you can challenge the positions while showing respect for the people presenting them.
3.	The Argument Principle	Because positions must be established by argument, when asked for reasons you must supply the best reasons possible.
4.	The Fallibility Principle	People acknowledge they could be wrong and must be willing to modify arguments or positions if they are shown to be wrong.
5.	The Listening Principle	People have an obligation to listen fairly to the arguments and claims of argument partners and to represent their positions and arguments fairly.
6.	The Principle of Charity	Argument partners demonstrate a good will effort to engage in discussion honestly and interpret their argument partner's arguments in a fair-minded way.
7.	The Burden of Proof Principle	The burden of proof — providing evidence or support for a claim or position — rests on the person defending a position.
8.	The Principle of Challenge and Response	People have a right and obligation to challenge the claims and positions of their argument partner, and when a challenge is raised they have a right to respond and an obligation (to the best of their ability) to provide a relevant and accurate response to the challenge.
9.	The Resolution Principle	An issue is considered resolved when argument partners agree: (1) arguments supporting one position are demonstrably superior to the arguments supporting the other position; and (2) the major challenges to the position have been adequately addressed.
10.	The Suspension of Judgment Principle	People agree to suspend judgment on an issue if no position is successfully defended or if two or more positions each have relatively strong arguments. The exception occurs when some action is required, in which case people should consider the relative consequences of the alternate courses of action versus the consequences of not acting.
11.	The Reconsideration Principle	Argument partners may re-open the issue if one of the arguments for the position adopted is found to be flawed or if a new defense is raised for one of the previously rejected positions.

QUICK QUIZ 1.4

Applying the Constitutive Rules of Argumentation

Each of the following is a move or response in an argumentation. Explain whether the individuals engaged in the interaction are adhering to the basic principles of argumentation. Identify which constitutive rules are violated (if any).

1. I do not care what your objection is. I know what I believe and I am not going to change my mind on the issue.
2. So far, your objections have not undermined my argument. Until they do, I am not agreeing with you on this.
3. That's just a typical feminist argument. And you know I do not agree with feminists on anything.

Answers to the Quick Quizzes are available on the Premium Website at www.criticalthinking2e.nelson.com.

QUICK QUIZ 1.5

Using the Constitutive Rules

Examine each of the following lines of dialogue from an argument exchange. Identify which constitutive rule the line of dialogue follows or violates and explain why.

1. You have challenged my claim that the government is hiding the remains of a crashed UFO at a secret air base. I admit I do not know where it is. But how do you know they are *not* hiding one?
2. We have been going at this for two hours. I think we have made some progress, and we've both refined our positions and reasons. However, we have not reached consensus on this. I suggest we go away and think about it.
3. You know, Fred, we reached agreement on that issue yesterday, but I was thinking about it overnight and realized one of the arguments you used to persuade me just does not work. Do you have some time now for me to run my challenge by you?

Answers to the Quick Quizzes are available on the Premium Website at www.criticalthinking2e.nelson.com.

1.8 Basic Dynamics of Argumentation

The constitutive rules define the basic framework and rules within which argumentation occurs, but they do not provide us with a model for the dynamics and possible moves and countermoves within an argument encounter. However, a model of argumentation dynamics does this.

Argumentation is a communicative process in which two (or more) positions or points of view use arguments to think through an issue in order to arrive at an understanding of it and its related claims. Although the dynamics of argumentation can be complex and quite free-flowing, they are nonetheless made up of a variety of discrete elements.

In an argument encounter, argument partners take one of two possible roles, advocate or challenger. Each may take either of the two roles at different stages of the discussion. In the Copyright Dialogue, Peter and Jean took on these roles. Peter takes the role of challenger, while Jean takes the role of defender. The defender stated a claim he wanted to defend, gave reasons for his claims, clarified terms and claims, and responded to challenges, while the challenger clarified the meaning of the key concepts and claims, asked for reasons, challenged the reasons, and restated and clarified his understanding of what had been said. The process can continue with the defender developing further reasons, and the challenger probing, clarifying, and challenging the reasons that are given. If the challenger raises a good challenge, the defender may modify his or her own reasons, introduce a new line of reasoning, and/or modify his or her position or conclusion as the evidence requires. The basic argumentation dynamic moves are illustrated in the Figure 1.5, below.

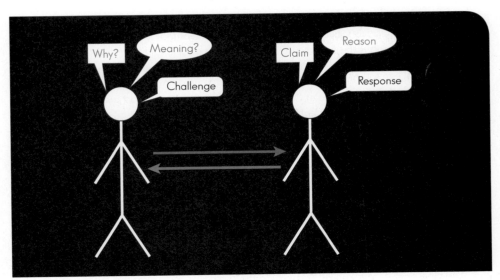

Figure 1.5 Argumentation Dynamics Diagram

The process of an actual argument encounter is likely to be more complex and nuanced than this suggests. There are nearly as many possibilities for how argumentation can play out as there are people to play them out. Throughout the process an argument partner can make any number of possible moves: some productively advance the inquiry, while others hinder it. Basic skills for conducting an effective argument include paraphrasing, formulating and critiquing arguments, supplying implicit reasons, examining presuppositions, using counterexamples, defending claims, clarifying meaning, and identifying and avoiding fallacies. (These will be explored in Module 10.)

The remainder of this text will help you develop the basic skills needed for being effective in argumentation, including: how to identify, structure, and evaluate arguments; clarify meaning; assess claims; develop and respond to challenges; analyze complex arguments; and present and defend arguments in both written and verbal contexts.

QUICK QUIZ 1.6

**Identifying Issues, Positions, and Arguments:
A Simple Argumentation Dialogue**

CONTEXT: The university student council has proposed a referendum on a supplemental health levy to pay for certain items not paid for by provincial health insurance. This includes some prescription drugs, physiotherapy, and chiropractic services. The levy will also provide basic health care for foreign students who are not covered by the provincial health care scheme. Two students are discussing the issue.

A: *I don't think we should support the supplemental health care levy.*

B: *Why not?*

A: *Because most people don't need it.*

B: *So you're saying that since only a few may need supplemental health insurance we shouldn't support it.*

A: *Yeah.*

B: *How do you know only a few need supplemental health insurance?*

A: *Because most students are covered by their parents' health insurance.*

B: *How do you know that?*

A: *I just assumed it.*

B: *I have some doubts, but let's suppose for the moment that it is true. So what you are saying is the only reason to support the additional health levy is if most students don't have supplemental health insurance coverage.*

A: *Yes.*

B: *So you don't think drivers in the province should have to support public transit since the majority of residents don't use it and don't need it?*

A: *I wouldn't agree with that.*

B: *What's the difference?*

For the simple example of argumentation above, identify:

1. The issue between A and B in the dialogue;
2. A's position in this dialogue if he takes one;
3. A's reason(s) for that position;
4. B's position in this dialogue, if she takes one; and
5. B's reason(s), if she gives any.

Examine each turn taken by A and B in the dialogue and, using the outline of a basic argumentation dynamic, identify the purpose of each turn in the dialogue — does it identify a position, state a reason, reformulate, challenge, or perform some other function?

Answers to the Quick Quizzes are available on the Premium Website at www.criticalthinking2e.nelson.com.

Module Summary

- Reasoning involves connecting and working through ideas.
- Critical reasoning involves the reflective examination of our reasoning.
- One form of critical reasoning is the critical evaluation of arguments and providing reasons for the claims we make.
- Opinions are unsupported claims, while supported claims are reasoned opinion.
- Claims with evidence that can be verified by others are called evidential claims.
- Arguments involve reasoned opinion or evidential claims.
- Arguments are about issues and taking a position and giving reasons for it.
- Arguments involve giving reasons for the claims we make, where reasons are sometimes called premises, and the claims being defended are called conclusions.
- Argumentation is the dynamic process of giving, challenging, and responding to challenges to our reasoning.
- Argumentation is defined by a set of constitutive rules that define the aim of the activity and the basic rules one should follow in this activity by defining good and bad argumentation.
- Argumentation is a dynamic process involving three main components:
  (1) the people arguing and the roles they take,
  (2) the content of what is being argued about, and
  (3) the process of argumentation.

Argumentation Exercise: Identifying the Key Elements of an Argument

Select one of the dialogues in the online Student Manual (Drug Testing or Huck Finn). For that dialogue:

1. Identify the issue and the positions and arguments taken;
2. Identify what each arguer is doing at each stage of the dialogue (presenting a position, asking for clarification, challenging a position); and
3. Identify which constitutive rules of argumentation are being used or broken at each exchange in the dialogue.

Writing Skills Exercise: Developing an Argument

Read one of the 2 online dialogues (Drug Testing or Huck Finn) and:

1. Identify one central issue addressed in the dialogue, one position, and one argument given to defend the position;
2. Identify an alternate position on that issue (one not given in the dialogue) and develop your own argument for it; and
3. Support your position with a good argument (a good argument involves giving and defending reasons for your position).

Present this in a one-paragraph argument, in which you identify the original issue, the original position and argument, and the alternate position and argument.

MODULE 2

Clarifying Meaning

LEARNING OBJECTIVES

After completing this module you should be able to:

1. Explain the role of language in reasoning and how the misuse of language can mislead in reasoning;
2. Explain and differentiate the key concepts having to do with meaning: a word (or term), a concept, and a thing, meaning (or sense), referent, and connotation;
3. Explain the role of context in determining meaning;
4. Identify and neutralize common problems of meaning, including vagueness, missing quantifiers and qualifiers, ambiguity, euphemisms, metaphors, and analogies;
5. Explain the different kinds of definitions, when to use them, the strengths and weaknesses of each, and the criteria for a good definition; and
6. Identify, differentiate, and be able to construct and use the different kinds of definitions appropriate to a given situation.

 A DIALOGUE ON COPYRIGHT AND PIRACY – CONTINUED

Jean: I take exception with some of the language you are using in your challenges.

Peter: Like what?

Jean: Well, you call it "piracy."

Peter: What's wrong with that? That's what it is.

Jean: When I think of piracy, I think of Spanish galleons and sea battles, or the contemporary pirates off Somalia.

Peter: What's wrong with that?

Jean: Downloading copyright material without paying for it is not the same thing. One involves violence and the other does not. Using "piracy" is prejudicial language.

Peter: Okay, I'll give you that, but "piracy" is a widely used word.

Jean: It may be, but it is still prejudicial.

Peter: Okay.

Jean: I have another problem with the word "theft." In some cases people are simply downloading digital copies of music they have already bought. So, they have paid for the music and are simply getting it in another format. Some cases may be theft, but not all.

Peter: I take issue with you on that.

Jean: Okay, but give me a minute. I read a case of a mother who videoed her two-year-old dancing to a piece of music and posted it on YouTube. The music company accused the mother of violating copyright and forced YouTube to remove it. Calling that "piracy" or "theft" simply seems wrong to me, and I think there is something wrong in the way the language is being used. Posing the issue in such language and assuming the words apply to all cases equally biases the issue in your favour.

Peter: Why do you say this biases the issue?

Jean: Because it gives preference to one side of the issue without considering the other side. Using "piracy," something no one would likely defend, presupposes the issue has been settled in favour of one side, and it is not obvious that it has been.

(to be continued)

Jean is challenging how language in this part of the dialogue has to do with the meaning of the words being used. Calling the downloading of copyright materials "piracy" or "theft" prejudices the issue in favour of one side. The words also carry connotations that tend to make the claims less than neutral, which can make clarifying the issues more difficult than they might otherwise be, and this is not helpful.

2.1 Introduction

To be effective in argumentation, we need to be clear in expressing our positions and the reasons for them, and be able to understand and help clarify an argument partner's arguments. After all, if we are not sure of what an argument partner means, we cannot know whether we agree or disagree.

In order to be able to clarify claims and concepts we need to understand how language is used and misused. This involves being able to understand the difference between the words used (or terms), the concepts (or the meaning of those words), the referents (or the things in the world picked out by those concepts), how the connotations (or the emotional and evaluative associations with words and concepts) affect the meaning of words, the role of meaning in context, and some of the problems associated with trying to express ourselves clearly and precisely (such as, vagueness, missing quantifiers and qualifiers, ambiguity, euphemisms, use of inference indicators, and misuse of metaphors and analogies). Knowing how to develop, use, and critique different kinds of definitions can help us clarify our use of language to make it more precise and effective – all of which are essential to argumentation.

The Copyright Dialogue at the beginning of this module illustrates some issues concerning language and meaning. Consider the following situation:

Anitha: Justice requires that we treat people with special needs differently.

Philippe: That's not justice. You can't be just if you are treating people differently.

If Anitha and Philippe do not clarify what they each mean by the word "justice," they are likely to engage in an unproductive discussion. Effective argumentation requires understanding precisely what is being claimed in an argument. Asking what is meant, identifying examples of justice, and defining the word is required to make sense of this disagreement. Consider another situation where meaning might not be clear:

> Obfuscation International and Corporate Mismanagement Enterprises announces a multiphasic strategic integrative alliance to leverage the functionality of their collaborative management solutions for a global win-win solution. The new cross-platform product initiatives will provide 24/7/365 distributed, dynamic, and innovative methodologies in a rapidly growing global economy in order to initialize new interactive opportunity structures, orchestrate mission-critical content, and incentivize holistic and compelling utilities for recontextualized multiphasic intermediate users and end users.

What exactly does the statement mean? This passage does not communicate clearly. Rather than expressing the ideas simply, the author has hidden the meaning behind jargon. Because of this it violates the truth-seeking principle (and its corollary, the unstated principle of clarity) that seeks to present our positions as clearly as we can.

Whenever we use language that hides (or obfuscates) our meaning, use words imprecisely, or without clearly defining them, we undermine effective argumentation, which requires the clear expression of ideas.

A related difficulty involves the use of code words, namely, words used with special meaning in a particular context. For example:

> Civilian contractors were employed to soften up the detainees.

Without knowing the precise meaning of the words within the context we do not know whether to accept this as true or challenge it. In the context of the United States' involvement in Iraq it takes on quite a specific meaning, but it is in a form of code because the terms are used in a special way to hide the meaning of what is being said. Decoded, the statement suggests mercenaries tortured the prisoners, which may not be what the author actually means. Some familiar contemporary words that serve the purpose of masking a statement's meaning include "collateral damage," "disanimate," and "misspoke." By using language that is less clear than more precise language the message hides the reality rather than showing it and this thwarts the aim of clear communication. Not understanding the claims our argument partners use, or of the texts we are reading, is a barrier to engaging effectively in argumentation.

2.2 Criteria for Effective Use of Language

For our language to be effective in communicating it should be clear, precise, accurate, and appropriate to the context. Language use is clear when we can be easily understood. This means key concepts have been defined or clarified and their meaning understandable. What does the author mean by "multiphasic strategic integrative alliance" in the above text? At best this is technical jargon, and more likely it is a meaningless jumble of words designed to impress and obscure the reality it purports to report on. The purpose of language is to understand and communicate. Something is *clear* if it can easily be understood correctly. A concept is clear if it can easily identify what it refers to accurately.

> Being **clear** means we can easily and accurately understand or express what is being said.

Language is ***precise*** when it is as exact as the context requires or allows. Calling Jack "overweight" may be precise enough in a casual conversation, but it would not be precise enough for a physician's chart or to determine weight load for a small airplane or parachute. A physician recording Jack's weight at 137.6953 kilos would constitute unnecessary precision. With respect to meaning we should strive to choose the most precise word that fits the situation. The words "overweight" and "obese" have different meanings in a medical context, and using "overweight" when one should use "obese" can result in a misdiagnosis. Similarly, asking for "yellow powder" in a chemistry lab may result in one getting sulphur rather than gold. Concepts can be used precisely or imprecisely: we increase our chances of using *precise* concepts when we select the most accurate one for the context and we will be ***imprecise*** when we select whatever comes to mind without carefully determining whether it is the most appropriate to the issue. Furthermore, a concept is precise when it involves all the cases that should be included in the concept (and excludes those that should be excluded), and imprecise when it involves being less exact, as in the case of when it is too broad (or covers more than should be included) or too narrow (or covers less than should be included).

> Being **precise** involves being as exact as the context requires or allows.
>
> Being **imprecise** involves being less exact than the context requires or allows.

2.3 The Various Functions of Language

The function of language can sometimes be identified through grammatical form: providing information is done with declarative sentences, asking questions is done with interrogative sentences (and often involve changes in intonation), and giving direction is done with imperative sentences. Other functions of language may not be associated with particular speech or grammatical forms: language can be used to express or arouse emotions, establish bonds (even intimate ones), or sever them. It can both create and resolve conflict, and it can also entertain us through stories, jokes, poetry, or drama.

Table 2.1 identifies some functions and examples of how language can be used for many purposes.

TABLE 2.1 Some Functions of Language

Function	Examples
To inform and describe.	Victoria is separated from Vancouver by a large body of water called the Strait of Georgia. The genetic revolution started with Gregor Mendel.
To question.	How do I get to Victoria from Vancouver in a hurry? Why do you say the genetic revolution started with Gregor Mendel?
To direct.	Insert Tab "A" in Slot "B". Make sure your essay has a thesis and a bibliography.
To express emotion.	I love you. That sucks.
To evaluate and assess.	The quickest way of getting from Victoria to Vancouver is by seaplane. Stealing is wrong.
To perform.	A *performative* utterance is one that simply by its utterance makes something happen: I pronounce you man and wife; and I sentence you to ten years in prison.

The above examples are not an exhaustive list, nor are the functions mutually exclusive. For example, storytelling can simultaneously arouse emotions, provide information, build solidarity with others, and create conflict with yet others.

Some uses of language can be confusing. Three such uses are irony, sarcasm, and rhetorical questions. Irony occurs when the meaning of a statement is opposite to what the statement literally means. In Mark Anthony's funeral oration in Shakespeare's *Julius Caesar* he refers to Caesar's murderers as "all honourable men," when, in context, the meaning is that they are not. Jonathan Swift's *A Modest Proposal* was written to bring the plight of the Irish under British rule to the attention of the English public. In it he proposed, in what seems a perfectly logical argument, that since the English were already making life unbearable for the Irish, the Irish should sell their infants at the age of two to the English to be eaten by them. In context, everyone saw the irony, and a price was placed on Swift's head. When presented with Swift's argument, some students have railed against Swift's inhumanity. The English government got the irony; some students did not. Calling the Titanic "unsinkable" is a bit of unintentional irony. The title of Alanis Morissette's song *Irony* is ironic because none of the things mentioned in the song involve irony.

Sarcasm involves using language to ridicule or mock someone or something. The statement "of course democracy is a great political system, look at how many have failed" uses irony to denigrate democracy. Groucho Marx's answer "No, Groucho is not my real name; I'm breaking it in for a friend." points out the stupidity of the person asking the question, while his statement "I never forget a face, but in your case I'll make an exception." mocks the person's looks. As with irony, what is literally being said needs to be interpreted in light of the speaker's intentions and the context.

A rhetorical question is a figure of speech that is framed as a question but which assumes a specific reply. As such, it is often an indirect way of making a claim without having to support it. Student in essay: "Isn't it true that evolution can't explain gaps in the fossil record? And isn't it true that if it can't do that, then it is not a very good scientific theory? And if it isn't a scientific theory, then why should it be taught in school?" In this passage the student asks a series of questions, assuming the answer to each. The tactic of using a series of rhetorical questions to make a point or, in this case, an argument, enables the author to make a series of points without having to defend them. While rhetorical questions can be used sparingly for emphasis, overuse often undermines the main point and can obscure the reasoning.

Our concern is with the informative and evaluative uses of language since these are what we primarily use in argumentation. The informative use of language conveys information through claims that can be true or false, while evaluative language expresses judgments or points of view. Clarity and precision are still qualities required for both.

QUICK QUIZ 2.1

The Functions of Language

What is the function of each of the following sentences?

1. I'm elated that Canadian women won the gold in hockey.
2. That is a job well done.
3. Wow!
4. Not one of the women on the team is a professional, but they all played like professionals.

Answers to the Quick Quizzes are available on the Premium Website at www.criticalthinking2e.nelson.com.

2.4 Language and Meaning

A language is a symbol system. Many languages are composed of words (sometimes called "terms") organized into meaningful structures (usually sentences). "Cat," "sat," and "mat" organized into a well-formed sentence might result in the sentence "The cat sat on the mat." (In this section, quotation marks are used to indicate the word itself, not the meaning, referent, or object represented by the term.) The informative use of language is intended to convey information about the world we experience.

Words are linguistic entities (sounds or their representation in writing) that convey a meaning. The word "cat" is itself not a cat, but signifies one of a group of objects we identify as cats. Many words represent ***concepts*** or the ideas we have of things. We can express a concept in a word ("cat"), a phrase ("Chicago blues"), a sentence ("Justice involves both fairness and equality"), or a set of sentences.

Concepts are one way we make sense of the "buzzing, blooming confusion" we encounter in this life. They provide us with categories for interpreting and organizing

Words are linguistic entities that convey a meaning.

Concepts are ideas we have of things.

our experiences and relating them to one another. Different concepts provide us with various ways of thinking. For example, calling someone a "detainee" rather than a "prisoner of war" involves choosing one concept over another. Although we are ultimately talking about the same person, the meanings of the terms differ considerably. The concept prisoner of war is tied to other ideas, and therefore connects to the world in a different way than the concept detainee does.

Sometimes disputes arise over which concept applies in a given situation. Labelling someone a "terrorist" invokes a set of categories that may blind us to other options for addressing them. It may also put an argument partner on the defensive because we may end up fighting over what words to attach to the situation, rather than over the situation, itself.

Most concepts can be understood by identifying three possible components. The first component of a concept is its **meaning** or **sense**, which is derived from a set of shared expectations or rules of use that members of a language community have about a given concept, and is often captured by a definition. Assigning a meaning to a concept is an attempt to establish the rules for its use. The meaning of some concepts is relatively invariant, while other meanings differ between social groups and change over time.

The second component of a concept is the **referent**, which is the object (thing, process, activity) the concept or word refers to. For example, the referent of the concept cat is each and every walking, meowing, furry creature we identify as a cat, while the referent of Snowball is an actual cat purring for attention. A referent may be many things (this is not an exhaustive list):

- A single object (such as, a cat, a plant, a bicycle);
- A process (such as, applying for a passport);
- A relationship (such as, with a brother);
- A property of something (such as, it being red, tall, bald);
- An action (such as, voting);
- An individual (such as, my friend Mary); and
- An abstract property (such as, justice).

Some words do not represent concepts, but instead help to demonstrate the relationship between concepts. For example, "the," "of," "very," "and," and "about" have no referents. Such words have a function in language (such as helping us construct grammatically correct sentences) without having a meaning in the usual sense of a referent.

Because meaning is based on the way a word is used, it is essentially contextual. Groups of language users may use a word and its related concept differently. Individuals might also use the same word differently in various contexts, as in Anitha's and Philippe's uses of "justice." To illustrate further, "cat" can refer to different things: a domestic feline; any member of the family Felidae (including the lynx, panther, lion, or tiger); a jazz musician or aficionado of jazz; anyone thought of as cool; a type of boat (a catamaran); the process of hoisting an anchor; the search for sexual partners ("catting" around); or malice (as in the case of cattiness).

Which concept is used and how it is used depends on variables such as the context of the utterance, the speaker, and the audience. Normally, the context establishes which of the possible meanings is intended. For example, when asked to let the cat out for the night, I do not release the mooring lines on the boat and cast it adrift.

In some cases we may agree on the meaning of a concept (for example, to steal means to take something that is someone else's property without that person's permission),

> The **meaning** or **sense** of a concept is derived from a set of shared expectations or rules of use that members of a language community have about a given concept, and is often captured by a definition.

> A **referent** is the object (thing, process, activity) that a concept or word refers to.

but disagree on its referent (or thing in the world it identifies). Although people might agree on the meaning of stealing and agree that taking a CD from a store without paying constitutes stealing, they might still disagree as to whether downloading a song through a peer-to-peer network without paying is stealing. They agree on the concept in its abstract sense, but not on its application in a specific context. What makes this process dynamic is that we often develop concepts in one context (say, taking material objects without paying is stealing), but when faced with a new context (say, taking information from the Internet without paying) we may apply the existing rules for the use of the concept in quite different ways, even though we agree on the concept's meaning and its original application. The issue here is whether we should apply the concept of material property developed in one context to a new referent in a new context. Alternatively, we may agree on a referent, yet disagree on the concept that should be applied to describe it (as in the case of questioning whether taking something without permission is always stealing).

QUICK QUIZ 2.2

The Role of Context

Consider possible alternate meanings for the claims below. Explain how the context might affect the meaning of the key terms or claims. How could they be interpreted in different contexts?

1. Meet me by the bank.
2. The President is a man of utmost honour, lives by the highest ethical standards, and tells only the truth.
3. We will ensure all children have access to child care.
4. Liberals are free-spending and irresponsible.

Answers to the Quick Quizzes are available on the Premium Website at www.criticalthinking2e.nelson.com.

Abstract concepts, adjectives, and adverbs often do not have a solitary, independent, or singular referent. Justice, truth, and integrity are not concrete things in the world, though they do refer to states of being. Similarly, being boring is not a specific concrete thing, but does describe (and evaluate) the way in which something is done.

Every day we use abstract terms such as "justice," "pornography," "family values," "torture," or "insurgent" without always clearly understanding either their meanings or referents. By identifying concrete situations where we would use such words we can start to understand the meaning of a given concept as it applies to a particular context, that is, the reality to which the word refers. By using more concrete words, identifying the referents of those terms, and providing definitions of the concepts we use, we can clarify our intent.

The third component of a concept is ***connotation***, which is not part of the concept itself or the criteria for identifying it, but the subjective and emotional associations we make with the concept or word. The literal meaning of the words "democracy" is a form of government in which political authority is ultimately held by those who are governed. Since Western nations typically consider this a good thing the word has a positive connotation.

> The **connotation** is the subjective and emotional associations we make with a concept or word.

Some words (such as, "friend," "justice," and "freedom") generally have positive connotations, while others (such as, "oppression," "inhumane," and "terrorist") generally have negative connotations, and still others (such as, "sidewalk," "bicycle," and "lamp") have neutral connotations. The connotation can vary depending on the audience (such as, "liberal," "socialist," "feminist," and "fundamentalist"). Some words – "anti" and "pro," for example – typically carry negative and positive connotations, respectively, regardless of what they are applied to. Newt Gingrich, a former Speaker of the U.S. House of Representatives, compiled a list of Optimistic Positive Governing Words that carry positive connotations and Contrasting Words that carry negative connotations.[1]

Words such as "candidly," "caring," "initiative," and "truth" generally carry positive connotations, while words such as "corruption," "cynicism," "patronage," and "self-serving" carry negative connotations. The widespread use of such words in political discourse for their connotative meaning, simply as labels to identify political positions, tends to short-circuit political discourse by moving it from a reasoned discussion of the issue to an emotional contest between our side (the good guys) and their side (the bad guys) without addressing the underlying reasons.

Connotations may also be personal (say, for someone who was bitten by a dog and breaks out in a sweat just hearing the word "dog") or may be shared (say, for those who have benefited by democracy or justice). Some connotations are common to most members of a language community, while others are much more specific to niche groups or even individuals, as some of the above examples demonstrate.

QUICK QUIZ 2.3

Words, Concepts, Referents, and Connotations

Identify the possible referents and meanings for the key concepts, and explain the meaning of the claim in each of the following. Where different referents and meanings are possible, identify these and show how the meanings of the claims might be affected.

1. Comment made during the Sponsorgate (Liberal advertising) scandal: The Liberals are corrupt.
2. Bikers are members of criminal organizations.
3. Intelligence is genetic.

Answers to the Quick Quizzes are available on the Premium Website at www.criticalthinking2e.nelson.com.

When dealing with words that have strong connotations, one way of avoiding the inferences they can lead to is to separate such words into one claim that identifies the literal meaning and another that identifies the emotive component. Consider the following example:

Fundamentalist Christians are trying to force their beliefs about evolution on others.

1 Mr. Gingrich's list can be found at Information Clearing House: http://www.informationclearinghouse.info/article4443.htm

In this example, "fundamentalists" and "force their beliefs on others" have strong connotations. For those who are not fundamentalist Christians, the word "fundamentalist" can raise a red flag, and for many the term is offensive.

The connotation can be neutralized by finding language that is less emotionally loaded and more neutral, and then identifying separately the emotive force of the claim. A *neutral claim* is a claim with little or no strong emotional connotation. The *emotive force* identifies the emotional nature (positive or negative) within the connotation and explains how it operates in the original claim. By reformulating the example above, we can see how this is done:

> Neutral claim: People with strong, conservative Christian religious convictions are trying to get others to adopt their views about evolution.
>
> Emotive force: The emotive force of this claim is strongly negative. Fundamentalists are expressing their opinions in a manner that the author of this claim thinks involves force or coercion or is in some other way unjustified.

Both "fundamentalist" and "force" have negative connotations.

In trying to get an audience to accept the neutral claim, emotionally laden elements are often used as the reason or justification to motivate the acceptance of an idea. By distinguishing between a claim and the connotations associated with it we can more easily understand and assess what the claim is and are less likely to be influenced by the connotation of the words.

Consider another example:

> The terrorists in Afghanistan want to take the country back to the Dark Ages.

The emotionally loaded words include "terrorists" and "take the country back to the Dark Ages."

> Neutral claim: Those resisting the occupation of Afghanistan by Allied forces want to bring about a more conservative society based on fundamentalist Islamic religious principles.
>
> Emotive force: These people are bad people, and their agenda is bad for the people of Afghanistan.

"Fundamentalist," as it is used here, may also be emotionally laden and may need neutralizing.

This technique is not a simple paraphrasing of the claim. Rather, it is an analysis of the claim that focuses on the meaning of what is being said and the referent so as to distinguish the informative content (neutral claim) from the connotative elements (emotive force). With the words neutralized, it is easier to examine the claims and determine if the emotive force provides any reason for accepting the literal claim. Usually it does not.

Prejudicial language involves using loaded or emotional words to influence people to think or act based solely on the emotional content of the claims, rather than on reasons to do with the issue itself. Prejudicial language can be either positive or negative and can strive to get an audience to accept or reject a claim or position.

> A **neutral claim** is a claim with little or no strong emotional connotation.
>
> **Emotive force** identifies the emotional nature (positive or negative) within the connotation.

Describing doctors accused of fraud as "quacks" prejudices us against their medical competency. In cases such as this one, the same technique used for neutralizing connotations can be used to neutralize prejudicial language. This involves translating a prejudicial claim into a neutral one, and then presenting the emotional or prejudicial language as a separate claim. The above could be translated into the following:

Neutral claim: Some medical doctors are being charged with fraud.

Emotive force: These medical doctors were poor physicians (or quacks). Referring to a physician as a quack is a way of dismissing the individual and distracting the audience from the actual issue.

QUICK QUIZ 2.4

Neutralizing Connotations and Prejudicial Language

In each of the following, identify whether there are **words** or **claims** with strong connotations. If so, neutralize the connotation by dividing the claims into the literal meaning and the emotive force.

1. The anti-choice terrorists have prevented abortion providers from doing their legal work. They have bombed their offices, killed them, and stalked their employees. These enemies of freedom need to be stopped.
2. [*Spoken by a U.S. commentator:*] Those spineless cowards who oppose the valiant U.S. efforts in Iraq are soft on terror and encouraging the murder of our brave fighting men and women.
3. We should be wary of legalizing gay marriage because if we change the definition of marriage to include same-sex people, then there appears to be no grounds for limiting marriage to just two people or prohibiting it between near relatives. The move to change the definition of marriage could result in legalizing polygamy and incest.

Answers to the Quick Quizzes are available on the Premium Website at www.criticalthinking2e.nelson.com.

2.5 Some Common Pitfalls in the Use of Language

Although our communicative goal in argumentation is to express ourselves in clear and accurate language, this does not always come easily. Sometimes we fail to speak precisely, falter in presenting our ideas, or simply do not realize we are not using language effectively. This section identifies some common mistakes and how to correct them.

Vagueness

A concept or claim is *vague* when its meaning or application is unclear, fuzzy, or inexact in the context of the purposes for which it is being used. The problem with this is that

> A concept or claim is **vague** when its meaning or application is unclear, fuzzy, or inexact in the context of the purposes for which it is being used.

you cannot determine with certainty how or when the concept would be applied. With a vague claim you cannot determine precisely what the claim means and under what conditions it would be true or false.

Let us imagine the police issued a bulletin to be on the lookout for a bald white male about 35 years old. "Bald" is vague in the context. Although there are clear cases of people who are bald (such as those without any hair on their heads), and although we can also identify clear cases of people who are not bald (such as those with a lot of hair on their heads), if we were to gradually add one hair at a time to a person without hair, at what point would the individual stop being bald? Is someone who has only a fringe of hair about the ears bald? There is no precise answer to this. Should I turn in every white male over 30 who is follicularly challenged, or only those with absolutely no hair on their heads? "Bald" is a vague concept in the context of the imagined police bulletin.

Ordinary use of language often involves some degree of vagueness. Whether or not this is a problem depends on the context and the degree of precision needed within that context. Consider a warning on a pesticide container:

Do not use near livestock or humans.

This warning is vague. How near is *near*? A metre? Two metres? Ten metres? Half a kilometre? Without more precise instructions I could cause harm to myself or to livestock. I am also not told whether it is safe to use in the vicinity of other kinds of animals (such as, cats and dogs). After all, technically they are not livestock.

When a concept is vague we do not know what it means or refers to in certain contexts. As a result we cannot clearly assess or act on the claim. Consider the following:

An interviewee is asked about experiences with respect to teamwork and answers "I learned many valuable lessons about teamwork."

Without elaboration this answer is vague. If the interviewee elaborates by providing specific examples and instances, then it is simply a poor start to a better answer.

The following are principles that will help in making statements clear and precise (and avoiding vagueness):

1. Be clear about what you are trying to express. If you do not know what you are trying to say you are more likely to be vague.
2. Select the precise words to express your meaning. Vague and sloppy language results when you simply use whatever words are at hand rather than trying to find the words that express your meaning exactly.
3. Use concrete rather than abstract words: where a vehicle can seat five adults comfortably, describe it as "seating five adults comfortably" rather than as "roomy."
4. When you do use abstract words, provide examples. The interviewee above could briefly describe an experience of being part of a team and explain how it was beneficial.
5. Use precise quantifiers rather than indefinite quantifying terms. Indefinite quantifying words include some, a few, many, near, far, young, and old. The pesticide instructions could be improved using this method and read "Do not use within 10 metres of where humans, livestock, or other animals travel."

The Missing Quantifier/Qualifier

A particular kind of vagueness arises from a missing quantifier or qualifier. A **quantifier** is a word that indicates how many members of a group a claim applies to. All, some, a few, none, and 47% are all quantifiers. Each quantifier determines the scope or range of application to a claim. "All swans are white" is different from "most swans are white," and is different yet again from "a few swans are white." In the absence of a quantifier, we tend to assume "all"; this can be misleading and result in assessing claims incorrectly.

A **qualifier** is a word that restricts a claim by limiting the kinds of things to which the claim applies. For example, the claim "drug users resort to crime to support their habit and are a threat to society" suggests all drug users are threats to society. Yet if pressed, someone making this claim would likely only be able to support that some drug users are threats. "Some drug users" would quantify the claim imprecisely, while "heroine users" would qualify the claim precisely. Quantifiers supply numbers, and qualifiers restrict claims by limiting them to kinds of things. Missing quantifiers and qualifiers leave the (mistaken) impression that all members of a class are relatively homogeneous and all have the property attributed to them. This hides the diversity and variation within the class being referred to.

In the debate over a Danish newspaper's publishing of cartoons depicting the prophet Mohammad, claims such as the following were made:

Muslims oppose free speech.

Subsequent discussions tended to treat all Muslims as one undifferentiated mass. People making such claims failed to correctly acknowledge the differences among individual Muslims within and between the various Muslim sects and communities. The missing quantifier often reflects a crude stereotyping of the group being discussed.

A universal claim (or one that applies to all) is sometimes used instead of a more restrictive claim when referring to a general tendency or feature that characterizes a large number or the majority of a group. For example:

> A **quantifier** is a word that indicates how many members of a group a claim applies to.

> A **qualifier** is a word that restricts a claim by limiting the kinds of things to which the claim applies.

Men leave child care up to women.

We tend to use the universal quantifier when none is provided, but in cases like this it would be more accurate and less misleading to formulate the claim more precisely by formulating it as follows:

Most men leave the majority of child care responsibilities to women.

Without knowing all the details this may be as precise as we can get. For a better argument it would be advisable to get accurate numbers.

The best way of avoiding problems with missing quantifiers and qualifiers is to recognize the differences within classes and formulate the claims in a much more restrictive way by providing an appropriate quantifier and/or qualifiers.

QUICK QUIZ 2.6

Missing Quantifiers and Qualifiers

In the following, identify claims with missing quantifiers and qualifiers, suggest possible differences and variations among the referents, and provide a more restrictive claim. If there are strong connotations, neutralize them. If the language is vague, you should note that and suggest how it could be made less vague.

1. Universities need to clean up their acts. All I read about are students getting out of control, having sex, posing for *Playboy*, drinking, and uttering racist remarks. The police regularly have to be called to homecoming at local universities, some of which were just voted the leading "party schools" in North America. What ever happened to going to university to learn?
2. Scientists defending evolution are opposed to religion.
3. *Said by one university faculty member to another:* "Students are getting worse. My recently assigned papers were so badly written I had to hand them back for rewriting. And the incidence of plagiarism is at epidemic proportions."

Answers to the Quick Quizzes are available on the Premium Website at www.criticalthinking2e.nelson.com.

Ambiguity

Ambiguity occurs when a word, phrase, or sentence has two or more distinct meanings, and when both make sense in the given context, so it is not clear which one is specifically intended. The difference between ambiguity and vagueness is that with ambiguous terms and claims there are two or more clear meanings but we cannot be sure from the context which is meant, whereas with vague terms and claims there is no clear and precise meaning.

Former President Bill Clinton's claim, "I did not have sexual relations with that woman," contained a convenient ambiguity in the meaning of the term "sexual relations." The term can mean "sexual intercourse" (in the narrow sense) or "any kind of sexual activity" (in the broader sense). Clinton was using the term in the narrow sense to deny that he and Monica Lewinsky had had sexual intercourse, while most people interpreted the term to mean he denied engaging in any sexual activity in the broader sense of the term.

> **Ambiguity** occurs when a word, phrase, or sentence has two or more distinct meanings, and when both make sense in the given context, so it is not clear which one is specifically intended.

A sociologist in a lecture identifies a particular religious group as a cult. A student who is a member of that religious group takes offence and challenges the claim. The instructor replies the religious group is precisely what it was characterized to be: a cult. The instructor is likely using "cult" in a specialized sociological sense to refer to an independent religious group in a context where there are a number of religious bodies and no one of them dominates, whereas the student is using "cult" in the more ordinary sense to mean a breakaway religious group often led by a messianic leader and assumed to be extremist in some way.

When confronted with a situation in which a claim seems obviously or unnecessarily controversial, and one side does not consider it as such, examine the passage to determine if one or more of the key terms is being used ambiguously. Try substituting alternate meanings to see if the claim can be made more acceptable.

QUICK QUIZ 2.7

Ambiguity

In each of the following, find any words that are used ambiguously and identify their alternate meanings.

1. The theory of evolution is just a theory. And theories are not factual, just speculative. Therefore, the theory of evolution is just speculation.
2. How can the doctor say my mother is dead? With the respirator she is still breathing.
3. Mathematics is a science. After all, it is taught in the faculty of science.

Answers to the Quick Quizzes are available on the Premium Website at www.criticalthinking2e.nelson.com.

Words That Conceal: Euphemisms, Doublespeak, and Code Words

Some uses of language intentionally hide what is being said and the underlying reality. Euphemisms and code words involve using imprecise terms (or phrases), or substituting less than fully precise language, to mask the meaning of a claim.

A *euphemism* involves using words to cast a positive light on situations that are not otherwise positive or pleasant. Euphemisms can be used to avoid giving offence, or to disguise what is being talked about. We use euphemisms for: (1) things considered unpleasant or potentially offensive, for example, death (such as, "passing on" "is now with God," or "didn't make it" instead of "died"), or sex, or excretion; (2) things considered too sacred to be uttered (such as, the name of the supreme being – itself a euphemism – that cannot be uttered in some religions); and/ or (3) covering up what it is we are referring to (such as, "wardrobe malfunction").

A particular kind of euphemism is *doublespeak*, which involves using an abstract or imprecise word (or phrase) in place of a concrete or precise one with the intent of concealing what is being said. Bureaucratese, a form of doublespeak, is composed of inflated language that can be seen in the following examples: "administrative assistant" for secretary, "sanitary engineer" for janitor, and "sunshine units" for radiation leaked from an improperly functioning nuclear power plant. Bureaucratese's well-known function of hiding the unpleasant truth of firing employees can be seen in the examples: "being laid off," "downsized," "right-sized," "restructured," and "realigned."

A euphemism involves using words to cast a positive light on situations that are not otherwise positive or pleasant.

Doublespeak involves using abstract or imprecise word (or phrase) in place of a concrete or precise one with the intent of concealing what is being said.

Military and political communications, where the function is to neutralize or distance oneself from what is being said, are full of doublespeak, as seen in the following examples: "Collateral damage" replaces "unintended civilian casualties"; "disanimate" replaces "kill"; and "effect regime change" replaces "overthrow the existing government." The neutral language of doublespeak results in a "death squad" becoming "a public safety unit," a "body bag" (originally, "a flexible coffin") becoming "a human remains pouch," and an "air attack" becoming "a protective reaction strike." In the sentence "The President misspoke," does "misspoke" mean she or he intentionally lied, unintentionally misstated something, or something else altogether? Doublespeak often creates unresolved ambiguity.

Code words involve a kind of ambiguity in which the context of a specific audience determines the meaning. For instance, some words have one meaning to the general public but a special meaning to a particular target audience. In hotly contested political issues a speaker might use code words to address supporters without having to be specific and thereby incite controversy. This is sometimes called "dog-whistle phrasing," a reference to the high-frequency whistle heard only by dogs because only the target audience hears what is actually being intended.

A social conservative speaking of "a return to family values" is using a dog-whistle phrase that might sound harmless to the public but has specific meaning to the conservative's specific audience. "Traditional family values" can be a code for many things: conventional gender roles (in which women are subservient to men); restricting marriage and child-rearing to heterosexual couples; opposing abortion, single-parent families, divorce, sex-education, and contraception. Since the term is not sharply defined people can apply whatever meaning they consider relevant and agree with. Since the phrase makes no overt claims, it cannot be challenged.

Euphemisms, doublespeak, and code words contribute to a lack of clarity and precision in language. The best way of handling these is to identify the referent and to translate the term, phrase, or claim into precise language.

> **Code words** involve a kind of ambiguity in which the context of a specific audience determines the meaning.

QUICK QUIZ 2.8

Words That Conceal

Translate the following into plain language.

1. *A military statement:* We made a pre-emptive reaction strike to neutralize the enemy. However, there was some civilian collateral damage. Several members of the coalition forces succumbed to friendly fire.
2. *Government policy statement:* The municipal government is committed to revenue-enhancement measures through cost recovery for nonessential programs.
3. *A corporate email announcement:* George Footloose has left the company, effective immediately.

Answers to the Quick Quizzes are available on the Premium Website at www.criticalthinking2e.nelson.com.

Hypostatization

Hypostatization (also called ***reification***: literally, making a concept into a thing) involves ascribing existence to abstract or conceptual entities and treating them as though they are concrete entities with the properties of agents. The claim "nature has

> **Hypostatization** (also called **reification**) involves ascribing existence to abstract or conceptual entities and treating them as though they are concrete entities with the properties of agents.

dictated that the sole purpose of sex is reproduction and any other purpose goes against the wishes of nature" is an example of a hypostatization because "nature," an abstract word referring to a variety of processes and activities, is being used as if it denotes a person who has intentions and wishes and can make pronouncements about those intentions. In the claim "we all have an obligation to society" the word "society" is being hypostatized because it is not a single entity but the totality of individuals and their relationships to one another. It is easy, though, to think of society as a concrete entity that makes demands and to whom we have collective obligations.

Not all uses of abstract or general terms result in hypostatization. Sometimes we use general terms as a form of shorthand for a more complex statement (such as when writing or speaking in an elliptical way to convey a much fuller meaning in an extremely condensed form). An *elliptical* use of language involves the use of a simpler or condensed statement for a more complex one. This can often lead to misunderstanding.

An **elliptical** use of language involves the use of a simpler or condensed statement for a more complex one.

The above claim about nature could mean that the sole function of sexual intercourse in the biological world is reproduction. This is a partial translation of the initial statement and therefore is elliptical since it does not personify nature, so there is no hypostatization. Nor does it carry the evaluative and normative overtones of the original statement. Hypostatization usually does not occur when we are speaking in a form of shorthand, but does occur when we interpret the general term as a concrete entity and ascribe properties and characteristics to that hypothetical entity. In any given context it can be difficult to determine whether a term is being used elliptically or is being hypostatized.

Almost any abstract entity (such as, art, history, love, society, the State, science, women, men, religion, and specific religions) can be hypostatized.

One way of handling a hypostatization is to translate the concept or claim into one that does not reify any terms (that is, treat them as things). If that can be done, then the original claim is elliptical. The above statement about society could be translated into a claim or set of claims that does not reify society. It might mean something like the following:

> Everyone who is a member of a social group has obligations not only to specific other members but to all members of the group by virtue of being a member of that group.

Since this does not reify the concept "society," we can conclude that the original statement was an example of elliptical shorthand, rather than a reification or hypostatization. Such translations can clarify meaning and may also identify what is contentious about a claim.

Hypostatized terms are often ambiguous. They may refer to a nonexistent abstract entity as a concrete thing, or they may be an elliptical way of saying something else. We have to examine the context to determine which is the case.

QUICK QUIZ 2.9

Hypostatization

In each of the following, determine if any terms are being hypostatized. If so, identify the term, explain how it is being hypostatized, and state the possible problems that could result from the hypostatization. If it is possible to treat the terms elliptically, provide an elliptical translation of the claim.

1. Poverty is stalking our nation's children.
2. Men believe women are inferior and seek to dominate and control them.

3. The nation demands that every citizen rally behind the war effort.
4. The gay community is trying to impose its views about marriage on the rest of society.

Answers to the Quick Quizzes are available on the Premium Website at www.criticalthinking2e.nelson.com.

Metaphors

A *metaphor* is a literary device in which a phrase that refers to one thing is applied to a different kind of thing. The metaphor "a tidal wave of illegal immigrants is flooding across the border" compares the number of illegal immigrants crossing the border to a tidal wave, a destructive, uncontrollable force. Metaphors often create vivid images and draw connections through comparisons of purported similarities without making the claims and connections explicit.

While we generally have no difficulty in understanding metaphors, the language used in them often fails to address crucial questions, in this case just how many immigrants are crossing the border and what constitutes a "tidal wave" of immigrants?

Metaphors can make our language come alive. However, they can also short-circuit critical reasoning and argumentation ("short-circuit" is itself a metaphor). Using the metaphor of a tidal wave when referring to illegal immigrants suggests a very large problem without clearly identifying the actual size or complexity of the problem. A metaphor may be used to illustrate a point, but if it replaces the reasoning and evidence required to support that point, it becomes problematic.

Metaphors and analogies are similar. Whereas a metaphor makes an implicit comparison between two different things, an *analogy* draws an explicit comparison between different things. For example: "The influx of illegal immigrants is like a tidal wave" is an analogy, because the statement is now an explicit comparison.

Metaphors are so deeply ingrained in our language we often do not notice we are using them. We talk of couch potatoes, short-circuiting thought, seeing through someone, lawyers grilling witnesses, the Canucks being toast this season, one's goose being cooked, poor social policy being a recipe for disaster, adding fuel to the fire, being burned up, out of touch, or hot for someone.

Metaphors are incredibly valuable. Not only do they enrich and enliven language, but they often enable us to see an issue more creatively and vividly. However, problems can arise when they obscure the reasoning, when we mistake the metaphor for the reality, or when the metaphors lead us to draw illegitimate inferences. A classic example of this is in the application of economic metaphors to war and genetics, as in the cases when we talk about whether the war in Afghanistan is "worth it," whether we are "too heavily invested," and what the long term "payoffs" will be. The use of such metaphors encourages us to think in terms of a certain framework drawn from economics that can distract us from other frameworks (say, ethical considerations about the war). Some geneticists talk about "competition" between genes, the different "investment strategies" of eggs and sperm, and their "payoffs." Sports, war, and evolutionary metaphors ("survival of the fittest") abound in business. Yet business is not simply a game, a war, or an evolutionary process. The problem arises when we reduce the complexities of the issue to a simpler version of a concept in order to understand the issue, but distort it while doing so.

A **metaphor** is a linguistic device in which a phrase that refers to one thing is applied to a different kind of thing.

An **analogy** draws an explicit comparison between two different things.

Before learning how to deal with metaphors we must be able to identify the metaphors that are being used. We do this by isolating the item under discussion and determining what it is being compared to. For example:

Item under discussion: immigrants crossing our borders

Is being compared to: a tidal wave, a flood

One way of addressing metaphors is to deal with them by translating them into language that does not contain metaphors. For example, "a large number of illegal immigrants are crossing our borders" clarifies the language and enables us to examine the claim more critically: the translation highlights the lack of precision in this particular claim by raising the question "how many is a large number?"

A second way to address metaphors is to generate a different one because it can help us see the same issue in a different light. For example, "our country is becoming a haven for hundreds of thousands of economic refugees" compares illegal immigrants to refugees and suggests the country is a haven or safe place. This conjures up quite a different image: by calling them economic refugees rather than illegal immigrants, this metaphor reframes the image and can lead us to question which (if either) is a more accurate portrayal.

These common pitfalls of language usage can give way to errors in reasoning if we base our reasoning solely on them. For example, ambiguity can lead to the fallacy of equivocation, while improper use of metaphor and analogy can lead to the fallacy of faulty analogy. (For more on fallacies, see Module 7.)

QUICK QUIZ 2.10

Metaphors

Identify the metaphors in the following statements and translate them into neutral language. Determine what is under discussion and what it is being compared to. Indicate whether or not the metaphors in each passage are likely to mislead and explain why.

1. *Politician during an election campaign:* Canadians are staggering under a massive tax burden. If elected, we will relieve the weight borne by the ordinary taxpayer.
2. There is a hole in that theory.
3. He spends his time wisely.

Answers to the Quick Quizzes are available on the Premium Website at www.criticalthinking2e.nelson.com.

2.6 Clarifying Meaning through Definitions

> A **definition** gives a word meaning by establishing a common understanding of a concept.

A **definition** gives a word meaning by establishing a common understanding of a concept. Different kinds of definitions have various functions. Understanding the different kinds of definitions, their purposes, and the criteria for good definitions can help you choose which kind to use in a specific situation.

Ostensive Definitions

An *ostensive definition* defines a concept by providing examples of it rather than outlining criteria for its use. Pointing to a cat, I could say "that is a cat" and in effect identify the referent (or a set of referents) for the term. However, this does not say anything about the meaning of the concept or what makes something a cat and not a dog. To clarify an ostensive definition further, I can use contrast to show what it is not, such as if I were to say "that is a cat" while pointing to a cat, then "and that is not" while pointing to a dog. This kind of definition is useful in introducing someone to a new concept and in providing the basis for developing other kinds of definitions. When used in conjunction with another kind of definition, the example serves as an illustration rather than as a definition.

An **ostensive definition** defines a concept by providing examples of it rather than outlining criteria for its use.

Operational Definitions

An *operational definition* defines a concept by prescribing a procedure or operation required to determine if something is the case or is occurring. The result of the procedure or operation is the concept being defined. This type of definition is most commonly found in science and the social science studies, policy studies, and organizational and governmental regulations. For example, *intelligence* is defined as the score achieved on a standardized IQ test, *relationship power* in this study is defined as marital decision-making as determined by responses to a standardized questionnaire on marital decision-making, and a *voting member* is defined as someone who has been a member of the union for three months.

An **operational definition** defines a concept by prescribing a procedure or operation required to determine if something is the case or is occurring. The result of the procedure or operation is the concept being defined.

Operational definitions typically provide technical criteria that can easily be measured. The advantage of a good operational definition is that it can ensure that the same procedure is used across different populations in a study so results are comparable. Some sociologists operationally define "relationship power" as someone who makes the most decisions in a relationship, and if other sociologists use the same operational definitions their results can be meaningfully compared. However, if another sociologist uses a different operational definition (say, "relationship power" is defined as someone who makes the financial decisions within the relationship) then the results cannot be meaningfully compared.

Different operational definitions are used for the same phenomena from one study to the next. This means one cannot easily or confidently compare the results of separate studies. If one study defines an "occasional smoker" as someone who smokes ten cigarettes a week, and another defines an occasional smoker as someone who smokes ten cigarettes a month, the two operational definitions are measuring different things but using the same name to do so.

Recognizing this is important in reading scientific and governmental studies. How researchers define such things as poverty ("an income of less than *x*," where *x* varies by study), unemployment, or pollution determines what they are measuring and how comparable the data from different studies are. In many cases the facts remain the same but what changes is how those facts are captured by an operational definition. This means what is called the poverty level or unemployment rate can vary simply by altering the operational definition of the words it seeks to define.

There are some difficulties with operational definitions. Because they relate to a given study and are very narrow in scope, they may not correspond to the way the words are used by others. Also, there may be more to *relationship* power or *intelligence* than the criteria the operations measure, besides which the operational definition may not measure what we normally mean by power or intelligence. Lastly, there is the problem of whether the operations used actually capture a useful sense of the concept.

Reportive Definitions

A **reportive definition** defines the meaning of a word by reporting how it is used within a language community. Dictionary makers commonly construct definitions by finding a number of instances of the word and then constructing reportive definitions. This is one of the most common forms of a definition.

Below is an example of a dictionary entry for the word "argue":

argue v.—*tr.* 1. To put forth reasons for or against; debate. 2. To attempt to prove by reasoning; maintain or contend. 3. To give evidence of; indicate: "*Similarities cannot always be used to argue descent*" (Isaac Asimov). 4. To persuade or influence (another), as by presenting reasons.—*intr.* 1. To put forth reasons for or against something; *argued for dismissal of the case*. 2. To engage in a quarrel; dispute. [ME *arguen* < OFr. *arguer* < Lat. *argu⁻ta⁻re*, to babble, chatter, freq. of *arguere*, to make clear.][2]

This reportive definition provides several different meanings of the word, each of which is a different but related concept. For some of the definitions it provides examples of the use of the word. It also indicates by reference to etymology (or origins) how the meaning of the word has changed over time, which reflects the constant evolution of language. For example, when the term "gay" was introduced into the English language it simply meant to be merry. However, over the course of time it has also come to mean homosexual. The term "bug," meaning insect, was metaphorically extended to include errors in software logic when a moth was found to have shorted out some of the circuits of an early computer. "Nice" once meant foolish, and the English word "lust" (derived from the German "lust" meaning any kind of pleasure) has now been narrowed to apply to a particular kind of sexual desire.

This shows us that language is fluid and contextual and the meanings of words change as members of a language community extend and modify the uses of the words. Since reportive definitions are simply accounts of how words are used in language, there are many examples of words that are used differently depending on the context or even on who in the language community is using it.

Essential Definitions

In searching for the meaning of a concept we must be clear as to whether we want a reportive or an essential definition. Whereas a reportive definition simply reports how a word is used in a given language, an **essential definition** seeks to identify the necessary and sufficient conditions for the use of a concept. In some cases essential definitions can correspond to ordinary usage.

One condition (say x) is a **necessary condition** for another condition (say y) if x must occur with y. And x is also a necessary condition for y if x must occur for y to occur. That does not mean if x occurs y occurs; only if y occurs x must have also occurred. For example, oxygen is a necessary condition for a fire, because for a fire to occur there must be oxygen; however, oxygen by itself is not sufficient to produce a fire.

2 "Argue." Def. *ITP Nelson Canadian Dictionary of the English Language*, 1997.

One condition (say *y*) is a ***sufficient condition*** for another condition (say *z*) if the presence of *y* is sufficient to define or bring about *z*. Thus, whenever *y* is present *z* is also present. For example, having an atomic number of 79 is a sufficient condition for something being gold, because if something is gold it has an atomic number of 79, and if something has an atomic number of 79 then it is gold. (See Module 4, Section 4.7 for more on necessary and sufficient conditions.)

An essential definition seeks to identify the conditions that either must be met, or would be adequate, for something to be a referent of a concept. In dictionaries some definitions are essential, but most are reportive. Occasionally, dictionaries may provide both kinds of definitions (for example, in the case of a word such as "gold").

Consider the word "gold" as applied to a metal commonly dug out of the ground and used for jewellery. One reportive definition might state that "gold is a precious metal used for jewellery and certain industrial applications." This is reportive because it tells how the word "gold" is used in a certain language community. There could well be a language community that does not value the metal we call gold and/or does not use it in the same ways. This reportive definition would change if we come to no longer treat gold as a precious metal or use it for jewellery or in industrial applications.

The conditions identified in a reportive definition may be neither necessary nor sufficient conditions for something to be gold. Now consider the following essential definition for gold:

> Gold is a soft-yellow, corrosion-resistant element with an atomic number of 79, atomic weight of 196.967, melting point of 1,063 degrees Celsius, and a specific gravity of 19.32.

This definition seeks to provide the necessary and sufficient conditions for identifying the metal gold. These conditions hold whether or not individuals realize gold has these conditions. This definition would change only if we discovered that gold had additional essential properties or that these properties did not distinguish gold from other elements (or metals). Most individuals who use the word "gold" and know the concept of it could not articulate these necessary and sufficient conditions, and if asked they are likely to cite a reportive definition. Nonetheless, both definitions are equally, though differently, true of the same referent.

The word "gold" is an easy example. It is a specific thing whose essential properties we can discover. "Sexual harassment" is more difficult because not only do people disagree as to its meaning, they also disagree as to what things constitute it. The disagreement is not just about the necessary and sufficient conditions for an agreed-upon set of objects, but also about what objects will be included in the class of things the word refers to. As the set of objects changes the necessary and sufficient conditions for members of that class will also change. As a result, a concept like sexual harassment may be dealing with a variety of related concepts, rather than one concept with a single essential definition.

Some words may not have necessary and sufficient conditions or may have only one of these. For example, the concept of a game has no necessary and sufficient conditions, yet virtually all of us can use the word accurately, identify what is and is not a game, and recognize problematic cases. At best, we can come up with reportive definitions (some possibly overlapping) for how the concept is used. We could say games are characterized by a cluster of conditions *p* through *z*. However, few games will meet all of these conditions and yet we are willing to call things that meet a substantial and undefined number of these conditions "games."

A **sufficient condition** is one whose occurrence is sufficient to produce or indicate the presence of another.

CLARIFYING MEANING **49**

Some abstract things (such as, justice, truth, freedom, and democracy) are particularly problematic. We sometimes treat them as having essential properties that define them, which may well be the case (if we can agree on the class of things the words refer to). However, often such words can refer to a variety of things, and different people will identify varying things that the words refer to. In such cases, there may not be one concept but several described by the same word.

Stipulative Definitions

In a ***stipulative definition*** an author specifies a meaning of a word in a particular context. This may be a new term or one already in the language in a given context. For examples,

By "pornography" I mean ...

By "metrosexual" I mean ...

In this essay, I use "democracy" to mean ...

Stipulative definitions can be a way of introducing a new concept into the language. Concepts such as "informed consent" and "sexual harassment" did not exist until relatively recently. They were introduced to identify phenomena that people wanted to draw attention to. Stipulative definitions can also be useful when there is not a clearly agreed-upon meaning for a concept, or when people wish to restrict a discussion to a particular aspect of a number of available meanings associated with a word. Since "pornography" and "democracy" are words with multiple and often contentious meanings, providing a stipulative definition (which may reflect a reportive definition) might be necessary to clarify what the words mean in a given context. Not only is the word "metrosexual" new to our language, but its meaning varies considerably, so providing a stipulative definition of it is a way to make sure the meaning is clear.

Stipulative definitions can cause problems with words already in use if the proposed definition is idiosyncratic or strays too far from common usage. Providing a stipulative definition of the word "pornography" as portrayals of sexual violence against women (as some have done) may reflect the perception of one group of language users without connecting it to the more general understanding of "pornography" used by others as any sexually explicit material, violent or not. Although this might add clarity to a specific discourse, it might also narrow the meaning of a word to a degree that blocks a broader discussion of an issue, thus creating a barrier to pursuing substantial understanding. Also, if a stipulative definition can be confused with a corresponding reportive or essential definition, it may create ambiguity in the use of the word, a problem that can be compounded if different people introduce multiple conflicting stipulative definitions.

One particular danger with using stipulative definitions occurs when one stipulates as a definition claims one is trying to establish, thus making the claim true by definition alone. For example:

I define "pornography" as sexual material that portrays violence against and degradation of women. I will show in this paper that pornography degrades women.

In this stipulative definition of "pornography" the author includes "degradation of women" as part of the definition, yet what he or she intends to show with the definition is *that* women are degraded by pornography. Since this is true by definition alone, there is nothing left to prove.

The concept of *"sexual harassment"* was invented to capture a phenomenon that had not yet been properly identified or named. According to the original definition, only women could be harassed, and only when in subordinate positions. As other related phenomena were identified and determined to be similar, the definition and concept changed and the term came to include the notion that both men and women could be sexually harassed and also that co-workers could sexually harass one another without either one of them being in a position of authority. The definition broadened to the point where it now covers more referents. In the process, however, it may have become more like the example of the word "game" than that of the word "gold" discussed previously, in that it refers to a cluster of conditions rather than a set of essential properties. Part of the difficulty in working out a definition of complex concepts like sexual harassment is that the boundaries of the concept are still not clearly identified. Developing the criteria for the meaning of the concept is an important step toward determining exactly which phenomena it applies to and which ones it does not.

Persuasive Definitions

A *persuasive definition* uses evaluative language in an attempt to convince people of a particular view. For example:

> Capitalism is the wilful exploitation of the poor through the exploitation of their labour.

This definition uses emotionally laden language (such as, "wilful" and "exploitation" in the definition above) and contains a particular view (such as, "capitalists exploit workers"), which is usually highly contentious as many people would disagree with it. A persuasive definition can be used to advocate on one's own behalf (as a politician would) or by an agent acting on behalf of another (as a political speech writer would).

Consider another two examples:

> Abortion is the killing of unborn babies.

> Abortion is the removal of an unwanted piece of tissue.

Each of these uses emotionally laden language (such as, "killing," "babies," "unwanted," "tissue") and each reflects a particular view the persuader wants others to take. In doing so, contentious issues are brought into the definition in a problematic way. A more neutral definition of abortion is available in the following example:

> Abortion is the termination of a pregnancy and the expulsion of an embryo or fetus from the mother's body.

This definition does not take a stand on the issue of killing or the status of the embryo or fetus. The stipulative definition of pornography (cited above) as the portrayal of sexual violence against and degradation of women is an example of both a stipulative and a persuasive definition.

One of the dynamics of argumentation is that people can use persuasive definitions as a way of establishing their substantive claims. If people can get others to accept a persuasive definition of a debatable word such as "pornography" or "abortion" they are well on their way to establishing their position, albeit by a faulty and poor form of argumentation.

A **persuasive definition** uses evaluative language in an attempt to convince people to take a particular view.

CLARIFYING MEANING   **51**

2.7 Criteria for Good Definitions

In addition to the criteria given for each type of definition above, the following criteria apply to virtually all definitions:

> The **scope** of a definition is the range of cases to which it appropriately applies.

1. *The definition should be of appropriate scope.* The **scope** of a definition is the range of cases to which it appropriately applies. A definition is too broad if the criteria include referents that are not instances of the definition. For example, defining "gold" as a yellow metal is too broad because the criteria "a yellow metal" includes other metals that are not gold. Thus, the criteria do not precisely limit the referent to only gold. Similarly, defining "pornography" as anything that denigrates women would include some advertising, anything misogynous, and some hate speech, none of which apply to the normal referent of pornography (that is, things having to do with portrayals of sex). Conversely, a definition is too narrow if it excludes significant referents it should include. Defining "sexual harassment" as the persistent unwanted sexual attention directed by male superiors toward female subordinates is too narrow because it excludes what should also be included (such as, same-sex sexual harassment, harassment of co-workers by co-workers, and female superiors of male or female subordinates).

   A definition can sometimes be both too broad and too narrow at the same time. For example, "sexual harassment involves the misuse of authority toward women" is both too broad and too narrow because not all misuses of authority toward women constitute sexual harassment and the definition excludes men as possible targets of sexual harassment.

2. *The definition should be phrased in neutral terms.* Emotionally laden terms and terms that skew a definition toward a particular perspective should not be used. The persuasive definitions of capitalism and abortion in the previous discussion are examples of non-neutral definitions.

3. *The definition should use words that are more clear than the terms they define.* The point of a definition is to explain the concept, and so if the terms used are less familiar than the term being defined the definition is not clear.

4. *The definition should be informative, not circular.* A circular definition is one that defines a concept in terms of itself, such as with the case of defining "arguer" as someone who argues—nothing is added by the definition and thus it is circular and not informative or helpful.

5. *The definition should not beg the question.* A definition begs the question when it includes as part of the definition the very thing that needs to be proven independently of the definition being used to do so. For example, defining "intelligence" as an innate mental trait measured by IQ tests assumes what still needs to be shown, namely, that intelligence is an innate trait adequately measured by an IQ test.

6. *The definition should be useful in the context.* Definitions are used in context, so if a definition is inappropriately used or does not apply to the context, then it is not useful.

Where there are alternate definitions, and some are contentious, the person advancing the definition should identify the alternative possibilities and justify the definition being used. For example,

> "Pornography" has been defined as "sexually explicit material which degrades women," as "sexual materials that arouse lust," and simply as "sexually explicit materials." In this essay, I will define "pornography" as any sexually explicit materials.

This leaves open the question of whether such materials do in fact degrade women as something we can investigate, and avoids the assumption that all pornography has a given effect of arousing lust. Thus, it does not build potentially controversial assumptions into the definition itself.

QUICK QUIZ 2.12

Criteria for Good Definitions

For each of the definitions in Quick Quiz 2.11, give the kind of definition each is and explain whether the definition meets the criteria for a good definition.

1. student
2. environmentalist
3. education
4. bachelor
5. suicide
6. euthanasia
7. student
8. motor vehicle

Answers to the Quick Quizzes are available on the Premium Website at www.criticalthinking2e.nelson.com.

Module Summary

- In order to engage in effective critical thinking, argument, and argumentation we must clearly, precisely, and contextually understand the meaning of concepts and claims.
- Meaning can be analyzed in terms of words, concepts (meaning), and referents.
- The meaning of a concept is influenced by the context in which it is used.
- Vague, ambiguous, imprecise, emotionally loaded language, and code words typically result in problems of meaning and understanding.
- One way of addressing potential problems of meaning is through definition.

Argumentation Exercise: Reasoning with Meaning

In the following dialogue, act as a coach to each of the argument partners by helping them clarify their meaning in the dialogue. Make sure to:

1. Identify where they may be disagreeing in the use of words, in the use of words in stipulative ways, or otherwise arguing in ways that are unclear and imprecise;
2. Where words are defined, identify what kinds of definitions are being used;
3. Suggest throughout what they could do at each stage to make their claims clearer and more precise; and
4. Identify what is going on at each stage in terms of the dynamics of argumentation (see Module 1).

Alphonse:	I tend to agree with Dr. King's argument that pornography is harmful.
Tali:	I disagree. It's not harmful. A lot of people view pornography and aren't harmed by it.
Alphonse:	Explain.
Tali:	I had to write a report on pornography for my psychology course and looked at some on the Web and it was nothing more than people having sex. What's so harmful about that?
Alphonse:	But it's full of all kinds of violence and degradation of women!
Tali:	What do you mean?
Alphonse:	It shows women as sexually subservient to men.
Tali:	But that's not violent.
Alphonse:	Of course it is.
Tali:	How so?
Alphonse:	Showing someone as inferior to another treats them in a violent way. It violates their equality as a human being. If that's not violent, then I don't know what is.
Tali:	I beg to differ.
Alphonse:	Look, pornography includes all kinds of images and videos that show children being abused, rape, and torture.
Tali:	That may be called pornography, but that's not what I mean by pornography. One can find those things, but that is not what most people think of when they think of pornography. It is simply people having sex with one another.
Alphonse:	Even if I grant you that, it still shows women as the sexual playthings of men, which is sexist, and sexism encourages men to treat women in a violent way, so it is harmful.
Tali:	How does it encourage men to treat women in a violent way?
Alphonse:	It encourages men to treat women as less than equal to men and that is violent.
Tali:	I don't accept that it encourages men to treat women as less than equal, or that if it did that behaviour is violent. Do you have any other arguments on how it is harmful?
Alphonse:	It is harmful to society. It undermines the social fabric that holds society together.
Tali:	How so?
Alphonse:	It damages the social cohesion of society.

Tali:	How so?
Alphonse:	It goes against the social consensus that defines us as a moral community.
Tali:	I think you are just going around in circles. Give me another argument.
Alphonse:	Pornography is harmful. A lot of people are offended by explicit sexuality.
Tali:	And a lot are not.
Alphonse:	Look, society has a moral code and pornography is against that moral code.
Tali:	Where do I find this moral code written?
Alphonse:	In the law books.
Tali:	But there is nothing in the legal code that prohibits pornography. There are laws against child pornography, but not against pornography per se. There is nothing against explicit sexual portrayals; the only restriction is displaying them in public.
Alphonse:	But society has a moral revulsion against the behaviour portrayed in pornography.
Tali:	Some people do. Some don't. How does that justify your saying society does?
Alphonse:	Look, I just know that Dr. King doesn't like pornography and neither do I.
Tali:	So give me a strong reason to support your opinion.

Writing Skills Exercise: Writing with Precision

Write a one-page essay that develops an argument. In your first version make the language in the essay as unclear, vague, imprecise, ambiguous, emotionally laden, and connotative as you can. Then rewrite the essay to be as clear, precise, and emotionally neutral as you can. Identify how each of the sentences is unclear, imprecise, and so on.

Analyzing Arguments

LEARNING OBJECTIVES

After completing this module you should be able to:

1. Define and correctly use key terms in argument analysis;
2. Identify and distinguish arguments from other kinds of textual discourse;
3. Use inference indicators to identify arguments and the component parts of arguments; and
4. Portray the structure of an argument using both standard form and arrow diagrams.

 A DIALOGUE ON COPYRIGHT AND PIRACY – CONTINUED

Jean: Let me see if I am characterizing your arguments correctly. You first claim I should not download copyright materials from the Web because we should always obey the law and there is a law against such downloading.

Peter: Yes, that is right.

Jean: So, you are claiming we should always obey the law, but consider this objection: it was once illegal for women to vote in Canada. Are you saying women (and some men) should not have challenged that law and sought to win the right to vote?

Peter: Of course not! It was an unjust law.

Jean: So, now you are saying we should only obey just laws?

Peter: Well, yes, because that is what laws are supposed to be.

Jean: But how do we determine what makes a law just or unjust? Consider for a moment that there are many people in Canada opposed to various current laws. Some are opposed to the fact that there is no law prohibiting abortion. Others are opposed to the laws prohibiting medically assisted suicide and pot smoking. In a recent case, an anti-gay advocate in Saskatchewan was charged with breaking the law prohibiting hate speech by distributing anti-gay materials and was charged under that law. Since these people consider these laws unjust, are they justified in breaking them?

Peter: Wait a minute — you are bombarding me with too many challenges!

Jean: Sorry for rushing, but I think the point is important. There are many laws people consider unjust. Must everyone obey all the laws, even those they consider unjust? Or to put it another way, what makes a law unjust enough that one can legitimately break it?

Peter: Again, too many questions. I think there are some important differences in the various cases you mention. Obviously it is not okay for everyone to pick and choose which laws they will obey and which they will not. In some of the cases you have mentioned (like women not having the right to vote), the law affects a sizeable part of the population and opposition to it seems justified.

Jean: Not that I disagree, but I am curious as to why?

Peter: Because men and women were being treated differently and there was no relevant difference that justified that treatment. The *principle of similar cases* (a fundamental principle of reasoning that likes should be treated alike and we are only justified in treating people differently if there is a relevant difference) holds here.

Jean: I can agree with you on that, and even though some people at that time thought women *were* relevantly different (not as rational as men, and hence not likely to be as reasonable in voting), that is clearly false.

Peter: Thank you. I know not all laws are unjust, but some have been and still are. And some people perceive laws to be unjust when they simply do not like them or find them inconvenient, and they often use the rhetoric of unjust without either understanding the term or using it correctly. So we have to sort through those to find the real cases where it may be justified to oppose a particular law, and separate them from those cases where the term is simply being misused. I want to argue that we should generally obey the laws unless they are obviously unjust and widely believed to be unjust.

(continued)

Jean: Okay, I understand your conclusion, but you are still assuming that the laws banning downloading of copyright material are just, which you need to show, and also that we should generally obey the law with a few exceptions.

Peter: Yes, that's what I am arguing.

Jean: Let's grant your reason that we should generally obey the law. Why do you think the laws making copyright piracy a crime are just? What is your argument for that?

(to be continued)

In this continuation of the dialogue, Jean and Peter's respectful conversation helps in developing an argument by clarifying claims, structuring arguments (by identifying the reasons), and modifying the conclusions. Developing these skills is the core of this module.

3.1 Introduction

The core of argumentation involves identifying, presenting, analyzing, critiquing, and responding to arguments. Before engaging in argumentation we must first be able to identify and analyze arguments, which is the focus of this module.

First, we need to verify that an argument is being given. Then we need to identify and distinguish the **components of the arguments**, the reasons and conclusion, from claims unrelated to the argument, and then portray the argument's structure. Inference indicators, and the positioning and meaning of the claims, will help us identify whether an argument exists and, if so, the function of each of its claims. Once this has been done, we portray the argument structure, identifying the relationship between the reasons and the conclusion, either in standard form or by using arrow diagrams (which can include challenges to claims and responses to those challenges).

> The **components of the arguments** are the reasons and the conclusion.

3.2 Identifying Claims

All arguments are based on claims. A *claim* consists of a complete thought, usually in the form of a complete sentence. It can be affirmed or denied, true or false, and evidence or support can be given to this end. Whereas claims are complete thoughts, non-claims are incomplete thoughts, not typically expressed as sentences, and do not make a claim that can be affirmed or denied.

"Bicycle," "red bicycle," "more energy-efficient than cars," and "cycle to work" are not claims since they do not express a complete thought. "My bike is yellow," "bicycles are more energy-efficient than cars," and "everyone should cycle to work" all express a complete thought and are claims. To *affirm a claim* is to accept or say it is true, whereas to *deny a claim* is to reject it or say it is false. A *negative* claim is one that negates, such as in the statement "the term *bicycle* does <u>not</u> include tricycles." To affirm a negative claim we simply repeat the claim, and to deny it we claim it is not true, as in the cases "the statement 'the term *bicycle* does <u>not</u> include tricycles' is not true" or "the claim 'bicycles do <u>not</u> include tricycles' is false" or "the term *bicycle does* include tricycles."

As mentioned in Module 2, not every utterance is a claim. Questions (such as, "who is the Prime Minister of Canada?"), imperatives (such as, "do exercise six before next week's class"), and exclamations (such as, "oh!") are not claims and are not functional parts of arguments.

3.3 What Is an Argument?

As explained in Module 1, an argument is a set of at least two claims that include one or more reasons and a conclusion. For each claim we can ask whether a reason has been given.

1. Health is a basic right. If something is a basic right, then society has an obligation to make sure people have access to that right. Therefore, society has an obligation to ensure that everyone has access to universal health care.

Analysis: This is an argument. The claim that society has an obligation to ensure that everyone has access to universal health care is controversial. Reasons are given to justify that.

Reason: Health is a basic right.
Reason: If something is a basic right, then society has an obligation to ensure that people have access to that right.
Conclusion: Society has an obligation to ensure everyone has access to universal health care.

2. All Canadian residents are entitled to health care, whether they can afford it or not.

Analysis: According to the criteria, this example is not an argument because it consists of one claim (the "whether" clause is a qualification of the claim, not a second claim). Although the claim may be controversial, no other claims are offered in support of it. An ***assertion*** is a claim that someone makes; it may be either supported or unsupported.

3. All Canadians are entitled to health care, whether they can afford it or not, because health is a basic good and it is the responsibility of society to make sure everyone has the access to the basic human goods.

> An **assertion** is a claim that someone makes; it may be either supported or unsupported.

Analysis: This is an argument. The first claim is contentious. The second and third claims are offered as reasons why all Canadians are entitled to health care.

> Reason 1: Society has a responsibility to ensure everyone has access to basic human goods.
> Reason 2: Health care is a basic good.
> Conclusion: All Canadians are entitled to health care.

4. All Canadian residents are entitled to a decent minimum of health care. Doctors and other health care professionals work hard to make sure health care is provided.

Analysis: There are two claims here and, although the first is controversial, neither claim is a reason for the other, that is, neither of the claims serves as an answer to the question *"why?"* for the other. (For more on identifying reasons and conclusions, see Section 3.4 of this module.) This passage is a ***description*** or a statement (or set of statements) that provides an account or report of the facts, details, or particulars of a situation, event, or topic – but not an argument.

5. The *Canada Health Act* was inspired by the work of Tommy Douglas and the Co-operative Commonwealth Federation in Saskatchewan. Although there was strong resistance to universal health care from the medical profession and insurance companies when it was initially introduced, the people of Saskatchewan embraced it. Seeing the popularity of Douglas's initiative, the Federal Government introduced a similar policy on the national level.

Analysis: Like the example above, this passage is a description, not an argument, because it only provides an account or report of the facts of the introduction of the *Canada Health Act*. No reasons are given for why it was introduced or why it was controversial, and there is no discussion of whether or not it should have been adopted. As well as being a description, the passage is a narrative. A ***narrative*** is a descriptive account that tells a story.

6. Many countries have since initiated state-run health care systems. Most European countries have such systems.

Analysis: This passage has two claims: the first ("Many countries . . .") might be confused with a reason, but it is actually an illustration; the second merely illustrates (or provides an example of) the first. An ***illustration*** is a statement that provides an example of another claim. An example is not a reason and this is not an argument.

7. Tommy Douglas introduced universal health care in Saskatchewan because as a boy he saw his father refused medical treatment.

Analysis: At first this might look like an argument because it has two claims and one of them is offered as a reason for the other ("*because*" indicates a reason). However, it is only an ***explanation***, that is, a statement (or set of statements) identifying the causes, context, consequences, factors influencing, or motivations of an object, process, state of affairs, or behaviour. Explanations are used to clarify such things or make them understandable by describing the relevant factors that produce them or the circumstances under which they occur. The passage above merely identifies Tommy Douglas's motivation for introducing universal health care in Saskatchewan, but it is not an argument.

A **description** is a statement (or set of statements) that provides an account or report of the facts, details, or particulars of a situation, event, or topic.

A **narrative** is a descriptive account that tells a story.

An **illustration** is a statement that provides an example of another claim.

An **explanation** is a statement (or set of statements) identifying the causes, context, consequences, factors influencing, or motivations of an object, process, state of affairs, or behaviour.

Explanations and arguments are often and easily confused because they both appear to be giving "reasons" for something. However, there are two critical differences between them. First, the conclusion of an explanation is usually not controversial. In the explanation above, it is assumed that it is a known fact Tommy Douglas introduced universal health care in Saskatchewan, so that is not contentious. What needs to be explained is the motivation for his actions. In an argument, on the other hand, the conclusion is often contentious. Second, in an argument you try to justify the contentious conclusion by relating it to more widely accepted reasons, whereas in an explanation you identify and connect other features (such as, causes, context, and motivations) that help make sense of what we already know. This confusion is compounded by the fact that the term *reason* is ambiguous as it can be used to mean motivation (or cause) or to mean the *reason* of an argument.

8. All Canadian residents are entitled to health care. Therefore, we should make sure everyone (including the homeless) receives a decent minimum standard of health care.

Analysis: This is an argument because there are two claims and the first is offered as a reason for the second (or the conclusion). And the conclusion is controversial: some would argue people should get health care only if they can afford it or if they qualify in some other way.

Reason: All Canadian residents are entitled to a decent minimum of health care.

Conclusion: We should ensure everyone (including the homeless) receives a decent minimum standard of health care.

The two fundamental components of an argument (the reason and the conclusion) are distinguished by their functions within a given argument. The claim being advanced (the conclusion) is controversial and in need of support or justification. In the context of an issue analysis it can also be called a "position" and in the context of an essay it is called the "thesis." The claim (or set of claims) advanced to support, defend, or justify the contentious claim is the reason because it provides support, justification, and, sometimes, evidence.

To identify an argument we need to determine the functions being performed by the claims. Any claim may function as a conclusion in one argument and a reason in another (that will be addressed in more detail with respect to intermediate conclusions).

QUICK QUIZ 3.2

Identifying Arguments

Identify whether the following statements contain arguments, illustrations, descriptions, or some other kinds of discourse. If they are arguments, identify the reasons and conclusions.

1. Céline took the job because she needed the money.
2. Céline had been looking for a job for six months. She had numerous initial interviews, but no follow-up interviews, and she was getting desperate.
3. Tuition fees should be raised because the cost of running universities, including hiring good faculty and increasing libraries and running laboratories, is rising.

(continued)

4. Although objectionable, racist materials should not be banned from schools.
5. The fundamental principles of justice demand that gay marriage be legalized.
6. Gay marriage should be legalized because everyone should be treated equally.
7. Second-hand smoke causes harm to others. Therefore, it should be banned in any area that the public has access to.
8. Marriage is a sacred institution and deserves to be preserved by the state.
9. If pornography causes harm, then it should be banned. Pornography causes harm. Therefore, it should be banned.
10. Pornography causes harm. Therefore, it should be banned.
11. Céline told her younger brother not to take philosophy in university because it would not help him get a job when he graduated.

Answers to the Quick Quizzes are available on the Premium Website at www.criticalthinking2e.nelson.com.

3.4 Identifying Reasons and Conclusions

Reasons and conclusions can be identified through meaning, through the use of words that indicate reasons or conclusions, or through their function within a passage.

Function: Why? Because …

Determining the structure of an argument using meaning requires understanding the claims in a passage, their relevance to one another, what each claim's function is in a passage, and the overall purpose of the passage. Is the passage trying to convince you of something? Is it trying to get you to accept a claim as true? Does it offer other claims in support of a claim? Is the passage simply a narration of a series of events, or is it a description of something? What is the overall purpose of the passage? Asking yourself these questions can help identify whether a passage is likely to contain an argument.

Once you have determined that an argument exists, examine its claims by looking for contentious ones. To do this, you want to ask questions such as "why is this true?" and/or "why should I accept it?" The claims that we can ask these questions about are likely to indicate a conclusion, while the answers to the questions are the reasons. It is usually easier to start by identifying the conclusion, or what needs to be justified, shown, or established, than by indentifying reasons, as we will see shortly.

Once you have tentatively identified the conclusion, ask yourself "why is this claim true?" or "why should I accept this claim?" Look for an answer in terms of a "because…". Finding other claims in the passage that provide answers (or that give a response to "because") can help you recognize the reasons.

In some cases you might start with the reasons. For example, an author may cite some obvious claims that people are likely to agree with, or give a set of data. In cases like these, the data are likely reasons and you need to start looking for the conclusions that follow from them. Ask yourself questions like "what follows from that?" or "what inferences does the author draw from this data?" to help identify the argument's conclusion.

If a passage has two claims that might be part of an argument, ask "why?" of one of them and see if the other provides a "because" (or a reason) for it. If so, an argument probably exists.

Inference Indicators

English contains a number of words and phrases that indicate one statement (or a group of statements) is functioning as a reason for another. Other words and phrases indicate that a given claim is functioning as a conclusion in an argument. These are called *inference indicators*. They indicate that there is a logical relationship between one claim (or set of claims) and another claim (or set of claims). The words and phrases listed below generally *but not always* indicate that the statement that follows is a reason. In the following list (which is not exhaustive), "R" a reason and "C" identifies a conclusion.

> An **inference indicator** is a word or phrase that indicates there is a logical relationship between one claim (or set of claims) and another claim (or set of claims) that function as reasons or a conclusion in an argument.

TABLE 3.1 Inference Indicators

In the following, "R" identifies a reason and "C" identifies a conclusion.

Kind of Indicator	Pattern	Example
Reason Indicators	C because R. C for the reason that R.	There will be increasing civil unrest because we are in a time of rising expectations and financial insecurity.
	In view of the fact that R, C. C. First, second, third.	In view of the fact that we are in a time of rising expectations and financial insecurity, there will be increasing civil unrest. There will be increasing civil unrest. For the reason that we are in a time of rising expectations and financial insecurity. There will be increasing civil unrest. First, we are in a time of rising expectations; second, there is financial insecurity; and third, we have a large underemployed population under thirty.
Conclusion Indicators	R, therefore C. R, thus C. R. It follows that C. R. Consequently C. R shows that C. R. So C. R demonstrates that C. R proves that C. R. Hence C.	We are in a time of rising expectations and financial insecurity. Therefore, there will be increasing civil unrest (any of the terms could be used instead of "therefore").

There are exceptions to the inference indicator words. For example, "since" can be used both to suggest time and to show logical connection:

> He has been acting strangely since taking his final exam.

"Then" often takes the role of indicator of sequence instead of the role of logical indicator:

> She went to class. Then she went to the bookstore. Then she went home.

In the second and third sentences, "then" shows a sequence of events.

"Thus" can both introduce a conclusion and also be used to summarize what comes before it:

> She wrote out her rent cheque, and then her hydro, cable, and student loan cheques. Thus, she quickly went through her hard-earned paycheque.

"Thus" in this passage acts as an indicator of a summary statement meaning "in this way." We are not trying to prove she went through her paycheque quickly, but rather we are outlining the steps that led to that result.

In analyzing a passage, circling any inference indicators helps guide us in identifying an argument:

> You should get the Orange computer rather than the IBIS because it is more reliable and less vulnerable to viruses.

Inference indicators are often misused. The one probably most widely misused is "therefore." Some writers begin many sentences with "therefore" whether it is appropriate or not. When an inference indicator's use is questionable, it is wise to test its validity by using one of the other two methods of identifying the structure of an argument (meaning, discussed above, and position, discussed below).

When you present your own arguments, using inference indicators to signal the reasons and conclusions can help make your arguments clearer and more compelling.

QUICK QUIZ 3.3

Identifying Inference Indicators

In the following passages, circle the inference indicator words being used, make note of any inference indicators being misused, and identify the reasons and conclusions by putting a "R" next to the reasons and a "C" next to the conclusions.

1. Marriage is sacred; therefore, it should be preserved.
2. We should allow gay marriage because if we do not we will be discriminating against people unjustly.
3. Marijuana should be outlawed: first, it is harmful; second, the claimed medical benefits are bogus; and finally, it undermines productivity and causes safety hazards in the work place.
4. The *Tour de France* has been happening since 1903; however, it did not achieve its current international prominence until after 1980.
5. Abortion is wrong; therefore, the fetus is a person, and therefore, anything that kills a person is wrong.

Answers to the Quick Quizzes are available on the Premium Website at www.criticalthinking2e.nelson.com.

Position

A third way of identifying the components of an argument is through their position within a passage. The conclusion of a more complicated argument can appear at the beginning or the end of a long passage or text. In a paragraph, it is often the first or last sentence. In an essay, it is often in the first or last paragraph, or both.

The Order of Reasons and Conclusions

Consider the following passage:

> The Canadian Government has been debating the legalization of marijuana. Not only is it considering legalizing marijuana for medical reasons, but it is also considering making possession of small amounts not a crime. Marijuana relieves symptoms of certain ailments (such as, glaucoma) and reduces the nausea caused by chemotherapy. However, I am opposed to any legalization. Marijuana is a harmful substance and once we allow it, our kids will find ways to get their hands on it and that will corrupt an entire generation.

Much of the early part of this passage simply sets up the argument by identifying the issue and the context. The argument comes in the final two sentences with the conclusion first and the reasons following.

The basic argument in this passage is:

Reason: Marijuana is a harmful substance.
Reason: Once we allow it, our kids will find ways to get their hands on it and that will corrupt an entire generation.
Conclusion: We should not legalize marijuana. Or, I am opposed to the legalization of marijuana.

The reason and conclusions in an argument can come in any order. When analyzing passages you will often find material that is not part of the core argument being made. Writers include illustrations, examples, descriptions, definitions of words, and explanations of claims being made. Since these often contribute to making the material easier to understand we cannot ignore them. However, they are not central to the analysis and evaluation of the argument.

Consider the following passage:

> Many high school students think it is cool to experiment with marijuana. After all, what is wrong with getting high? And marijuana is not harmful, especially compared to heroin or tobacco. So what is the problem? Many of our parents used marijuana when they were young and most of them turned out all right. Most people in Canada see nothing wrong with a little recreational use of marijuana. Consequently, I see no reason to ban it.

Much of this passage consists of material not part of the logical structure of the argument (such as anecdotes, illustrations, and examples) rather than the components of an argument. Only toward the end of this passage is an argument presented.

We can *paraphrase* or reword the argument in this passage as follows:

Reason: Marijuana does no harm.
Reason: It is widely accepted.
Reason: Many have used it and most turned out all right.
Conclusion: It should not be illegal.

> A **paraphrase** involves restating in one's own words the core meaning of a passage or text.

In both of these arguments the central claims have been paraphrased. While *paraphrasing* involves restating in one's own words the core meaning of a passage or text, an ***argument paraphrase*** seeks to capture the core argument in the original text or dialogue. This is especially useful in verbal argumentation since most of us are often trying to find a way of presenting an argument for the first time and we often do not initially phrase our ideas in the clearest and most precise way. Having an argument partner assist us through paraphrasing can help us understand what we are really trying to say. Paraphrasing serves a number of functions. First, it helps people understand what is being said in the original passage, text, or discussion. Second, it captures the core meaning and eliminates extraneous words and statements. Third, it helps people understand what they are arguing. And fourth, it helps establish a rapport between argument partners, giving the defender the sense that the argument has been understood. It is important to note that paraphrasing differs from ***summarizing***. In paraphrasing we strive to find the logical connections, whereas in summarizing we are usually repeating in our own words the order of ideas as they are presented in the passage, text, or discussion, without necessarily capturing the logical connections among the claims.

QUICK QUIZ 3.4

Identifying Arguments and Providing Inference Indicators

In the following passages, identify the basic argument and provide the appropriate inference indicator words to help the reader follow the passage. You may re-order the sentences or paraphrase where necessary.

1. Abortion should be banned. It is morally wrong to kill an innocent human.
2. Capital punishment does not allow people to be rehabilitated and it is immoral.
3. Kittens need to be trained. Instinct only goes so far with higher mammals. What is not governed by instinct needs to be taught. Kittens are higher mammals.
4. Most people believe woolly mammoths became extinct because of the Ice Age. This explanation is not satisfactory. Mammoths have been found entombed whole in glaciers in Siberia. Glaciers form and move too slowly to entomb woolly mammoths suddenly. The glaciers came later than the woolly mammoths. The mammoths were clearly the first alien abductions. Nothing else makes sense.
5. Everyone should wear a seat belt. This should be mandatory. Not wearing one increases the risk of death. When people are injured or killed in car accidents their families are devastated. We all have an obligation to our family. And we all have an obligation to society. Not wearing a seat belt results in more injuries which have to be paid for by the rest of society.

Answers to the Quick Quizzes are available on the Premium Website at www.criticalthinking2e.nelson.com.

3.5 Portraying Argument Structure: Standard Form

Portraying the structure of an argument involves identifying the different components of arguments and their relationship to one another in that particular argument and then displaying them in a visual way. There are two common ways of showing an argument's structure: standard form and arrow diagram.

To portray an argument using ***standard form*** we begin by writing out each reason on a separate numbered line. We then separate the reasons from the conclusion with a straight line and write the conclusion below it. Three dots forming an equilateral triangle (∴) are used as a conclusion indicator, which is placed in front of the conclusion statement. The three dots symbolize the word "therefore." For easy reference the claims can be numbered as shown in the example below:

1. First reason

2. Second reason (if there is one)

∴ 3. Conclusion

Consider the following argument:

> By virtue of being human, all people are entitled to the basic necessities of life. Health care is a basic necessity of life. Therefore, everyone is entitled to health care.

In this case we can determine what the reasons are and what the conclusion is, and then put the argument in standard form.

> **Portraying the structure of an argument** involves identifying the component parts of argument and their relationship to one another in that particular argument and then displaying them in either standard form or an arrow diagram.

> The **standard form** of an argument is a way of displaying the structure of an argument with each claim on a separate numbered line with the reasons above and the conclusion below a line. The conclusion is also indicated by three equilateral dots (∴).

Using standard form, this argument would be portrayed as follows:

1. By virtue of being human, all people are entitled to the basic necessities of life.

2. Health care is a basic necessity of life.

∴ 3. Everyone is entitled to health care.

There are no strict rules for the order of the reasons if there are more than one. However, it is useful to group them so claims that are connected appear together. In this case we have put the more general reason first.

As previously discussed, a claim that functions as a reason in one argument may function as a conclusion in another. Consider the following:

By virtue of being human, all people are entitled to the basic necessities of life. Health care is a basic necessity of life. Therefore, everyone is entitled to health care. And since the homeless are no less human than others, they are entitled to health care.

There are two arguments in this passage. The conclusion of one acts as the reason for the other, thereby linking them. We can portray this argument in standard form as follows:

1. Simply by virtue of being human, all people are entitled to the basic necessities of life.

2. Health care is a basic necessity of life.

∴ 3. Everyone is entitled to health care.

4. The homeless are no less human than others.

∴ 5. The homeless are also entitled to health care.

QUICK QUIZ 3.6

Portraying Standard Form

Portray the following arguments in standard form.
1. All tortoiseshell cats are female. Felicity is a tortoiseshell cat. Felicity is female.
2. According to reports of the sightings of the Loch Ness monster, it would be an enormous size — at least six metres in length and a ton or more in weight. An aquatic creature of that size would have to eat literally tons of food each month. Yet, the loch has a far smaller food supply than that. The reported sightings must be wrong.
3. Although Lance Armstrong has won seven *Tour de France* races to Eddy Merckx's five, Merckx is the better cyclist. Armstrong has won only

seventy-one classic races, including the *Tour* and the five stages he has won within the *Tour*. Merckx has won 471 classic races, including his stages within the *Tour de France*. Although they are both amazing and both legends, Merckx is the better all-round cyclist.

4. *Context: A couple had planned to go camping.* "I think we should stay home. It is going to rain all weekend."

5. I recommend we fire Farah. She has been making decisions not within her job description and then contacting agencies and saying her decisions are company policy. She has been warned twice that this is unacceptable behaviour and it contravenes corporate policy, but she has not listened or learned. If she continues, she will cause serious problems not only externally to the company's relationships but internally as well. She has to go.

Answers to the Quick Quizzes are available on the Premium Website at www.criticalthinking2e.nelson.com.

3.6 Portraying Argument Structure: Arrow Diagrams

Portraying arguments using standard form works well for relatively simple arguments with a single line of reasoning. However, once arguments become more complex and involve several lines of reasoning the standard form can become quite cumbersome and ineffective. To address these cases, an alternate way of displaying the structure of an argument uses arrows and numbers. This is called an ***arrow diagram***.

Here is a method for generating arrow diagrams:

1. Draw square brackets [ ] around each claim in the text.
2. Number each claim separately (starting from the first claim in the passage through to the last). Note that some sentences may contain multiple claims and each claim (<u>not</u> each sentence) is assigned a separate number. (If some claims are not used in the argument, they can be dropped when diagramming the structure.)
3. Circle inference indicators.
4. Use arrows to portray the structure of the argument (the blunt end of the arrow indicates the reason and the pointy end the conclusion). Normally in the arrow diagram the conclusion is at the bottom of the diagram.

> An **arrow diagram** displays the structure of an argument using arrows to identify the reasons in relation to each other and to the conclusion.

Paraphrasing the argument first is sometimes helpful in order to focus on the core elements of the claims. Construct the paraphrase and use the above strategy on the paraphrased argument. This works especially well with passages that have a lot of extraneous material or ones in which the basic claims in the argument need to be stated more clearly.

Consider the following argument:

[You should major in psychology] because [you are good at dealing with people.]

Bracketing, numbering, and circling inference indicators would produce the following:

1   2

[You should major in psychology] (because) [you are good at dealing with people].

Diagramming using arrows would portray an argument structure that looks like this:

$$2 \\ \downarrow \\ 1$$

All arguments with one reason and one conclusion are diagrammed this way.

If there is more than one reason in the argument we can diagram it in one of two ways: as convergent or linked. In a *linked argument* the two reasons are related to one another and must be considered part of the same argument. In a *convergent argument* each reason is independent and stands entirely on its own.

In such arguments each reason is represented by its own arrow shown here:

1

[Legalizing marijuana will make a dangerous drug available to our kids.]

2

Furthermore, [there are no proven medical benefits to it.] (Therefore),

3

[we should not legalize marijuana.]

In this argument reasons 1 and 2 are unrelated reasons for the third reason (or the conclusion). Each addresses a different feature of the debate over legalizing marijuana: (1) a dangerous drug being made available to kids, ; and (2) the drug's medical uses. When this is the case we treat each reason as individual. This is a convergent argument. This argument's diagram would be as follows:

By contrast, consider the following linked argument:

1   2

[We would not knowingly expose our children to harm.] [Legalizing marijuana

3

would expose them to a harmful substance.] (Therefore), [we should not legalize marijuana.]

In this argument reasons 1 and 2 reinforce one another, and when taken together provide stronger support than when the reasons are taken separately. The reasons would be treated as one unit in this argument's arrow diagram:

To show that the reasons are linked, we join them with a plus sign and draw a line underneath them to indicate that they are to be taken as one argument. When we diagram an argument with *linked reasons*, we are claiming the reasons linked by the plus sign need to be considered together. This is called a *linked argument*.

Arrow diagrams are particularly useful when diagramming more complex arguments, including arguments with multiple reasons and sub-arguments and several lines of reasoning, all leading to the same conclusion. You can combine standard form and arrow diagrams by connecting the statements with arrows (although this is a less common form of diagramming). The second argument above could be displayed as follows:

We would not
knowingly expose our   +   Legalizing marijuana would
children to harm.   expose them to a harmful
                                                      substance.

_____

∴ We should not legalize marijuana.

One primary purpose in drawing the structure of an argument is to be able to see at a glance what reasons are being supported and what reasons are being offered in support. Since most arguments are written in prose, their structures are not always immediately apparent. Diagramming an argument helps to visually see and better understand the arguments being analyzed and also provides a convenient way of explaining the arguments to others.

QUICK QUIZ 3.7

Using Arrow Diagrams

Portray the arguments in Quick Quiz 3.6 using arrow diagrams.

Answers to the Quick Quizzes are available on the Premium Website at www.criticalthinking2e.nelson.com.

3.7 Diagramming Complex Arguments

The arguments presented thus far have been relatively simple. However, many of the arguments we encounter are more complex than this. For example:

> I can't write the exam because I am sick, and besides, my grandmother died and I have to go to the funeral.

By numbering and bracketing we get:

>   1   2
> [I can't write the exam] (because) [I am sick], and besides, [my
>
>   3   4
> grandmother died] and [I have to go to the funeral].

Our convention is that we number claims consecutively in the text, starting with 1. Although we have three reasons and one conclusion in this argument, not all of the reasons are inherently related. Being sick and having a dying grandmother have no clear connection to one another. If two sets of reasons are relatively independent of one another, and either could be treated as separate reasons for the same conclusion, then it is best to treat them as independent arguments (or independent lines of reasoning). We could portray the argument in standard form as follows:

Standard Form Diagram 1:

2. I am sick.

∴   1. I cannot write the exam

Standard Form Diagram 2:

3. My grandmother died.

4. I have to go to the funeral.

∴   1. I cannot write the exam.

In this case, if the viewer does not read the conclusions, he or she will not know there are two independent arguments in it. Portrayed in an arrow diagram the structure is more obvious:

This is a convergent argument overall; 3+4 is a linked argument within the overall argument.

Consider the following passage:

> Smoking in public places should be banned because it causes harm to others. It is harmful to others because second-hand smoke can cause cancer, asthma, or lung disease.

This argument is also complex, but has a different structure.

Standard Form Diagram 3:

1. Second-hand smoke can cause cancer, asthma, or lung disease.

∴   2. Smoking is harmful to others.

∴   3. Smoking in public places should be banned.

Using an arrow diagram, this would be displayed as follows:

Arrow Diagram 3:

1

↓

2

↓

3

In this case, we have one reason (1) that acts as a reason for a conclusion (2), that in turn acts as a reason for yet another conclusion (3). One claim has two functions: it serves as a conclusion of one argument and a reason for another. More specifically: (1) is a ***basic reason*** because it is a starting point of an argument for which no further justification is given (and as such it is undefended); (2) is an ***intermediate conclusion*** because it is a conclusion for at least one reason and a reason for yet a further conclusion; and (3) is the ***final conclusion*** because it completes the argument. When the conclusion of one argument becomes the reason for another conclusion, the argument is called a ***serial argument***.

Consider the following:

> We should not legalize marijuana. Although some will experience minor health benefits with its legalization, these benefits are outweighed by the increase in the number of people who will be attracted to this dangerous drug if it is legalized. In order to prevent more people from becoming addicted, it should not be made legally available for any purposes.

Some of the basic claims are repeated and some may be redundant, which often is the case when people make arguments. The following paraphrase (supplying inference indicators) captures the basic logic in the passage, while eliminating the redundancies and extraneous claims:

> We should not legalize marijuana. If we legalize it for any reason, more people will become addicted and we do not want that to happen.

By bracketing, numbering, and identifying inference indicators, we get the following:

1
[We should not legalize marijuana.] [If we legalize it for any reason

2

3
more people will become addicted], and [we do not want that to happen].

Portraying this in standard form, we get the following:

Standard Form Diagram 4:

2. If we legalize it for any reason more people will become addicted.

3. We do not want that to happen.

∴　1. We should not legalize marijuana.

A **basic reason** is a claim that is a starting point of an argument for which no further justification given.

An **intermediate conclusion** is a claim that serves as a conclusion of at least one reason and a reason for yet another conclusion.

A **final conclusion** is the last conclusion of a serial argument.

A **serial argument** is an argument within an argument where the conclusion of one argument serves as the reason for another conclusion.

ANALYZING ARGUMENTS **73**

Portrayed with an arrow diagram, we get the following:

Arrow Diagram 4:

$$\underline{2+3}$$

$$\downarrow$$

1

When the reasons are clearly linked to one another, are on the same topic, and if taken together help strengthen the argument, they are treated as a unit. In the above argument, the reasons provide a stronger argument when linked. If we were to treat them as distinct arguments we would have to provide additional reasons to link them to the conclusion and the additional reasons would duplicate the already stated claims.

When reasons could be considered separately, and if when considered separately they provide independent reasons for the conclusion, they should be treated as independent. Consider the following:

> We should not legalize marijuana for any reason. If we legalize it, it would only induce more people to try it and to become addicted. Furthermore, marijuana is a harmful drug. By legalizing it we would be condoning the use of an unsafe substance. And we do not want to do that.

Using bracketing and numbering we come up with the following:

1
[We should not legalize marijuana for any reason.]

2
[If we legalize it, it would only induce more people to try it and to become addicted.]

3
Furthermore, [marijuana is a harmful drug].

4
[By legalizing it we would be

5
condoning the use of an unsafe substance]. And [we do not want to do that].

Standard Form Diagram 5:

2. If we legalize it, it would only induce more people to try it and to become addicted.

∴ 1. We should not legalize marijuana for any reason.

3. Marijuana is a harmful drug.

4. By legalizing it we would be condoning the use of an unsafe substance.

5. We do not want to do that.

∴ 1. We should not legalize marijuana for any reason.

We end up with the following:

Arrow Diagram 5:

$$2 \searrow \quad \underline{3+4+5} \swarrow$$
$$1$$

The arrow diagram portrays more clearly the structure of the argument by showing how its components parts function. We have two independent arguments, one made up of three reasons, and both leading to a common conclusion. Each of the sets of reasons can support the conclusion.

QUICK QUIZ 3.8

Interpreting Arrow Diagrams

Explain the meaning of each of the following arrow diagrams by identifying the reasons and conclusions:

1. $1 \searrow \quad 2 \downarrow \quad 3 \swarrow$
    4

2. $\underline{1+2} \searrow \quad 3 \downarrow \quad \underline{4+5} \swarrow$
    6

3. $\underline{1+2} \downarrow \qquad 7 \downarrow$
    $3 \searrow \quad 4 \downarrow \quad \underline{5+6} \swarrow$
    8

Answers to the Quick Quizzes are available on the Premium Website at www.criticalthinking2e.nelson.com.

QUICK QUIZ 3.9

Diagramming Complex Arguments

Portray the structure of the following arguments.

1. Marriage is a private matter between individuals. The state has no right to interfere in the private affairs of its citizens. Therefore, the state has no right to prohibit gay marriage.
2. The state does have a right to regulate marriage, including gay marriage. The state is entitled to enforce morals and values, and sexual relations between individuals of the same sex are immoral and an abomination to God. Moreover, marriage is fundamentally about conceiving and raising children and gay couples cannot do this. So the state has a right to prohibit gay marriage.

(continued)

3. The recent dramatic increase in gas prices is a good thing because it will result in less drain on oil reserves. We are running low on oil reserves and need to conserve them.
4. Capital punishment is not effective as a deterrent. It is a form of cruel and unusual punishment. And we risk killing innocent people by supporting capital punishment, because some innocent individuals have been convicted of what would be capital crimes. Therefore, capital punishment should not be allowed.
5. The Atlantis portrayed by Plato (and on which all later stories of the lost continent are based) could not have existed. Plato claims Atlantis was an extremely advanced culture that existed 10,000 years before his day in the Atlantic Ocean, was destroyed by tidal waves and earthquakes, and sank to the bottom of the sea virtually overnight. Extensive mapping of the Atlantic Ocean floor reveals neither the kind of rock that continents are made of, nor a land mass even approximating the presumed size of Atlantis. From geology we know that tidal waves and earthquakes cannot cause a land mass of Atlantis's alleged size to sink to the ocean bottom, much less overnight. Nor is there any evidence for any kind of advanced civilization existing 10,000 years before Plato. Plato's story is a myth.

Answers to the Quick Quizzes are available on the Premium Website at www.criticalthinking2e.nelson.com.

3.8 Analyzing Passages with Mixed Prose

Many passages that contain arguments also contain extraneous material, which may include background information, examples and illustrations, definitions, descriptions, elaboration, repetitions of the basic claims, explanations, and/or simply irrelevant information. When analyzing a passage for its argument we want to remove the extraneous material and focus on the argument structure. To do so:

1. Read the passage.
2. Circle inference indicators and underline key concepts in the passage.
3. Examine each sentence for its role in the passage. What does each claim do in the overall context of the passage? Among other things, a sentence may:

   • Contain a claim that acts as a reason or conclusion in an argument;
   • Set the stage with relevant background information;
   • Provide information to help the reader understand an issue;
   • Define an issue;
   • Provide examples or illustrations;
   • Define key words;
   • Restate what is being said in a slightly different way; and/or
   • Make an aside or digression from the main point.

Many or all of these functions are useful in presenting an argument in prose. However, when analyzing an argument we are looking for only what is essential to the logic of the argument. To identify what is essential:

1. Identify the main point (conclusion) of the passage. You may find a stated claim that captures the main point exactly. In some cases you may need to formulate the main point in your own words.
2. Check the conclusion against the passage. How do the other claims fit with this claim?

3. Identify the structure of the argument by relating the reasons to the conclusion.
4. If there are any unclear, ambiguous, or vague words that are central to the argument, clarify them.

Consider the following passage:

> The debate over gay marriage has become particularly heated over the past two years. By gay marriage, I mean the right of same-sex couples to enter into a legal union that gives them the rights normally shared by heterosexual couples who marry. Gay men and women have demanded they be given the legal right to marry. Many conservatives have rejected the idea on the grounds it will undermine the sanctity of marriage. I contend we should allow gay marriage because if we do not we will be denying a significant segment of the population the basic rights shared by the rest of the population.

Bracketing and numbering the basic claims we get the following:

1
[The debate over gay marriage has become particularly heated over the
2
past two years.] [By gay marriage, I mean the right of same-sex couples to enter into a legal union that gives them the rights normally shared by
3
heterosexual couples who marry.] [Gay men and women have demanded
4
they be given the legal right to marry.] [Many conservatives have rejected the idea on the grounds this will undermine the sanctity of marriage.]
5
(I contend that)[we should allow gay marriage](because) [if we do not we will
6
be denying a significant segment of the population the basic rights shared by the rest of the population].

The key to extracting the argument from such a passage is to examine each sentence to determine its role:

Statement 1: provides information about the escalation of the controversy;
Statement 2: defines gay marriage;
Statement 3: presents the position of one side in the debate;
Statement 4: presents the position of another side in the debate ("on the grounds that" could be interpreted as a reason indicator);
Statement 5: is preceded by a conclusion indicator and identifies a controversial claim;
Statement 6: is preceded by a reason indicator and gives a reason for the controversial claim.

Claims 1 through 4 provide background information, but are not part of the argument. Although there is an argument within 4, it is not the main argument of the passage. That is given in claims 5 and 6:

6. If we do not allow gay marriage we will be denying gay people basic rights shared by the rest of the population.

∴ 5. We should allow gay marriage.

ANALYZING ARGUMENTS **77**

An analysis involves not just analyzing the arguments in the passage, but interpreting the passage and trying to clarify its meaning. Sometimes when we do this we end up with something other than what was intended. Some passages are simply muddled, so when interpreting them we may have to say "if the author means *x* by this" (where *x* is our reconstruction) "then here is what is right or wrong with this argument."

Consider the following argument:

> Evolutionary theory is just a theory. As such it is not factual, and if it is not factual, it has not been established. So, it is simply speculative. Therefore, we should not trust it.

The conclusion of this argument states we should not trust evolutionary theory and the reasons given are that it is just a theory (or speculative) and not factual.

In this argument the word "theory" is ambiguous. In everyday life we often talk about "that's just a theory, not a fact," where theories are speculative and not established, while facts are. The word "theory" is used differently in science and means a set of interconnected claims used to explain a type of phenomena. Some theories in science are highly speculative with no observational results (such as, string theory) and others are so widely established they are treated as "fact" (such as, Newton's theory of gravity). If the author is using the everyday sense of the word "theory," then he or she is simply wrong about evolutionary theory being merely speculative. We have moved here to assessing the argument by analyzing some of its claims. What is important is realizing there are alternate reconstructions and the different reconstructions make a difference to what argument is being offered and the acceptability of that argument.

QUICK QUIZ 3.10

Identifying Arguments in Passages, with Extraneous Material

In the following passages, identify whether or not there is an argument. If there is no argument, explain why there is not. If there is an argument, identify the basic argument. Pay special attention to extraneous material, and do not include it in your analysis. If there is extraneous material, make sure you explain why the material is irrelevant to the argument.

I. (1) Transgender people are individuals who believe their proper genders are different from the sex of the bodies they inhabit. (2) Some transgender people seek to change their bodies to conform to what they feel is their proper gender identity. (3) Some psychiatrists have argued that these individuals have a serious personality disorder and that such attempts at transformation are signs of this. (4) I disagree. (5) They do not have a personality disorder at all. (6) Psychiatrists have failed to provide any evidence to the contrary. (7) Moreover, if it were a personality disorder, transgender people would have the various characteristics of a personality disorder. (8) Generally speaking, they do not have these characteristics. (9) This is just another example of psychiatrists trying to impose their narrow values on anyone they see as different.

II. (1) Marijuana is an addictive drug like heroin and cocaine. (2) It has become widely available in Canada. (3) Much of the marijuana available in Canada is grown domestically. (4) Once grown only in fields, it is increasingly being grown in grow-houses (houses taken over by drug dealers and used to grow marijuana). (5) Because it is addictive, marijuana should not be legalized for either medical or recreational uses. (6) There are far more effective drugs that could be used medically. (7) Because it is addictive, it should not be used recreationally.

III. (1) Hate speech should not be prohibited. (2) It is simply speech. (3) Some people find what is called "hate speech" upsetting. (4) However, many people find many things upsetting. (5) For example, some people find particular ads upsetting. (6) Others find violence in movies upsetting. (7) Some people find same-sex couples upsetting. (8) Some find even the mention of such things upsetting. (9) Causing upset is not sufficient grounds for the prohibition of anything. (10) If we did that, we would prohibit all kinds of unpopular ideas and beliefs. (11) Hate speech is simply speech. (12) All speech, even unpopular and unpleasant speech, should be tolerated. (13) It is far better to counter such verbal communication with good arguments than to suppress it. (14) No, hate speech should not be suppressed.

Answers to the Quick Quizzes are available on the Premium Website at www.criticalthinking2e.nelson.com.

3.9 Diagramming Challenges and Responses

The conventions for diagramming and displaying arguments do not yet provide us with an easy way of diagramming challenges and responses. A ***challenge to a claim*** involves a denial of a claim. Other challenges could be to the logic of an argument, to adequacy of meaning, or to presuppositions and implication. A ***response*** to a challenge is a challenge to the challenge, or the denial of the challenge. In effect, a challenge says claim x is false because y (the challenge); a response to a challenge says challenge y is false (or to be rejected) because of z. So as not to get confused by using the same notation as for a reason and a conclusion, we will use a wavy arrow $\rightsquigarrow$ to indicate the relationship between a challenge and a claim or between a response and a challenge.

> A **challenge to a claim** involves a denial of a claim.
>
> A **response** to a challenge is a challenge to the challenge, or the denial of the challenge.

$$
\begin{array}{c}
R \\
\rightsquigarrow \\
C
\end{array}
$$

This is read as *C* is not true (is false) because *R*. In this case, *R* is a reason for rejecting *C*. A response to a challenge is read the same way.

$$
\begin{array}{c}
A \\
\rightsquigarrow \\
R \\
\rightsquigarrow \\
C
\end{array}
$$

ANALYZING ARGUMENTS **79**

We read this diagram as *C* is false because *R*; and *R* is rejected (false) because *A*.
Consider the following argument:

	1	2
ORIGINAL:	[Abortion is immoral] (because)	[the fetus is a person.]

CHALLENGE: [The fetus is not a person]^{not 2} (because) [a person is a moral³

agent], and [moral agents are capable of making decisions]⁴.

[Fetuses cannot make decisions,]⁵ (so) [they cannot be treated as⁶
moral agents.]

RESPONSE: [Infants are not capable of making decisions]⁷, yet [we treat them as⁸
persons.]

This can be diagrammed as follows:

$$\underline{7 + 8}$$

$$\wr$$

$$\underline{3 + 4 + 5 + 6}$$

$$\wr$$

$$2$$

$$\downarrow$$

$$1$$

This notation reads as follows: 2 supports 1; 2 is false because of 3 and 4 and 5 and 6; and 7 and 8 deny 3, 4, 5, 6.

QUICK QUIZ 3.11

Diagramming Challenges and Responses

Diagram the following arguments using the notation for challenges and responses.

1. A: *The Adventures of Huckleberry Finn* is racist because it uses the N-word over 200 times and that is offensive to many people.
   B: The dictionary uses the N-word and it is not racist.
   C: The dictionary is defining the term and *The Adventures of Huckleberry Finn* uses the term to refer to a group of people.

2. A: Euthanasia is immoral because it denies an individual autonomy.
   B: It does not deny an individual autonomy; rather, it allows the individual to choose how and when he or she will die, and that is upholding an individual's autonomy.

3. A: Pornography is degrading to women because it shows women in sexual positions.
   B: It shows men in sexual positions. Is it not degrading to men as well?
   C: No. Men have positions of power in society and cannot be degraded whereas women are degraded by being shown in sexual positions.

Answers to the Quick Quizzes are available on the Premium Website at www.criticalthinking2e.nelson.com.

Module Summary

- The central unit of analysis in argumentation is the argument.
- Arguments are composed of claims that can be affirmed or denied, true or false.
- An argument consists of at least two claims, one of which (the reason) is provided as the justification for the other (the conclusion).
- We use inference indicators, meaning, and position to help identify arguments and distinguish between the reasons and the conclusion.
- In order to display the structure of the argument (the relationship between the reasons and the conclusion), we diagram the argument, using either standard form or an arrow diagram. We can also diagram challenges to the claims in the argument and responses to those challenges.

Argumentation Exercise: Identifying the Structure of an Argument in a Dialogue

Examine the A Dialogue on Piracy and Copyright at the beginning of this module. Briefly portray the structure of the argument in that dialogue, using either standard form or arrow diagrams.

Writing Skills Exercise: Presenting the Structure of an Argument in Paragraph Form

In many essays you will have to summarize the structure of an argument for the reader in order to analyze and critique it. Presenting the structure in paragraph form is better for most audiences. Examine the following arrow diagram of the argument, then write one paragraph outlining the structure of the author's argument, using the inference indicators to help identify the overall structure of the argument.

1. Barry Bonds should not be allowed into the Baseball Hall of Fame.
2. His trainer claims he took steroids.
3. Barry Bonds used steroids.
4. Steroids are banned in baseball.
5. Barry Bonds developed significantly physically within a few years.
6. The Baseball Hall of Fame honours those who excel and reflect well on baseball.
7. Taking steroids does not reflect well on baseball.
8. Barry Bonds denies he took steroids.

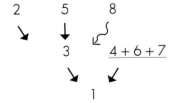

ANALYZING ARGUMENTS **81**

Assessing Deductive Arguments

LEARNING OBJECTIVES

After completing this module you should be able to:

1. Explain the difference and distinguish between non-deductive and deductive arguments;
2. Explain and apply the criteria for assessing deductive arguments;
3. Define and apply key terms in assessing argument structure;
4. Distinguish between a valid argument and an invalid argument, as well as a sound argument and an unsound one;
5. Explain why a given deductive argument is valid or invalid using the topics model and the patterns model;
6. Supply missing reasons for a deductive argument; and
7. Identify and challenge invalid arguments using the argument counterexample method.

 ## A DIALOGUE ON COPYRIGHT AND PIRACY – CONTINUED

Jean: As I understand your argument, if something is unjust then we should ban it, and we should ban downloading copyright material, so downloading copyright materials is unjust. But isn't that putting the cart before the horse? It's also an invalid argument because it affirms the consequent.

Peter: I think you are right. I have to review my logic. If it affirms the consequent it won't work. I need to think about the unjust argument a bit more. I could formulate it that if something is unjust then it should be banned, but I am not sure I could defend that yet.

Jean: Let's try another argument and you can think about that one.

Peter: Okay, consider this one. If downloading copyright material is legal, then we would be allowing theft, but we shouldn't allow the downloading of copyright material, so we shouldn't allow theft. That works.

Jean: I'm afraid it doesn't. You have given another invalid argument. This time you have denied the antecedent because you could claim that if downloading copyright material is legal, then we would be condoning theft, and we shouldn't condone theft, so we shouldn't make downloading copyright material legal.

Peter: I'm confused. I guess I need to review valid and invalid arguments.

Jean: Okay, let's do that.

(to be continued)

4.1 Introduction

In this dialogue, Peter formulates two arguments: both fail to establish the conclusion because they are invalid. Jean will help him formulate a valid argument. Part of formulating and assessing effective arguments requires knowing and using the criteria for a good argument. Although both deductive and non-deductive arguments use the same general criteria, they differ in how they apply the criteria. A ***deductive argument*** is one in which accepting the reasons logically requires that we accept the conclusion or we contradict ourselves. A ***non-deductive argument*** is one in which the reasons, if accepted, provide plausible or probable grounds for accepting the conclusion, but do not logically require that we accept the conclusion. In this module we will examine deductive arguments and what makes for good and bad deductive arguments.

We assess both deductive and non-deductive arguments on two sets of criteria: whether the reasons adequately support the conclusion (assessing the structure of the argument, which consists of criteria of relevance and sufficiency), and the content (assessing whether the reasons are true). This module shows how to assess the structure of deductive arguments; the next module examines assessing non-deductive arguments.

We give an argument because we have some doubts about the truth of the conclusion or because we want to identify the reasoning, assumptions, and claims that support a given conclusion. We are trying to show that the conclusion rests on claims that are more readily accepted than the conclusion, and provide a strong or compelling reason to accept the conclusion. This means that not only must the reasons be true, but they must also adequately support the conclusion. If an argument meets all of these conditions, it is said to be *sound or cogent,* depending on whether it is deductive or non-deductive.

For the reasons to support the conclusion they must be relevant to the conclusion, as well as sufficient to support the conclusion. To say one claim is *relevant* to another is to assert that the truth or falsity of the first claim is linked to establishing the truth or

A **deductive argument** is one in which accepting the reasons logically requires that we accept the conclusion or we contradict ourselves.

A **non-deductive argument** is one in which the reasons, if accepted, provide plausible or probable grounds for accepting the conclusion.

falsity of the second claim. To say one or more claims are *sufficient* to establish a second claim is to assert that their truth assures or guarantees the truth of the second claim.

Both deductive and non-deductive arguments provide reasons that support the conclusion but differ in the strength of that support. Deductive arguments guarantee the truth of the conclusion by providing sufficient grounds for the truth of the conclusion, whereas non-deductive arguments can only provide, at best, very strong reasons, but not sufficient grounds, for the conclusion. This module examines the logical conditions for good deductive arguments, namely, validity and invalidity. It introduces two methods for determining validity (logical patterns and the topics model) and one method for demonstrating invalidity (the counterexample method). Patterns and the topics model provide means for supplying the assumed reasons needed to make an argument valid. Module 5 addresses non-deductive arguments.

4.2 Deductive and Non-Deductive Arguments

Consider the following argument:

1. Beethoven was the greatest composer of the nineteenth century.

∴ 2. The moon is made of green cheese.

If someone were to offer this as an argument we would doubt both his or her seriousness and sanity. Even if the reason were true there appears to be no connection or relationship between it and what it is supposed to justify. There simply is no relevance between composing music and the composition of the moon.

Consider another argument:

1. Beethoven was the greatest composer of the nineteenth century.

∴ 2. Every university student should study Beethoven.

In this argument the reason does constitute a possible ground for accepting the conclusion because it is the kind of claim that would be relevant to establishing the conclusion. However, it is not sufficient by itself to establish the conclusion. That Beethoven was the greatest composer of the nineteenth century might be a reason for some people to study him, but not necessarily for all university students to study him. To guarantee this conclusion we would need an additional claim or claims that connect Beethoven's being the greatest composer of his time to making it compulsory for all university students to study him or other great composers.

Now consider the following argument:

1. Beethoven was the greatest composer of the nineteenth century.

2. Every university student should study the great composers.

∴ 3. Every university student should study Beethoven.

In this argument the reasons are not only relevant reasons for the conclusion but, if accepted, they would be sufficient to establish the conclusion because you could not accept the reasons and deny the conclusion (if you did you would contradict yourself). Arguments with this kind of structure, in which accepting the reasons logically forces us to accept the conclusion, are called deductive arguments.

However, not all arguments are of this type. Consider the following argument:

1. I bought this coffee in the college dining hall.

2. It is overpriced.

∴ 3. All coffee sold on campus is overpriced.

Although the sample is relevant to establishing that all coffee on campus is overpriced, it is not sufficient. The reasons provide weak grounds for accepting the conclusion. Thus, even if we accept the reasons we are not logically forced to accept the conclusion. To infer that all coffee on campus is overpriced we would need to know several additional things (such as, how many coffee outlets there are on campus, whether they are controlled by one body that sets a common price or whether they all set their own price structures, what each charges, what constitutes a fair price for coffee, and so on).

The price of coffee argument is a non-deductive argument, or one in which the reasons provide plausible or probable grounds for the conclusion but do not absolutely guarantee it. In the following non-deductive argument the reasons provide probable grounds for accepting the conclusion; however, accepting the reasons does not guarantee that the conclusion is true.

1. Ninety-seven percent of the part-time faculty voted to go on strike.

2. Nayla is a member of the part-time faculty.

∴ 3. Nayla must have voted to go on strike.

Although this non-deductive argument provides strong grounds for accepting the conclusion, accepting the reasons does not guarantee the truth of the conclusion because Nayla might be one of the three percent who voted not to go on strike. In this case, the reasons provide strong but not conclusive support for the conclusion.

Non-deductive arguments are judged in terms of the strength of the support they provide for accepting the conclusion. That strength can range from very weak (as in the price of coffee example above) to very strong (as in the example involving Nayla).

Both deductive and non-deductive arguments require that the reasons be relevant to the conclusion. Where they differ is in whether or not the sufficiency condition is met. In a deductive argument the reasons fully support or guarantee the conclusion. In a non-deductive argument the reasons only partially support the conclusion by providing a degree of probability for the conclusion. The rest of this module discusses the criteria for assessing deductive arguments.

Identifying Deductive and Non-Deductive Arguments

For each of the following:

(A) portray the structure of the argument;
(B) identify whether the argument is deductive or non-deductive; and
(C) assess whether the reasons are relevant and sufficient to establish the conclusion.

1. Daphne is a cat. All cats are playful. Therefore, Daphne is playful.
2. Nigel is a dog. Some dogs are playful. So Nigel is playful.
3. The defendant knew the victim. She had the motive to want him dead, was in possession of a weapon that could have been the murder weapon, was in the vicinity where the victim was killed, and was seen by three eyewitnesses talking to the victim just before he was killed. Therefore, she must have killed him.
4. If something is immoral it should be illegal. Adultery is immoral. So it should be illegal.
5. I did not receive any mail last week, yet there were no holidays. My mailman must be falling down on the job.

Answers to the Quick Quizzes are available on the Premium Website at www.criticalthinking2e.nelson.com.

4.3 Assessing Deductive Arguments: Validity

> A deductive argument is **valid** if accepting the reasons logically requires us to accept the conclusion without contradicting ourselves.
>
> A deductive argument is **invalid** if we can affirm the reasons and deny the conclusion.

Deductive arguments are assessed in terms of validity and invalidity. A deductive argument is **valid** if accepting the reasons logically requires us to accept the conclusion; accepting the reasons and denying the conclusion would result in a contradiction. This makes validity a function of the structural relationship between the reasons and the conclusion. A deductive argument is **invalid** if we can affirm the reasons and deny the conclusion without contradicting ourselves.

The following is a valid argument:

1. All mammals nurse their young.

2. Whales are mammals.

∴ 3. Whales nurse their young.

> A deductive argument is **sound** if it is valid and has true reasons.

This is valid because we cannot assert the reasons are true and deny the conclusion. This is also a **sound argument**, or a deductive argument that is valid and has true reasons.

Not all valid arguments are sound. Consider the following argument:

1. All mammals nurse their young.

2. Alligators are mammals.

∴ 3. Alligators nurse their young.

Again, *if* we accept the reasons in this argument we must also accept the conclusion or consequently contradict ourselves. The argument is valid. However, in this argument, one of the reasons happens to be false. So, although the argument is *valid*, it is not *sound*.

We can also have valid arguments in which the reasons are false and the conclusion is true. For example:

1. Mammals lay eggs.

2. Alligators are mammals.

∴ 3. Alligators lay eggs.

This argument is valid. If we accept the reasons we must accept the conclusion because there are no circumstances under which we could accept the reasons and not accept the conclusion. However, in this case, the reasons are in fact false, but the conclusion happens to be true.

Validity is a structural property of the relationship between the reasons and the conclusion. It says the reasons are related to the conclusion in such a way that accepting the reasons guarantees the truth of the conclusion without saying anything about the content of the reasons, that is, whether they are true or false.

Knowing an argument is valid does not assure us that the conclusion is true. Validity is concerned simply with the relationship between the reasons and the conclusion, with relevance and sufficiency. A valid argument may have any of the combination of true and false reasons, as outlined in Table 4.1. An invalid argument, on the other hand, may have any combination of true and false reasons and conclusions. That is, with an invalid argument, the truth of the reasons does not guarantee the truth of the conclusion. Because the relationship between the reasons and conclusion is not properly established, knowing the truth of the reasons tells us nothing about the truth of the conclusion.

An invalid argument can have true reasons and a true conclusion (number 4, below), but the truth of the conclusion is not the result of the relationship between the reasons and the conclusion. It is true for other reasons. Only a valid pattern ensures the truth of the conclusion follows from the truth of the reasons (number 1 below). This is why determining validity is so important. Validity, a structural feature of the relationship between the reasons and the conclusions, guarantees that *if* the reasons are true, then the conclusion must be true. The next section examines some ways of determining valid argument structures.

TABLE 4.1 Truth, Validity and Invalidity

	Validity	Reasons	Conclusion	Example
1.	Valid	True	True	All cats are mammals. All mammals nurse their young. ∴ Cats nurse their young.
2.	Valid	False	False	All cats are alligators. Alligators are reptiles. ∴ Cats are alligators.
3.	Valid	False	True	All cats are alligators. Alligators nurse their young. ∴ Cats nurse their young.
4.	Invalid	True	True	All cats are mammals. All dogs are mammals. ∴ All cats nurse their young.
5.	Invalid	True	False	All cats are mammals. All dogs are mammals. ∴ All cats are dogs.
6.	Invalid	False	False	All cats are alligators. All alligators are vegetarians. ∴ All cats are vegetarians.
7.	Invalid	False	True	All cats are alligators. All cats lay eggs. ∴ All alligators lay eggs.

QUICK QUIZ 4.2

Validity Comprehension

In the following list determine:
(A) Which of the following statements are true and which are false; and
(B) If the statement is false, explain why.

1. A valid argument can have true reasons and a false conclusion.
2. A sound argument must be valid.
3. A sound argument can have false reasons.
4. A valid argument must have a true conclusion.
5. Validity is an indication of the truth of the claims in the argument.
6. Soundness is an indication of the truth of the claims in an argument.
7. Validity is concerned with the relationship of the claims to one another.

Answers to the Quick Quizzes are available on the Premium Website at www.criticalthinking2e.nelson.com.

4.4 Valid Argument Patterns

Validity is a structural feature of how terms or statements are related to one another within an argument. An argument is considered valid, not by the truth of its reasons, but by the relationship of its reasons to one another. We call this relationship the **logical structure** (or the **logical form)** of an argument. Since we are not concerned with an argument's substance when determining validity, we need only to look at the structure (the logical form) and not the content (the truth of the reasons) of the argument.

There are two types of logical structure of arguments. One relates terms or categories to other categories, which is called *categorical logic*. An example is "All logicians are mad" because it says everything that fits the category of being a logician also fits the category of being mad. The second relates claims to one another, which is called *propositional logic*. An example is "If I drop this chalk, then it will break" because it states a relationship between the claims "I drop this chalk" and "it will break" without asserting either is true. **Logical terms** are terms that show the relationship between terms or claims within an argument. Some logical terms relate one category to another, some relate claims, and some are used in both kinds of arguments.

Table 4.2 identifies the kinds of logical terms found in categorical and propositional claims. **Categorical claims** relate categories of things to one another (such as, cats, mammals, intelligent). **Propositional claims** relate claims to one another (such as, Socrates is mortal, Socrates will die someday).

The statement "If there is life on Venus, then there must be water on Venus" contains the logical term "If … then …" and the content terms "there is life on Venus" and "there is water on Venus." We can identify the logical structure of the statement by replacing the content terms with variables (a, b, c, etc.). The logical structure of the statement is "If a, then b."

> The **logical structure** (or **logical form**) of an argument is the logical relationship between the terms or claims of an argument.

> **Logical terms** are terms that show the logical relationship between claims or terms within an argument.

> **Categorical claims** relate categories of things to one another.
>
> **Propositional claims** relate claims to one another.

TABLE 4.2 Logical Terms

Categorical	Propositional	Both
All … are … e.g., All cats are mammals. e.g., All chalk breaks. (All chalk is the kind of thing that breaks.)	If …, then … e.g., If something is a cat, then it is a mammal. e.g., If I drop this chalk, then it will break.	… and …. Cats are mammals and alligators are reptiles.
… is (a) … e.g., Socrates is a cat. e.g., Socrates is mortal.	Either … or … e.g., Socrates is either a cat or a reptile. Either we go to a movie or we go for a nice supper.	Not … Cats are not reptiles.
Some … are e.g., Some cats are mammals.		
No … is a … No cats are reptiles.		

ASSESSING DEDUCTIVE ARGUMENTS **89**

The statement "There is life on Venus" contains no logical terms and is simply translated as *a*. The statement "There is no water on Venus" contains the logical term *not* and would be translated as "not *b*."

Consider the following argument:

1. If there is water on Venus, then there may be life on Venus.

2. There is water on Venus.

∴ 3. There is life on Venus.

We can determine this argument's logical form by identifying the logical terms and the content terms and replacing the content terms with variables. Each repetition of a content claim gets the same variable. Replacing the content terms with variables in each of the above claims in the argument would give us the following logical form for the argument:

1. If a, then b

2. a

∴ 3. b

This is a valid argument form. (We discuss why this is the case in Section 4.6.) Any argument with this logical form is valid because one cannot logically accept its reasons and deny its conclusion. Knowing this logical form enables us to identify and determine the validity for any argument having this form.

Because arguments are *valid* or *invalid* solely in terms of their logical form we can determine the validity of an argument solely by examining its logical form. Some logical forms are valid and some are invalid. A valid form will never produce an invalid argument, and an invalid form will never produce a valid argument.

Logicians have developed a number of different ways of establishing validity (such as, truth tables, Venn diagrams, and logical derivations). Using each of these requires mastering a somewhat technical set of skills. Less formal methods of determining validity and invalidity include identifying the most basic common argument patterns, the topics model, and the method of argument counterexample. Since our purpose in this text is not to become logicians but to develop the skills for critical thinking and argumentation, we will focus on the less formal methods.

QUICK QUIZ 4.3

Identifying Logical Terms and Content

For each of the statements below:

(A) identify the logical terms and content terms in each of the following; and
(B) turn the content terms into variables.

1. Either I study for the exam or go partying with my friends.
2. Some stars are relatively cool compared to our Sun.
3. No stars are as cool as a planet.
4. If I am late for the interview, I will not get the job.
5. All cats chase mice.

Answers to the Quick Quizzes are available on the Premium Website at www.criticalthinking2e.nelson.com.

4.5 Necessary and Sufficient Conditions

Some claims used in arguments identify relationships between two states of affairs. Some examples are: "If there is water on Venus, then there is likely life on Venus"; "You will pass this course on the condition that you get a "C" on the final"; "Oxygen is a necessary condition for fire"; "An "A" on the final is a sufficient condition for passing this course." If *a* occurs, then *b* will occur. Conditional claims relate one state of affairs or condition to another state of affairs or condition.

We can identify two types of conditions: necessary and sufficient. A ***sufficient condition*** is one that, if it occurs, is sufficient to produce the condition that depends on it. For example, a sufficient condition to establish the presence of oxygen is for there to be a fire, because if there is a fire, then there must be oxygen present. In a course where one exam makes up 100 percent of the grade, passing the exam is a sufficient condition for passing the course. However, if the final makes up only 40 percent then passing it by itself would not be sufficient to pass the course. A given result may have various, independent conditions sufficient to bring it about. Fire is a sufficient condition for establishing the presence of oxygen; so, too, is oxidation and the presence of aerobic organisms. These conditions can occur independently of one another. The presence of any is sufficient to show oxygen is present. A claim that is a sufficient condition for another is one whose truth is sufficient to establish the truth of the second claim.

A ***necessary condition*** is a condition that must be present for the resultant condition to occur, but by itself is not sufficient to produce the resultant condition. For example, oxygen is a necessary condition for fire; however, oxygen is not sufficient to produce fire because a number of other conditions must be met if fire is to occur (such, as some burnable material and raising the burnable material to its flash point.)

A necessary condition does not need to be a sufficient condition, although in some situations it can be; and a condition may be a sufficient condition without being a necessary condition. Dropping the chalk is sufficient to break it. However, dropping the chalk is not necessary for breaking it, nor does the fact that the chalk is broken mean it was dropped. A sufficient condition may be one of several ways of producing the result, so the presence of the result need not indicate that a particular sufficient condition occurred.

We can express necessary and sufficient conditions in a number of ways. Some examples are: "Fire needs oxygen"; "To get a "B" on this essay you will have to do a critical review of five papers"; "If there is a fire, then oxygen must be present."

We sometimes talk of sets of necessary conditions, sets of sufficient conditions, or sets of necessary and sufficient conditions. A set of conditions is two or more of the relevant conditions that together would be either necessary or sufficient. For example, "Oxygen, burnable material, and raising the material to its flash point are sufficient to produce a fire."

> A **sufficient condition** is one that, if it occurs, is sufficient to produce the condition that depends on it.

> A **necessary condition** is a condition that must be present for the resultant condition to occur, but by itself is not sufficient to produce the resultant condition.

4.6 Conditional Claims

> **A conditional statement** is a single claim that asserts that one state of affairs is conditional upon another.

A *conditional statement* is a single claim that asserts that one state of affairs is conditional upon another. It does not state that either is true, only that if one is true the other will be true (if the conditional statement as a whole is true). More precisely, a conditional claim relates a sufficient and necessary condition.

The following is a conditional statement:

If he is a logician, then he is mad.

It claims that a person is mad under certain conditions (if he or she meets the condition of being a logician). In effect, the claim is the same as the claim "All logicians are mad." It does not claim the only condition for being mad is being a logician: that claim would be only logicians are mad, which is a different claim.

This statement contains the logical term "If ... then ..." and the content terms "he is a logician" and "he is mad." Substituting a different variable for each of the content terms in the statement (*a* for "he is a logician" and *b* for "he is mad,") we get the following statement:

If a, then b.

"If ... then ..." is the most common form of a conditional claim. A conditional statement is a single claim and it always consists of two conditions, one of which is dependent in some way on the other. A conditional statement cannot be broken into its component parts unless we have further information. From the statement "If he is a logician, then he is mad" we do not know that anyone is a logician, much less that he is mad. All we know is the condition – that *if* someone meets the condition of being a logician, then he is mad.

> **The antecedent** is the claim after the "if" in a conditional statement.
>
> **The consequent** is the claim after the "then" in a conditional statement.

In the conditional statement "If *a*, then *b*," the *a*, called the *antecedent* (because it comes before the "then" and after the "if"), is a sufficient condition for *b* and *b*, called the *consequent* (because it comes after the "then), is a necessary condition for *a*.

"If ... then ..." is the basis for identifying the antecedent and the consequent. Other variants of the conditional are identified below, under "Translating Claims into the Conditional Form." No matter how a conditional is worded, it can always be translated into the base form "If *a*, then *b*."

In a conditional claim the antecedent is a sufficient condition for the consequent. However, the consequent is only a necessary, not a sufficient, condition for the antecedent. There can be multiple sufficient conditions that could produce the same result (or consequent). For example, we can raise the kindling temperature of burnable material with a match, a lightning strike, or spontaneous combustion. Each is sufficient to produce the result, fire.

QUICK QUIZ 4.5

Identifying Antecedents and Consequents

In the following, identify the antecedents and the consequents.

1. If the sun is powered by nuclear fusion, then its life span is far longer than anyone expected.
2. We will go to the party if I can borrow the car.
3. If the province raises tuition fees, fewer students will be able to go to university.

Answers to the Quick Quizzes are available on the Premium Website at www.criticalthinking2e.nelson.com.

4.7 Conditional Argument Patterns

One of the most common argument patterns is the conditional argument. A **conditional argument** is an argument that contains at least one conditional (if …, then …) statement. Identifying the patterns will enable us to identify any argument that fits the pattern as either valid or invalid. All arguments fitting a valid pattern are valid and all arguments fitting an invalid pattern are invalid.

We can identify the pattern by using the technique introduced above for identifying the logical structure of an argument. We identify the logical and content ter~
the argument and then substitute variables for the content terms. As l~
consistent about substituting the same letter for the same conte~
an argument, we can portray the logical structure of the a~
below, by following through with the substitution ~

1. If he is a logician, then he is mad~

2. He is a logician.

∴ 3. He is mad.

With substitution, this becomes:

1. If a, then b

2. a

∴ 3. b

A **conditional**
argument is an
argument t~
at l~

In this argument, the conditional statement is "If *a*, then *b*," *a* is the antecedent and *b* is the consequent.

To understand validity we need to understand what we can do with a claim. With any given claim we can either affirm it or deny it. To *affirm a claim* means we say the claim is true. By affirming the claim "Saindon is a logician" we are saying this claim is true. To *deny a claim* is to say the claim is false. By denying the claim "Saindon is a logician" we are saying "It is false (or not the case) Saindon is a logician" or, more simply, "Saindon is not a logician." We can deny either affirmative or negative claims. Denying an affirmative claim would produce a negative claim:

Saindon is a logician.

would become

Saindon is not a logician.

Denying this negative claim (it is not the case that Saindon is not a logician) would, in turn, produce a positive claim:

Saindon is a logician.

Affirming and denying claims is a function of what we do. It is not be equated with whether the claim does or does not contain a "not." Given these basic functions of affirming and denying we have four possibilities with the conditional claim "If a, then b." We can affirm or deny the antecedent or consequent. If we portray the structure by stating the conditional on the first line, and what is done to the conditional on the second line, we can easily see the logical structure of the argument. It also gives us the name of the pattern, for the name of the pattern is given by what the second reason in the argument pattern does. The four conditional argument patterns are represented in Table 4.3.

TABLE 4.3 Conditional Argument Patterns

Name	Pattern	VALID/INVALID
Affirm the antecedent	If a, then b, a ∴ b	VALID
Deny the antecedent	If a, then b, Not a ∴ Not b	INVALID
Affirm the consequent	If a, then b, b ∴ a	INVALID
Deny the consequent	If a, then b, Not b ∴ Not a	VALID

To illustrate, we will use the following claims as substitutions for *a* and *b:*

a = I drop the chalk.

b = The chalk will break.

Making these substitutions, we get:

Affirming the antecedent — VALID

1.	If I drop the chalk, the chalk will break.	If *a*, then *b*
2.	I dropped the chalk.	*a*

∴ 3. The chalk broke.   ∴ *b*

There are no conditions under which if the reasons were true the conclusion could be false. That is, if the reasons are true, the conclusion cannot possibly be false. If I drop the chalk and it does not break, we have shown that the first reason is false, not that the argument is invalid. To show the argument to be invalid, we would have to find a condition in which both reasons could be true and the conclusion could be false. And we cannot find that.

Denying the antecedent — INVALID

1.	If I drop the chalk, the chalk will break.	If *a*, then *b*
2.	I didn't drop the chalk.	not *a*

∴ 3. The chalk must not be broken.   ∴ not *b*

This argument is invalid because both reasons could be true and the conclusion could be false. Just because I did not drop the chalk does not mean it is not broken. It could have rolled off the table when I set it down, I could have snapped it with my fingers, or sat on it. So both reasons could be true and the conclusion false – the chalk is broken.

A conditional statement claims that if (or whenever) *a* occurs, then *b* will follow. If I drop the chalk, then it will break. However, the chalk could break for a number of other reasons. My not dropping the chalk does not tell me anything about the current state of the chalk, that is, whether it is broken or unbroken.

Affirming the consequent — INVALID

1.	If I drop the chalk, the chalk will break.	If *a*, then *b*
2.	The chalk is broken.	*b*

∴ 3. I dropped the chalk.   ∴ *a*

Again, this is invalid. The reasons could be true but the conclusion false. I might have sat on the chalk and broken it, or it might have rolled off the table. Dropping the chalk is just one way of guaranteeing (according to *a*) that the chalk will break. However, it can be broken in a number of other ways. Knowing that if I drop it, it will break, and that it is broken does not make it possible for me to infer I that must have dropped it.

Denying the consequent — *VALID*

1.	If I drop the chalk, the chalk will break.	If *a*, then *b*
2.	The chalk isn't broken.	not *b*

∴ 3. I didn't drop the chalk.   ∴ not *a*

If we know the conditional is true and the consequent is false, then we must know that the antecedent is also false.

Now that you know these four basic conditional argument pattern, you can handle the vast majority of conditional arguments you encounter. By simply identifying the logical pattern of an argument you can determine whether any given conditional argument is valid or invalid.

QUICK QUIZ 4.6

Determining Validity: Conditionals

In each of the following:

(A) portray the structure of the argument;
(B) determine whether or not the argument is valid or invalid; and
(C) show validity or invalidity by labelling the claims with variables and identifying the argument pattern.

I. 1. If Watson's fingerprints are found on the money, then he committed the robbery.
   2. His fingerprints are not on the money.

∴ 3. He did not commit the robbery.

II. 1. If the moon has an atmosphere, then there would be few signs of impacts with meteors.
   2. There are signs of a large number of meteor impacts on the moon.

∴ 3. The moon does not have an atmosphere.

III. 1. If Mars is inhabitable, we would find water on Mars.
   2. We found water on Mars.

∴ 3. Mars is inhabitable.

IV. 1. If I park here overnight, I will get a ticket.
   2. I have to park here overnight.

∴ 3. I will get a ticket.

Answers to the Quick Quizzes are available on the Premium Website at www.criticalthinking2e.nelson.com.

Translating Claims into the Conditional Form

Some conditional claims are not stated in the "If *a*, then *b*" form, but can be translated into it. For example, "*a*, unless *b*" can be restated as "If *b*, then not *a*."

Other types of statements that appear not to be conditionals at all can often be rewritten as such. Universal claims such as "All cats are mammals" can be expressed as a conditional "If something is a cat, then it is a mammal." Similarly, "No cats are reptiles" can be expressed as either of the following conditionals "If something is a cat, then it is not a reptile" or "If something is a reptile, then it is not a cat." Table 4.4 shows how claims can be turned into conditionals.

TABLE 4.4 Translating Other Claims into Conditionals

Claims	Equivalent Conditionals	Examples
All *a*'s are *b*'s.	If something is an *a*, it is a *b*.	All cats are mammals. = If something is a cat, it is a mammal.
a on the condition that *b*.	If *b*, then *a*.	It is a mammal on the condition that it is a cat. = If it is a cat, then it is a mammal.
No *a*'s are *b*'s.	If something is an *a*, then it is not a *b*, *and* If something is a *b*, then it is not an *a*.	No cats are reptiles. = If it is a cat, then it is not a reptile, *and* If it is a reptile, then it is not a cat.
Only *a*'s are *b*'s.	If *b*, then *a*, and if *a*, then *b*.	Only fourth-year students may take this course. = If you take this course, you are a fourth-year student.
a unless *b*.	If *b*, then not *a*, *and* if *a*, then not *b*.	John goes home on weekends unless he has a test on Monday. = If he has a test on Monday, John does not go home on the weekend, *and* If John goes home on the weekend, then he does not have a test on Monday.

4.8 The Conditional Chain Argument

One further set of arguments uses the conditional pattern. A ***conditional chain argument*** is an argument that reasons from one set of conditional claims to another set of conditional claims. For example:

> **1.** If I spend my student aid grant on books, then I will not be able to eat well during the term.

> **2.** If I am not able to eat well during the term, then I will not get good marks.

> ∴ **3.** If I spend my student aid grant on books, then I will not get good marks.

This has the logical form:

> If a, then b
>
> If b, then c
>
> ∴ If a, then c

Table 4.5 identifies the valid and invalid conditional chain patterns.

> **A conditional chain argument** is an argument that reasons from one set of conditional claims to another set of conditional claims.

TABLE 4.5 Conditional Chain Arguments

Name	Pattern	VALID/INVALID	Example
VALID Conditional Chain	If a, then b. If b, then c. ——— ∴ If a, then c.	VALID	If you go shopping, then I will cook supper. If I cook supper, then you can do the dishes. ——— ∴ If you go shopping, then you can do the dishes.
INVALID Conditional Chain	If a, then b. If a, then c. ——— ∴ If b, then c.	INVALID	If something is a cat, it eats mice. If something is a cat, it is a mammal. ∴ If something eats mice, it is a mammal.

4.9 The Disjunctive Pattern

Another common argument pattern is the either/or pattern. This is based on a claim of the logical form "either *a* or *b*," called a ***disjunction***. For example:

> Either I study for the exam or I will fail it.

> **A disjunction** is a claim of the logical form "either *a* or *b*."

The components of the disjunction (in this case "I study for the exam" and "I will fail it") are called the **disjuncts**. Logically, it does not matter which disjunct comes first and which second. A disjunction normally has two disjuncts. However, it may have three or more (although grammatically *either* takes only two disjuncts, logically it may take two or more). For example:

> I will take either psychology, fine arts, or economics next semester.

The disjunctive claim becomes the basis for a disjunctive argument in the same way the conditional claim becomes the basis for a conditional argument. As with the conditional form we can either affirm or deny a disjunct to construct an argument. There is one valid and one invalid disjunctive argument form.

For the claim "Either *a* or *b*" to be true at least one of the two disjuncts must be true, although it is possible that under certain conditions both could be true (I may study for the exam and still fail it). Therefore, the minimum condition for a disjunction being true is that one of the claims must be true. Hence, we can draw a valid inference if we know the disjunction is true and one disjunct is false: the remaining disjunct must be true. Table 4.6 identifies the disjunctive argument patterns.

> **A disjunct** is one of the alternatives in a disjunction.

TABLE 4.6 Disjunctive Argument Patterns

Name	Pattern	VALID/INVALID	Example
Denying a Disjunct	Either *a* or *b*. Not *a*. ∴ *b*.	VALID	Either I study for the exam or I fail it. I did not study. ∴ I will fail the exam.
Affirming a Disjunct	Either *a* or *b*. *a*. ∴ not *b*.	INVALID	Either I study for the exam or I fail it. I did study. ∴ I will not fail the exam.

Since it is possible that both claims in a disjunction can be true, knowing that one is true tells me nothing about the truth of the other. I might have studied for the exam and still failed. The reasons would be true but the conclusion could be false, and that would make the argument invalid.

The disjunctive forms are based on the fact that in most disjunctive statements, the statement can be true if either disjunct is true or if both are. Thus, knowing that one disjunct is true does not guarantee that the other is false. However, knowing one is false does guarantee that the other is true. And that is the only way to guarantee a true conclusion from a disjunctive claim. As mentioned above, in the claim "Either I study for the exam or I will fail it" it is possible that I both study and fail the exam. When the disjunction includes the possibility that both are true (such as, either *a* or *b*, or both) it is called an **inclusive disjunction** claim.

Another kind of disjunctive claim, however, is more restrictive: "Either I study or I do not study, but I cannot do both." In this kind of disjunctive claim, knowing the truth of one *does* guarantee the falsity of the other. This is called an **exclusive disjunction** claim and occurs with disjuncts whose truth conditions are linked so that asserting one automatically denies the other. They have the form "Either *a* or *b*, but not both," such as in the example "Either I study for the exam or I do not study, but I cannot do both."

> An **inclusive disjunction** is one in which both disjuncts may be true.

> An **exclusive disjunction** is disjunction in which only one of the disjuncts can be true.

In some situations, we present an exclusive disjunction without the words "but not both." "Either I study or I do not" looks like an inclusive disjunction but is actually an exclusive disjunction. The disjunctive patterns built on the inclusive disjunction form apply to both kinds of disjunction.

QUICK QUIZ 4.8

Assessing Disjunctive Arguments

In the following:

(A) portray the structure of the argument; and
(B) identify whether the argument is valid or invalid.

1. Either Harris did it or his wife is lying. His wife is not lying. So he must have done it.
2. Either the circuit breaker has tripped or the TV's circuit board has gone. The circuit breaker has tripped. So the circuit board is okay.
3. Either we improve our response time in getting to fires or more people are going to die needlessly. I guess more people are going to die needlessly, because we cannot improve our response time.

Answers to the Quick Quizzes are available on the Premium Website at www.criticalthinking2e.nelson.com.

4.10 Conjunctions

A **conjunction** is a claim of the logical form *a and b*, where *a* and *b* are both themselves claims. A **conjunct** is one of the claims in a conjunction. We identify the logical form of a conjunction by replacing the content terms with variables. For a conjunction to be true, both conjuncts must be true. If we have the claim "Cats are mammals and alligators are reptiles" the logical form is "*a and b.*" The claim is true if both *a* and *b* are true. If either is false, the claim is false. A **conjunctive argument** is an argument involving a conjunction as a main reason or as a conclusion. As with disjuncts, the order of the conjuncts in a statement makes no difference to the logical validity of the pattern. The English terms "and," "but," "yet," "still," "furthermore," "also," "however," "although," and "moreover" typically work as conjunctions.

> A **conjunction** is a claim of the logical form *a and b*, where *a* and *b* are both themselves claims.
>
> A **conjunct** is one of the claims in a conjunction.
>
> A **conjunctive argument** is an argument involving a conjunction as a main reason or as a conclusion.

TABLE 4.7 Conjunctive Arguments

Name	Pattern	VALID/INVALID	Example
Affirming a Conjunct	*a and b* ∴ *a*	VALID	1. Birds evolved from reptiles and humans evolved from proto-mammals. ∴ 2. Birds evolved from reptiles.

Denying a Conjunct	a and b not b _____ ∴ not a	INVALID	1. Birds evolved from reptiles and humans descended from proto-mammals. 2. Birds did not evolve from reptiles. _____ ∴3. Humans did not evolve from proto-mammals.
Introducing a Conjunct	a b _____ ∴ a and b	VALID	1. Birds evolved from reptiles. 2. Humans evolved from proto-mammals. _____ ∴3. Birds evolved from reptiles and humans evolved from proto-mammals.

4.11 Complex Argument Patterns

The various structures we have identified thus far can be combined to create more complex argument patterns. For example, we can have an argument that combines a conditional and a disjunction in the following:

1. If a, then b or c

2. a
_____

∴ 3. b or c

In the above argument, the antecedent is affirmed, the consequent is a disjunction, and the argument is valid. It says that if a given antecedent is true, then one of two outcomes is possible, but we do not know which. Consider, however, the following:

1. If a or b, then c

2. a
_____

∴ 3. c

This structure says that if one of two possible antecedent conditions (a or b) is true, then a given consequent (c) is true. In this case, the antecedent is a disjunction. We know a disjunction is true if one of the disjuncts is true. Since we know that a is true, and a disjunctive claim is true as long as one of the disjuncts is true, then we know the claim "a or b" is true and we can infer "c." Contrast this with the following:

1. If a and b, then c

2. a
_____

∴ 3. c

The preceding is not a valid argument. The claim "*a* and *c*" is a conjunction. For a conjunction to be true both conjuncts must be true. In the argument as stated we have affirmed only *a*. Until we know that *b* is true we cannot conclude that *c* is true.

We can sometimes construct complex arguments using the various simple patterns:

1. If *a*, then *b* or *c*

2. *a*   Affirms the antecedent — VALID

∴   3. *b* or *c*

4. not *b*   Denies the disjunct — VALID

∴   5. *c*

The first argument above is a conditional argument, while the second is a disjunctive one. In these particular examples both arguments are valid. It is possible, however, for one of the inferences to be valid and the other invalid, as in the following example:

1. If *a*, then *b* or *c*

2. *a*   Affirms the antecedent — VALID

∴   3. *b* or *c*

4. *b*   Affirms the disjunct — INVALID

∴   5. not *c*

QUICK QUIZ 4.9

Complex Argument Patterns

Consider the following patterns. Are they valid or invalid? Explain.

I.   1. If *a* then *b* or *c*
    2. not *b*

∴   3. not *a*

II.   1. Either *a* or *b*
    2. not *b*

∴   3. *a*

4. If *a*, then *c* or *d*

∴ 5. *c*

III. 1. If *a* or *b* or *c*, then *d* or *e*
2. *a*
3. not *d*

∴ 4. *e*

IV. 1. If *a* and *b*, then *c* or *d*
2. *a*
3. *b*
4. not *c*

∴ 5. *d*

V. 1. If *a*, then *c* and *d*
2. *a*
3. not *d*

∴ 4. *c*

Answers to the Quick Quizzes are available on the Premium Website at www.criticalthinking2e.nelson.com.

So far we have identified only some valid and invalid argument forms. Arguments without a clear logical pattern, or with a different logical pattern from the ones we have encountered, need to be assessed using the method of counterexample or the topics model.

4.12 The Topics Model

The arguments we have encountered thus far deal with the logical relation between claims. Another category of reasoning involves topics. "A cat is a mammal" relates two categories of things or topics to one another in one claim. A *topic* is a subject for discussion, a term in a claim. A claim connects these topics (other logicians call these "categories"). In the preceding, "cat" would be a topic and "mammal" another topic.

An alternate model that works for determining validity as well as helping in constructing arguments, analyzing issues, engaging in argumentation and writing essays is the *topics model*, which is a method for determining validity by connecting the topics in the conclusion with the topics in the reasons. The topics model works by identifying the key terms (topics) in the conclusion and comparing those with the topics in the reasons.

A topic is a subject for discussion, or a subject about which we can say something. In this context, a topic is usually the grammatical subject, verb phrase, or object of a sentence. Occasionally, it may be a qualifier: an adjective or adverb.

Critical Thinking helps one in dealing with life.

> A **topic** is a subject for discussion, a term in a claim.

> The **topics model** is a method for determining validity by connecting the topics in the conclusion with the topics in the reasons.

"Critical Thinking" is one topic and "helps one in dealing with life" is another topic. We can say something about "Critical Thinking," and we can say something about "things that help one in dealing with life."

We can identify the topics in a claim by drawing a single line under the first and a double line under the second (we can also number them "1" and "2") as follows:

1   2
<u>Critical Thinking</u> <u><u>helps one in dealing with life</u></u>.

Relevance and sufficiency are established by connecting the topics in the reasons with the topics in the conclusion. If none of the topics in the conclusion appear in the reasons, then the reasons are irrelevant to the conclusion. That is the case with the Beethoven and the moon-is-made-of-green-cheese argument in Section 4.3. Using the underlining and numbering technique, the Beethoven argument would look like this:

3   4
1. <u>Beethoven</u> was <u>the greatest composer of the nineteenth century.</u>

∴ 2. <u>The moon</u> is <u><u>made of green cheese</u></u>.

1   2

From this it becomes clear that none of the topics in the conclusion are mentioned in the reasons. Thus, the reason is irrelevant to the conclusion. For the reasons to be relevant to the conclusion they must address the same topics as the conclusion.

If only some of the topics in the conclusion are mentioned in the reasons, then the reasons, though likely relevant, are insufficient to establish the conclusion. For example:

1. Murder is immoral.

∴ 2. Abortion is immoral.

In this argument, although "immoral" is mentioned in both the reason and the conclusion, "abortion," the topic of the conclusion, is not mentioned in the reason. For the argument to be valid, "abortion" would have to be mentioned in the reasons.

Validity of an argument is established by properly linking the various topics in the reasons with the topics in the conclusion. If the topics mentioned in the reasons are not connected appropriately to those in the conclusion, validity cannot be established.

To use the topics model to determine validity, start by identifying the separate topics in the conclusion. To keep things clear we underline and number the topics in the conclusion. Focus on the subject of the sentence as one possible topic, and the verbs and objects as others. Remember that important qualifiers may be additional topics. Next, identify the topics that recur in the reasons and give them the same underline pattern and number. New topics are assigned a different number and underline. This has been done in the following argument:

3   2
1. <u>Murder</u> is <u><u>immoral</u></u>.

1   2
∴ 2. <u>Abortion</u> is <u><u>immoral</u></u>.

In this argument, there are three topics:

1. murder (occurs only in reason);
2. abortion (occurs only in conclusion); and
3. immoral (occurs in both reason and conclusion).

The conclusion has two topics: "abortion" and "is immoral." "Murder" is a new topic introduced in the reason. It gets a different underline and a new number.

The topic "abortion" is not mentioned in the stated reason. Unless we mention "abortion" and connect it to the topics in the conclusion, we cannot be sure the conclusion follows from the reason(s). For the conclusion to be established, we need reasons that say something about all of the topics that are present in the conclusion. This provides us with a basic rule for validity: *For an argument to be valid, all of the topics mentioned in the conclusion must be mentioned in the reasons.* The above argument, as stated, fails this basic rule.

Consider the above argument with this additional reason:

      1   4

A. Abortion is the <u>taking of a human life</u>.

      3   2

1. <u>Murder</u> is <u>immoral</u>.

---

      1   2

∴ 2. <u>Abortion</u> is <u>immoral</u>.

When adding an unstated reason to an argument, we label it with a capital letter to identify that it is something we have added. This distinguishes it from the author's explicit claims.

Adding this reason would satisfy the condition. However, the argument would still not be valid. Neither "abortion" nor the fourth topic, "the taking of a human life," has been connected to the other two topics, "murder" or "is immoral."

This demonstrates a second rule for determining validity: *for an argument to be valid, all of the topics mentioned in the conclusion must be connected to the topics in the reasons, and those must be connected to one another.* Since "abortion" is already connected with "is immoral" in the conclusion, the only other term it can be connected with in the original argument without making the argument more complex is "murder." Instead of adding the reason above and introducing a new topic, we can add the following reason to the existing argument to make it valid:

      1   3

A. <u>Abortion</u> is <u>murder</u>.

      3   2

1. <u>Murder</u> is <u>immoral</u>.

---

      1   2

∴ 2. <u>Abortion</u> is <u>immoral</u>.

"Abortion" is connected to "murder" and "murder" is connected to "is immoral." Now "abortion" can logically be connected to "is immoral."

Another way of using the topics model to make an argument valid is to recognize that we can ask two linked questions of any claim, each dealing with one of the topics in the claim. One question will focus on the verb –object in a conclusion claim and will indicate a general set of conditions that must be met for the claim to be true. A second question will focus on the subject and identify something that fits those conditions. Likewise, the reason involving the verb –object topic will usually be more general than the reason involving the subject topic. Applying this, we get the following two questions (where x is the verb –object topic and y is the subject topic):

1. Under what conditions does/is something x?

2. Does y meet those conditions?

Applying this to the abortion argument where x is "immoral" and y is "abortion" we get:

1. Under what conditions is something immoral?

The first question is general. It asks nothing specific about abortion or any other moral action. However, the answer will give us a condition or set of conditions under which any action is immoral. We can then apply that to the second question.

The second question is asked with the first one in mind. What we want to do is to connect the topic in the second question with the answers generated by the first question. The following question does this:

2. How does abortion meet the conditions for something being immoral?

The two questions are linked. An answer to one provides information about answering the second. Applying these to the argument in question we get the following:

1. Under what conditions is something immoral?

Something is immoral if it involves murder. This equals "murder is immoral."

2. Does abortion meet those conditions?

Abortion does meet those conditions: It is a form of murder. = Abortion is murder.

The argument must answer both questions in order to establish relevance and sufficiency. If it answers only one of the questions the argument is incomplete because the reasons, as stated, are relevant but not sufficient. If it answers both, the reasons are relevant and sufficient to establish the conclusion. This topics model can help us determine the validity of an argument. It does not guarantee soundness. For that we must ensure our answers to the questions are true.

The topics model is extremely useful both in developing arguments and in engaging in argumentation. We will develop this further in Modules 10 and 11.

4.13 The Counterexample Method for Showing Invalidity

The *method of counterexample* is a means of showing that an argument pattern is invalid; however, it will not show us that an argument pattern *is* valid. If you encounter an argument you believe is invalid you can use this method to confirm its invalidity. A **counterexample** is a specific example that shows either a specific claim or an argument pattern is false. Here we develop the method of counterexample for argument patterns.

Since a valid argument is one in which the reasons, if true, must lead to a true conclusion, if we can show that the pattern of an argument can have true reasons and a false conclusion we have shown that the argument pattern cannot be a valid one.

> A **counterexample** is a specific example that shows either a specific claim or an argument pattern is false.

Consider the following argument:

1. All logicians have Ph.D.s.

2. All college teachers have Ph.D.s.

∴ 3. All logicians are college teachers.

In identifying the argument pattern we look for the logical connectives (listed in Table 4.2). We then substitute a letter, or variable, for each same statement consistently throughout. Finally, we try to find a substitution for the letters that will give us true reasons and a false conclusion. If we can find such a substitution we know the argument pattern is invalid. Not being able to find a substitution does not prove the argument is valid, however, because it may simply be a testament to our limited imagination in finding a substitution.

In the above argument, we can make the following substitutions:

a   for "logicians"
b   for "have Ph.D.s"
c   for "college teachers"

This gives us the following argument structure:

1. All *a*'s are *b*'s

2. All *c*'s are *b*'s

∴ 3. All *a*'s are *c*'s

If we can now find substitutions for *a, b,* and *c* that will make the reasons true and the conclusion false, we will have found a counterexample for this argument form. In other words, we will have shown that with this argument pattern it is possible to have true reasons and a false conclusion, which confirms that this pattern is not valid. Remember that for a pattern to be valid it must *always* lead from true reasons to true conclusions.

One substitution for the above could be the following:

a = cats

b = mammals

c = dogs

Simple biological categories like these tend to work well, since the connections become quite obvious, and it becomes clear when the reasons are true and the conclusion false. The above substitutions give us the following invalid argument:

1. All cats (*a*'s) are mammals (*b*'s).   True

2. All dogs (*c*'s) are mammals (*b*'s).   True

∴ 3. All cats (*a*'s) are dogs (*c*'s).   False

It is now clear this is an invalid argument form. Any argument having this form will be invalid even if the reasons and conclusion happen to be true.

QUICK QUIZ 4.12

Using Argument Counterexamples to Show Invalidity

For each of the following arguments provide a counterexample:

1. All logicians are mad. Saindon is not a logician. Saindon is not mad.
2. Some logicians are mad. Saindon is a logician. So Saindon must be mad.
3. Anyone who works hard will pass the course. I have not worked very hard. It looks as though I will not pass.
4. If you do not have perfect attendance, then you will not be entitled to a bonus at the end of the year. I had perfect attendance. So I will get the bonus.
5. Treating animals kindly is a sign that individuals will treat other people kindly. Michael doesn't treat his dog very well. He must not treat his wife very well.

Answers to the Quick Quizzes are available on the Premium Website at www.criticalthinking2e.nelson.com.

4.14 Assumed (or Missing) Reasons and Conclusions

In many deductive arguments the arguer does not present all of the reasons needed to prove validity. Such arguments have an assumed or missing reason. An ***assumed*** or ***missing reason*** is a claim that is required by the argument to establish relevance or sufficiency (or, preferably, both) between the reasons and the conclusion.

Similarly, an author sometimes does not explicitly state the conclusion. In such situations the argument has an unstated conclusion. A ***missing*** or ***unstated conclusion*** is a conclusion that follows from the stated reasons in an argument but is not explicitly stated by the author.

The purpose of supplying a missing reason or conclusion is to identify all of the assumptions necessary to make an argument valid. It can help us analyze and critique the argument by showing what the argument is committed to.

When supplying a missing reason or conclusion we try to meet two conditions: (1) where possible, we supply a missing reason or conclusion that makes an argument valid rather than invalid; and (2) given a choice between supplying either a true or a false missing reason we supply a true reason. These are necessary to satisfy the truth-seeking principle and the principle of charity discussed in Module 1. Meeting both conditions may not always be possible because the author may have simply given an invalid argument or an argument that assumes a false claim. In such cases, we should indicate that the argument cannot be reconstructed soundly and explain why.

To identify and supply missing reasons we can use either argument patterns or the topics model.

> An **assumed** or **missing reason** is a claim that is required by the argument to establish relevance or sufficiency (or, preferably, both) between the reasons and the conclusion.

> A **missing** or **unstated conclusion** is a conclusion that follows from the stated reasons in an argument but is not explicitly stated by the author.

Using Argument Patterns to Supply Missing Reasons and Conclusions

Using valid argument patterns to supply missing reasons and conclusions is relatively straightforward.

1. Identify the existing pattern of the argument from the stated claims.
2. Start with the conclusion, then examine the reasons.
3. If there is a conditional, compare the existing parts of the argument with the valid argument forms.
4. Supply what is necessary to make the argument valid.
5. If there is no conditional, then supply the conditional necessary to make the argument valid.
6. If it is a categorical argument, you can use the topics model to supply the missing claims.

For example:

  1. Ali told Ellen he inflated his expense report.

  _____

∴ 2. Ali is dishonest.

This argument has two claims. The pattern is

  1. a

  _____

∴ 2. b

Comparing this structure to the valid argument patterns we could make this valid by either matching the affirming the antecedent or denying the consequent pattern. If we try to affirm the antecedent, we need to supply "If a, then b" (If Ali inflated his expense report, he is dishonest). If we try to deny the consequent, we need to supply "If not b, then not a (If Ali is not dishonest then he did not tell Ellen he inflated his expense report). We have to insert the negatives into the statement because the claim in the argument is a positive. To act as a denying the consequent argument it would have to be denying a negative claim.

In this situation, the simplest of these two methods is affirming the antecedent:

  A, [If a, then b]

  1. a

  _____

∴ 2. b

Or, in prose:

  A. [If Ali inflated his expense report, then he is dishonest.]

  1. Ali told Ellen he inflated his expense report. (Treat as equivalent to "Ali inflated his expense report.")

  _____

∴ 2. Ali is dishonest.

To identify where we have supplied missing claims in an argument diagram we put square brackets around the claim and identify it with a capital letter instead of a number. This makes it easier for us when examining our analysis to see what we have supplied and check whether it is faithful to what the author was arguing.

Depending on the context of the argument we may sometimes want to make the conditional a general claim rather than a specific one, as in the example "If someone inflates his expense report, then he is dishonest." It is not just Ali's inflating his expense report that is dishonest. Anyone who inflates his or her expense report is dishonest. Making the claim broad gives us the general conditions, not just conditions as they apply to Ali.

Which valid pattern to use (affirming the antecedent, denying the consequent, or the valid disjunctive form) will depend on what makes the most sense and is most enlightening in a given situation. Any pattern that makes the argument valid, if it is a valid argument, is acceptable. If an argument is invalid, however, no matter which pattern you use, it will not be possible to make it valid. Consider the following:

1. If the breeding grounds had been contaminated by lead, the birds would have stopped nesting.

∴ 2. The breeding grounds must have been contaminated by lead.

The only possible missing reason here ("The birds have stopped nesting") would give us an invalid argument as it affirms the consequent.

QUICK QUIZ 4.13

Using Valid Patterns to Supply Missing Reasons and Conclusions

Identify the structure of the argument. Using the valid argument forms, supply the missing reasons or conclusions for the following arguments. If you cannot make the argument valid, explain why not.

1. We want to reduce speeding, so we should use red-light cameras.
2. If he is a good lawyer, he reads the fine print in contracts. So he is not a good lawyer.
3. If something is intellectually challenging, it is not designed for a mass audience. So university is not designed for a mass audience.
4. If he is a good lawyer, he reads the fine print in contracts. So he does not read the fine print in contracts.
5. If we do not stop obesity now, the next generation will have shorter lifespans and health costs will increase, and we do not want either of those.
6. If we raise tuition fees then we will have fewer students and a less educated public. But we do not want that.

Answers to the Quick Quizzes are available on the Premium Website at www.criticalthinking2e.nelson.com.

Using the Topics Model to Supply Missing Reasons and Conclusions

The topics model can also be used to supply missing reasons. Steps for doing so include identifying, numbering, and underlining the topics in the conclusion, then the stated ones in the reasons, and supplying a claim that will connect the unconnected topics. Using the questions we used to assess validity can also help.

Using the argument below, we will walk through these steps.

I. Identify, number, and underline the topics in the conclusion.

    1. Saindon is a logician.

---

           1   2

∴ 2. <u>Saindon</u> is <u>mad</u>.

II. Identify, underline, and number the stated topics in the reasons.

           1   3

    1. <u>Saindon</u> is a <u>logician.</u>

---

           1   2

∴ 2. <u>Saindon</u> is <u>mad</u>.

III. List the topics in the argument.

- Saindon
- mad
- logician

"Saindon" is used twice, the other two terms once. "Saindon" is connected to each of the other two terms. The other two terms ("mad" and "logician"), however, are not connected to one another. These need to be connected.

IV. Using the topics model, work from the conclusion and identify the questions that need to be answered for the argument to be valid.

1. Under what conditions is someone mad?
2. Does Saindon fit those conditions?

V. Which, if any, question is answered by the stated reason? If neither is answered by the stated reason, then the reasons are likely irrelevant to the conclusion. In our example, the stated reason identifies a condition that Saindon meets—he is a logician (Question 2). We can infer that being a logician is a condition for being mad, which will give us the answer to Question 1: Anyone who is a logician is mad.

Another way of using this is to notice that "Saindon" appears in both the reason and the conclusion. "Is mad" and "is a logician" each occur only once in the argument, so these are the two terms that need to be connected in the reasons for the argument to be valid. The missing reason is:

A. [All logicians are mad.]

Which gives us the following valid argument:

A. [All logicians are mad.]

1. Saindon is a logician.

∴ 2. Saindon is mad.

In supplying a missing reason or conclusion we are trying to supply only what is minimally necessary, given the materials in the existing argument, to make the argument valid. For example, although we could supply any of the following as possible missing reasons, none of them will enable us to connect the terms in the argument:

A. [Saindon has been diagnosed with a mental disorder.]

B. [Logicians are odd people.]

C. [Logicians spend their lives interacting with arguments rather than people.]

None of these would make the argument valid. Each introduces a new term that would then have to be connected to the existing terms in the conclusion.

QUICK QUIZ 4.14

Using the Topics Model to Supply Missing Reasons

Portray the structure of the following arguments and use the topics model to supply the missing reasons for each argument. Identify the two questions for each conclusion and show how the stated reason and missing reason answer those questions.

1. Fred should not be allowed to drive. He drives dangerously.
2. Creationism should not be taught in biology classrooms because it is not science.
3. Stem cell research can help in the search for a cure for Alzheimer's disease. Therefore, we should support stem cell research.

Answers to the Quick Quizzes are available on the Premium Website at www.criticalthinking2e.nelson.com.

4.15 Assessing Soundness

A deductive argument is said to be *sound* if it is valid and has true reasons. Assessing an argument for soundness involves first assessing it for validity and then determining whether the reasons are true. We start with validity because we want to make sure the reasons actually are relevant and sufficient to establish the conclusion. If the reasons are not relevant or sufficient to support the conclusion, then the arguer has not given a good argument. Checking validity also enables us to determine what the argument is committed to. We can use any of the techniques in this module to determine if the argument is valid or invalid. If an argument is invalid, then we can stop the assessment because the arguer has not established the conclusion and soundness is not possible.

To assess the truth of the claims, examine each claim in the reasons. Is each sufficiently clear and precise in context that you know what would count as evidence for and against it? Is it a claim that is either widely known or acceptable to everyone who would likely read the argument, or if it is contentious has it been supported by independent lines of argument? If a claim is false, doubtful, or contentious, develop your reasons to show why it is, and how that affects the argument.

Do not simply accept the reasons because you agree with the conclusion. Test the truth of the reasons. Under what conditions could they be false? One of the most common errors in reasoning is ***confirmation bias***. This occurs when we look for evidence to support our claims rather than for the possible evidence that might disconfirm or challenge our claims. Our natural tendency is to search for confirmations rather than disconfirmations. In most cases we can find some evidence that will support our position, especially if we have to interpret the evidence. Since we can usually find some evidence that could be interpreted to support our prior positions, finding evidence that confirms those positions does not necessarily prove them to be true. Rather, what we need to do is subject our positions to a more rigorous test by looking for the evidence that might disconfirm our basic position.

Consider the following:

> Withholding information is the same as lying. So withholding information is wrong.

The argument can be analyzed as follows:

1. Withholding information is the same as lying.

A. [Lying is wrong.]

∴ 2. Withholding information is wrong.

We have supplied the missing reason (A). The argument is valid. We can show this using the topics model:

> Under what conditions is something wrong?
>
> *Something is wrong if it involves lying.* = Lying is wrong.
>
> Does withholding information fit those conditions?
>
> *Withholding information is the same as lying. (Stated)*

Alternatively, we could translate the missing reason into a conditional "If something involves lying, it is wrong." The argument then becomes a standard affirming the antecedent.

However, the argument is not sound. Although we can think of some exceptional circumstances in which the stated reason could be interpreted as true, the stated reason (1) is false. Withholding information is not always the same as lying. Professors withhold information about their personal lives from their students without lying to them because it is none of their business. If professors withhold information from their students about the specific contents of the final exam, it would also not be lying. However, lying might be intentionally telling students a false date for the exam. Therefore, lying and withholding information are not the same. Here we have used a claim counterexample to show that the reason as formulated is false, and the argument is not sound.

It is not sufficient to assert a claim is false. We also need to provide reasons why it is false. To do this, we need to construct an argument. Consider the following passage:

> We are justified in torturing and even killing terrorists without trial or due process. Terrorists have no concern for the rights of the innocent citizens they

Confirmation bias occurs when we look for evidence to support our claims rather than for the possible evidence that might disconfirm or challenge our claims.

slaughter. Therefore, we should not grant them any rights once we have caught them.

We can analyze this argument as follows:

A. [If (people have no concern for the rights of others), then (they should not be given any rights themselves).]   If *a*, then *b*.

1. Terrorists have no concern for the rights of the innocent citizens they slaughter.   *a*

∴ 2. We should not grant them any rights once we have caught them. (*I treat this as the same as "we are justified in torturing and even killing terrorists without trial or due process," because this simply explains "not grant them any rights.")* *b*

"A" is a missing reason supplied to make the argument valid. With this claim, the argument is valid because it affirms the antecedent.

The argument, however, is not sound. Reason 1 may be false, but we have no evidence to indicate it is. However, the missing reason, "A" is false. If we were to accept its claim, then we are saying we would be justified in denying rights to anyone accused of a crime. One could argue that anyone who commits a crime has shown he or she has no concern for the rights of those whose rights were violated by the crime itself. Furthermore, if this is applied to everyone accused of a crime, then those who are accused would lose their rights simply on the grounds of having been accused, not on the grounds of having been convicted. Since the arguer is referring to due process and a trial as part of the rights being denied, this would mean we could simply imprison or execute people on the grounds of their having been accused of a crime, not on the grounds of their having been convicted. This would result in many innocent people being falsely imprisoned and/or convicted. And this would not be just. The missing reason is unacceptable.

If a passage contains several independent lines of argument supporting the conclusion, then we need to examine each line of argument. As long as there is one sound argument, the arguer has made a case for his or her conclusion.

QUICK QUIZ 4.15

Assessing Soundness

Assess the following arguments for soundness using the skills developed thus far. Give reasons for your assessments of validity and of soundness.

1. Teachers should not be allowed to strike because their going on strike disrupts students' learning.
2. We should censor anything that is crude and offensive. And much of rock music is certainly crude and offensive. So we should censor it.
3. The novel *The Adventures of Huckleberry Finn* uses language that many consider racist. Therefore, the novel is racist and promotes racism.

Answers to the Quick Quizzes are available on the Premium Website at www.criticalthinking2e.nelson.com.

Module Summary

- There are two basic types of arguments, non-deductive and deductive, classified according to the degree of support the reasons give the conclusion.
- Support is based on the relevance of reasons to the conclusion and the sufficiency of the reasons in establishing the conclusion.
- Deductive arguments seek to provide indisputable support, whereas non-deductive arguments provide probable support for the conclusion.
- We can assess the support (relevance and sufficiency) separate from the acceptability of the reasons.
- The support in deductive arguments is assessed in terms of validity or invalidity.
- We can determine validity and invalidity through identifying argument forms or patterns and through the topics model.
- We can show invalidity through the method of argument counterexample.
- Once we have assessed a deductive argument for validity, we can assess it for soundness by determining whether the reasons are in fact true.
- A sound argument is valid and has true reasons.

Argumentation Exercise: Developing an Argument

Help Peter in the dialogue at the beginning of this module by formulating two sound arguments (other than the one given in the dialogue itself) on the issue of downloading copyright material being theft. If one or more of your reasons is challengeable, defend it with a sub-argument that is sound.

Writing Skills Exercise: Putting a Deductive Argument into Flowing Prose

Write a one-paragraph argument in which you present the argument developed in the Argumentation Exercise in prose as a paragraph.

MODULE 5

Assessing Non-Deductive Arguments

 A DIALOGUE ON COPYRIGHT AND PIRACY— CONTINUED

Peter: I want to go back to a couple of your arguments. In a previous discussion, you claimed that Internet piracy (sorry, downloading of copyright material without authorization) harms no one. What do you base that on?

Jean: Various artists have encouraged downloading of their songs and said it actually helps them.

Peter: How many artists?

Jean: I don't know, a lot.

> **Peter:** Let's grant that a significant number do. Have you heard of any that oppose it?

> **Jean:** Yeah, a few.

> **Peter:** Have you done a study of the number in each camp?

> **Jean:** No, why should I?

> **Peter:** Well, you may have a biased sample. Without systematically counting those musicians for and against, you don't know how many, or the characteristics of each, or why they take the position they do. It doesn't give you a strong basis for your generalization.

> **Jean:** So you are saying that I should do an analysis of those who support and oppose downloading? I haven't got the time for that right now. Let me try another argument.

> **Peter:** OK.

(to be continued)

5.1 Introduction

Many arguments we encounter are not deductive arguments. In this dialogue, Jean offers a generalization and Peter points out some of the difficulties with his generalization.

Deductive arguments establish a connection between the reasons and conclusion, the relevance and sufficiency of which can be assessed solely in terms of logical form (as measured by validity). Various non-deductive arguments do not have such a relationship between their premises and conclusions and require that we examine the content to determine relevance and sufficiency. In such arguments, the premises provide support for the conclusion, but do not guarantee it. Instead of validity and invalidity, we say that the reasons weakly, strongly, or very strongly support the conclusion, depending on how well the relevancy and sufficiency conditions are met. If the reasons are true and strongly support the conclusion, we say that the argument is *cogent*.

> An non-deductive argument is **cogent** if the reasons are true and strongly support the conclusion.

Some of the most common types of non-deductive arguments include inductive generalization, causal argument, argument from analogy, and appeal to authority. There are other types of non-deductive reasoning; however, this module focuses on the most common types.

5.2 General Claims and Generalizations

We can distinguish between a summary, a generalization, and a general claim. A *summary* is the uniting of a set of observations in a general claim. The claim "I observed ten instances of people driving badly and eight of these people were driving SUVs" could be summarized as "80 percent of those observed driving badly were driving SUVs." Rather than enumerating each of the cases, they are summarized in a simple statement or set of statements. We can show that a summary is false by showing that the observations it is based on are false or that the summary is inaccurate.

> A **summary** is the uniting of a set of observations in a general claim.

A *generalization* is the result of a process of reasoning from a limited number of cases to a broader range of cases. "I observe three people driving badly were driving

> A **generalization** is the result of a process of reasoning from a limited number of cases to a broader range of cases.

SUVs. I conclude all SUV drivers are bad drivers." The conclusion generalizes from a smaller set of instances than the population we generalize to. We cannot directly observe a generalization, although we can observe the instances it is based on and assess the inference from those instances to the generalization. We can show that a generalization is false by showing that the observations it is based on are false, the inference is erroneous, or the scope of the conclusion is too broad. The **scope** is the range of instances to which a claim applies. "All drivers" is more general than "all SUV drivers," which in turn is more general than "most SUV drivers I have observed today."

A **general claim** is a claim about a group or class with no indication of the process of reasoning behind it (such as, "All SUV drivers are bad drivers"). No observations that the general claim is based on are identified. Indeed, a general claim may be based on no observations at all. A generalization is a process of inference from a smaller number of cases to a large class of instances. Many people make general claims without having thought about either the evidence those claims are based on, or the adequacy of the inference from the evidence to the general claim. General claims can be addressed either by asking for the evidence they are based on (in which case we can treat them as generalizations), or by giving counterexamples (such as, "My cousin drives an SUV and is a good driver"). A counterexample for a general claim involves giving a specific example that shows the generalization to be false. "I saw several SUV drivers today driving well" is a counter example to the claim "All SUV drivers are bad drivers."

Assessing Generalizations

Generalizations are the result of a process of inference from a limited number of cases. The person making the inference makes a limited number of observations and draws a conclusion about the whole set of things that the observations are assumed to apply to. For instance, I note that the chalkboards in five classrooms on campus are green and draw the general conclusion that all chalkboards on campus are green.

To decide whether or not this is a good generalization, we need to know about the accuracy of the observations, and other things as well: the population, the sample, the representativeness of the sample, the variability and frequency of the items in the sample, and any possible bias.

The group of things we are drawing the conclusion about is called the **population**. In the example above the population we are interested in is that of all chalkboards on campus. The set of things we actually observe in order to draw the generalization is called the **sample**. In the example above, the sample is the chalkboards in the five classrooms visited.

For an inference to a generalization to be a good inference, not only must the original observations be accurate, but the sample must be **representative** of the population. To be sure the sample is representative, we need to assess whether the sample we have selected adequately represents the variability in the population and the frequency of that variability. **Variability** refers to the range of difference or variation within the population in respect to relevant characteristics, while **frequency** refers to how often those characteristics occur within a population. If we are trying to judge the proportion of coloured balls in a jar, variability would depend on whether there are two colours or ten, while frequency would refer to the relative proportion of the colours to one another: one red to one white (1:1), two red to one white (2:1), or ten red to one white (10:1), in the case of two colours; one red to two black to two blue to five green to ten white (1:2:2:5:10), in the case of five colours. Chalkboards can be black or green—that is their variability. The proportion of green to black on this campus would be the frequency. At the start of a study, we may know neither of these.

In examining the sample, we need to discover if there is anything about the sample that might be biased. In a **biased sample**, the representativeness is skewed in some way so that not all of the variability and frequency among the items will have an equal chance of being in the sample. If all of our observations of chalkboards were made in classrooms in one building, that might indicate a limitation, or bias, in our sample. We might generalize more reliably about the chalkboards in that building than about all chalkboards on campus. Based on other information we may or may not be able to extend our generalization. For example, if we knew that all the classrooms on campus were built at the same time by the same contractor, we might be able to generalize more reliably about all classrooms on campus. However, if we realize that the various buildings on campus were built over a thirty-, fifty-, or hundred-year time span and by various contractors, we might have less confidence in our generalization about all chalkboards on campus. If we know that prior to 1960 only black chalkboards were made, and that between 1960 and 1980 green chalkboards gradually replaced them, we might be able to refine our estimates of frequency and our conclusions.

If we are sure that every item in a population is identical (that is, there is no variation), then a sample of one would be sufficient to establish the basis for a generalization. If we are trying to judge the colour of identical balls within a jar, then a sample of one is sufficient. However, once there is variability within a population we need to know what the relevant differences are and how frequently they occur in order to know whether a sample is representative. If there is a great deal of variability in the population (five colours of balls), then a substantially larger sample would be required for us to be sure we have captured both the range of variability in the population and the frequency of that variation. If we do not know the range of variation (how many colours of balls there are), then it is more difficult to establish a representative sample.

This takes us into the realm of probability and statistics. Although we do not have the space in this text to go into all of the conditions that make for good generalizations, we can identify some of the major features. A **reliable generalization** meets the conditions outlined in Table 5.1.

> In a **biased sample**, the representativeness is skewed in some way so that not all of the variability and frequency among the items will have an equal chance of being in the sample.

> A **reliable generalization** is one that meets the basic conditions for reliability.

TABLE 5.1 Criteria for a Reliable Generalization

1.	It is based on evidence, that is, on observations of a number of cases.
2.	The observations are systematic, that is, they have been gathered using organized criteria rather than anecdotally.
3.	The evidence is identified.
4.	The population is identified or easily inferred.
5.	The sample is identified
6.	The sample is representative of the population.
7.	The range of variation in the population is identified or easily inferred.
8.	The generalization does not over-generalize the sample in relation to the population, that is, it has an adequate scope.

To defend a generalization as reliable, we should establish each of these conditions.

Challenging a generalization as being unreliable involves challenging it on one or more of these conditions. Although these eight conditions are rarely met explicitly except in some scientific and social-scientific literature, enough information is often given or is implicit in the context to allow us to judge the reliability. We can use the criteria for a reliable generalization given above to help us develop our ability to assess generalizations.

Limitation of scope refers to limiting the population about which we are generalizing.

Both generalizations and general claims are easier to defend if they are limited in scope. While scope is the range of cases covered by a claim, ***limitation of scope*** refers to limiting the population to which we are generalizing. Instead of generalizing about all chalkboards, we can restrict our generalizations to one specific building, or buildings constructed after 1980. Generally, questions of scope have to do with *qualifiers* (such as, *all, some, most, a few, 51 percent, more than half, two-thirds* and so on.) Qualifiers can also be such things as "buildings on campus built after 1980," "SUV drivers in downtown Montreal," and "homicides in the city this year." The more precise we can be with these and the more limited in scope the conclusion is, the more likely it is that we can defend the claim. Conversely, the more wide-ranging and less qualified the general claim is, the easier it is to challenge. For more on generalization (especially errors in generalizations) see the fallacy of hasty generalization in Module 7.

QUICK QUIZ 5.1

Assessing Generalizations

In the following, identify the population and the sample, and assess whether the sample is likely to be representative of the population. Using the criteria specified in the text, Table 5.1, how reliable would you judge the conclusions reported to be? Justify your reasoning.

1. A radio journalist interviews five people at a parking lot in the city about their views on what the Government should do about rising gasoline prices. Four of the five think the Government should intervene to lower the gas tax. The journalist reports 80 percent of the population think the Government should lower the gas tax.

2. A student surveys a class of 60 students on whether they approve of a proposal to introduce a student health levy. Forty-five of the 60 students interviewed agree with the proposal. The student concludes that 75 percent of the 10,000 students at the University support the proposal.

3. A student surveys a cross-section of 200 students, balanced for year of study, gender, ethnicity, and major, on whether they approve of a proposal to introduce a student health levy. One hundred and fifty students agree with the proposal. The student concludes that the majority of the 10,000 students at the University are likely to support the proposal.

4. Most people think the Government should lower the taxes on gas.

Answers to the Quick Quizzes are available on the Premium Website at www.criticalthinking2e.nelson.com.

5.3 Causal Arguments

A *causal inference* involves drawing a connection between two states of affairs and inferring that one causes the other. Although some causal inferences involve generalizations, they do not have to. The claim that a specific automobile accident was caused by alcohol and speeding involves a causal inference but does not involve a generalization. However, saying alcohol and speed cause most automobile accidents is both a general claim and a causal inference. In order to establish a causal connection we need to establish the conditions identified in Table 5.2.

> A **causal inference** involves drawing a connection between two states of affairs and inferring that one causes the other.

TABLE 5.2 Criteria for Establishing Causation

1.	***Temporal priority***: the cause must come before the effect or be nearly simultaneous with it.
2.	***Spatial connection between the two events***: the cause and the effect must be connected in some way; a cause may produce an effect at a distance, but we then need to understand the intervening mechanism.
3.	***Covariance***: the two things must vary together; as one increases the other increases, or as one decreases the other decreases. This is usually established through correlation.
4.	A ***reasonable mechanism***: one that establishes the connections between the two items and shows which causes which and why. This is what helps establish the cause.

The purpose of a causal argument is to establish that one event is the result of another or that one event caused another. To establish a cause–effect relationship we must establish two things: (1) that the cause temporally preceded and was spatially connected with the effect, and (2) that the effect would not have occurred without the cause. Ideally, in order to establish the second condition we normally have to establish the mechanism by which the cause produces the effect. Without that we merely have a correlation.

A *correlation* is a claim that two things vary together. For example, the more people smoke, the more likely they are to get lung cancer. A ***direct correlation*** is one in which the two variables either increase or decrease together (that is, as one increases the other increases, or as one decreases the other does as well). The preceding claim is a direct correlation. As people smoke more, their likelihood of getting lung cancer increases, and as they smoke less the likelihood decreases. An ***inverse correlation*** is one in which the two variables vary in opposite directions: as one increases the other decreases. For example, in the claim "the more leafy green vegetables and fruits a person eats the less the likelihood of that person getting colon cancer," eating leafy greens and fruits and contracting colon cancer are inversely correlated.

Establishing a correlation does not establish a causal connection between the two instances. For example, I am always exhausted when I arrive home from teaching class and my cats always meet me at the door when I get home. Although there may be a perfect correlation, we cannot conclude that my being tired causes my cats to meet me at the door, because my being tired is caused by a long day and my cats greet me in the hope of getting fed. The two variables, though correlated, are independent of one another.

In order to establish cause, we need to establish a mechanism. In the example of smoking, extensive research has been done to establish some of the causal mechanisms linking smoking and lung cancer. This includes identifying the ingredients in tobacco smoke, the effects of those on lung tissue, genetic predispositions, and so on. Some of these mechanisms have been well enough established that we can say smoking causes lung cancer.

That we usually have imperfect rather than perfect correlations complicates establishing cause. In a ***perfect correlation***, in every instance in which one of the correlated items varies the other also varies. We know smoking causes lung cancer. However, not everyone who smokes gets lung cancer, and some of those who do not smoke (and are not exposed to smoke) do get lung cancer. This is an ***imperfect correlation***, or a correlation in which only some instances are associated with one another and vary together. In this case, not every change in one produces a change in the other. What we do know is that a much higher percentage of those who smoke get lung cancer than those who do not.

The problem with establishing a perfect connection between smoking and lung cancer is that what we identify as the cause is only one of several conditions that produce the effect. Often we need conditions *a, b,* and *c* to produce effect *p*. Other conditions, *d, e,* and *f* may act as ***countervailing causes***, or factors that inhibit the action of another cause. And other factors *g, h,* and *j* may independently cause *p*. Yet we do not know all of the conditions *a* through *j*. Moreover, when we are dealing with something like smoking and lung cancer there are numerous variables that lead to the effect. Smoking may produce it, but so too may air pollution. Furthermore, smoking does not necessarily cause cancer in everyone who smokes, although it does increase the likelihood of a smoker getting cancer. Knowing the mechanisms helps us make the correct connection between the cause and the effect, even when we do not appear to have a perfect correlation.

A **correlation** is a claim that two things vary together.

A **direct correlation** is one in which the two variables either increase or decrease together.

An **inverse correlation** is one in which the two variables vary inversely to one another.

In a **perfect correlation**, in every instance in which one of the correlated items varies, the other also varies.

In an **imperfect correlation**, only some instances are associated with one another and vary together.

A **countervailing cause** is one that inhibits the action of another cause.

Scientific and academic methods of research have developed quite detailed methods for establishing causal connections. Our focus here is not on those more detailed methods, but on how we attribute cause in everyday life. Often we attribute cause when only one of these conditions for causality has been met, usually temporal priority, spatial connection, or covariance. When this occurs we have committed an error in reasoning (specifically, the fallacy of false cause, discussed in Module 7).

Consider the following claim:

> There is a high incidence of exposure to pornography in New York City and there is a high incidence of rape in New York City. Therefore, pornography causes rape.

This is a common type of argument. We will grant the claims that there are both a high incidence of exposure to pornography and a high incidence of sexual assault in New York City, but is that sufficient to establish the causal connection? Applying the conditions for causality, we get the analysis outlined in Table 5.3.

TABLE 5.3 Analyzing a Proposed Causal Connection Using the Criteria for Establishing Causation

	Criterion	Analysis
1.	Temporal Priority	The argument does not establish that exposure to pornography comes before sexual assault. There was likely a high incidence of sexual assault before pornography became widely available in New York in the 1970s. This suggests that other variables lead to sexual assault. Did the rates of sexual assault increase after pornography became widespread? Adding this information might support a conclusion about causation.
2.	Spatial Connection	While there appears to be a spatial connection (both exposure to pornography and the high incidence of sexual assault occur in New York City), nothing establishes that the individuals exposed to pornography are the ones who commit sexual assault. We also do not know what happens in the absence of pornography. Are there areas that do not have exposure to pornography in which the incidence of sexual assault is low? Without a comparison group, we do not know whether it is the exposure to pornography or something else that produces the effect.
3.	Covariance	The argument establishes a minimal correlation (that both happen often in New York City). However, it does not establish there is covariance. At best, there could be an imperfect correlation. It is possible some people exposed to pornography do not commit rape and some people not exposed to it do.
4.	Reasonable Mechanism	The argument does not identify a mechanism that would show how viewing pornography causes rape.
5.	Overview	This is a poor argument; at best it may establish one of the three conditions for a causal connection.

5.4 Argument from Analogy

An *analogy* is a statement that compares two different things and suggests they are similar. For example, the eye is like a camera, DNA is like a code, business is like nature (a struggle for survival of the fittest). All of these point out similarities between two different things.

An *argument from analogy* is an argument that draws a parallel from a better known or less controversial case to a less well known or more controversial case, and concludes from a known trait of the first to something controversial or unknown about the second. For example, because your brain is like a computer, short term memory is RAM (that processes what is in immediate memory), the hard drive is the same as long term memory, and computers can recall anything, therefore, humans should have the capacity to recall anything they have experienced.

The logical structure of an argument from analogy has the following form:

1. A is like B.

2. A has characteristics 1, 2, 3, x.

3. B has characteristics 1, 2, 3.

∴ 4. B has characteristic x.

> An **analogy** is a statement that compares two different things and suggests they are similar.

> An **argument from analogy** is an argument that draws a parallel from a better known or less controversial case to a less well known or more controversial case, and concludes from a known trait of the first to something controversial or unknown about the second.

Martin Luther King's speech "*I Have a Dream*" uses an extended argument from analogy by comparing Lincoln's emancipation of the slaves to a promissory cheque on which America had defaulted. Darwin's argument for natural selection in *The Origin of Species* is based on an extended analogy between artificial selection and natural selection.

The strength of an argument from analogy can range from providing a strong reason for accepting the conclusion to being a fallacy of faulty analogy. (See Module 7 for the fallacy.)

Consider the following argument:

> Humans have a face, four limbs, and are capable of abstract thought; chimpanzees have a face and four limbs; therefore, chimpanzees must be capable of abstract thought.

We can represent the form of this argument as follows:

1. Humans are like chimpanzees.
2. Humans have a face, four limbs and are capable of abstract thought.
3. Chimpanzees have a face, four limbs.

∴ 4. Chimpanzees must be capable of abstract thought.

Whether the argument provides good reason or not depends on the following conditions identified in Table 5.4.

TABLE 5.4 Criteria for Assessing an Analogy and Application, Applied to the Human-Monkey-Intelligence Argument

	Criterion	Meaning	Application	Assessment
1.	*Truth of the reasons*	Are the two objects being compared similar in the way being claimed?	In the above example, humans and chimps both have a face and four limbs.	True
2.	*The relevance of the characteristics*	Are the known similarities (a, b, c) relevant to the unknown x?	Are the characteristics being compared (having a face and four limbs) actually relevant to the conclusion (being capable of abstract thought)?	As stated, not relevant. We know many creatures have these without being capable of abstract thought. If the argument had focused on the regions of the brain known to be responsible for abstract thought (such as, the prefrontal cortex) then the similarities would be relevant and the argument considerably stronger.

(continued)

TABLE 5.4 Continued

	Criterion	Meaning	Application	Assessment
3.	*The number of shared characteristics (a, b, c . . .)*	Generally the more shared relevant characteristics, the stronger the analogy.	Only two characteristics are identified (having a face and four limbs).	Very weak. Increasing the number of relevant characteristics would strengthen the conclusion. Showing similarity in brain structure in the prefrontal cortex (the area responsible for abstract thought) would increase the number of relevant characteristics shared.
4.	*The variety of shared characteristics (a, b, c . . .)*	The greater the variety, the stronger the analogy.	The two things compared (having a face and four limbs) are both structural characteristics and, hence, of the same kind.	No variety. Focusing on the similarity of the two in the structure and operation of the prefrontal cortex (the area of the brain associated with abstract thinking), the ability of chimps to do tasks associated with abstract thinking (such as, tool making, foresight, and problem-solving), would strengthen the analogy by increasing both the number and variety of relevant shared characteristics.
5.	*Disanalogy*	A ***disanalogy*** is a significant dissimilarity that challenges the conclusion. Even if two objects are similar in a lot of relevant ways, there may still be important dissimilarities between them that might cast doubt on the conclusion.	For example, human brains are substantially larger than chimp brains and size affects cognitive functioning (including ability for abstract thought). Chimps also do not have language skills, which some contend is central to abstract thinking. There may also be other differences in structure and function that would limit the scope or kind of conclusion we could draw from this analogy.	The disanalogy is too strong for the original analogy to hold.

A **disanalogy** is a significant dissimilarity that challenges the conclusion.

Searching for the disanalogies can be a way of challenging an analogy. It can also be a way of discovering the limitations with our analogies and require us to modify the conclusions accordingly. The disanalogies between chimps and humans above (which need significantly more elaboration) may point out that chimps have abstract thinking on only a very limited level.

Analogical arguments are used in a variety of fields, including biology, economics, business, cognitive science, philosophy, law, and moral reasoning. They are often used as methods of discovery to move from known similarities to discovery of further similarities. Recognizing that DNA is a chemical code (drawing the analogy between a chemical structure and information) led to the explosion that became the genetic revolution of the latter part of the 20th and beginning of the 21st centuries. Analogies are also used as ways of explaining difficult ideas. Many people have trouble understanding electricity and electrical circuits, but presenting the flow of electricity as analogous to hydraulics (the flow of liquids) often helps their understanding of electricity.

QUICK QUIZ 5.4

Assessing Analogies

In each of the following, identify the argument from analogy by putting it into the argument from analogy form. Assess the adequacy of the analogy using the criteria for assessing arguments from analogy in Section 5.4.

1. A CEO of a company is like the general of an army. Both are responsible for leading. Both are entrusted with authority. And you don't change generals in the middle of a battle. So we shouldn't change CEOs when the company is the middle of a crisis.

2. All pigeon varieties descended from the common Rock Pigeon (just as all dogs started from the wolf). Through selective breeding (artificial selection), pigeon fanciers have been able to produce an incredible variety of pigeons by selecting for specific traits they wanted to emphasize. The results are pigeons of various hues, configurations, with all sorts of exaggerated characteristics (such as, fantails and ruffs). Man, by selecting those traits he fancies, has been able, over generations, to produce those characteristics he desires, whether in pigeons, corn, or dogs. So, too, do we find in nature an incredible variety of species — birds, reptiles, mammals. And, just as in artificial selection, there are many offspring in a given generation with varying characteristics. Only some survive to pass on their characteristics. Over time, certain characteristics emerge and come to define different species. The selector in natural selection is nature herself, who rewards with survival those whose characteristics are most fit for their given environment to enable them to survive. (Hint: the compared terms are *natural selection* and *artificial selection*.)

3. Rape is just one reproductive strategy in all species. Randy Thornhill studied scorpionflies and found they employed three reproductive strategies — courtship, seduction, and rape. He also found that all three strategies were equally successful in producing offspring. Humans employ the same three strategies. So we have reason to believe rape is simply one co-equal reproductive strategy in humans. Further, since scorpionflies are driven by biological instincts to mate and to adopt these strategies, we have reason to believe that men who rape are driven by the same instincts and, therefore, just like scorpionflies, are not responsible for their actions.

Answers to the Quick Quizzes are available on the Premium Website at www.criticalthinking2e.nelson.com.

5.5 Appeals to Authority or Experts

When we know little about a particular subject and do not have the time to become an expert in that subject, we appeal to those who are authorities or experts. Such appeals can be legitimate or illegitimate. The conditions for a legitimate appeal to authority are as follows:

TABLE 5.5 Conditions for a Legitimate Appeal to Authority

	Criterion	Correct Use	Incorrect Use
1.	There is a body of empirical knowledge or field about which someone could be an expert.	Science, what the law says, administrative procedures, the ethical theory of Immanuel Kant.	Morals, what one ought to do, political views, how one should vote.
2.	There is consensus within the field on the results being cited.	Areas within a field where virtually all experts agree (there are occasional individuals who do not accept the prevailing view).	Areas within science where there is controversy over the results and/or interpretations of law.
3.	The person appealed to is an expert in the field.	A classical physicist on Newton's theory.	A biologist on Newton's theory.
4.	The expert is identified (and credentials noted).	"Professor Douglas Futuyma, author of the best-selling text, *Evolution*, and a widely recognized expert on speciation, cited as an authority on speciation.	"Scientists agree ..." is too general.
5.	The expert could substantiate his expertise with a survey of the evidence if required.	An expert witness at a trial who has published numerous peer-reviewed research works and surveys of the research.	An "expert" witness at a trial who has no research or published material on the topic on which he is testifying.
6.	The expert does not have a conflict of interest.	An expert whose research was funded by an independent body (e.g., the National Research Council of Canada).	An expert whose research was funded by Reynolds Tobacco who is testifying on the effects of smoking on health.

There must be a body of empirical knowledge (based on observation of the world) about which the expert can testify. A *field* or ***body of knowledge*** is an area of inquiry where there is widespread consensus on the basic claims, evidence, and theories, based on evidence available to anyone, and this consensus is recognized by others as authoritative.

We appeal to an ***expert*** (or someone who knows the body of knowledge) to cite the knowledge gathered within a given discipline. If there is no field or body of knowledge about a subject, there can be no expert knowledge of that area, and hence no experts. The sciences and many other academic fields have bodies of knowledge about which there is widespread agreement.

Some areas are not fields about which we can have empirical knowledge (such as, in ethics, religion, and aesthetics), although in such areas we can have reasoned opinions. For example, an expert in the area of ethics could testify about the theories and practical implications of various ethical theorists, but not about what the "best moral course of action" for someone might be, because the former is part of an academic study about which agreement is possible and the latter is not. Any disinterested inquirer could investigate and discover what theories of morality have been proposed and developed. However, when it comes to giving a judgment invoking normative criteria, there is no agreement on which normative criteria take precedence. Hence, there is no expert opinion in the case of what one *ought* to do. Similarly, a theological scholar could testify about the doctrines of a particular church (such as, what they are, when they were passed, how they have been interpreted, any disputes about them), but not about which religion is "the true religion." Ultimately, on such issues, people have to make their own decisions, based on their own judgments.

A Catholic theologian, knowledgeable about the Catholic Church's view on abortion, can give an authoritative answer as to what that view is. There is a body of knowledge about the Catholic Church's stand on abortion. It is a matter of public record and as a doctrine of the Church there is consensus among Catholic theologians on it. However, we cannot ask for the Christian view on abortion, for there are a variety of conflicting Christian views on the subject. If we want the answer to "Is abortion morally justified?" there is no expert or authority who can answer the question.

Not only must there be a body of knowledge, there must be ***consensus within the field***. In some fields where we can have knowledge (such as, some areas of inquiry in science), we may not have consensus. In such situations the expert testimony can only tell us there is a lack of consensus. Experts cannot be used, in their capacity as experts, to testify that one side is truer than the other in such a situation because the evidence does not establish that. If there is no consensus then we have to justify why we prefer one expert's support of the position to another's opposition of it. And to do that we need to supply independent evidence for their positions.

The requirement for consensus on the subject within a field does not mean absolutely every expert must agree. Within virtually any field a few mavericks can be found who challenge the general opinion. So by consensus we mean the agreement of the vast majority of people working within the field and knowledgeable of the relevant evidence. The fact that a few doubt the claim does not destroy the consensus.

This explains one of the common strategies used in legal trials that confuses many lay people. Lawyers call opposing experts to give their opinions. Sometimes, however, the experts are not equal. One lawyer may use a well-recognized authority and the other may use someone on the fringes of the discipline. If both are well-recognized experts and one's view differs from the consensus within the field, the maverick

> A **field** or **body of knowledge** is an area of inquiry where there is widespread consensus on the basic claims, evidence, and theories, based on evidence available to anyone, and this consensus is recognized by others as authoritative.

> An **expert** is someone who knows a body of knowledge.

> **Consensus within the field** occurs within a body of knowledge when the vast majority of experts agree on the relevant basic claims.

ASSESSING NON-DEDUCTIVE ARGUMENTS

(the one whose view differs) is testifying, not necessarily as an expert, but on his or her reasoned opinion. This strategy is often used by lawyers in an effort to suggest there is no consensus on the subject.

That those within a field agree (i.e., have reached consensus) on certain facts and ideas within their field does not mean those facts and ideas are, in some ultimate sense, true. Instead, what this means is that, according to the criteria and standards of evidence used within the field at this point in time, the "facts" are the best we have. Virtually all scholars working in this area agree on this, and new evidence, the development of more sophisticated measuring devices, and/or new criteria may lead them to reject these facts and ideas later on.

Often people with few or no relevant qualifications pose as experts. Some of the key people cited as "experts" in the climate change debate were physicists, not climatologists. Some of the same people were also cited as experts by the tobacco industry in its fight against bans on smoking. As lay people, when assessing whether or not someone is an expert, we need to consider such things as the person's involvement with the field. We can do this by asking such questions as "is our expert a scholar recognized by peers as knowledgeable and worthy of citing," or someone on the fringes of the field? Is he or she doing research in the field? Is he or she cited by others? Does our expert belong to professional societies? Does he or she have proper credentials and qualifications? None of these guarantees the person is an expert; however, if we are going to cite someone as an expert and expect that person's claims to further our argument, we should at the least investigate his or her credentials, qualifications, and standing within the field. For an appeal to be a legitimate appeal to authority, it needs to satisfy the criteria identified in Table 5.6.

TABLE 5.6 Criteria for a Legitimate Appeal to Authority

	Criterion	Use
1.	There should be a body of knowledge.	We use expert testimony because we do not have the technical knowledge or the time to master a body of knowledge.
2.	There should be consensus in the field in the status of knowledge in that field.	An expert is not testifying about his or her opinion, but about the consensus in the field. If there is no consensus, then we have to examine the evidence independently.
3.	The person cited should be an expert in the specific field of knowledge.	An expert in biology is not necessarily an expert in physics and an expert in microbiology is not necessarily an expert on evolutionary theory.
4.	The expert must be identified.	We need to know who the expert is to assess his or her credentials to determine if he or she is reliable, credible, and knowledgeable.
5.	The claim of the person's expert status must be supported.	What has the expert done that establishes any claim to his or her expertise?

| 6. | The expert should be unbiased and he or she should not be in a conflict of interest or have an identifiable bias. | If the expert owns shares in the company he or she is testifying about, has research funded by the group he or she is supporting, or has a history of selling his or her research skills to the highest bidder, then his or her testimony is suspect. This does not mean the person's claims are false, but only that they are potentially tainted by the member's association with the company. It also does not even mean the person is consciously distorting his or her assessment of the evidence. However, because an employee could be subconsciously influenced, it is better to have a neutral expert who could make the same claims. |

QUICK QUIZ 5.5

Assessing Appeals to Experts

Treat each of the following claims as an appeal to authority. Identify what body of knowledge is being appealed to and who is being appealed to as an expert. For each of the following claims, determine, using the criteria for a proper appeal to authority, whether the person being appealed to would qualify as an appropriate authority for the claims being made.

1. A news broadcaster gives an opinion on a current political event.
2. The author of a popular book on negotiating strategies makes claims about the most effective way to negotiate. The claims are based on twenty-four years' experience of negotiating in various contexts.
3. Pollution Probe (an environmental organization opposed to nuclear energy) testifies at a public hearing on the re-opening of Ontario's nuclear generating facilities that such a move would be costly and environmentally unsound.
4. Wayne Gretzky, a hockey superstar, claims in an advertisement that Motrin is a good medication for arthritis.
5. A management consultant who teaches negotiation is called as an expert witness to testify at a trial about whether a contract was negotiated in good faith.

Answers to the Quick Quizzes are available on the Premium Website at www.criticalthinking2e.nelson.com.

QUICK QUIZ 5.6

Assessing Experts

What expertise would be required to establish someone as an expert on the following topics? Be as specific as you can. To the best of your knowledge, are these fields of knowledge about which expert testimony is possible?

1. The claims of astrology.
2. The truth of astrology.
3. The origins of humankind.
4. International banking policy.
5. The effects of the Roe – Wade decision (a United States Supreme Court decision on the legal acceptability of abortion).

Answers to the Quick Quizzes are available on the Premium Website at www.criticalthinking2e.nelson.com.

Expert Opinion versus Informed Opinion

It is all too easy to say someone is not an expert and, therefore, we should dismiss his or her opinion. However, some people can have an informed opinion without meeting all of the criteria for being experts on the issue. A sportscaster who is knowledgeable about hockey could have an informed opinion on the likelihood of a particular team winning the Stanley Cup. Despite there not being consensus on an issue like this (nor a field of knowledge and thus no experts proper), some individuals' opinions are more informed than others.

We need to distinguish between expert opinion, informed opinion, and uninformed opinion. Expert opinion relies upon there being a body of knowledge, consensus about that knowledge, and a person having expertise in that body of knowledge. The expert testifies to the state of knowledge about which there is consensus in the field.

Yet in many cases we rely on *informed opinion*, or the opinion of an individual who is knowledgeable about a particular subject, even though there may not be consensus on that subject. Each year, at the beginning of the hockey season, various informed observers are asked their opinions about the likely rankings at the end of the season. The opinions are based both on the person's knowledge of the teams' strengths and weaknesses and their knowledge of hockey in general.

Much of what takes place in modern political, social, athletic, and entertainment discourse is opinion. Whether it is informed depends on our assessment of who is making the comments, their knowledge, and their reasoned consideration of the issues. Someone who has extensive experience and has thought about an issue is more likely to give an informed opinion than someone who has not. At best, informed opinion becomes information we ought to consider, not expertise we ought to accept in the absence of contrary evidence. And if it is backed by reasoning and evidence, then we have grounds for making our own judgment.

> **Informed opinion** is the opinion of an individual who is knowledgeable about a particular subject.

QUICK QUIZ 5.7

Experts, Informed Opinion, and Opinion

In each of the following, identify whether the appeal is made to expert opinion, informed opinion, or just opinion. Explain.

1. My brother, who has worked as a motorcycle mechanic for 30 years, says Harley-Davidson motorcycles are more reliable than Suzukis.
2. Based on an extensive survey about motorcycles, Consumers, Union reports Harley-Davidson motorcycles are more reliable than Suzukis.
3. Dr. Hamm in the physics department says Harley-Davidson motorcycles are more reliable than Suzukis.

Answers to the Quick Quizzes are available on the Premium Website at www.criticalthinking2e.nelson.com.

5.6 Inference to the Best Explanation

An **inference to the best explanation** is a non-deductive argument in which the conclusion is offered as an explanation for the facts cited in the reasons.

Consider the following:

1. Fred was desperate to get his bookie off his back.
2. Fred bought a gun the day before the bank robbery.
3. He was seen getting into a white 1998 Blazer two miles away from the robbery, fifteen minutes before the robbery.
4. A 1998 white Blazer was the getaway car.
5. Although the robbers were masked, Fred's height and weight fit the description of one of the bank robbers.
6. Fred cannot account for where he was at the time of the robbery.
7. Fred paid off his bookie debt the day after the robbery.

∴ 8. Fred robbed the bank.

The conclusion is not a deductive certainty. However, the probability that Fred is one of the bank robbers is strong. If we just had the first two and last two reasons, we would have doubt about Fred's guilt. As additional pieces of evidence tie Fred to the time and location of the robbery, the probability that Fred was involved increases. Nonetheless, we could imagine a situation in which all of the reasons are true and the conclusion false (Fred did not rob the bank). Fred might have gotten the money through other illegal activities or by engaging in something he considers shameful. Casting doubt on the truth of the stated reasons or providing *alternate explanations* for the facts in the reasons decreases the probability of the conclusion.

> An **inference to the best explanation** is a non-deductive argument in which the conclusion is offered as an explanation for the facts cited in the reasons.

TABLE 5.7 Criteria for Defending and Challenging an Inference to the Best Explanation

Criterion	Defending	Example	Challenging	Example
True premises	Support premises with adequate evidence.	Introduce evidence about how insistent Fred's bookie was.	Show one or more premises is false.	Show that the description of the robber was not a close approximation to Fred.
Plausibility of the premises	Show that the premises and their assumptions are plausible.	Establish that Fred had a bookie and that this bookie was known to use force on those who did not pay up.	Show that one or more of the premises or the explanation relies on unproven or doubtful ideas.	Show that Fred doesn't know how to drive and suffers from motion sickness in a car. (The explanation assumes he got to the bank in the car.)

(continued)

TABLE 5.7 Continued

Criterion	Defending	Example	Challenging	Example
Simplicity of the explanation	Show that the explanation relies on few or no unproven claims and assumptions. i.e., Occam's Razor. (p. 137)	Establish that the explanation that Fred did it involves fewer unsupported claims and assumptions than the alternatives.	Show that the explanation is unduly complex or requires unnecessary and unproven assumptions.	Show that it would take too long for the Blazer to get to the bank from where Fred got into it.
Completeness of the explanation	Show that the claims are linked together. Establish additional links.	Show that Fred knew the other thieves. Show that Fred had a history of robbing banks.	Establish new facts that the existing explanation cannot explain.	Fred's motion sickness. Fred was having an affair and was somewhere else at the time.
Absence of alternatives	Show that the explanation provides a better explanation of what needs to be explained than the alternatives.	Fred robbed the bank is the only explanation or the only one that adequately explains the facts.	Show an explanation that is as good as or better than the existing one. Introduce agreed upon facts that cannot be explained by the alternatives.	It wasn't Fred. The eyewitness was mistaken; the bookie had given Fred an extension; Fred was having an affair and was with someone else at the time.

The central strategy for improving an inference to the best explanation is to show how a given alternative does explain the relevant facts better than possible alternatives.

One way of examining an inference to the best explanation is by considering one or more alternate possible explanations and applying these criteria to them. Where an alternate is not given, we need to come up with one. To illustrate, consider the following example:

> Someone reports seeing a UFO. When I ask why the person believes that it was a UFO, the response was that it was an unusual light in the sky that could not be identified.

The argument could be represented as follows:

1. Someone saw an unusual light in the sky.
2. The person could not explain it.

∴ 3. It was a UFO.

Alternate explanations for the conclusion include that it was a satellite, Venus, a meteor, or a plane. Each of these is plausible. The hypothesis that it was a UFO is less plausible. A claim is *plausible* if, given a background set of information, the claim could be true, is supported by independent evidence, and is likely or worth considering. The UFO hypothesis above is minimally plausible in the sense there have been numerous reports of UFOs. However, there is little or no solid evidence for their existence, and good evidence against them. At best, the existence of UFOs is highly controversial. By contrast, each of the other alternatives has independent and / or empirical evidence and each has been mistaken many times for a UFO. Those alternates are more plausible than the UFO hypothesis. An implausible alternative might be that my friend was witnessing angels crossing the multidimensional barrier from the seventh dimension. Nothing in our background knowledge supports such a claim. The seventh-dimension claim also fails the criterion that the conclusion adequately explains the facts. It is not clear how angels would produce what was observed.

> A claim is **plausible** if, given a background set of information, the claim could be true, is supported by independent evidence, and is likely worth considering.

The alternate explanations are simpler in the sense that they involve postulating fewer new entities, and the explanation involves fewer unsupported assumptions. This is called **Occam's Razor**, or a principle for evaluating alternate hypotheses which states that, given two alternatives, so long as there are no differences in the observed consequences, we should prefer the one with the fewest principles or assumptions. In other words, if there are two explanations for the same phenomenon and the repercussions of accepting either are the same, we should choose the simplest unless the more complex one explains more. In the UFO example, satellites, landing jets, Venus, and meteorite sightings are all simpler explanations than the UFO alternative. The UFO alternative posits an unknown entity for which there is no independent evidence, whereas there is independent evidence for each of the others.

> **Occam's Razor** is a principle for evaluating alternate hypotheses which states that, given two alternatives, so long as there are no differences in the observed consequences, we should prefer the one with the fewest principles or assumptions.

An explanation is more *complete* if it links together more of the relevant considerations than the alternatives. An alternate explanation for Fred that did not address premises 3, 6, or 7 would be less complete and, hence, a less satisfactory explanation.

In assessing an inference to the best explanation argument, consider what additional information would strengthen or weaken the argument. When possible, check that information out. For example, if you are considering the Venus alternative to the UFO hypothesis, you might investigate where Venus was at the time of the sighting. Discovering that Venus was not visible at that time would rule out that alternative. Finding out that when Fred entered the Chevy Blazer he was wearing the same clothes that the bank robber was reportedly wearing would strengthen the case against him. Part of assessing an inference to the best explanation is identifying what additional evidence would count for or against the proposed explanation.

Assessing Inference-to-the-Best-Explanation Arguments

Formulate the following arguments. Assess each argument in terms of strength — very strong, strong, weak — and explain why you assess it that way. Use the criteria for assessing inference-to-the-best-explanation arguments.

1. Raj and Janet are friends. They have studied together all year. They sat next to each other in the exam. Not only did they both get the same letter grade on the exam, but both got the same questions right and most of the same questions wrong. They must have cheated on the exam.

2. The Loch Ness monster has to exist. Hundreds of people have seen the creature over the centuries. Furthermore, there are photographs and even videotapes of the monster.

3. Gasoline prices go up at the beginning of a long weekend and down just after. And this happens all over the country. This shows that the major oil companies are controlling gas prices.

4. The developer withdrew $25,000 from his business account. He then immediately called a local city alderman and met him fifteen minutes later in an underground parking garage. Over the next week, $23,000 was deposited to the alderman's account in five deposits. All deposits were in $100 bills. The alderman claims that the money was a gift from his father-in-law. However, there is no evidence of withdrawals from the father-in-law's account and no independent evidence for the source of the money. The alderman spoke strongly for a proposal favouring the developer over the next few months and convinced many of his colleagues to support the developer's proposal. I contend that the alderman took a bribe from the developer.

Answers to the Quick Quizzes are available on the Premium Website at www.criticalthinking2e.nelson.com.

Module Summary

- The premises in non-deductive arguments can provide only some degree of probable support for the conclusion.
- Accepting the reasons in a strong non-deductive argument does not guarantee the absolute certainty of the truth of the conclusion.
- Some non-deductive arguments are stronger than others.
- Different kinds of non-deductive arguments (inference to the best explanation, generalizations, causal arguments, appeals to authority, arguments from analogy and inference to the best explanation) rely on different criteria and each needs to be assessed in terms of the criteria relevant to it.

Argumentation Exercise: Analyzing an Argument from Analogy in a Speech

Examine Reverend Martin Luther King's *"I Have a Dream"* speech (available on the Web), focusing on the argumentative appeals. Who are his primary and secondary audiences? A primary audience is the one that is directly being addressed; a secondary audience are other possible audiences that might hear and respond to the speech. What are the key appeals made in this speech to those audiences? Which ones are supported by arguments? Are there appeals that are not supported by arguments? If Reverend King were speaking to a group of legislators and trying to convince them to change the laws to provide more equality, how might his appeals change? If he were speaking to a group of philosophy or pre-law students, how might his appeals be different? Would his arguments change?

Writing Skills Exercise: Analyzing an Argument from Analogy in a Speech

Examine Martin Luther King's "I Have a Dream" speech (available on the Web) again, and this time assess the argument from analogy in that speech using the criteria outlined in Section 5.4 and Table 5.4. Is it a good argument from analogy? Write a two-paragraph analysis and assessment of the analogy in the speech. The first paragraph should state your reconstruction of the argument from analogy using the model outlined in this chapter. The second should state your assessment of the analogy.

Assessing Claims

A DIALOGUE ON COPYRIGHT AND PIRACY—CONTINUED

Peter: You have been challenging my position in some detail; now I want to examine your claims a bit.

Jean: Okay.

Peter: You claim it is okay to download copyright material without paying for it, correct?

Jean: Yes.

Peter: As I understand it, you have argued three things: first, everyone does it.

Jean: Yes.

Peter: Second, it does not really harm anyone.

Jean: Right again.

Peter: Third, it is not really theft.

Jean: Right again.

Peter: Let's take each of these in turn. First, you claim everyone does it. How would you establish that? I am someone who doesn't do it.

Jean: Well, most people do it.

Peter: Again, how would you establish that?

Jean: Well, I suppose I could do a survey. I know an organization that defends artists' rights that claims a lot of people do it.

Peter: So, ultimately we could resolve how many people do it by some kind of facts, either determining the number of downloads or a survey of some sort?

Jean: Yes, I suppose so.

Peter: Okay, granting a lot of people do it, why does that justify it? A lot of people cheat on their income taxes. Does that justify it?

Jean: I think it does. After all, what everybody does is natural, isn't it? And if something is natural, doesn't that make it okay?

Peter: It may be common, but that does not necessarily make it natural or justify it. Being natural and being common are two different things. Let's sort this out a bit. What people do and how frequently something is done can be determined by checking the facts. What is justified or not is an ethical issue. We can't simply resolve it by a head count. You would not want your spouse to cheat on you, would you, or your friend to lie to you, just because some number of people do so regularly?

Jean: Absolutely not!

Peter: So, why not?

Jean: It is just not right.

(continued)

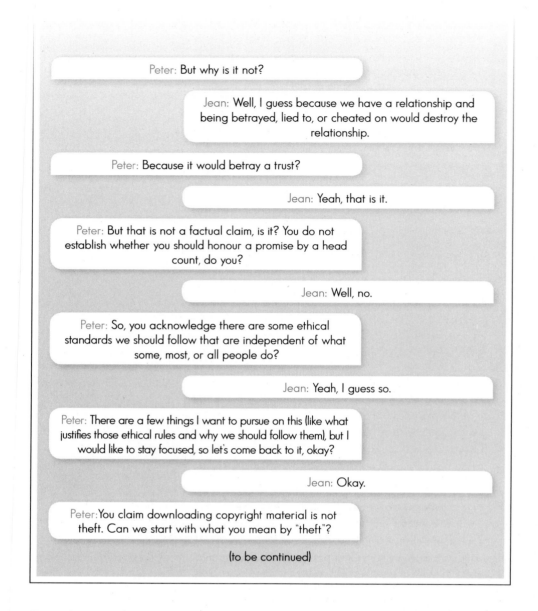

Peter: But why is it not?

Jean: Well, I guess because we have a relationship and being betrayed, lied to, or cheated on would destroy the relationship.

Peter: Because it would betray a trust?

Jean: Yeah, that is it.

Peter: But that is not a factual claim, is it? You do not establish whether you should honour a promise by a head count, do you?

Jean: Well, no.

Peter: So, you acknowledge there are some ethical standards we should follow that are independent of what some, most, or all people do?

Jean: Yeah, I guess so.

Peter: There are a few things I want to pursue on this (like what justifies those ethical rules and why we should follow them), but I would like to stay focused, so let's come back to it, okay?

Jean: Okay.

Peter: You claim downloading copyright material is not theft. Can we start with what you mean by "theft"?

(to be continued)

In probing Jean's position, Peter starts to disentangle the several different kinds of claims: empirical (about what is factually the case), conceptual (about the meaning of the words being used), and normative (about what should be the case as assessed by some morally relevant criteria). Arguments commonly hinge on one or more of these kinds of claims. Learning how to identify and assess the different kinds of claims is necessary for assessing the content of an argument as a whole.

6.1 Introduction

Good arguments require a combination of good structure and content. This module focuses on the content of an argument by looking at the different kinds of claims arguments use and the conditions under which they can be thought of as acceptable or unacceptable. (Module 3 discussed identifying claims and distinguishing them from other kinds of utterances.)

Not all claims are the same. Different claims require different evidence or support and have different ways for determining their content: empirical claims rely on observations about the world to establish their acceptability in terms of truth or falsity; conceptual claims rely on our knowledge of language to establish their acceptability;

and normative claims (including ethical ones) rely on judgment according to some morally relevant criteria to determine their acceptability.

We use the term "acceptability" (rather than "truth") when discussing conceptual and normative claims because "true" applies strictly to empirical claims (though it is still a measure of their acceptability). The measure for an empirical claim's *truth* is different from the measure of conceptual and normative claims' *acceptability*. In addition to assessing claims based on their content we can use tools such as counterexamples, presuppositions, and corollaries to determine their meaning and acceptability.

QUICK QUIZ 6.1

Preliminary Quiz: Kinds of Claims

Before continuing, examine the list of claims below. For each claim, identify whether it is empirical, conceptual, or normative, and consider how you would establish that it is true or that it is false. Identify the specific evidence that would be required to prove or disprove each of the following claims. Be as specific and detailed as you can. You do not need to gather evidence. Rather, you are being asked *what would count as evidence* for or against the claim. If you are unsure about what kind of evidence would be relevant, explain your uncertainty. If there are several possible interpretations of the claim's meaning that would affect how you would assess the acceptability of the claim, explain. Having identified the specific evidence that would count for or against each of the claims, examine your list and analyze it to see what different *kinds* of evidence are used.

A Note on the kinds of evidence used:

1. Empirical evidence is based on observation;
2. Conceptual evidence is based on the meaning of concepts; and
3. Normative evidence based on criteria used to evaluate.

Examples of claims:

1. The chalkboard in my critical thinking classroom is green.
2. Every chalkboard on this campus is green.
3. Every chalkboard ever made has been green.
4. It is in the nature of chalkboards to be green.
5. Caesar crossed the Rubicon in 49 B.C.E.
6. The Earth is 4.5 billion years old.
7. Water freezes at 32 degrees Fahrenheit (or 0 degrees Celsius).
8. The atomic number of gold is 79.
9. Scientists believe AIDS is not one single virus but several kinds of viruses.
10. AIDS is caused by HIV.
11. Getting unauthorized information about an exam prior to that exam is cheating.
12. This classroom is overcrowded.
13. *Pornography* is any depiction of sex or nudity that degrades women or children.
14. Pornography degrades women and children.
15. Prostitution is immoral.
16. Humans are by nature selfish.

Answers to the Quick Quizzes are available on the Premium Website at www.criticalthinking2e.nelson.com.

6.2 Kinds of Claims

Different kinds of claims require different kinds of evidence: empirical claims are based on observational evidence; conceptual claims are based on meaning; normative claims are based on criteria of evaluation; and mixed claims are based on some combination of the three.

Before examining these in more detail it is worth noting that we can take the following three approaches to dealing with the acceptability of a claim:

1. We can *accept* the claim as true or acceptable;
2. We can *suspend judgment* if there is insufficient evidence to establish the claim (a variant of this is to show that the claim is problematic or there is some reason for doubting it, even though neither the claim nor its evidence has conclusively been shown to be erroneous); or
3. We can *reject* the claim as unacceptable or false (if it does not meet the specified measures for the type of claim it is).

6.3 Empirical Claims

Empirical claims are ones whose truth is ultimately established by observation of the world and/or the inferences we make based on those observations. (Inferences, such as generalizations, causal claims, and appeal to expert testimony, are discussed in Module 5.)

We know the chalkboard in the next classroom is green by *observing* it. We know Lance Armstrong won the *Tour de France* seven times by *watching* the sixth and seventh races and by *reading reports* by those who were there for the other five; and we know he has been stripped of his title for illegal doping by *reading the report stripping him of his titles*. We know an electron is a bundle of energy and not a particle by relying on the *testimony of experts* who have studied electrons and made observations about them. We know gay couples are entitled to spousal benefits at their respective places of employment by *consulting the companies' written policies*. All these claims are confirmed by some kind of observational evidence: observing directly, referring to some kind of authoritative document, or getting information from an authority. Ultimately, their acceptability in terms of truth (or falsity) rests on observations about the world. Table 6.1 identifies and gives examples of different types of empirical claims.

> An **empirical claim** is one whose truth is ultimately established by observation and/ or the inferences we make based on those observations.

TABLE 6.1 Types of Empirical Claims & Examples

	Type of Empirical Claim	Example
1.	Personal sensory observation.	The text I am reading is printed on white paper.
2.	General knowledge based on the observations of others.	Caesar crossed the Rubicon in 49 B.C.E
3.	Generalizations based on some or many observations.	All swans are white.
4.	Theoretical knowledge capable of being tested by observation.	A falling body accelerates at the rate of 32 feet per second per second.
5.	The factual testimony of experts.	Scientists believe some cancers are genetic and others are environmental.

Each of these is a kind of empirical claim. Ultimately, their truth (or falsity) is determined by some observation independent of human belief. The claim about swans is in fact false. However, it is still an empirical claim since its truth (or falsity) depends on some observation or inference based on observation. In this case, it is shown to be false by the discovery of black swans in Australia. Consider the following:

> Somewhere in the Universe is a planet other than Earth inhabited by intelligent beings capable of space travel.

This is an empirical claim, yet we do not know if it is true or false because we have not yet been able to make the appropriate observations (though in time we may be able to). While we do not know the actual truth (or falsity) of the claim, it is still an empirical claim since its truth (or falsity) could only be established by observation through one of our senses. A claim's status as empirical relies on whether observations are the kind of evidence that would establish it as true (or false), not on whether we have actually made the observation. In other words, knowing a claim is empirical only tells us about *the kind of claim* it is, not about its actual truth (or falsity).

The various kinds of empirical claims have different considerations relevant to establishing their truth, as illustrated in Table 6.2. Consider the following kinds of observational claims in terms of their reliability:

TABLE 6.2 Types of Empirical Claims and Their Evidence

	Types of Empirical Claims	Evidence
1.	Direct and immediate observation.	"The chalkboard in front of me is green."
2.	Report of a past observation.	"The last time I was in class I noted the chalkboard in the room was green."
3.	Report of a direct observation made by another person.	"Mary told me the chalkboard in room 230 is green."
4.	A second-hand of a direct observation made by a third party.	"Mary says one of her classmates reported the chalkboards in her class room were also green."
5.	A summary of observations.	If I have observed ten classrooms with chalkboards on campus and Mary has observed another ten in different buildings, then I could claim "all the chalkboards we have seen on campus are green."
6.	An inference drawn from an observation.	"Green chalkboards must be easier to read, since they are used in newer buildings, whereas black chalkboards are typical of older ones."

(continued)

TABLE 6.2 Continued

	Types of Empirical Claims	Evidence
7.	A generalization inferred from one or more direct observations.	"In the ten classrooms I visited, all of the chalkboards were green, so all the chalkboards in this University must be green." (A generalization differs from a summary in that it goes beyond what was actually observed and draws an inference to a wider group than was actually observed, as discussed in Module 5.)
8.	Causal inferences from observations.	Green chalkboards must be easier to read, since they are found in newer buildings.
9.	Expert testimony by someone in a position of knowledge.	"The person in charge of building maintenance for the University says all chalkboards on campus are green."

Although these are all empirical claims, there are some important differences: the first five claims (in Table 6.2) are direct observation reports or memories of someone's direct observation, while the remaining four claims go beyond direct observation to inferences and judgments.

Direct Observation Reports

A **direct observation report** is a report based on the direct observation of someone.

Direct observation reports are based on direct observations made by someone. Their truth differs depending on how proximate the report is to the observer. Memory reports are less reliable, and become less so over time as memories fade and become distorted. Reports of second or third parties depend on the accuracy of their observations, along with other factors. Table 6.3 identifies some of the ways we judge observations, along with some examples.

TABLE 6.3 Criteria for Evaluating Observation Reports and Examples

	Criteria for Evaluating	Examples
1.	How reliable the observer is.	Geon claimed to see a UFO but tends to exaggerate.
2.	How attentive the observer is when making the observation.	Besides he was making out with Alex and had other things on his mind.
3.	How recent the observation was.	He reported the sighting was a month ago.

4.	How systematic the observation was.	He does not remember what time it was or what part of the sky it was in.
5.	How detailed the report is.	And he simply said the UFO moved quickly and disappeared.
6.	Whether the report is or can be confirmed by independent witnesses or independently confirmed observations.	Alex was there but did not see it, and though he was on the flight path for the nearby military base, the military base has no confirmations of anything unusual that night, and no military planes were operating during the time period of the reported sighting.
7.	The categories used to report the observations.	"I saw a bright light in the night sky" versus "I saw a UFO."

Other Observation Reports

The last three categories of observation reports in Table 6.2, items 6 through 9, are somewhat different: generalizations (which include scientific laws) go beyond what we immediately observe to incorporate claims about a whole group or class of things; causal connections involve inferences that one situation caused another situation; expert testimony is usually about the general knowledge within a field of study and is a mixture of observation and inference, as well as opinions within that field. Although all of these are empirical claims (because their acceptability in terms of truth or falsity is ultimately based on observations), they go beyond the directly observable.

QUICK QUIZ 6.2

Assessing Empirical Claims

In each of the following, identify the empirical claim, the evidence offered for it, and how reliable each claim is, based on the evidence.

1. When in Scotland last year, I visited Loch Ness and saw a number of photographs of the Loch Ness monster. It is a forty-foot-long dinosaur-like creature that lives in the loch.
2. Although there are no photos of the Loch Ness monster from before 1900, we do have over a dozen drawings. All of these show a seagoing dinosaur-like creature.
3. Ancient dinosaur-like creatures must exist because they have been seen and the Loch Ness monster is a good example of one.

Answers to the Quick Quizzes are available on the Premium Website at www.criticalthinking2e.nelson.com.

6.4 Conceptual Claims

Conceptual claims are claims about the meanings of words and expressions such as, "a bachelor is an unmarried male." The acceptability of such claims is determined by examining language and its use, rather than by examining the physical world.

> A **conceptual claim** is a claim about the meanings of words and expressions.

Conceptual claims have to do with the meanings of concepts and words, and are neither true nor false in the same way that empirical claims are. As discussed in Module 2, dictionaries can be a helpful starting point for clarifying the meaning of a word. For instance, if you do not know the definition of "euthanasia" and you are presented with a claim on the subject, your first resource might be a dictionary. However, a dictionary definition is not independently a sufficient tool for considering all conceptual problems. For example, it would not help answer the following questions: "was Canada a *democracy* before the introduction of voting rights for women?"; "do animals feel *pain?*"; or "is a fetus a *person?*" Instead, we need to explore how the concepts of "democracy," "pain," and "person" are used in language and (in some cases) make decisions about their proper use. (We will discuss how to deal with these kinds of issues of concept in Module 9.)

The criteria for assessing the acceptability of a conceptual claim are its use in language (or within a particular conceptual system), the purpose for which the concept is being used in a given context, and whether or not a given proposed meaning contributes to communicating effectively. In reviewing definitions, we normally do not discuss their truth (or falsity), but rather talk about whether they help us communicate, capture the accepted or a specific use of the concept, identify key features associated with the concept, or their accuracy in reflecting common or specific meanings. Similarly, we judge a conceptual claim by its ability to help us understand the concept, its consistency with the use of the term within language, and its usefulness in interpreting the world. For example, if we use "a yellow metal" as the meaning of the concept *gold,* it may be sufficient for trying to distinguish it from aluminium or tin, but it would not be sufficient for trying to distinguish it from iron pyrite (or fool's gold). Likewise "yellow metal" would not be sufficient for a chemist or jeweller but might be in another context (such as, someone reporting a ring she had found to the police).

QUICK QUIZ 6.3

Assessing Conceptual Claims

Identify which of the following are conceptual claims or involve a conceptual issue, and explain why.

1. Objectifying women is wrong.
2. Objectifying women means treating them as less than human.
3. Objectifying women results in their being treated as less than equal to men.

Answers to the Quick Quizzes are available on the Premium Website at www.criticalthinking2e.nelson.com.

6.5 Normative Claims

> A **normative claim** is one that expresses or prescribes a value.

Normative claims are ones that express or prescribe a value. There are claims about what should or should not be, about what states of affairs are good or bad, and/or desirable or undesirable. For example, "Stealing is wrong;" "This term paper deserves a grade of 'B';" and "*The King's Speech* was a great movie."

We can distinguish two kinds of normative claims based on the kind of support offered for them: the first is a ***preference claim***, which simply expresses a personal preference (such as, "I like broccoli"), and the second is a ***criterial claim***, which is based on some kind of general criterion or criteria for judging or evaluating (such as, "this paper deserves a 'B'"). In our language from Module 1, a preference claim is simple opinion and a criterial claim is reasoned opinion.

In a preference claim, the only ground given for the claim is the individual's personal preference or evaluation (such as, whether someone does or does not like, prefer, or want something). The only real challenge to a preference claim is to the person's sincerity in making the claim. For example, "you say you hate broccoli, but yesterday you told Andrey you eat it at least three times a week. Are you sure you hate broccoli?"

By contrast, a criterial claim uses at least one criterion or standard for evaluating that extends beyond the individual's preference. The criteria for giving a paper a "B" can be articulated, defended, and challenged. Because they are based on more than preference alone, criterial claims can be argued about, defended, and determined to be appropriate or not in a given circumstance.

These two types of normative claims can be easily confused. For example, "that was a good movie" might simply be someone's way of saying "I liked it" (just as one would say "I like broccoli"), or it might be based on some critical standards of evaluation (such as, "that was a good movie because it was well cast, and had a good plot and innovative cinematography"). Which it is depends on context and whether reasons are or can be given for the claim. In the latter case, the movie evaluator is providing criteria for determining whether a movie is good or bad. By presenting the claim in a way that allows multiple people to also make a similar evaluation, the criteria are rationally defensible (and challengeable), unlike with a preference claim that is tied to a specific individual.

The best way of determining whether someone is making a preferential or criterial claim is by asking "why?" If the answer indicates specific criteria, it is a criterial claim, whereas if it indicates an individual's opinion, it is simply a preference claim.

To assess the acceptability of a criterial normative claim we must identify the criteria for evaluation, determine whether what is being evaluated meets the indentified criteria, and decide whether the criteria are the best possible ones for assessing that specific thing in the specific circumstances. Applying this to the movie example above, we would ask the following questions: (1) "what criteria are being used to evaluate the movie?" (2) "does the movie meet these criteria?" and/or (3) "are these the best possible criteria for evaluating this movie for this purpose?"

Often we simply get the normative judgment without any justification for it. Since the claim "this paper deserves a 'B'" does not provide any criteria for evaluation we have to probe it with the question "what criteria are being used that justify this paper being given a 'B'?"

Normative criterial claims are evaluations because they assert judgments about what states of affairs are good or bad, desirable or undesirable, should or should not be pursued. Claims such as "insider trading is wrong" depend upon the application of some evaluative criteria. Thus, assessing normative claims depends upon three separate activities identified in Table 6.4 below.

Normative criteria are always ***evaluative*** because they enable us to evaluate or judge different alternatives. Table 6.4, identifies the tasks involved in assessing normative claims. In the example in Table 6.4, essays that are focused, well-structured and

A **preference claim** is one based on a personal expression of preference.

A **criterial claim** is one based on some general criterion or criteria for evaluation.

Evaluative means using criteria to evaluate or judge different alternatives.

well-argued, and lack grammatical or spelling errors, are more highly valued than those that are unfocused, poorly structured and argued, and contain grammatical and spelling errors. In an English composition course, one might use other criteria, placing more importance on style and creativity than being analytical. Which criteria are chosen will depend on the purposes in evaluating.

TABLE 6.4 Assessing Normative Claims

	Task	Examples
1.	Identifying the purpose for making the assessment.	We will use different criteria for English literature, sociology, and philosophy essays. What is my purpose for evaluating student essays? Is it to see if they have met learning objectives and help them develop their understanding or simply to pass them through the course?
2.	Identifying a criterion (or set of criteria) to be used for evaluation in this context.	A "B" term paper should meet the following criteria: (1) address the issue; (2) be reasonably well-structured; (3) demonstrate high competence with the material; (4) adequately develop an argument to support a conclusion; and (5) have few or no grammatical or spelling errors.
3.	Applying a criterion (or set of criteria) to a specific situation.	This paper meets the criteria for a "B" paper in the following way . . . .

Weighting criteria involves giving priority to some criteria over others.

In addition to these basic dimensions for assessing normative claims we may also weight and defend our criteria. ***Weighting criteria*** involves giving priority to some criteria over others. For example, we might place more weight in assessing an English essay on interpretation of the text and originality than on research; for a science report we might place more weight on research than on writing style; for a philosophy critique we might place more weight on detailed analysis of the arguments than on secondary research. Weighting is done in terms of our purposes for evaluation.

Because different people give weight to criteria differently when evaluating something, some may draw the conclusion that such evaluations are all relative. But this ignores the fact that different evaluators may give weight to criteria differently because they are evaluating for different purposes. For example, a scientist will likely give less weight to style, whereas a creative writing instructor may give style significant weight.

Defending criteria involves showing that the criteria being used and the weight given to them are the best (or better than any alternative criteria) available. Criteria can be defended by showing they are the best suited for accomplishing the purposes of evaluation in the context. For the purpose of teaching philosophy, a colleague might argue that we cannot expect students to develop an original, coherent argument of their own until they have examined and analyzed the works of others, and we should make the first assignment a critique of a text rather than an original essay, whereas a statistician may argue that one statistical test is better than another for a particular purpose and the one we have proposed using will not sufficiently discriminate between alternatives.

Assessing Normative Claims

Normative claims can be defended on the basis of the criteria used to make their evaluations, namely, by clearly identifying which are being used, demonstrating that they are the best possible criteria for the specific situation, and showing clearly how they apply to the situation. Conversely, normative claims can be challenged on the basis of the criteria used to make their evaluations, namely, by showing they have not been clearly identified (or they are self-contradictory or confused), determining that they are not the best possible criteria for the situation, and demonstrating they have not been thoroughly applied in the specific situation (or that applying them leads to a different evaluation).

Aesthetic, Practical, and Ethical Claims

Various types of subject matter give us a second way of categorizing normative claims. They can be divided into aesthetic, practical, and ethical categories. An **aesthetic claim** is a normative claim concerned with art and beauty, the criteria for which depend on the kind of material being assessed (such as, novels, movies, sculpture, architecture, painting, photography) and may consider such things as proportion, contrast, harmony, realism, non-realism, craftsmanship, plot, writing style, cinematography, directing, and character portrayal.

A **practical claim** is a normative claim concerned with decisions about appropriate courses of action. Some examples of practical normative judgments are evaluating student papers, the comparative merits of different university programs, the choice of best MP3 player, and the comparative merits of different social policies (in terms of costs, infrastructure required, feasibility considerations, etc.).

An **ethical claim** is a normative claim concerned with issues of right and wrong behaviour, fairness, equity, duty, obligation, and justice. When we claim certain actions are right or wrong, moral or immoral, just or unjust, fair or unfair, we are claiming that the actions satisfy some criteria of evaluation based on ethical considerations. These criteria, or ethical principles, are based on an understanding of what is and is not desirable behaviour for us as humans.

Anything can be evaluated in any of these three ways. For example, we can evaluate a movie as good using aesthetic criteria of craftsmanship if its plot is well developed, its acting is well done, and its script is well written; we could also evaluate it as good using practical standards if it earned a lot of money; and we could evaluate it as ethically bad if it is thought to result in the possible corruption of youth.

Although the words "morals" and "ethics" are often used interchangeably we can use them to distinguish between two kinds of discourse. **Morals and morality** will be used in this text to refer to the specific principles, rules, and behaviours of individuals and groups, whereas **ethics** will be used in this text to refer to the systematic and rational examination of those moral rules and principles of individuals and groups, as well as to the developing of a system of conduct based on rational grounds. For example, we can say whether the morals (or the specific moral code and practices) of a given society justify slavery. In that sense we are describing the moral principles that the society follows. This is different from talking about the ethics of that practice, which would ask the question "is this the way we should treat people?" An ethical judgment, which appeals to a value or set of values independent of the specific code of that particular society, might answer the above question with "the moral code of a society condoning slavery is unethical in its treatment of those individuals it enslaves."

An **ethical principle** is a normative claim that identifies a core human value and enshrines it in a general claim. Such values include things like happiness, fair treatment, justice, and the promotion of human well-being. Some ethical principles that capture some of these values include such pronouncements as "individuals ought to act so as to create the greatest good or the greatest happiness for the greatest number of people," "individuals ought to act so as to ensure that each person is treated fairly," and "individuals ought to act so as to ensure human well-being" (where well-being is characterized as ensuring access to those goods and the development of those traits essential for humane treatment of others, like health, personal security, food, shelter, autonomy, freedom of thought and action, and so on). How the ethical principles are to be implemented and which specific rules follow from them is not specified, because part of ethical reasoning involves working out the meaning of such principles and how they apply in specific situations.

An *ethical rule* is a rule of behaviour or judgment that identifies a specific kind of action as right or wrong (such as, "stealing is wrong" or "you should not lie"). Ethical rules are concerned with a relatively specific kind of action. If we probe deeper to find out why stealing is or should be wrong, we may come up with a variety of reasons. For example, someone might say stealing is wrong because it violates a basic agreement we have with others in our society to treat them fairly. In this case, there is a basic principle, namely, we have an agreement with others in our society to treat them fairly. Within this framework, taking someone's property without permission is treating them unfairly. The basic value enshrined in this principle is the fair treatment of all members of one's society. Different ethical systems can be based on different fundamental values (such as, obedience to the will of a deity, satisfying the needs and wants of human beings as living creatures, respect for the autonomy of individuals, and human choice, are but a few that have served as the foundations of ethical systems).

Ethical rules and principles operate in ethical arguments in the same way normative criteria work in normative arguments, that is, they identify a criterion (or set of criteria) to be applied to a situation in order to evaluate it. Where we agree on an ethical rule we can use it as a basic principle in an argument, and where we disagree on an ethical rule, we have to back up the rule with more general and accepted ethical principles.

In defending moral judgments, we use the same kind of criteria used with criterial normative claims:

1. What ethical criteria are being used in this situation?
2. Do the criteria apply to this situation?
3. Are the best possible criteria being used, given the purposes of the evaluation?

The difference is that we use specifically ethical criteria when defending moral judgments, namely, ethical principles or ethical rules and the underlying moral values on which they are based.

Consider the following argument:

1. Michel stole some money from Aine's purse.

2. Stealing is wrong.

∴ 3. Therefore, what Michel did was morally wrong.

An ethical rule "stealing is wrong" is used to show Michel's actions were immoral. We could challenge this by showing the criteria do not apply in this situation, as would be the case if Michel borrowed the money with Aine's approval and did not steal it. This does not invalidate the ethical rule; it simply says it does not apply in this situation. Alternatively, we could also challenge it by arguing that the criterion can be overridden by a more important value given the situation, that is, the criterion being used is not the best possible or most appropriate under the circumstances. For example, Michel did steal the money, but he stole it to buy medicine for his sick wife, without which she would have died. In this case we are claiming there is another ethical rule that overrides the first, such that stealing (or other unethical behaviour) can be excused when it is done for a higher purpose.

The second challenge rests on identifying an alternate ethical value and arguing that the alternate value overrides the stated one in a given situation. The "no-stealing" rule defends the value of private property, while the "stealing-is-justified-to-save-a-life" rule defends the value of preserving life. The claim is that saving a life overrides the value of private property in certain circumstances. In this case, we would need to give an argument why the obligation to save a life overrides the obligation not to steal in certain circumstances.

This helps explain why some people assert that normative claims are subjective or mere matters of opinion, because different individuals in different situations may invoke different normative criteria as relevant and appropriate. While this does show variability in assessments and criteria, it does not mean we cannot argue and reason about the criteria and their application. Nor does it show that ethical reasoning is merely a matter of personal opinion because we can give arguments and reasons for why the obligation to save a life overrides the obligation to respect private property under certain conditions. Not everyone will agree that the obligation to save a life always overrides the obligation to respect private property in all cases. Nor will everyone agree that it overrides the obligation to respect private property in a specific case. But the important issue here is that we can argue about these and search for the most reasonable position. Thus, such judgments are not mere matters of individual preference but are reasoned opinions based on criteria of evaluation about which we can also reason.

Ethical judgments are not objective in the sense that empirical claims are, that is, based on observational evidence drawn from an independently existing external world. Whether the earth is 4,000 years old or 4.6 billion years old, whether there is a prehistoric creature in Loch Ness, or whether certain forms of cancer are genetic or environmental can ultimately be decided by observational evidence and inferences based on that evidence.

Ethical judgments are not decided in this way but are decided by appealing to ethical principles that are based on values regarding what constitutes human flourishing. We can and do argue about which values take precedence in specific situations, and we can argue about which values generally take precedence over others. Despite difference in ethical beliefs, we do reach agreement on some ethical rules and values in some areas (such as, with the beliefs that slavery and genocide are morally unjustifiable, and that children should be protected from harm). Admittedly, difficult cases arise (such as, whether the duty to protect from harm applies to child soldiers), and the judgments we make are neither at the level of mere opinion, nor are they evidential claims. Rather, they are reasoned opinions based on appeals to fundamental ethical values, and such values are not purely arbitrary in the way preferences and opinions can be. A ***core human value*** is one based on the kind of beings we are and the kind of things that enhance human well-being. They can be seen in the claims that it is better to be alive than dead, healthy than diseased, autonomous than subservient, free than enslaved. These are not just arbitrary values because it makes a difference to our lives and to the life of any human being, whether we are the former or the latter in each category. Given the alternative, no one would reasonably choose to be dead rather than alive.

That said, human values can and do come into conflict. Individuals have to make choices between living enslaved or dying resisting tyranny. In the last stages of a devastating cancer and suffering incredible pain, some individuals may be faced with a choice between continuing to live, knowing there is only more intense suffering ahead, and ending their life. No one value is absolute in all situations and contexts. Individuals are sometimes forced to make difficult choices between competing and equally significant values, and they can benefit by doing so using the tools of critical thinking to weigh the alternatives, consider the positions and the arguments for them, and make the most informed choice possible at the time and for that situation. It is not arbitrary, subjective, or just personal opinion, but a reasoned opinion based on fundamental ethical principles and human values, and the best reasoning we can bring to bear on the issues.

> A **core human value** is one based on the kinds of beings we are and the kinds of things that enhance human well-being.

We can defend ethical claims by clearly identifying the criteria being used, defending the criteria as the best possible for the situation, and showing clearly how the criteria apply to the situation. Conversely, we can challenge ethical claims by showing that the criteria have not been clearly identified and asking for a clear statement of the criteria, showing that the criteria are self-contradictory or confused, demonstrating that the criteria are not the best possible ones for the situation, and showing that the criteria have not been thoroughly applied in the situation or that applying them leads to a different evaluation.

The fact that we can challenge ethical judgments does not make them simply a matter of personal preference, or subjective, because the judgments can be based on reasoning. We can agree on values, and even which values apply and take precedence in certain situations. For example, respect for human autonomy entails that slavery and the subjugation of people (such as, women) are ethically unacceptable, whereas respect for life entails that we do not wantonly and without sufficient justification take someone's life. While there may be circumstances in which those values may be overridden by others, what remains true is that behaving ethically requires you to provide sufficient justification for overriding those values, and that makes them subject to reason and rational discussion.

QUICK QUIZ 6.6

Identifying Ethical Claims

For each of the ethical claims below, identify:

(A) the ethical claim being argued for;
(B) the criteria being invoked; and
(C) other possible criteria that might challenge these criteria.

1. The United States should be condemned for systematically using torture in its conducting of the war on terror and the war in Iraq. Torture violates the basic human rights of its victims.
2. Paying women less than men for doing the same job is immoral. Therefore, we should not do it.
3. A student charged with a breach of the rules of a university should have the right to a fair hearing before a disinterested party and the right to counsel at such a hearing. This is only a matter of basic justice.

Answers to the Quick Quizzes are available on the Premium Website at www.criticalthinking2e.nelson.com.

6.6 Mixed Claims

Mixed claims are claims whose criteria for acceptability depend on some combination of empirical, conceptual, and normative criteria. They can be conceptual-empirical, conceptual-normative, or empirical-normative. The claim "computers are not capable of human thought" involves both conceptual (what do we mean by "capable of human thought") and empirical (do computers have those characteristics?) dimensions. The claim "anything that causes harm to another is immoral" involves both conceptual (what do we mean by "causing harm?") and ethical (what are our criteria for something

> A **mixed claim** is a claim whose criteria for acceptability depends upon some combination of empirical, conceptual, and normative criteria.

being immoral?) dimensions. The claim "Alphonse's stealing of the watch was wrong" involves an empirical assessment (did Alphonse steal the watch?) and a normative assessment (was his stealing of the watch wrong?).

QUICK QUIZ 6.7

Identifying Mixed Claims

Identify any mixed claims in the list below. Determine which are conceptual-empirical, conceptual-normative, or empirical-normative. Explain what would be required to determine the claim's acceptability.

1. The Conservatives have the best policy on child care.
2. Feminism is making a comeback among female university students.
3. Low-income earners have greater health problems and lower life expectancies than middle- and high-income earners.

Answers to the Quick Quizzes are available on the Premium Website at www.criticalthinking2e.nelson.com.

6.7 Additional Tools for Challenging Claims

Thus far we have considered the kinds of evidence relevant for assessing different kinds of claims, and the kinds of evidence that would make a claim acceptable or unacceptable. One common type of claim we encounter is a *general claim* (defined in Module 5). Now we will discuss how counterexamples can be a basic technique for challenging general claims.

Counterexamples

> A **counterexample** is a specific instance or case designed to show the limitations (unacceptability or falsity of) a general claim.

A *counterexample* is a specific instance or case designed to show the limitations (unacceptability or falsity of) a general claim. It is a key tool in argumentation as most arguments contain general claims of some sort. Providing a counterexample will test the acceptability of a general claim.

Different kinds of general claims require different kinds of counterexamples. Consider the example:

All cats are black.

Since the claim is in form "all *a*'s are *b*," if we can find one *a* that is not *b* we have shown the claim is false. In other words, we need to find a specific instance of a non-black cat in order for the counterexample to work. If we just say "some cats are not black" we are simply asserting the contrary of the statement without providing any support for our counterclaim being true. On the other hand, if we give a specific example or instance (such as, saying "My cat Pandora is white") we have provided evidence. We have thereby shown that the original claim is false by showing there is at least one cat it does not apply to. Consider the following example:

If this is water, it will boil at 100 degrees Celsius.

This claim has the form of a conditional statement "if *a* then *b*." We can counterexample this by identifying conditions under which *a* (the antecedent or term following the "if," as described in Module 4) could occur and *b* (the consequent or the term following the "then," also described in Module 4) would not occur. This claim is probably true under most normal conditions (such as, if the liquid has no contaminants like salt, if it is at sea level, if the barometric pressure is normal, and so on). If some or all of these conditions are not met, the liquid will not boil at 100 degrees Celsius. These are the normal *reservations, exceptions,* or the *unless conditions* that indicate exceptions to a general claim. Normally, pointing these out might be considered picky, but under certain conditions it might be necessary to do so. The claim "water boils at 100 degrees Celsius" assumes the normal conditions of being at sea level because at a significantly higher altitude water boils at a lower temperature. If we are trying to boil water to cook something, and are at a higher elevation, the liquid may boil at 95 degrees Celsius, and this temperature may not be high enough to kill certain bacteria.

When we make a general claim we are saying all instances of a particular kind should be treated alike. We call this the ***Principle of Similar Cases***, which holds that all things that are alike should be treated alike. The corollary of this is that whenever we encounter any two things appearing to be alike and propose to treat them differently we must provide some justification for the difference in treatment, that is, we must show that they are significantly different in some way. We might, to coin a term, call this the ***Principle of Significant Difference.***

In short, counterexamples are designed to show that two things which appear to be similar are not, and can legitimately be treated differently. In the following dialogue, the argument partners are using counterexamples to challenge one another.

> The **Principle of Similar Cases** holds that all things that are alike should be treated alike.
>
> The **Principle of Significant Difference** holds that if we propose to treat two things differently that appear to be the same, we must provide some reason for doing so.

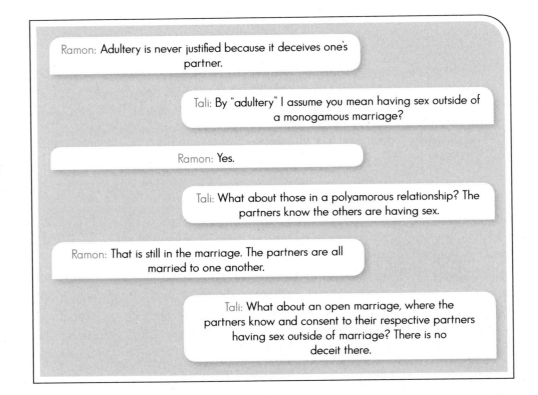

Ramon: Adultery is never justified because it deceives one's partner.

Tali: By "adultery" I assume you mean having sex outside of a monogamous marriage?

Ramon: Yes.

Tali: What about those in a polyamorous relationship? The partners know the others are having sex.

Ramon: That is still in the marriage. The partners are all married to one another.

Tali: What about an open marriage, where the partners know and consent to their respective partners having sex outside of marriage? There is no deceit there.

In this exchange, Tali gives several counterexamples to show that there are situations in which having extramarital sex does not necessarily involve deceiving one's partner. Now that Ramon's initial argument has been challenged, he has several possible alternative strategies to choose from. He can:

The **scope of a claim** is the range of cases to which a claim applies.

1. *Accept the counterexample as relevant and withdraw or modify his claim.* In response to the counterexample "black swans are found in Australia," a defender can restrict the scope of the original claim. The **scope of a claim** is the range of cases to which a claim applies. For example, "swans are white" implies a universal scope because it applies to all swans; "all swans outside of Australia are white" has a limited universal scope because it applies to those swans not found in Australia; and "some swans are white" is more limited and somewhat indefinite in scope. One strategy in argumentation is to limit the scope of our claim, which is a form of modifying our claim. Alternatively, we could simply withdraw the claim and admit we were wrong about the colour of swans.

2. *Reject the counterexample as not relevant.* In response to the counterexample with the claim "newborn swans are brown," a defender can respond by clarifying that he or she is referring to adult swans, not newly hatched ones.

When making a general claim we are asserting that all instances of that claim are true, and the counterexample is designed to show that either the claim is false or it is limited in scope.

QUICK QUIZ 6.8

Counterexamples

For each of the following claims identify at least one possible counterexample.

1. All SUV drivers are a menace on the roads.
2. If a person is a financial success then he or she is a good person.
3. In making all of their decisions Chief Executive Officers have in mind the best interests of the stockholders.
4. Everyone who uses a public roadway should have a motor vehicle licence or be banned from using it.

Answers to the Quick Quizzes are available on the Premium Website at www.criticalthinking2e.nelson.com.

Presuppositions

Presuppositions and corollaries are additional tools for assessing claims.

A **presupposition** is a claim that logically precedes another claim and must be true for the claim it precedes to be true.

A **presupposition** is a claim that logically precedes the one under consideration. This means the presupposition must be true in order for the claim under consideration to be true. For instance, if "*a*" is to be considered true, then a prior claim "*p*" must be true, and alternatively if "*p*" is false, then "*a*" must be false as well. The prior claim "*p*" is the presupposition; all claims have one or more presuppositions.

Suppose you are presented with the following argument:

> A student tells her instructor she could not write the exam because her father died and she had to attend the funeral.

This seems to be acceptable grounds for the student not having written the exam. However, the instructor discovers her father died several years before. The problem is not the that argument has unacceptable (or false) claims in the obvious ways, but rather the claim "my father died" presupposes her father had been alive near the time of the exam and his funeral was going to be held at or near the time of the exam. Although the student has not made an explicit claim about this, the claims she does make presuppose them, which is false. If the presupposition of one or more of the reasons of an argument is false, then the argument is defective and should not be accepted. In general, if the presupposition of any claim is false, then the claim itself is false.

Consider the following:

> We need to make our meetings more democratic by ensuring that every member has a significant say.

The above claim presupposes the following claims:

- I belong to a group that holds meetings;
- The group has already held some meetings;
- Meetings can be made more democratic;
- Meetings should be more democratic;
- The meetings the group has held have not been democratic or not as democratic as they could be;
- Something in the meetings has prevented at least one and possibly more members from having a significant say in the proceedings; and
- Democracy is assured by ensuring every member has a voice.

We might challenge a number of these claims, including the claim that meetings should be democratic and the claim that past meetings have not been democratic. In critically assessing a passage, we want to focus on those presuppositions that are most significant.

There are various kinds of presuppositions (the list is not exhaustive):

- *Existence:* A claim may presuppose the existence of something (the claim about making meetings more democratic presupposes we are holding meetings);
- *Properties:* Properties of the thing talked about are assumed (i.e., meetings can be democratic);
- *Relations:* A claim may presuppose that one thing is related to another in a certain way (i.e., I belong to a group); and
- *Context:* A claim may presuppose features of the context (i.e., in a specific organization, the context presupposes meetings should be democratic).

Consider the following claim, made in the context of a Christian Minister telling the story of the exodus of the Israelites from Egypt:

> Moses led the Israelites out of Egypt and to the Promised Land.

Before continuing, examine the above claim using the various kinds of presuppositions listed above:

Existence: Moses, Israelites, Egypt, and the Promised Land are all presupposed to exist and we know what the Promised Land is.

Properties: Moses was the kind of person who could be a leader.

Relations: Moses was the leader of the Israelites. The Israelites were capable of being led (or the Israelites were willing to follow a leader). Egypt was not the Promised Land. One can get from Egypt to the Promised Land. This happened in the past (led is the past tense and a temporal relation).

Context: The Bible's story of the exodus of the Israelites truthfully tells the story of a real event. The Israelites were enslaved in Egypt.

We can contrast textual and contextual presuppositions. *Textual presuppositions* are presuppositions based on the claims actually made in the text (in this case, the Israelites were in Egypt), and *contextual presuppositions* are those based on the context of the passage (in this case, the Biblical account is of an actual event).

The contextual presuppositions require knowledge of the Biblical context and all that goes with this particular story, just as the contextual presuppositions in the earlier example require knowledge of a university's examination policies.

The context includes how and why a story is being told or a set of claims is being made. In some cases the context is set within the passage, and in other cases the passage presumes common cultural knowledge. For example, a claim made about a legal or political system may presuppose common knowledge about the system referred to, as in the case of a claim made about the legal system in Quebec, which may presuppose different things from a claim made about the legal system in the rest of Canada, given that Quebec operates under the Napoleonic code, while the rest of Canada operates under the English system of common law.

Some claims related to a given claim may not be presuppositions. For instance, the claim "Moses was an Israelite" is not a presupposition because given the original claim it might be possible that Moses led the Israelites out of Egypt but was not himself an Israelite. For that we need independent knowledge because someone who leads a group is not necessarily a member of that group.

QUICK QUIZ 6.9

Presuppositions

Identify the presuppositions in the following claims. Using the list of kinds of presuppositions might be helpful here. Identify at least one claim related to the claims in the passage that is not a presupposition of the claim given.

1. You need to replace your engine because it has over 350,000 km on it.
2. Kidnapping, torture, and extortion are legitimate strategies in waging war.
3. Marijuana should be legalized for medical reasons.

Answers to the Quick Quizzes are available on the Premium Website at www.criticalthinking2e.nelson.com.

Corollaries: Implications and Consequences

A *corollary* is a claim that follows from an explicit statement. For example, "The Canucks have a much improved team this year." This claim has the corollary: the Canucks should win more games this year than last year. Any statement, whether or not it is part of an argument, can have a corollary.

There are two key differences between presuppositions and corollaries. A presupposition is a claim that must be true if the claim in question is to be true, whereas a corollary is a possible consequence. Presuppositions are logically prior to the claim in question, whereas a corollary is a possible consequence that would follow if the claim turns out to be true.

One way of challenging a statement is to show that its corollary (the claim that follows from it) is false, unacceptable, or otherwise problematic. If the statement is the conclusion of an argument, and the corollary is not true or unacceptable, either something is wrong with the argument used to support the conclusion, or the argument has been framed in too narrow a way (such as, if a key issue in the situation has not been addressed by the argument). An example of the latter would be proposing a project, presented with good reasons for undertaking it, but with the costs being prohibitive.

Consider the following claim:

> A study has shown that astrologers have been far more accurate than stock analysts in predicting market variations.

If we accept the claim as true, then one corollary is if we want to make money in the stock market we are more likely to do so by following the advice of astrologers. Yet if we have reason to doubt that (say, because astrologers have been inaccurate in predicting my future), then we might reject the claim.

Consider the following claim:

> Israel should accept Hamas's offer to return to the peace table.

If we accept this claim as true, there may be a number of corollaries. One might be that Israel's actions will be seen as conferring legitimacy on Hamas, offer, which may be objectionable to Israeli leaders and therefore something they will not want to do.

When identifying a corollary we are in effect determining what will follow from the claims in question if we accept them as true. By showing there are unacceptable corollaries we generate reasons for rejecting the original claim. To be clear, we have not shown the claims are false, only that there are grounds for considering the claims problematic and possibly unacceptable.

There are two significant types of corollaries: consequences and implications. A *consequence* is a causal effect of the state of affairs described in a claim. A consequence of building a domed stadium in the centre of a city is that there will be an increase of traffic in the downtown core. An *implication* is a symbolic effect that follows from a claim. An implication of building a domed stadium in the centre of a city is that such a move signals that the location is considered more important or valuable than others in the region. The first has to do with the causal effects of the stadium's location, and the second with the meaning or significance of the stadium's location.

A **corollary** is a claim that follows from an explicit statement.

A **consequence** is a causal effect of the state of affairs described in a claim.

An **implication** is a symbolic effect that follows from a claim.

Presuppositions differ from corollaries in that they are claims that must be true if another claim is true, whereas implications and consequences are possibilities (all other things being equal). In identifying corollaries it is important to know something about the social, political, and personal (among others) contexts surrounding the things in the statement.

For example, consider the claim:

> Paul Bernardo was convicted of first-degree murder.

In the Canadian context, the consequence of this is that Paul Bernardo will spend a minimum of 25 years in a federal penitentiary. In the context of the Canadian *Criminal Code,* the consequence of this is the minimum sentence before parole can even be considered. The consequence may be different in other jurisdictions. One of the significant attributes of implications and consequences are that we sometimes require content knowledge of the claims in order to identify a corollary.

QUICK QUIZ 6.10

Corollaries

Identify the implications and consequences for the following claims/situations.

1. Situation: Marijuana is going to be legalized for medical reasons.
2. Situation: A student is trying to get an exemption from the rule that she cannot take a particular course without first taking its prerequisite. In talking with an advisor, she is caught lying about a grade in a previous course, and why the low grade was received.
3. Claim: Tuition for general undergraduate education will increase next year by 10 percent.

Answers to the Quick Quizzes are available on the Premium Website at www.criticalthinking2e.nelson.com.

Module Summary

- The assessing of claims is central to assessing the cogency or soundness of arguments.
- Empirical, normative, conceptual, and mixed claims require different kinds of evidence to make them acceptable.
- Empirical claims are ultimately based on observations and/or inferences from those observations.
- Challenging empirical claims means challenging the reliability of the observations, the inferences from the observations to the generalizations or causes, or the expertise of the authorities.
- Conceptual claims are claims about the meanings of concepts and are ultimately checked by how the words are used in language.
- Normative claims are claims of value and are based on identifying and defending standards or criteria of evaluation. Unlike preference normative claims, criterial normative claims can be argued and reasoned about.
- In addition to knowing the kinds of evidence relevant to different claims, two additional ways of challenging claims are through their presuppositions and corollaries.
- General claims can be challenged with counterexamples.

Argumentation Exercise: Replying to a Challenge

Continue the dialogue between Ramon and Tali (page 157) by developing how Ramon could respond to Tali's challenges by (a) rejecting her counterexamples (or showing they are not a relevant difference); and (b) accepting her counterexample as relevant and limiting the scope of his claim. Develop several further counterexamples Tali could raise and give possible responses for Ramon. Identify the kind of response.

Writing Skills Exercise: Supporting Your Claims

Write a one page argument essay (an essay in which you defend an argument). The essay should contain at least two of conceptual, empirical, and normative claims. For each statement in the essay:

1. identify the kind of claim;
2. whether the claim needs support (i.e., is contentious or could be challenged);
3. whether the claim is supported; and
4. what kind of claim it is.

MODULE 7

Fallacies

LEARNING OBJECTIVES

After completing this module you should be able to:

1. Explain what a fallacy is;
2. Identify and distinguish different kinds of fallacies;
3. Identify and explain how a fallacy occurs within a passage;
4. Neutralize a fallacy;
5. Avoid committing fallacies in your own writing;
6. Distinguish between look-alike fallacies; and
7. Determine when an argument that appears to be a fallacy is not a fallacy.

 ## A DIALOGUE ON COPYRIGHT AND PIRACY – CONTINUED

Peter: Jean, you have claimed that piracy, sorry, downloading of copyright materials, is ethical. Why do you say that?

Jean: Well, it's obvious. Everyone knows that it's not unethical.

Peter: So your argument is that it is ethical because it is obvious? That's not an argument! It is just a claim that something is obvious to you. That is not good enough. It is not obvious to me, and I am the one you are trying to convince. Why do you think it is obvious?

Jean: Everybody does it and no one considers it unethical.

Peter: So your argument is that because everyone does it and no one considers it unethical, then it is ethical? That was once true for slavery. It was widely done and not considered unethical. So was slavery unethical?

Jean: Of course it was. What I am trying to say is that it is widely done, and if it is widely done then those doing it must consider it ethical.

Peter: Maybe they just haven't thought about the ethics of it?

Jean: That's possible.

Peter: Let's take your other reason, why do you think it is widely done?

Jean: A study I read says so.

Peter: Who did the study? What credentials does she or he have? Have other studies confirmed this?

Jean: Some study I read.

Peter: You are using an unnamed study by an unknown author. Why should I accept that as authoritative? Can you give me any more information about the study?

Jean: I read a survey online, reporting the research of a professor at some university who found that over 80% of university students download illegal material regularly, and that 54% of them do not consider it unethical even if it is illegal. If the majority of people have no ethical concerns, then it must be okay.

Peter: Let's grant that the research was well-conducted and that the study is sound. That is still not a good enough reason. You are saying that if something is popular enough, then it is ethical. That is a fallacy of appeal to popularity. Just because a lot of people do something doesn't make it right. A lot of people once thought it was ethical to not allow women to vote and that didn't make it ethical.

(continued)

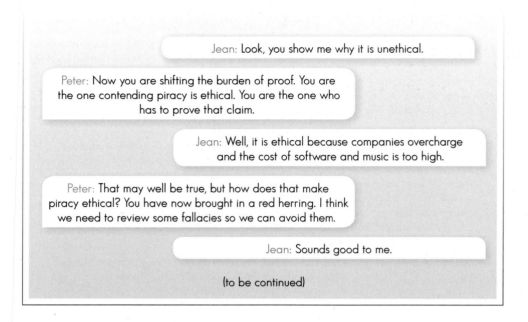

Jean: Look, you show me why it is unethical.

Peter: Now you are shifting the burden of proof. You are the one contending piracy is ethical. You are the one who has to prove that claim.

Jean: Well, it is ethical because companies overcharge and the cost of software and music is too high.

Peter: That may well be true, but how does that make piracy ethical? You have now brought in a red herring. I think we need to review some fallacies so we can avoid them.

Jean: Sounds good to me.

(to be continued)

7.1 Introduction

In the above dialogue, Jean has used a number of particularly bad arguments in developing his position. The mistakes he makes in the dialogue do not simply involve false reasons and assumptions. Rather, he commits a series of what are called "fallacies." A ***fallacy*** is a pattern of reasoning that is fundamentally erroneous. Whereas an argument with a false claim involves a specific false claim or assumption, a fallacy is a pattern of faulty reasoning that can be found in many different arguments. Learning to identify the various fallacies can help us identify them when they occur in a new situation.

A fallacy meets the following two conditions:

1. It is a pattern of reasoning, not a specific error; and
2. There is something fundamentally flawed about that pattern of reasoning.

The flaw in the pattern of reasoning can vary. It can result from reasons no one should accept, from a significant error in the reasoning, from an error in the use of language, or from a failure to meet the constitutive rules of argument in a basic way.

In everyday language, we sometimes refer to a false claim as a fallacy. What we mean is that the claim is false. In this text and in the study of logic as a whole, the term "fallacy" refers to an inference or a pattern of reasoning that is fundamentally erroneous. Under our terminology, *claims* are false and only *arguments* can be fallacious.

Avoiding fallacies requires that we hone our understanding of the criteria for the various fallacies, and pay attention to the context of claims and arguments. The following identifies some of the ways that we mistakenly cry, "Fallacy!"

False claims are not fallacies. If someone says "Canada became a country in 1800" that is simply a false claim, not, properly speaking, a fallacy.
Nor are all faulty arguments fallacies. For example:

1. If I study hard I will pass the exam.
2. I studied hard.

∴ 3. I should have passed the exam but did not.

> A **fallacy** is a pattern of reasoning that is fundamentally erroneous.

This is a faulty argument, but not a fallacy, because the first reason is false. Studying hard is no guarantee of a pass. A student must also understand the material and be competent in test-taking. It is a simple error of fact, not a pattern of faulty reasoning.

Merely being a poor argument does not make an argument a fallacy. The argument must have a pattern of poor reasoning that is fundamentally erroneous. Not all faulty arguments meet that condition. A faulty argument may simply have a false reason, have insufficient evidence for a conclusion, or be unclear. None of these are in themselves fallacies.

What does it mean to say a fallacy is "a pattern of faulty reasoning?" Consider the following argument:

1. Sophie is a lesbian.
2. Lesbians are all radicals trying to destroy the family.

∴ 3. We should not accept what Sophie has to say about abortion.

Something is wrong with this argument. It is not just that some of the claims are false (that all lesbians are radicals, all lesbians are trying to destroy the family, or the presupposition that one's stand on abortion is an attempt to destroy the family). These are all problems with this specific argument. However, there is something fundamentally wrong, not just with this particular argument or the specific claims in it, but with the pattern of reasoning that this argument exemplifies.

We can identify the pattern of reasoning in an argument by substituting variables for the content terms in the argument (much as we did in Module 4 to identify the patterns of deductive reasoning). Using variables for content terms, the argument structure is:

1. Person p (Sophie) says y (supports abortion).
2. Person p has characteristic c (is a lesbian).
3. c is viewed as discrediting (lesbians are trying to destroy the family).

∴ 4. We should not accept what p has to say (or y is false)

This argument structure is fundamentally flawed. It is saying we should dismiss someone's argument, not because of a flaw in the argument, but because of a personal characteristic of the person advancing the argument. Let us examine a similar argument:

The Leader of the Opposition in the provincial legislature challenges the Premier about a possible conflict of interest involving a Cabinet Minister. The Premier's response is to suggest members of the legislature should disregard the challenge because the Leader of the Opposition is "sleazy."

This has the following structure:

The Leader of the Opposition advanced a charge that a member of the Government is involved in a conflict of interest.

The Premier's response, formulated as an argument, is the following:

1. The Leader of the Opposition is sleazy.

∴ 2. We should disregard his charges. (= His charges are false.)

Although the content of this argument and that of the preceding one are quite different, both have a common pattern:

> We should reject what someone says because of who he or she is, not what they actually argue.

In both cases the arguments are being dismissed, not because they have been shown to be wrong, but because of the something about the person asserting them (such as, Sophie is a lesbian or the Leader of the Opposition is alleged to be a sleazy politician). It is not just that there are specific false or questionable claims in the Sophie and Leader of the Opposition arguments. Rather, a fundamentally flawed pattern of reasoning is being used. To say a *pattern of reasoning* is being used is to say there is a structure to the reasoning. To say it is *fundamentally flawed* is to claim that there is something about the pattern of reasoning that should not be accepted.

This pattern of reasoning (that *p*'s arguments should be dismissed because of who he or she is, or what he or she has done, or other beliefs he or she have) is fundamentally flawed for two reasons. First, the reasons provided are not good ones for accepting the conclusions because, even if they were true, they are irrelevant to showing that the arguments are not sound. The only way of showing that the arguments are faulty is to assess them, and the reasons of the rebuttal do not do that. Second, this pattern of reasoning violates several of the constitutive rules of argumentation, specifically the truth-seeking principle, the respect principle, and the argument principle (see Module 1). *Argumentation* is about assessing the claims and arguments for a position, not assessing the character or associations of person making the claims. This *argument pattern* fails that.

Fallacies are patterns of reasoning that undermine the basic aim of argumentation, which is the pursuit of truth about an issue. Fallacies prevent us from discovering possible points of agreement and disagreement; they also thwart the possibility of reaching a resolution on an issue.

The idea that fallacies are a pattern of erroneous reasoning is similar to the idea of validity in that the error is a structural or patterned error (see Module 4). *Affirming the consequent* is a pattern of reasoning that is always erroneous, regardless of the specific content. It is a fallacy, as is *denying the antecedent*. Any argument with a fallacious pattern of reasoning is always a fallacious argument. The kind of structure or pattern differs between validity and fallacies. With validity, the structure is a formal pattern related to the conveying of truth. With fallacies, the structure relates to the aim and constitutive rules of argumentation.

The more common fallacies have names based on how the error occurs. The particular pattern of argument, illustrated above with the Sophie and the Leader of the Opposition arguments, involves attacking the person rather than the person's position. It is called *ad hominem*, which translates as "to the man," because we attack the person rather than the reasoning. A fallacy's name refers to the specific pattern of bad reasoning it commits.

Each of the fallacies in this module has been expressed using these four steps:

1. Identify examples of a type of faulty reasoning.
2. Abstract from the examples their particular patterns of reasoning, which are the criteria for the fallacy.
3. Identify why this pattern of reasoning, as a pattern of reasoning, is faulty. This can be done in one of two ways:

(i) by showing how the pattern violates one or more of the constitutive rules of argumentation, or

(ii) by showing that such a pattern of reasoning does not guarantee the truth of the conclusion.

4. Provide a descriptive name for the pattern of reasoning.

Rather than going through this entire process with each fallacy, we will use a simpler form that gives the name of the fallacy (#4 above), the criteria for the fallacy (#2), a brief explanation of why it is an error in reasoning (#3), and one or several paradigm examples (#1) of the fallacy. The examples provided in the text are designed to be clear and unambiguous examples of the specific fallacy. When we encounter fallacies in everyday life, however, they are not always so clear, and critical assessment is required to identify them.

By identifying the fallacy, showing what is wrong with its reasoning, and explaining how the error in reasoning manifests itself in a particular argument, we can neutralize the fallacy.

QUICK QUIZ 7.1

Understanding Fallacies

For each of the following, state whether the claim is true or false.

1. A fallacy as used in this text is a false claim.
2. All bad arguments are fallacies.
3. In challenging a fallacy, one should attack the person for making the mistake in reasoning.
4. A fallacy is a violation of one of the constitutive rules of argumentation.
5. In challenging a fallacy, it is sufficient to be able to name the fallacy committed.
6. Any error in reasoning is a fallacy.
7. All fallacies are bad arguments.

Answers to the Quick Quizzes are available on the Premium Website at www.criticalthinking2e.nelson.com.

When we encounter arguments with fallacies in the real world, the fallacies will not always be evident and may not precisely fit the criteria. Passages may commit multiple fallacies, and it may be challenging to disentangle them. Also, some fallacies resemble one another and we may have difficulty trying to decide between several types. **Lookalikes** are fallacies that have similar characteristics and are commonly mistaken for one another. In such cases, the existing criteria might not be precise enough for the purpose, and we might have to adopt further criteria to help us distinguish between the *lookalikes*. Finally, some things that appear to be fallacies may not be fallacies. For instance, name-calling is not necessarily a fallacy, but in the context of dismissing someone's argument, it is a fallacy.

The context and the function of the utterance within a context are critical in determining whether or not a fallacy has been committed. Saying the Leader of the Opposition is "sleazy" is a fallacy if it is used as part of an argument to dismiss what he or she has to say. If it is simply a comment on a particular political manoeuvre he or she has engaged in, it is not.

> **Lookalikes** are fallacies that have similar characteristics and are commonly mistaken for one another.

The context is often not specified in examples given to illustrate and learn fallacies. In the absence of background, consider various possible contexts and how they might affect whether or not a fallacy is being committed. In more complex examples, context will be specified.

7.2 The Fallacies

The remaining part of this module examines twenty of the most common types of fallacies, numbered I to XX in Roman numerals. These fallacies fall into three general categories: A, B, and C.

This presentation goes beyond the traditional approach of simply naming the fallacy, identifying the criteria, and giving some examples. It adds material on distinguishing situations and contexts in which what appears to be a fallacy may be a legitimate argument, how to neutralize a fallacy, and ways of distinguishing lookalikes (different fallacies that are often confused). We will first introduce one cluster of fallacies, then address when something which can be mistaken for a fallacy is not a fallacy, how to neutralize a fallacy, and ways of distinguishing lookalikes. We will introduce this basic approach with the first group of fallacies, and then apply the same approach to the later groups.

There are many ways of classifying fallacies. Sometimes different fallacies can be identified by the same name, and sometimes the same fallacy can be identified by different names (for instance, *ad hominem* can also be called "attacking the person"). What is most important about fallacies is not whether we know their names, but being able to recognize that there is an error in the reasoning, what exactly the error in reasoning is, and being able to explain and neutralize the fallacy. These criteria for fallacies are more significant than the name. An argument can commit more than one fallacy at a time. Identifying just one, however, is sufficient to show that the argument is not cogent.

The fact that an argument or appeal is fallacious does not mean its conclusion is false. What it means is that the reasons given for that conclusion are irrelevant, insufficient, or false. The conclusion of a fallacious argument could be true, just as the conclusion of an invalid argument could be true, but in both cases the conclusion is true on grounds other than having been established by the reasons given for it.

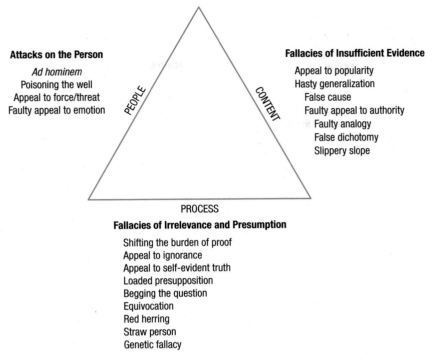

Figure 7.1 Fallacies and the Dimensions of Argumentation

If we use the model of the dimensions of argumentation (content, process, and people – introduced in Module 1), we can organize fallacies according to which dimension of argument a specific fallacy violates.

This is illustrated in Figure 7.1, which organizes fallacies according to the dimensions of argumentation they primarily violate: attacks on the person, fallacies of content (insufficient evidence), and fallacies of process (irrelevance and presumption).

A. Fallacies Involving the Person

These include *ad hominem,* poisoning the well, appeal to force or threat, and (faulty) appeal to emotion. These violate the basic aim of argumentation, which is to establish the truth of a claim through reasoned argument. All of these involve attacking the person or trying to influence the person (either one's argument partner or the audience) by attacking or dismissing the person's arguments, and doing so by means of attacking the person or appealing to irrelevant appeals (such as, threat or emotion). Doing this violates the Constitutive Principles of truth-seeking, respect, and argument (discussed in Module 1).

B. Failure of Process: Irrelevance and Presumption

These include shifting the burden of proof, appeals to ignorance, appeals to self-evident truth, loaded presupposition, begging the question, equivocation, red herring, straw person, and the genetic fallacy. Such appeals, whether intentional or not, undermine the very process of argumentation by making it difficult to discover the truth through rational means. They also violate a number of Constitutive Principles, including truth-seeking, respect, burden of proof, and argument.

C. Fallacies of Insufficient Evidence

These fallacies provide reasons that may be relevant but are insufficient as given to establish their conclusions. Fallacies in this category include appeal to popularity, hasty generalization, false cause, faulty appeal to authority, faulty analogy, false dichotomy, and slippery slope.

7.3 Fallacies Involving the Person

These fallacies involve appeals that address the people side of an argumentation, either by attacking the person, appealing to emotion, or seeking to discredit one's argument partner (and thereby the partner's argument) in the eyes of another. These violate the following Constitutive Principles of Argumentation: the truth-seeking, argumentation, respect and burden of proof principles.

I. *Ad Hominem* (Attacking the Person) Fallacy

Ad hominem literally means "to the man." An ***ad hominem fallacy*** involves attacking the individual, rather than the individual's arguments, as a way of dismissing the individual's arguments. Often such attacks misrepresent the person's character. However, even those that do represent the person accurately violate the basic principles of argumentative discourse. Calling people "sleazy" does not show that their arguments are incorrect. The fallacy can also appeal to the person's beliefs, character, or actions, if these are seen as discrediting. In argumentation, we are assessing the person's arguments, not character, because even someone of poor character and judgment can make good arguments. The assumption of the *ad hominem fallacy* is that someone who is evil or ignorant or does not share our views or is otherwise flawed cannot present a sound argument, which is a faulty assumption.

There are several versions of this type of argument.

Abusive Ad Hominem Fallacy

The **abusive ad hominem fallacy** involves making a personal attack on another person's expertise, character, intelligence, good faith, or other personal characteristic to try and show that the person's argument or position should not be considered.

> Example 1: Why do you accept Professor Richards's claims that most men abuse women? She's one of those man-hating radical feminists who want to castrate all men. How could she have anything unbiased to say on this?

The attack here is on a person, not the arguments she has presented. The speaker is trying to get the listener to accept that Professor Richards's arguments are faulty. This appeal is not based on an examination of her arguments, but on the claim that she is a feminist. The arguer is also trying to discredit all feminists by portraying them as man-hating. Even without this attack on feminists, the argument is an *ad hominem fallacy* because it attempts to discredit Professor Richards based on her politics.

Circumstantial Ad Hominem Fallacy

The **circumstantial ad hominem fallacy** involves trying to show that an individual's argument should be rejected because of the individual's personal circumstances and

An ***ad hominem fallacy*** involves attacking the individual, rather than the individual's arguments, as a way of dismissing the individual's arguments.

The **abusive ad hominem fallacy** involves making a personal attack on another person's expertise, character, intelligence, good faith, or other personal characteristic to demonstrate that the person's argument or position should not be considered.

The **circumstantial ad hominem fallacy** involves trying to show that an individual's argument should be rejected because of the individual's personal circumstances and relationship with the subject of the argument.

relationship with the subject of the argument. It suggests the person being attacked has a personal interest in the matter and hence is not objective, trustworthy, or sincere.

> Example 2: The officer in command of the West Coast naval detachment has argued in favour of an increase in the personnel under his command and the addition of new equipment. He has presented a detailed case with statistics that seem to show he needs these in order to fulfill his mandate. In response, a challenger replies this is all a smoke screen because the officer's real motive is to increase his own importance and stature in the military. Therefore, his argument should be rejected.

The challenger seeks to discredit the officer by pointing to his personal reasons for advancing his arguments and suggesting that he has a personal stake in the outcome. This is intended to discredit his arguments. However, the arguments themselves have not been addressed. A basic principle of rational dispute is that we evaluate claims on the basis of the evidence given for them, not on the characteristics of the person offering the claim.

In some situations, what appears to be an *ad hominem* fallacy is not a fallacy. The challenge is justified. If someone is testifying based on his or her experience and there are good grounds for doubting the person's powers of observation, memory, or truthfulness, then such a challenge would be legitimate. For example, if a person is testifying in a criminal trial, raising the fact that he has been convicted of perjury would be a relevant fact to offer for consideration in judging his testimony. Challenging a witness on the grounds she was going to receive a more lenient sentence for testifying would also be a relevant challenge because it calls into question her motives for telling the truth, and, hence, is relevant to establishing their trustworthiness. Thus, it is not an *ad hominem fallacy*. The challenge may not be sufficient, especially if there is corroborating evidence for the testimony. Similarly, if a medical doctor was called to testify on the medical competence of a colleague, then the relationship may indicate bias in the testimony and may be a legitimate challenge (say, if they have co-authored articles together or are friends).

QUICK QUIZ 7.3

Ad Hominem Fallacy

(A) Identify whether an *ad hominem* fallacy has been committed in the following.

(B) For those that are *ad hominem* fallacies, explain how the criteria for this fallacy apply in the example; and

(C) For those that are not, explain why you do not consider it to be an *ad hominem* fallacy.

1. A Conservative speaking about his Liberal opponent in a provincial election: "My opponent is simply repeating the liberal tax-and-spend ideas that have proved bankrupt in the past." (Implication: You should not vote for him.)

(continued)

2. A Liberal challenging Prime Minister Harper *(paraphrased)*: "I would urge you to look at Mr. Harper's policies over the past four years. He has taken the nation from a substantial surplus to a massive deficit. He is the first Prime Minister since the Depression to preside over a net loss of jobs. He has led the nation into an unjustified and costly war that is taxing the Canadian economy. He has been cited for contempt of Parliament and rammed through Bills without adequate discussion. He has enriched the wealthiest 10% at the expense of the middle class and poor. Are these the policies you want continued for another five years?"

3. Dr. Khan was a member of the committee who authored the report. I doubt we can accept anything he has to say in favour of it.

Answers to the Quick Quizzes are available on the Premium Website at www.criticalthinking2e.nelson.com.

II. Poisoning the Well Fallacy

The fallacy of **poisoning the well** involves attempting to put an opponent in such a position that anything he or she says is dismissed prior to the opponent being heard. The arguer does this by discrediting the opponent before he or she is able to say anything.

Example 1: Anyone who disagrees with our position is (a) obviously repressed (Freudian); (b) a running-dog lackey of the capitalist imperialist warmongers (communist); (c) a male chauvinist; (d) an irrational women's libber; (e) an uptight prude; (f) a foe of the family; (g) a friend of big business; and so on.

Example 2: My opponent is not noted for his fondness for the truth.

The arguer in example 1 labels those who disagree with the position as a way of discouraging criticism. The arguer in example 2 attempts to discredit the opponent by accusing him or her of being a liar. Both serve to discredit the opponent prior to their arguments being considered or even presented.

These may not appear as arguments in themselves. However, in context, they can be portrayed as such:

1. *x* has a particular characteristic or is associated with a certain position or people.

2. This characteristic or association is disreputable.

∴ 3. *x*'s position should not be considered, whatever his or her reasons.

Since this strategy is designed to discredit what an opponent says before he or she has a chance to present an argument, it is an illegitimate argumentative move.

The fallacy of **poisoning the well** involves attempting to put an opponent in such a position that anything he or she says is dismissed prior to the opponent being heard.

III. Fallacy of Appeal to Force or Threat

The fallacy of **appeal to force** or **the threat of force** occurs when, instead of offering rational grounds for a position, the arguer uses or threatens to use coercion to get another to do something or to accept an idea. Such an appeal violates the truth-seeking principle, the respect principle, the argument principle, and the resolution principle.

Consider the following:

> Example 1: I don't think it would be wise to run a story on my son's driving escapades. After all, my firm does thousands of dollars of advertising business with your paper.

Expressed as an argument:

1. My firm does thousands of dollars of advertising business with your newspaper.

2. If you run a story on my son's driving escapades I will withdraw that advertising business.

3. You do not want to lose my advertising dollars.

∴ 4. You should not run the story on my son's driving escapades.

> Example 2: Refugees who come to this country from other cultures have no right to try to preserve their own customs and beliefs. If it were not for us taking them in, they would be dead. If they keep on insisting on their cultural integrity, we should ship them back home.

> The fallacy of **appeal to force** or **the threat of force** occurs when, instead of offering rational grounds for a position, the arguer uses or threatens to use coercion to get another to do something or to accept an idea.

This can be expressed as in standard form as follows:

1. If refugees from other cultures insist on cultural integrity and retaining their own customs and beliefs they should be shipped back to their homelands.

2. If they are shipped back home (= if we do not take them in and let them stay), they will die (= if they return home they will die).

A. [They do not want to die.]

∴ 3. They should not insist on cultural integrity.

Each of these arguments, instead of presenting evidence and reasons for a position, involves an attempt either to persuade by a threat or use of force, or to silence by threatening an undesirable state of affairs. In the first case, the implicit threat to withdraw advertising dollars is not a relevant reason for not running a particular story. Legitimate reasons might be that the story is not newsworthy, has been improperly researched, or is old news. In the second example, refugees are being threatened with being returned to homelands they have fled unless they relinquish their cultural identities, instead of reasons being provided for why they should integrate into the mainstream.

QUICK QUIZ 7.5

Appeal to Force or Threat

(A) Identify which of the following arguments is an appeal to force or threat.
(B) For those that are, explain how the criteria for this fallacy apply in the example; and
(C) For those that are not, explain why you do not consider it to be a fallacy of appeal to force or threat.

1. *A professor to a student who has challenged her argument:* "I suggest you remember who is marking your paper before you continue this line of reasoning."
2. *Spoken by a Canadian Cabinet Minister:* "If the United States continues to engage in unjust and unfair restrictions on Canadian softwood lumber imports, Canada will have no choice but to take the issue to arbitration and to impose countervailing restrictions on U.S. imports to Canada."
3. *Manager to an employee:* "I do not care if you think the 1-2-3 accounting program will do a better job and cost less. Remember you are working for me and if you do not support it I will give you a bad performance appraisal."

Answers to the Quick Quizzes are available on the Premium Website at www.criticalthinking2e.nelson.com.

The fallacy of **appealing to emotion** involves appealing to emotions (such as pity, shame, flattery, disgust, sympathy, or some other emotion) instead of reasons as a way of persuading someone to believe or to do something.

IV. Fallacy of Appeal to Emotion

The fallacy of **appealing to emotion** involves appealing to emotions (such as pity, shame, flattery, disgust, sympathy, or some other emotion) instead of reasons as a way of persuading someone to believe or to do something.

Consider the following:

Example 1: You should hire Mae. She has a disability and has not been able to get a job. I know she is quite depressed and giving her a job would really boost her self-esteem.

Example 2: I need an "A" to get into law school. I know I did not show up for class and turned in only some of my assignments but if I do not get into law school my parents will be heartbroken and my father, who has a serious heart condition, will be terribly crushed.

Formulated as arguments, both of these examples have as a major reason an appeal that one should have pity on someone and take action based on feelings rather than on solid reasons.

Expressed in standard form, example 2 looks as follows:

1. If I do not get into law school my parents will be heartbroken.

2. My father has a heart condition and will be crushed.

A. [You do not want these things to happen.]

∴ 3. You (the Professor) should give me an "A."

The appeal is for the professor to consider the possible consequences for the student's family and the fact the professor would not want these on his or her conscience. However, if grades are based on performance, then this is an irrelevant appeal to an individual's personal circumstances. More specifically, it is an appeal to the professor to have pity on the student's parents, innocent parties to the situation.

Emotions are not good reasons because they are usually irrelevant to the issue. The potential law student is asking for an "A," not because of her performance, but because of the effects that her not getting an "A" will have on her parents. The possible effects on the parents are irrelevant to whether the student deserves an "A" in the course. Emotions can be useful in motivating one to pursue an issue, and they can also serve as the basis for exploring an issue further. If we believe strongly that Mae should be hired, emotion can serve as the basis or impetus for seeking better reasons than the ones given. However, by themselves emotions are not reasons, and when offered as reasons they are fallacious.

QUICK QUIZ 7.6

Appeal to Emotion

(A) Identify which of the following passages involves an appeal to emotion fallacy.
(B) For those containing a fallacy, explain how the criteria for this fallacy apply in this example; and
(C) For those that do not, explain why you do not consider it a fallacy of appeal to emotion.

(continued)

In addition to identifying fallacies, we need to learn to identify when an argument that looks like a fallacy is not one, how to neutralize a fallacy, and how to distinguish lookalike fallacies.

When Is a Fallacy Not a Fallacy?

Now that we have a few fallacies to work with, we can introduce some additional considerations and skills that will help us with the rest of the fallacies. These include distinguishing fallacies from non-fallacies, distinguishing lookalikes, and neutralizing a fallacy.

If you have done the last four Quick Quizzes, you will have noticed that not all of the exercises commit the fallacy in question. Once we learn about fallacies, we tend to see them everywhere, including where there are none. Sometimes in looking for fallacies we identify anything that meets part of the criteria for a fallacy as being a fallacy. For example, we confuse name-calling with an *ad hominem,* or a general claim with a generalization. In some cases, we confuse other kinds of faulty arguments with fallacies (such as, arguments with faulty reasons, or invalid arguments).

Fallacy/No Fallacy?

Ad Hominem and Poisoning the Well

Fallacies are failures of argumentative communication and of reasoning. If you are intending to discredit someone or heap invective on them, and you are not in an argumentative situation, then it is not a fallacy. It may be disrespectful, it may be bad manners, it may even predispose me not to listen to what the person says later in an argument, and most important, it may destroy the basis for any future discussion with that person. However, none of these make it a fallacy. There is an exception, however, with the form of poisoning the well called "hostile climate," which we will examine below.

> The Prime Minister's Press Secretary says in a private conversation with a colleague that George Bush is a moron. She is overheard by a reporter and the comment is publicized.

Some might suggest the Press Secretary's words are a *fallacy of abusive ad hominem* because she utters something discrediting and disrespectful about George Bush. However, in this context, she is simply making a comment on President Bush's obtuseness. Since fallacies are errors in reasoning, and this is not an argument but just name-calling, there is no fallacy here. In this context, even the fact that the Press Secretary's comment may predispose me not to listen to the U.S. President when he gives an argument does not make it a fallacy. But if we were to prejudge George Bush and use this comment as a reason for dismissing his arguments, then we would commit the fallacy. The following is a fallacy:

> George Bush's taxation policies should not even be considered because George Bush is a moron.

In this case, the arguer dismisses George Bush's taxation policies without presenting an argument against them and instead attacks George Bush as a person. This makes it is an *ad hominem* fallacy.

Context can make a critical difference in whether an utterance is a fallacy. Calling George Bush a moron in a situation in which his arguments are being considered (even if not directed to a specific argument) might be a form of poisoning the well, since it sets up a predisposition within that context to discredit whatever Bush has to say. If reasons are given, however, the same claim may not be a fallacy:

> Look, we all know that George Bush is a moron. We all know that his taxation policies are simple-minded and should not be accepted. Let me show you what I mean. His policies will increase the differential between the poor and middle-class and the wealthy. They benefit only the wealthiest one percent, and put the burden on the poorest in society. The policies are based on a discredited theory of trickle-down economics that will only increase the national debt, not diminish it, as he thinks. And they are likely to stall economic growth and put us into a recession, if not a depression.

In this context, the claim "George Bush is a moron" is not a fallacy. The arguer in this passage has provided reasons (whether one accepts them or not) suggesting why Bush's economic policies are unacceptable ("simple-minded"). Although the arguer is trying to discredit Bush's position, he is doing so by presenting arguments (which themselves need to be evaluated and considered) relevant to dismissing Bush's position, indicating that he is taking Bush's arguments seriously and not employing a poisoning the well fallacy.

Fallacies are committed in arguments and in reasoning. Simple name-calling or labelling does not constitute giving an argument and *normally* does not involve a fallacy. However, there are some borderline cases. Rush Limbaugh, a radio/TV commentator, tends to label and dismiss anyone he dislikes. For example, feminists have become "feminazis." Women who argue that women have a right to reproductive control of their bodies become "sluts" and their arguments are dismissed on those grounds alone. Indeed, Limbaugh's diatribes invite the audience not to even consider what the targets of his invectives have to say. Since Limbaugh's job is to comment on people's views and since he is, at least implicitly, inviting us to dismiss those views solely on the basis of the labels he uses, his labels do amount to a form of poisoning the well. It is a slightly different kind than the one discussed earlier in this module; whereas the original form of poisoning the well refers to uttering a specific claim, usually directed to a specific issue of a specific opponent, Limbaugh commits the fallacy by establishing a hostile climate in which anything said by the opponent (and in the case of our example, the opponent is a whole class of people: all feminists) is automatically dismissed. The ***hostile climate variant of the poisoning the well fallacy***

> The **hostile climate variant of the poisoning the well fallacy** involves establishing a climate where anything said by the target group is dismissed as not being worthy of consideration.

involves establishing a climate where anything said by the target group is dismissed as not being worthy of consideration. This differs from the more traditional form of poisoning the well in that he sets up a we-they dichotomy: Everything "we" say and accept is accepted unquestioningly, and everything "they" say is rejected simply because "they" are not "us." In effect, Limbaugh develops an environment for feminists and their supporters in which their views cannot be considered fairly or objectively, or even considered. Since his behaviour involves a rejection of their positions and implicitly their arguments before they can even be expressed, an argument context exists making this is a fallacy, specifically, a poisoning the well fallacy, hostile climate version.

This differs from the "George Bush is a moron" situation above because there the Prime Minister's Press Secretary states an opinion or vents her frustration. However, it does not occur in an argument context and does not involve a wholesale dismissal of anything or everything George Bush says. At least, it is not obvious that it does. By the principle of charity we ascribe the best interpretation to an utterance. We do not select a possible worst-case scenario and treat that as the norm.

In general, a passage is not a fallacy (i) if it is not an argument or not part of an argumentation context, (ii) when the context indicates that there is further information that needs to be considered in making a charge of fallacy, or (iii) when the criteria for the fallacy are not fully met.

Fallacy/No Fallacy?

Force/Threat vs. Warning

Not all threats or warnings are fallacies. In the fallacy of appeal to threat or force, an arguer tries to coerce someone through the use of force or a threat of use of force. This may include depriving someone of something he or she has a legitimate right to, or abusing a position of power:

> *Manager of the department to a new hire:* I want your support at the Board meeting. Remember I am doing your performance appraisal this week.

This is a form of coercion and a fallacy, because the manager is not offering reasons for support but is suggesting the person's support should be based on her career aspirations. A performance appraisal is supposed to evaluate an individual's relevant work-related performance. Voting with one's manager simply because he or she could give you a bad performance appraisal is not a relevant consideration for voting a particular way at the Board meeting.

On the other hand, we often issue legitimate warnings to change someone's behaviour:

> *Supervisor to habitually tardy employee:* "If you continue to come in late I will have to report it in your next performance appraisal."

In such circumstances the supervisor is issuing a warning quite within his or her role.

Part of the difficulty in sorting out the difference between an improper appeal to force or threat and a fair warning is in determining whether the appeal is legitimate based on the roles, obligations, and duties of the parties involved. Whether someone is performing the duties of his or her job description is a relevant consideration in doing a performance appraisal. Voting with the boss on a proposal one does not accept is not relevant to a performance appraisal.

Whether a fallacy is committed in such cases may also depend on the options available. Whether someone is given a choice and allowed to make a decision (even if the options are not fully open or acceptable), or forced into a situation where there are no options, also helps us distinguish between an appeal to threat or force and the issuance of a legitimate warning about behaviour. The employee has a choice to continue coming in late and has been warned about the consequences of such behavior. The supervisor is reminding the person of her role as an employee. In the example involving the Board meeting, the employee has been hired for her expertise, which includes providing an honest assessment of issues, not just blindly doing what the manager wants.

Simple coercion is not a fallacy. A police constable telling a suspect to drop his weapon and raise his arms or he will be shot is not engaging in an argument. The constable is giving an order that is coercive and under most circumstances it is legitimate. Thus, it is not a fallacy.

Fallacy/No Fallacy?

Appeals to Emotion

We sometimes think any argument involving emotion is a fallacy. However, emotion can play a legitimate role in argumentation. Being passionate about an issue gives us information about our argument partner. We often believe certain reasons or lines of argument are more important than others and express that in the way we argue, and there is nothing illegitimate about this. Expressing such passion can help our argument partner sort through the various reasons we may give. Where emotion becomes a fallacy is when it replaces reasons with passion. Whether we do or do not share emotions on a given issue, the emotions by themselves do not provide us with a reason for believing something.

Lookalikes

Lookalikes are fallacies that look similar to and/or are often confused with one another. Confusion frequently occurs because some of the criteria for fallacies are similar and require further differentiation. Two such fallacies that are confused are *ad hominem* and poisoning the well.

An *ad hominem* fallacy occurs when an arguer attacks the person rather than the person's arguments, usually, though not always, as a way of challenging an individual's specific arguments. A poisoning the well fallacy occurs when an arguer attempts to discredit someone or someone's arguments before they have been given.

Both of these are fallacies of irrelevance because each attempts to discredit a claim or a person based on irrelevant criteria. Rather than examining the claims and arguments, the arguer either attacks the person's character directly or tries to discredit the person in front of an audience. What these fallacies have in common is a misguided target. The *ad hominem* is a direct criticism of the opponent and his or her circumstances. Poisoning the well is more contextual. While it is an attack on the person, and thus similar to an *ad hominem,* its context is different. It tries to discredit, not a specific claim or argument, but anything the opponent might offer by undermining the opponent before he or she has the opportunity to say anything.

Paradigm Cases

Ad hominem: All I need to do to show my opponent's arguments are not acceptable is to point out that he is constitutionally incapable of telling the truth.

Poisoning the well: My opponent is not known for his integrity. I do not think we need to consider what he has to say on the issue.

Both fallacies are typically directed to third parties (an audience). What distinguishes them is the *ad hominem* typically seeks to discredit a particular argument (usually after the argument has been given), whereas poisoning the well typically seeks to discredit anything the opponent has to say (usually before the person speaks).

QUICK QUIZ 7.7

Lookalikes: *Ad Hominem* and Poisoning the Well

(A) Identify and explain which fallacy (if any) is committed in each of the following; and

(B) Explain how each might be confused with one of its lookalikes.

1. Aristotle's comments on women can safely be ignored because he simply reflects the patriarchal society of the fifth century B.C.E.
2. We should reject the arguments in *The Bell Curve* that blacks have lower I.Q.s than whites and are disproportionately involved in social problems because the authors are known racists.
3. Pravar: "Martina Lieberman in the biology department claims gay men are born that way because evidence shows brains of gay men are structurally different from the brains of heterosexual men. So we do have proof there is a biological basis to being gay."
Sergei: "Of course she's going to say that. She's a lesbian, isn't she?"

Answers to the Quick Quizzes are available on the Premium Website at www.criticalthinking2e.nelson.com.

Neutralizing Fallacies

To **neutralize a fallacy** means to render the fallacy ineffective by showing what is wrong with it. We do this by identifying the fallacy (or error in reasoning), indicating what is wrong with the argument's reasoning, explaining how the criteria for the fallacy apply to a particular argument, and why we should not accept it.

The process of neutralizing fallacies outlined in Table 7.2 has been designed to be used when dealing with an audience unfamiliar with fallacies and needing to be shown the full process of reasoning that neutralizes the fallacy. If the audience knows the fallacies, a shortened form of this process will suffice. To illustrate the method, we will use the Sophie example from above, page 167.

To **neutralize a fallacy** means to render the fallacy ineffective by showing what is wrong with it.

TABLE 7.1 Neutralizing a Fallacy

	Step	Explanation	Example
1.	Summarize the argument in which the fallacy occurs.	Identify the place in the argument where the fallacy occurs. This normally involves identifying the reason and conclusion in the argument. If the fallacy is in the context or process of reasoning identify that. Briefly summarize.	1. Sophie is a lesbian. ∴ 2. We should not accept what she has to say about abortion.
2.	Name the fallacy.	Give the name of the fallacy if it is one you know.	*Ad hominem, circumstantial.*
3.	Identify the criteria for the fallacy.	Give the explicit criteria for the *ad hominem fallacy.*	The circumstantial *ad hominem* is committed when one uses circumstances about an individual that are irrelevant to their argument to reject their argument.
4.	Apply the criteria to this particular argument.	Demonstrate for the audience how the criteria that define the fallacy apply in this specific case.	The arguer is dismissing Sophie's argument on abortion on the grounds she is a lesbian.
5.	Challenge the fallacy.	Show what is wrong with this particular argument as a fallacy and why this argument should not be accepted.	Being a lesbian is irrelevant to whether or not Sophie's arguments are cogent. What needs to be addressed are her arguments and not her sexual preference. This form of argument violates the truth-seeking, respect, and argument Constitutive Rules.

One common error people make in challenging a fallacy is to challenge one of the claims in the argument as false (such as, not all lesbians are radicals who want to destroy the family). While this shows an error in the argument (one reason is false), it does not show what is wrong with the argument in terms of a fallacy. The process of neutralizing a fallacy shows what is wrong with the fallacy *as a fallacy*.

QUICK QUIZ 7.8

Neutralizing Fallacies

Use the steps for neutralizing a fallacy to neutralize the fallacies in the preceding Quick Quiz 7.7.

Answers to the Quick Quizzes are available on the Premium Website at www.criticalthinking2e.nelson.com.

Putting It All Together: Presenting the Critique as Prose

In some situations we may want to incorporate a critique of a fallacy as part of an essay or other written submission. We can translate the critique developed in Table 7.1 above into fluid prose:

> The author of the Sophie argument outlined above is contending that Sophie's views on abortion should be rejected because she is a lesbian and opposed to the family, without addressing her specific arguments. This is a circumstantial *ad hominem* fallacy. Rather than challenging her views, the author attacks her sexual orientation as the basis for dismissing her views. Her sexual orientation is irrelevant to the arguments she has made. If the point of the discussion is to examine the acceptability of Sophie's views, then the argument needs to address those explicitly, not irrelevant issues such as her sexual orientation.

A briefer presentation of the critique for those who are likely to know and understand fallacies might be as follows:

> The author of the Sophie argument outlined above is contending that Sophie's views on abortion should be rejected because she is a lesbian and opposed to the family, without addressing her specific arguments. This circumstantial *ad hominem* fallacy is unacceptable as her sexual orientation is irrelevant to proving or disproving her arguments on abortion.

In some situations, we will need to lay out all five steps for neutralizing the fallacy and lead the audience through the reasoning process. In others, simply providing the brief summary is sufficient to show an audience what is wrong with the argument. The most important thing in critiquing a fallacy is identifying it and demonstrating what is wrong with the pattern of reasoning *as a pattern of reasoning in that particular argument.*

QUICK QUIZ 7.9

Translating Critiques into Prose

Translate your critiques of the fallacies in Quick Quiz 7.8 into both full and brief prose passages.

Answers to the Quick Quizzes are available on the Premium Website at www.criticalthinking2e.nelson.com.

7.4 Fallacies That Undermine the Argumentation Process

These fallacies involve moves that undermine the basic principles of argumentation (such as, the truth-seeking, respect, burden of proof, and argumentation principles). These fallacies, in effect, derail the attempt to find out the truth about an issue. The fallacies in this grouping include the fallacy of shifting the burden of proof, the fallacy of appeal to ignorance, the fallacy of self-evident truth, the fallacies of loaded presupposition, begging the question, equivocation, red herring, and straw person, and the genetic fallacy.

V. Fallacy of Shifting the Burden of Proof

The person who introduces a claim has the obligation to defend that position (the Burden of Proof Principle). The fallacy of *shifting the burden of proof* occurs when the arguer defending the position shifts the burden of proof to the challenger.

> Example 1: Aleksandra has introduced the claim that pornography causes harm and therefore should be banned. When Mikko challenges her to show that pornography causes harm, she replies "Can you prove it does not?"

If successful, Aleksandra has shifted the burden of proof. She is the one who has introduced the position, and, therefore, has an obligation to defend her claims. Her move here suggests that Mikko must instead show that her claim is false. When the arguer requires that a critic provide a reason for not accepting the claim, the arguer has reversed or shifted the burden of proof.

The fallacy is not committed if one argument partner asks the other to support the claim or points out that they are advancing a claim but have not supplied evidence or support for the argument and needs to do so.

> Example 2: Mikko: Aleksandra, I thought you were arguing it causes harm. It is your responsibility to provide evidence for that, not mine to show that it does not.

In this situation Aleksandra is presuming her position has been established and is requiring Mikko to provide evidence to the contrary.

> The fallacy of **shifting the burden of proof** occurs when the arguer defending the position shifts the burden of proof to the challenger.

QUICK QUIZ 7.10

Shifting the Burden of Proof

(A) Identify whether or not one of the persons involved has shifted the burden of proof in the following, and explain how it is done; and

(B) If the burden of proof has not been shifted, explain why the argument might be confused with a shifting the burden of proof fallacy.

1. The advocates for gay marriage keep claiming the legalization of gay marriage is necessary to ensure civil rights. Yet they have not shown what these rights are, nor how legalizing gay marriage ensures them. Before we can continue they must support those claims.

2. You will have to show me why I should not believe in astrology before I will consider giving it up.

3. I do not believe man ever went to the moon. What evidence have you got to show he did?

Answers to the Quick Quizzes are available on the Premium Website at www.criticalthinking2e.nelson.com.

VI. Fallacy of Appeal to Ignorance

Despite its name, this fallacy does not amount to claiming one's opponent is ignorant on the issue. Rather, the fallacy of **appeal to ignorance** uses an opponent's inability to prove something as evidence for the truth of the arguer's own conclusion. There are two versions of this: (i) if you cannot prove it is wrong, it must be right, and (ii) if you cannot prove it is right, it must be wrong. Either way, no evidence has been given for the conclusion. The argument rests entirely on the fact that no evidence has been offered.

Example 1: There must not be any intelligent life in outer space because no one has been able to prove there is.

Example 2: No one has proven to me that the company was not responsible for the Westray coal mine disaster. Until someone does, I stand by my claim that it was the carelessness of the company that led to the deaths of those miners.

These arguments amount to: "There is no evidence, so I will hold as true whatever claim I want to." One basic principle of argumentation is that we accept claims only if argument or evidence is provided to support them.

The fallacy of appeal to ignorance is sometimes confused with the fallacy of shifting the burden of proof. Although both lack evidence for the conclusion, in the former the arguer takes the lack of argument for the opposing side as reason for accepting the arguer's position, while in the latter the arguer is evading giving reasons for a position they are obligated to defend by asking his argument partner to disprove it.

QUICK QUIZ 7.11

Appeal to Ignorance

(A) Identify if an appeal to ignorance is committed in any of the following.

(B) If it has, explain how the criteria for the fallacy apply in this example.

(C) If it has not, explain why you do not consider it to be a fallacy of appeal to ignorance.

1. You haven't shown me that abortion is wrong, so it must be okay.
2. You need to show me that passive euthanasia is wrong. So far, I haven't seen an argument against it.
3. Nessie [the Loch Ness monster] must exist. No one has been able to show she doesn't.

Answers to the Quick Quizzes are available on the Premium Website at www.criticalthinking2e.nelson.com.

VII. Fallacy of Self-Evident Truth

The fallacy of **self-evident truth** involves the arguer presenting a contentious position in need of defence as being self-evident and not in need of defence. In effect, the arguer assumes that the position is so obvious and the reasons so well-known that it does not require reasons.

> Example 1: Women should not be in decision-making positions. Isn't it obvious they are more emotional than men? And since women are more emotional, they are likely to make decisions based on emotions rather than reasons.

In this case, a contentious claim is presented as obvious and not in need of defence. The arguer assumes that it is obvious women are more emotional than men, and no reasons are given. The arguer then uses this to conclude that women should not be in decision-making positions. The self-evident truth fallacy violates the argument principle and the reason principle.

Terms such as the following *may* signal an appeal to self-evident truth:

> It is self-evident that . . .
> It is obvious to everyone that . . .
> No one can deny that . . .

The implication is that anyone who fails to see the statement's self-evident nature is deficient in some way. It is only when these terms are used as substitutes for arguments that they become a fallacy.

However, we must be careful, because the terms above can also be legitimate inference indicators that may simply signal a conclusion of an argument. Contrast the previous argument with the following:

> Example 2: Women go through far more hormonal swings than men do. They menstruate once a month, at which time their hormones vary widely. They go through menopause, during which their hormones vary widely. Men do not suffer from such variations in their hormone levels. It is obvious that women are therefore more emotional than men.

The phrase "it is obvious that" is used in this context as an inference indicator because reasons have been given for the claim that follows. Since reasons have been given it is not an appeal to self-evident truth. The argument, however, is not cogent.

The terms may also be used to summarize what is considered accepted within a given realm of discourse. When an economics professor says "it is obvious that classical economics has serious deficiencies," she is summarizing the state of knowledge about classical economic theory. If there is doubt about her claim, we could challenge her and she could provide the relevant reasoning. In this situation, no fallacy has been committed. Rather, "it is obvious" is being used to indicate that she is summarizing the consensus within a field. The fallacy occurs when the claim being made is contentious, no evidence is offered to support it, and the proponent assumes or asserts that the claim is so well-known and accepted or so self-evident as not to need defence.

VIII. Fallacy of Loaded Presupposition

A presupposition is a claim that logically is prior to a claim that is being asserted. The claim that someone could not come to your party because they had to visit an aunt in hospital presupposes they have an aunt and she is in hospital. (For more on presuppositions see Module 6.)

The **_fallacy of loaded presupposition_** (also called *fallacy of many questions, fallacy of loaded questions,* and *fallacy of complex questions*) involves making a claim or asking a question that has a contentious presupposition buried in it and not independently defending the presupposition. It often occurs when someone presents several issues together and assumes an answer to one implies an answer to another without adequately defending the initial assumption. In effect, this presents a false starting point in the argumentation. An arguer can think he or she is addressing one question or assessing one claim, assuming a prior one has been answered when it has not been. This fallacy consists of presenting a claim with a highly doubtful, false, or misleading presupposition. It is often committed by asking a question with one or more debatable assumptions.

> Example 1: Why is it that children of divorced parents are less emotionally stable than children raised in unbroken homes?

This complex question presupposes a questionable claim: children from divorced homes are emotionally less stable than children from intact homes. The rush to answer the stated question may commit us to a false presupposition.

Often this rule is violated by hidden presuppositions that are not explicitly stated and defended. Consider the following:

> Example 2: The scandalous Liberal Goods and Services Tax needs to be rejected if the country is to regain its economic health.

This claim asserts not only that the Liberals introduced the tax, but that it was scandalous. Normally, such adjectives are not defended. The claim also presupposes that the country had economic health (whatever that means) before the Liberals introduced the tax.

The **fallacy of loaded presupposition** involves making a claim or asking a question that has a contentious presupposition buried in it and not independently defending the presupposition.

Notice that the fallacy of presupposition does not have to occur in the argument as a whole. Each of our examples has illustrated the use of the fallacy in individual claims. Accepting the claim requires accepting the presupposition within it.

QUICK QUIZ 7.13

Loaded Presupposition

(A) Identify which of the following arguments are fallacies of loaded presupposition.
(B) For those that are, explain how the criteria for this fallacy apply in the example; and
(C) For those that are not, explain why you do not consider it to be a fallacy of loaded presupposition.

1. We cannot accept the fiscally unsound and morally bankrupt policies of the opposition. They would only lead us down a path we should not take.
2. The objectionable notion that intelligence is genetically determined is one of the central tenets of sociobiology.
3. When did you stop beating your wife?

Answers to the Quick Quizzes are available on the Premium Website at www.criticalthinking2e.nelson.com.

IX. Fallacy of Begging the Question (Circular Argument)

The fallacy of ***begging the question (or circular argument)*** occurs when one assumes what he or she has set out to prove. Typically, an arguer proves a conclusion by giving reasons; however, in presenting an argument involving the fallacy of begging the question, the arguer takes as an undefended reason the conclusion he or she originally intended to prove. This is sometimes called "circular reasoning" because the arguer starts and ends with the same basic claim. When trying to prove a given claim, he or she offers as a reason for the claim some variant of it, and by doing so in effect offers no independent reason for the conclusion.

> Example: All claims of the Bible are true because they are the words of God Himself. We know the Bible represents the word of God because its writers were divinely inspired. The Bible makes it clear that the Biblical writers wrote "at direction" and the truth of Biblical statements is beyond doubt.

Paraphrasing this makes the circularity of the argument clear. The claim is little more than "the Bible is true because it is true." But what the arguer has to show is that the Bible is true.

There are several variants of this:

• The ***logical equivalence (or definitional) form of begging the question*** occurs when the reasons and conclusion say the same thing but in different words.

The fallacy of **begging the question (or circular argument)** occurs when one assumes what he or she has set out to prove.

The **logical equivalence (or definitional) form of begging the question** occurs when the reasons and conclusion say the same thing but in different words.

Example 1:   Socialism is wrong because it is government control of the means of production.

"Government control of the means of production" is a definition of socialism, not a reason against it. No reason has been given to show that there is something wrong with government control of the means of production. The logical equivalence form of begging the question may, as it does in this case, involve substituting a definition for a concept, as though one is giving a reason.

Example 2:   A: Pornography degrades women.
               B: Why do you say that?
               C: Because I define pornography as anything that degrades women.

The definition that pornography degrades women is used to support the (presumably empirical) claim that pornography degrades women. The claim "pornography degrades women" has been made true by definition. Yet that is what needs to be established.

- The **interdependence form of begging the question** occurs when the reasons are acceptable only if we have already accepted the conclusion or some important aspect of the conclusion.

> The
> **interdependence form of begging the question** occurs when the reasons are acceptable only if we have already accepted the conclusion or some important aspect of the conclusion.

Example:
Customer: "You can be assured of any money you lend to me will be repaid because I am a trustworthy person."
Bank manager: "How can I be assured of that?"
Customer: "Well, Frank Lucci will vouch for me."
Bank manager: "How do I know he is to be trusted?"
Customer: "That's easy. I will vouch for him."

In this case, the customer's trustworthiness is vouched for by Mr. Lucci, and Mr. Lucci's trustworthiness is vouched for by the customer. In order to accept the conclusion, we must accept the claim offered as a reason, but that requires accepting the conclusion. The claims depend mutually on one another for support. No independent support has been given.

QUICK QUIZ 7.14

Begging the Question

(A) Identify which of the following arguments are fallacies of begging the question;
(B) For those that are, explain how the criteria for this fallacy apply in this example; and
(C) For those that are not, explain why you do not consider it to be a fallacy of begging the question.

1. Euthanasia is wrong because it involves helping someone to end his or her life.
2. Women are less rational than men because they can't reason as well as men.
3. Democracy is a form of government in which the leaders are elected and represent the will of the people. Using that definition, the government of

Vulcan is not a democracy. The so-called elections are shams, and the leaders represent only the will of the power brokers.

Answers to the Quick Quizzes are available on the Premium Website at www.criticalthinking2e.nelson.com.

X. Fallacy of Equivocation

The *fallacy of equivocation* is committed when an arguer uses one word or phrase that has two different meanings, and different meanings are used in the argument. This shift of meaning affects the reasoning. The fallacy of equivocation usually occurs when a word used to mean one thing in a reason is used to mean something different in another reason or in the conclusion. The shift in meaning can make the claims appear to be true and the argument sound. However, when the word is paraphrased or the difference in meaning identified, it becomes clear that the conclusion does not follow from the reasons. In effect, an arguer asserts one claim with a given word in the reason and a different claim with the same word in the conclusion.

> Example: I don't see any reason for us to listen to the Superintendent of schools on the textbook issue. We need to hear from someone who has authority in the field of education. Our Superintendent doesn't have enough authority to keep students or teachers in line. Nobody respects her orders.

This example equivocates between "authority" meaning an expert in a particular discipline and "authority" meaning the power to influence or control the behaviour of others. If we paraphrase this portion of the argument we get the following:

1. The Superintendent does not have the power to influence the students' or teachers' behaviour.
2. We should listen only to someone who is an expert on the textbook issue.

∴ 3. We should not listen to the superintendent of schools about the textbook issue.

With this paraphrase, it is clear that the reasons are talking about two different things and do not support the conclusion. Reasons 1 and 2 use the word "authority" in two different ways, and neither is sufficient to establish the conclusion.

The **fallacy of equivocation** is committed when an arguer uses one word or phrase that has two different meanings, and different meanings are used in the argument.

QUICK QUIZ 7.15

Equivocation

(A) Identify which of the following arguments are fallacies of equivocation;
(B) For those that are, explain how the criteria for this fallacy apply in the example; and
(C) For those that are not, explain why you do not consider it to be a fallacy of equivocation.

(continued)

1. Men and women are clearly not equal. They differ in various attributes. Men are stronger; women more verbal. So how can one say that we ought to treat them equally?
2. Active euthanasia is morally justified. When a doctor administers a lethal injection, he or she is not killing the patient. Rather, the disease is killing the patient. If a person is responsible only when he or she actually kills someone, then the doctor is not responsible for the death. The disease is.
3. We shouldn't teach critical reasoning because critical reasoning teaches people to argue and arguments create conflict and dissent between people.

Answers to the Quick Quizzes are available on the Premium Website at www.criticalthinking2e.nelson.com.

XI. Red Herring Fallacy

The **red herring fallacy** involves introducing an irrelevant issue into an argument to confuse or sidetrack discussion of the issue. The image is taken from fox hunting, where a red (salted and cured) herring (a smelly fish) used to train hounds, would be dragged across a trail to throw the dogs off a scent. In the case of argumentation, a red herring is the introduction of information that is seemingly related to the topic at hand, but is in fact irrelevant and used simply to distract the listener from the issue.

Example: My opponent has claimed I have stolen from the public purse and enriched myself. Ladies and gentlemen, I have introduced and passed Bills benefitting this community, opposed unscrupulous developers and those who would destroy family values, and opposed video parlour games.

Instead of addressing the issue of whether the speaker has stolen from the public purse, the argument points to his or her contributions about which everyone can probably agree. By focusing on this positive aspect, the speaker diverts attention from the original charge. A red herring can be used both in response to a challenge and to defend a position.

QUICK QUIZ 7.16

Red Herring

(A) Identify which of the following arguments are red herring fallacies;
(B) For those that are, explain how the criteria for this fallacy apply in the example;
(C) For those that are not, explain why you do not consider it to be a red herring fallacy.

1. Eugenics is a failed science. After all, it was used by the Nazis as a justification to eliminate over six million people (such as, Jews, gypsies, homosexuals, and the mentally challenged).

2. In response to the charge that she has mismanaged the union, been ineffectual as Chair, played partisan politics, and been ineffectual in negotiations, Chandra Johnson argues that the charges should be dismissed because they are merely an attempt to discredit her because she is a woman and the members obviously don't believe a woman should run a union.

3. My opponent has argued that we should implement a national child-care program that would ensure that all parents have access to universal child care for all children up to the age of six. While there are good reasons for a program like this, and my opponent has advanced them, there is one critical and overwhelming objection - the cost. We, as a society, simply do not have the resources to fund this project and, therefore, we can't introduce such a program.

Answers to the Quick Quizzes are available on the Premium Website at www.criticalthinking2e.nelson.com.

XII. Straw Person

The ***straw person*** (originally "straw man") ***fallacy*** occurs when a simpler or distorted argument is attacked instead of a stronger one. *Straw person* refers to a dummy (literally, a straw person) that can be attacked or burned in effigy. The dummy is an oversimplified representation and can be attacked easily without fighting back. In argument it refers to attacking an oversimplified version of an argument or position instead of the more complex and well defended original. By substituting a weak or distorted argument or position for a stronger one the arguer can easily challenge the weaker one. This fallacy can be committed by caricaturizing a position or argument, by misrepresenting an argument, by distorting it in subtle or not so subtle ways, or by picking the weaker or weakest of the arguments for a position when there are stronger ones available.

> The **straw person** (originally "straw man") **fallacy** occurs when a simpler or distorted argument is attacked instead of a stronger one.

> Example: In a tract called "Six Bridges No Evolutionists Can Cross," a fundamentalist preacher attempts to refute the theory of evolution. He argues that Darwin cannot explain individual variation (such as, why some people have blue eyes and others have brown ones). He concludes, therefore, there is no reason to believe evolution took place.

Although it is true that Darwin could not explain individual variation (because he had an inadequate theory of heredity, which he acknowledged), modern evolutionary biology *can* explain the variations in traits. Attacking Darwin's original theory is not a refutation of evolutionary theory as it now stands, but only a challenge to an early stage of the theory. Scientific theories develop over time. As our knowledge advances we often discover earlier versions of a theory are false. However, later versions usually address and correct those weaknesses. More recent arguments and statements in evolutionary theory are stronger and not subject to this same criticism.

Detecting this fallacy requires knowing the original claim and being able to show how it has been modified or distorted in the discussion. A variety of moves can produce a straw person fallacy, including simplification of a claim, exaggeration of a claim, generalization beyond what is reasonable, omission of nuances and qualifications, changing the meanings of terms, and making a relative claim absolute.[1]

Original claim: Mary was upset at her mother's funeral.
Simplification: Mary is emotional.

In the above case, the simplification omits the qualifications and context of the funeral. The conclusion suggests Mary is often, usually, or always emotional, which is not supported by the context.

Original claim: Mary gets emotional when she thinks about her mother's death.
Exaggeration: Mary is always emotional.

In the exaggeration above, the exaggeration ignores the context and qualifications in the original claim.

Original claim: Some men are insensitive.
Generalization: All men are insensitive.

In the generalization above, the claim changes from one that is limited in scope to one that is not.

Original claim: If you want to graduate with honours and stand a good chance of getting into graduate school you will have to get almost all "A"s.
Omission of nuances: My advisor told me I need all "A"s to graduate.

In this example, the second claim changes the scope and ignores the difference between graduating and needing almost all A's to get into graduate school, and substitutes "to graduate."

Original claim: Voluntary passive euthanasia is allowed by the Canadian Medical Association's Code of Ethics.
Changing the meaning of terms: The Canadian Medical Association encourages euthanasia.

Usually this is not done quite so obviously. In this example, two terms have been changed: "allowed" to "encourages" and "voluntary passive euthanasia" to the unqualified "euthanasia."

Original claim: The Canadian Medical Association allows voluntary passive euthanasia under certain exceptional circumstances.
Making a qualified claim absolute: The Canadian Medical Association allows euthanasia.

The final example omits the qualifications *voluntary passive euthanasia* and *under certain exceptional circumstances* thereby turning a limited claim into an absolute one. Whenever a claim seems a bit too easy to challenge and involves some kind of overly general claim or seems a bit ludicrous, it is worth checking the original source to see if a straw person fallacy has been used.

Some straw person fallacies occur intentionally: the original position is deliberately distorted. However, many are the result of sloppy scholarship, poor listening skills, inattention to the position of the other, or an attempt to develop a strong challenge to a strong position.

---

1 van Eemeren, Frans H., and Rob Grootendorst. *Argumentation, Communication and Fallacies: A Pragma-Dialectical Perspective.* Hillsdale, N.J.: L. Erlbaum, 1994.

XIII. Genetic Fallacy

The *genetic fallacy* attempts to show that a claim or idea is false or should be discounted because of its origins. Because the source of the idea is tainted or disreputable, the idea is deemed to be such also. Various kinds of origins can potentially discount an idea (such as historical or ideological associations, and psychological needs and motivations). This is treated as a fallacy of irrelevance, rather than one of insufficiency, because the origins of an idea or position or claim are irrelevant to the truth of the claim.

> The **genetic fallacy** attempts to show a claim or idea is false or should be discounted because of its origins.

> Example 1: Astrology is patently false; after all, it originated in the superstitious mumbo-jumbo of ancient Greek religion, something no one believes now.

In the above argument, astrology is being dismissed because of its origins in "superstition." That an idea may have once been part of folk knowledge or superstition does not prove that there is no evidence for it now. A variant of this fallacy is the attempt to justify a belief or practice because of its origins.

> Example 2: Astrology is true. It originated with the ancient Babylonians and has existed for centuries.

Genetic Fallacy and Provenance

A genetic fallacy occurs when a person dismisses a position or argument based on the origins of the position or argument. In some conditions, an appeal to the origins of a position or story may be relevant in assessing the account, and the fallacy is not committed.

The term *provenance* literally means origins or source. When used in the art world, it means tracking the piece of art back to the artist who made it and establishing its authenticity. A failed or questionable provenance indicates that we cannot establish the connection between the work of art and the purported artist. We can also examine the provenance of a story or position.

The story of Atlantis as a lost continent is widely known. Various authors have written books claiming that Atlantis existed. However, by tracing the provenance of the story, we discover there is a solitary source of the story: the philosopher Plato. Not only was Plato writing about something that allegedly happened 10,000 years before he lived, he also introduced the story as a myth to make a philosophical point. In this case, identifying the provenance of the story can cast doubt on its truth, and challenging the provenance is not a genetic fallacy.

Another example is the story of flying saucer crashes at Roswell, New Mexico, in 1947. Tracing the story's provenance we discover that until 1980 there was no story of crashed saucers or recovered alien bodies and that the story was promulgated by the same individual who manufactured the mystery of the Bermuda Triangle. While this looks like a form of genetic fallacy, in that we are discrediting a story or argument based on its origins, in this particular case it is not. The provenance of the story is directly relevant to establishing the truth of the claims of flying saucer crashes at Roswell.

QUICK QUIZ 7.18

Genetic Fallacy

(A) Identify which of the following arguments are genetic fallacies;
(B) For those that are, explain how the criteria for this fallacy apply in the example; and
(C) For those that are not, explain why you do not consider it to be a genetic fallacy.

1. Sergei: "As a rule of thumb, you can convert miles to kilometres by multiplying miles by 1.6."
   Pravar: "Don't you know that you shouldn't say 'rule of thumb?' It's a sexist term. It refers to a nineteenth-century English law that says a man can beat his wife as long as he uses a stick no bigger than the diameter of his thumb. By using it, you are condoning wife abuse."

2. Liberalism as a political philosophy and guide for social policy is a nineteenth-century idea. How could it possibly provide guidance in the twenty-first century?

3. We have to rethink Liberalism. It was founded in the nineteenth century as a guideline for social reform. However, many of the assumptions on which it was based no longer stand.

Answers to the Quick Quizzes are available on the Premium Website at www.criticalthinking2e.nelson.com.

7.5 Fallacies of Insufficient Reason

The fallacies included in this section generally have reasons that are or could be relevant under some conditions. However, as presented in a given argument, the reasons given are insufficient to establish the conclusion. These fallacies violate various dimensions of the argumentation principle and the basic considerations for arguments laid out in previous modules. They include: appeal to common practice, belief or popularity, faulty appeal to authority, hasty generalization, false cause, slippery slope, false dichotomy, and faulty analogy. The criteria for constructing good causal arguments, generalizations, analogies, and legitimate appeals to authority have are laid out in Module 5. The fallacious versions of those arguments violate the criteria for the good versions of those arguments.

XIV. Fallacy of Common Practice/Popularity

The *fallacy of appeal to popularity, common belief,* or *common practice* rests on making a claim that something is true and should be accepted because it is widely believed, accepted, or done. This fallacy has a number of variants. While we could distinguish the many variants, and give different names and criteria for each one, this would only make our task more difficult. We will use one name and identify several of the variants. A number of different kinds of appeals are included under this label. We could separate them as different fallacies or focus on the commonalities. What unites the various versions is that the attempt at justification is made through an appeal to common practice or the popularity of a belief, rather than through an attempt to establish that it is true for particular reasons.

> The **fallacy of appeal to popularity, common belief,** or **common practice** rests on making the claim something is true and should be accepted because it is widely believed, accepted, or done.

TABLE 7.2 Variations of the Fallacy of Appeal to Popularity

Variant	Criteria	Example
Appeal to popularity.	If something is popular it must be acceptable or true.	Everyone accepts that business is cutthroat, so it must be acceptable.
Inverse of appeal to popularity.	If something is not popular or accepted it must be false.	No one agrees polygamy is acceptable, so it must not be.
Appeal to tradition.	Since we have always done something in a given way, we must continue to do so, or it must be true.	Music has always been part of the curriculum. How can the government even think of removing it for fiscal reasons?
Appeal to common belief.	If something is commonly or widely believed, it must be true.	Everyone knows the world is flat, Columbus, so I would not recommend sailing too far from land.
Appeal to common practice.	If something is commonly done, it must be justified.	Everyone uses formal logic in teaching critical thinking, so it must be the best way for students to learn critical thinking.

(continued)

TABLE 7.2 Continued

Variant	Criteria	Example
Appeal to group membership (or patriotism).	If you are a member of a given group, then you must believe a certain set of ideas.	If you are a Muslim, you must support the rights of the Palestinians.
Appeal to novelty or change.	If something is new or different, it is better; conversely if something is not recent or current, it must be worse.	That idea cannot be right because a nineteenth century author came up with it. Mill's ideas on liberty are mid-Victorian and must be wrong. Aristotle lived 2500 years ago; how could he have anything valuable to say about ethics?
Appeal to dislike of eccentric, unusual, or uncommon habits, beliefs, lifestyles, clothes, etc.	If something is unusual, it must be false or bad.	So few people practice religion x; so, it cannot have anything to say about spirituality.
Appeal to racial, religious, or social prejudices.	These appeals to common preconceptions and ideas are made on the assumption that others share them and they do not have to be argued.	All true Canadians support x. All Muslims believe y. We know homosexuals are z.

Some of these may raise legitimate issues and concerns. Mill's arguments on liberty were written in the mid-nineteenth century, and he made some questionable claims based on his historical-cultural situation. However, much of his argument on liberty and freedom of expression does apply today. Simply to dismiss his ideas as "outdated" because they were written 150 years ago ignores those elements of his writing that may still have currency today. It is legitimate to point out that a given text or set of arguments may have been written in a different time and place for different circumstances, but it is not legitimate to dismiss all of the text and arguments on these grounds without a careful examination and argument.

The contraries of these variants (that since everyone believes or does *x*, *x* must be wrong or bad) are also included in the generic fallacy of appeal to common practice. They are based on the contrarian notion that whatever the majority believes must somehow be wrong. Whereas the typical version of this fallacy involves appealing to popular sentiment, to common practice, to the way things have always been done, the contraries involve the dismissal of tradition and common belief as wrong simply because they are traditional or common.

Example 1: Immanuel Kant wrote his philosophy in the eighteenth century; therefore, his ideas are dated and wrong. [Although simplified for illustration, this is commonly encountered in philosophy courses.]

Example 2:   Although Thomas Aquinas's views on marriage may have been correct for his time, they are dated and do not fit the twenty-first century.

The only reason given for Aquinas's or Kant's ideas being wrong is that they are from a different time and place. This is a contrary version of the appeal to common belief. Nothing specifically is argued about why their ideas do not apply, other than that they were not developed today. If we substitute "Newton's law of gravity" for "Aquinas's views on marriage" we can see the problems with such an argument. We do not automatically dismiss Newton's law of gravity because it is "dated and does not fit the twenty-first century." While there are scientific challenges to Newton's theory, a challenge and dismissal of Newton's laws requires that we examine his actual ideas and arguments, not when they were written. The same holds true for the ideas of Kant and Aquinas.

Under some conditions, some of these appeals may provide grounds for re-examining a given set of claims or arguments. For example, the fact that Aristotle wrote his ethics for an elite class and condoned slavery may lead us to examine to what extent his ethics is committed to these values and the extent to which they are separable. However, our grounds for challenging his ideas would be, not that they are from another time and place, but that they commit him to things that are false or unethical. Charles Darwin's views about women and sex were shaped by his mid-Victorian background. A caution that his views should be more carefully examined because of this would be legitimate, but it should not be grounds for dismissing the theory of evolution or natural selection because they were not written in the twenty-first century. Furthermore, the fact that the majority of people in a given society do not accept Darwin or evolutionary theory does not show it is false. That requires argument and evidence, which an appeal to common belief short-circuits.

QUICK QUIZ 7.19

Common Practice/Popularity

(A) Identify which of the following arguments are appeals to common practice or popularity;

(B) For those that are, explain how the criteria for this fallacy apply in this example; and

(C) For those that are not, explain why you do not consider it to be a fallacy of appeal to common practice or popularity.

1. You're an essentialist? No one believes in essentialism anymore.
2. The Canadian legal system is based on the core values of tolerance, equality, respect, and social justice. This proposal violates all of these and should be rejected.
3. I don't see how you can argue that pornography is beneficial. Society disagrees and rightly bans it.

Answers to the Quick Quizzes are available on the Premium Website at www.criticalthinking2e.nelson.com.

XV. Faulty Appeal to Authority

Some appeals to authority are quite legitimate (Module 5, Section 5.5, identifies the conditions for a legitimate appeal to authority). We are not and cannot be experts in everything. We need to appeal to authorities to substantiate some of our claims. Appeals to authority are justified when:

1. There is an identifiable field of knowledge;
2. The person appealed to is an authority in that field;
3. The authority's knowledge of the field is current;
4. There is general consensus within that field on the topic under discussion;
5. The authority is clearly identified; and
6. The authority's testimony does not put the authority in an obvious conflict of interest.

> A fallacy of faulty appeal to authority occurs when there has been a significant breach of one or more of the conditions for a legitimate appeal to authority.

A *fallacy of faulty appeal to authority* occurs when there has been a significant breach of one or more of these conditions for a legitimate appeal to authority, such as when there is no field of knowledge, the person is not an expert or is not current, there is no consensus in the field, the expert is not identified, or the expert is in an obvious conflict of interest.

These criteria are arranged in order of importance. If there is no field of knowledge, there can be no appeal to authority. Not identifying the authority is a lesser charge that could be corrected. When one or more of these conditions are not met, the appeal is a faulty appeal to authority.

> Example 1: Linus Pauling, a double Nobel prize-winning chemist, has argued that mega-doses of vitamin C will increase a person's life span. Surely, if such a noted scientist claims this is true, it must be true.

Linus Pauling is indeed a double Nobel laureate, but he is not an authority in the field of medicine and vitamin C. This violates condition 2; he is not an authority in the field in question.

> Example 2: J. Philippe Rushton, a noted Canadian psychologist, argued that head size and I.Q. are strongly correlated, and black people have smaller head sizes than white people.

The arguer fails to note that the claim about the relationship between head size and I.Q. has been substantially disproved by many scientists for over 100 years. This appeal violates condition 4 because this statement is not based on a consensus in the field. Unfortunately, as in this case, we are not always able to determine whether some of the conditions are met without further investigation.

> Example 3: Numerous scientists critical of the research on global warming have questioned whether global warming is occurring, and whether or not it is caused by human actions. So, until we get full consensus, we should be wary of instituting any policies on carbon emissions.

This argument seems to raise concerns about item 4 because there is not a consensus in the field; that is, it seems to contend that there is a lack of consensus in the field on the issue. However, the claim that there is a lack of consensus is a false charge. The vast majority of researchers on global warming agree that it is occurring and is caused by human agency. The problem here is whether there is a legitimate or manufactured lack of consensus. Those charging no consensus are a small number of scientists, and they are not experts in the field of global warming. Furthermore, one discovers the doubters have also been involved in arguing that smoking does not cause cancer ("there is no consensus"), that the ozone layer was not being harmed ("there is no consensus"), and a number of other politically sensitive issues. Further investigation reveals these same researchers have also been consultants for the tobacco industry and the petroleum industry, both of whose practices might be curtailed by clean air laws, and so on. In other words, they fail to meet the basic criteria for being experts. Part of the problem with citing experts and counter-experts is that it can be difficult for the layperson to know which experts to believe and when the charge of lack of consensus is legitimate and when it is a political stratagem to obscure and hinder political action. This does not mean appealing to experts is always or often illegitimate, but it does mean we often need to go beyond the claim "the experts say" or "the experts disagree."

Although ideally all of the conditions should be met for the appeal to authority to be legitimate, in practice, usually some of the conditions are not explicitly stated. Whether the absence of a condition within a passage indicates a faulty appeal or simply a concise presentation of a case is something we have to judge in context. For example, rarely is it stated that a purported expert does not have a conflict of interest. It is not usual for an expert's credentials to be explicitly identified and defended. The challenge of determining such criteria is often left to those questioning the appeal. Sometimes the expert is not identified. Depending on the context, this can be a minor or serious problem. If the expert is not identified in an academic paper, it is a serious problem. If the expert is not identified in a popular newspaper article, it may be grounds for withholding judgment until we find out who it is, but it is likely not grounds for a charge of fallacy, just sloppy writing.

QUICK QUIZ 7.20

Faulty Appeal to Authority

(A) Identify which of the following arguments are faulty appeals to authority;

(B) For those that are, explain how the criteria for this fallacy apply in the example; and

(C) For those that are not, portray the argument and explain why you do not consider it to be a fallacy of faulty appeal to authority.

1. Don Cherry, a noted hockey announcer, appears as a spokesperson for a leading auto insurance company, claiming that it has the lowest rates in the industry.

2. My art history professor says that the *Mona Lisa* is the most beautiful painting in the Western world. I guess it must be.

3. A: There are only about 30,000 genes in the human genome.
   B: How do you know that?
   A: I read a study that claimed that.

Answers to the Quick Quizzes are available on the Premium Website at www.criticalthinking2e.nelson.com.

XVI. Hasty Generalization

The **fallacy of hasty generalization** is committed when an arguer violates the criteria for a good generalization.

The **fallacy of hasty generalization** is committed when an arguer violates the criteria for a good generalization, usually by using a small or unrepresentative (biased) sample or by generalizing beyond the limits of the population. (The criteria for a good generalization were outlined in Module 5, Section 5.4.)

> Example: The notorious serial sex killer Paul Bernardo viewed pornography. So did Ted Bundy, another notorious serial sex killer. This shows all serial sex killers view pornography.

In this example, the arguer generalizes by stating that since Paul Bernardo and Ted Bundy both viewed pornography, all serial sex killers view pornography. (Do not confuse a hasty generalization with a false cause, in which the inference would be that pornography is the reason the individuals became serial sex killers. That is a different kind of argument.) The arguer is assigning to all cases the attributes of two probably unrepresentative cases. A hasty generalization occurs when the data insufficiently support the conclusion drawn from that data.

QUICK QUIZ 7.21

Hasty Generalization

(A) Identify which of the following arguments are hasty generalizations;
(B) For those that are, explain how the criteria for this fallacy apply in the example; and
(C) For those that are not, explain why you do not consider it to be a fallacy of hasty generalization.

1. Book prices sure have gone up. I bought my texts for the fall, and they were double the cost of last year's.
2. I have asked six of the ten support staff what they would like for lunch. They all agreed on the salmon. Since everyone wants it, we should order salmon for everyone.
3. People who support euthanasia also support abortion. Liz supports euthanasia, so she must support abortion.

Answers to the Quick Quizzes are available on the Premium Website at www.criticalthinking2e.nelson.com.

XVII. Fallacy of False Cause

The **fallacy of false cause** is committed when the arguer fails to establish all of the conditions for a causal connection.

The **fallacy of false cause** is committed when the arguer fails to establish all of the conditions for a causal connection. The most common kind of false cause argument involves mistaking a correlation or spatial or temporal connection for a cause. (Module 5, Section 5.4, identifies the criteria for a good causal inference.)

Some advocates of capital punishment argue that since capital punishment was abolished the crime rate has been increasing. The argument can be formulated as follows:

Example: Ever since capital punishment was abolished the crime rate has been increasing. The abolishment of capital punishment is the reason there is more crime.

This argument has two errors. The first is that a purported correlation has been confused with a causal relationship. Two things are said to have occurred around the same time; therefore, one must have caused the other. However, many factors can affect the crime rate. Capital punishment is only one. Demographers know crime rates fluctuate systematically with the number of unattached (unmarried or not bound by strong family ties) and underemployed males in the population. As their numbers vary, so too do rates of violent crimes and crimes against property. If the percentage of unattached and underemployed males has been on the rise in the same time period, that may account for the increase in crime. The second problem is that the stated correlation does not exist. The murder rate in Canada in 1976, when capital punishment was abolished was 3.03 per 100,000; from 1998 to 2004, it was 1.82. In this case, the false cause fallacy rests on a fictitious correlation.

A common strategy for challenging a possible false cause is to show that there is another possible cause for the result. This does not prove that the alternative is the cause, only that another possible, reasonable cause could explain the result, and thus the offered cause has not been established.

QUICK QUIZ 7.22

False Cause

(A) Identify which of the following arguments are fallacies of false cause;

(B) For those that are, explain how the criteria for this fallacy apply in the example; and

(C) For those that are not, explain why you do not consider it to be a fallacy of false cause.

1. A recent government study has found that smoking and education are inversely related. The lower a person's education, the more likely he or she is to smoke, and the more difficulty that person has in quitting smoking. Obviously, being less educated causes people to smoke. The solution to getting people to stop smoking, therefore, is to develop a more educated populace.

2. When the City repaved the street in front of my house on Monday, severe vibrations shook my house. Tuesday it rained, and the foundation of my house started leaking. The vibrations obviously cracked the foundation in my basement. The City should be held responsible for damaging the foundation of my house.

3. Several South Korean scientists have announced that they have found a prevention for stomach cancer. They fed kim chi (pickled cabbage) to a test group of subjects and compared their rates of stomach cancer with those of people who did not eat kim chi. Those fed the kim chi had a 25% lower rate of stomach cancer than those who did not eat the cabbage. The scientists have concluded that kim chi has an inhibiting effect on the development of stomach cancer.

Answers to the Quick Quizzes are available on the Premium Website at www.criticalthinking2e.nelson.com.

XVIII. The Slippery Slope Fallacy

The *slippery slope fallacy* occurs when the arguer suggests that one action will set off a sequence of others that will lead to an inevitable end result, which is usually seen as undesirable. This fallacy rests on the idea that if you take the first step, you are committed to a "slippery slope" of unspecified intermediate steps and a far-off, harmful outcome. While pointing out the long-term effects of an act can be a legitimate argument strategy, slippery slope is a fallacy because the consequences are distant, questionable, suggested to be inevitable, and usually unconnected to the first step.

> Example 1: Professor to class: "I do not permit questions in my class because if I allow one student to ask a question then everyone starts asking questions and before you know it there is not enough time for my lecture."

In this example, the professor jumps from the allowing of one question to the result that everyone will ask questions, and from there to the result that time will run out. It is not certain that allowing one question will lead to a barrage of questions. Furthermore, the instructor is not helpless to say "no" if there are too many questions. The causal connection is neither inevitable nor obvious.

While most slippery slope fallacies involve negative consequences, there is a positive version of the slippery slope fallacy. In this version the positive first step leads to positive consequences.

> Example 2: *Preacher at door to resident:* All you need to do is accept the Lord into your heart and let Him guide you and all of your worries will be over. You will find happiness and prosperity.

In this version of the argument, the act of accepting the Lord into one's heart will lead up that slippery slope to happiness and prosperity.

QUICK QUIZ 7.23

Slippery Slope

(A) Identify the slippery slope fallacies in the following arguments;
(B) For those that are, explain how the criteria for this fallacy apply in this example; and
(C) For those that are not, portray the argument and explain why you do not consider it to be a fallacy of slippery slope.

1. We can't allow abortion. Once we start killing innocent babies in the womb, there is nothing to stop us from killing the elderly, the disabled, or anyone deemed undesirable. We become no better than the Nazis with their gas chambers!

2. I can't take that first drink. I'm an alcoholic. I know that if I have one drink, I will be in the gutter tomorrow. I can't stop myself.

3. *Argument given in response to a proposal to fund a school exclusively for black students who are at special risk of dropping out of the school system:* We can't fund schools exclusively for black students. If we do, then every ethnic and religious group will want its own school, and that will be the end of public education. And we don't want that to happen.

Answers to the Quick Quizzes are available on the Premium Website at www.criticalthinking2e.nelson.com.

XIX. False Dichotomy

The fallacy of *false dichotomy* (also called *false dilemma* or *false alternative*) occurs when the arguer presents only two alternatives, as though they exhaust the range of possibilities and there are no other alternatives, and then forces a choice between the two.

> Example: A person has to choose between the Bible and evolution. There is no need of salvation if man never fell. (TV televangelist)

The arguer is presenting the alternatives as mutually exclusive and forcing a choice between them, when they are not mutually exclusive options. In this situation one could choose both or neither.

A fallacy is not committed if there are only two legitimate, logical, or practical alternatives. This is called an *exclusive alternative* because a person can choose only one or the other. If a student is faced with two alternatives (such as, studying for an exam or going to a party) and these are the only two practical alternatives, then the choice between staying home to study for the exam or going to the party is a legitimate exclusive alternative. It is also a *practical exclusive alternative* in which, practically speaking, a person cannot do both. A *logical exclusive alternative* is one in which a person cannot logically do both (such as, in the case of either studying for the exam or not). A false dichotomy presents alternatives that are neither practically nor logically exclusive. The basic way to challenge a false dichotomy is to show that there are other viable alternatives.

> The fallacy of **false dichotomy** (also called **false dilemma** or **false alternative**) occurs when the arguer presents only two alternatives, as though they exhaust the range of possibilities and there are no other alternatives, and then forces a choice between the two.

QUICK QUIZ 7.24

False Dichotomy

(A) Identify which of the following arguments are fallacies of false dichotomy;

(B) For those that are, explain how the criteria for this fallacy apply in the example; and

(C) For those that are not, explain why you do not consider it to be a fallacy of false dichotomy.

1. *George Bush in a speech to the American people:* "If you are not supporting us, then you are supporting the terrorists. Anyone who opposes our policy, including the Democratic opposition in Congress, is only helping the terrorists in Iraq."

2. Either we save for a down payment on a house by cutting out all luxuries, or we allow ourselves the luxuries of lattes, new clothes, and vacations, and forgo saving for a house. I, personally, can't forgo the little luxuries of life. So it looks like we won't get the down payment for a house.

3. Either we raise taxes and break an election promise, or we don't raise taxes and keep an election promise. However, we need the additional revenue from taxes. So it looks like we'll have to break an election promise.

Answers to the Quick Quizzes are available on the Premium Website at www.criticalthinking2e.nelson.com.

XX. Faulty Analogy

A fallacy of **faulty analogy** occurs when an arguer draws an inappropriate comparison between two things. (Criteria for analogies are discussed in Module 5, Section 5.5.)

Analogies can be a good way of developing and generating ideas. However, analogical arguments can commit the fallacy of faulty analogy if the stretch is too great between the items being compared, that is, if the properties being compared are superficial or if the stated similarities do not apply. Consider the following:

1. The world is like a machine.
2. The world has many intricate parts that fit together.
3. Machines have inventors.

∴ 4. There must be a supreme being who invented (created) the world.

This argument compares two things:

  i. the world
 ii. a machine

Machines have properties:

  a many intricate parts that fit together
  b creators (inventors)

The world has properties:

  a many intricate parts that fit together

Therefore, the arguer contends the world has the other property of the analogy, *b*.

In a faulty analogy the properties of the first half of the analogy either are superficial (i.e., the *analogues* or items being compared do not have much in common) or do not apply to the second half of the analogy (the world is not a machine). The argument is consequently not sufficient to establish the conclusion.

Analyzing an analogy requires identifying:

1. The two things being compared;
2. The properties characterizing the first analogue;
3. The properties characterizing the second analogue; and
4. The inference from the properties of the first analogue to the properties of the second.

Our natural tendency is to focus on the similarities between the analogues. One way to challenge an analogy is to identify important differences between them and explain why, as a result, the analogy does not work. In the above analogy we might call attention to the fact that we have seen machines designed and constructed. We have no such clear evidence that the world has been similarly designed and constructed. Another challenge would be to show that the world is not a machine, but rather a set of organic and inorganic features that interconnect.

Consider the following argument:

> Example: No one objects to the practice of a physician looking up a difficult case in medical books. Why, then, shouldn't students taking a difficult examination be permitted to use their textbooks?

This can be diagrammed as follows:

1. Students' textbooks are like physicians' medical books.

2. Physicians use their reference books to look up difficult cases.

∴ 3. Students should be allowed to use their textbooks on difficult examinations.

The two analogues are:

i. Students' textbooks; and
ii. Physicians' medical reference texts.

Students' textbooks are being compared to physicians' reference books.

The problem is that the similarity between physicians and students is superficial. The doctor's knowledge has already been tested and certified. The students' have not. The functions of referring to a text are, therefore, different. For this argument to work, the arguer would have to establish that the two functions do not significantly differ. This is a faulty analogy.

Having analyzed the analogy, exposing a faulty one further involves showing:

1. The ways in which the two items are different; and
2. How that difference affects the conclusion being drawn.

QUICK QUIZ 7.25

Faulty Analogy

(A) Identify which of the following arguments are faulty analogies;
(B) For those that are, explain how the criteria for this fallacy apply in the example; and
(C) For those that are not, explain why you do not consider it to be a fallacy of faulty analogy.

1. The State is like a ship. Just as a ship needs a strong captain – one who insists on unyielding obedience – to command it, the State requires a strong leader whom all the citizens must obey.
2. Business is a struggle for survival in which only the most competitive should survive. For this reason, the Government should not provide support to businesses. If businesses cannot survive on their own, they should not be supported by government handouts.
3. Nature is a book open to everyone to read. If we do not understand it, it is simply because we have not read it carefully enough. And like a book, nature requires an author. Its author is God.

Answers to the Quick Quizzes are available on the Premium Website at www.criticalthinking2e.nelson.com.

Lookalikes: Hasty Generalization, False Cause, Slippery Slope

These fallacies are similar in various ways. False cause and slippery slope are both causal fallacies. In the case of false cause, because two claims are associated, we infer that one causes the other, even when no causal connection has been clearly established. Slippery slope, also a form of causal argument, says if a person does *a* then another event, *z*, will inevitably follow. That is: doing *a* causes *z*. Where false cause establishes a causal relationship between two things based on usually one condition (temporal or spatial proximity, correlation), slippery slope claims a cause exists when none has been established. Furthermore, in slippery slope an arguer is not just invoking a cause, but invoking a causal sequence: *a* causes something, which causes something else, which causes *z*. A third difference between the two is that with slippery slope, the causal outcome is usually an undesirable one: taking the first drink causes one to become an alcoholic. The slippery slope is used in an argument to get another person to reject the initial step (or the *a*): do not take that first drink. A false cause does not have these conditions.

Hasty generalization is more commonly confused with false cause than with slippery slope. A hasty generalization draws a general conclusion from an unrepresentative or insufficient sample. On the basis of one corrupt politician, we conclude that all are corrupt. This is often confused with false cause because some people are unclear on the difference between generalizing and attributing cause. To further complicate things, passages can commit both the fallacy of hasty generalization and the fallacy of false cause.

Paradigm Cases

Hasty generalization: You have been late for work twice now. You are always late.

False cause: I went to the show the night before my exam and failed my driver's test the next day. Going to the show caused me to fail the driver's test.

Slippery slope: If you take one drink you will become an alcoholic. Therefore, you should not take the first drink.

QUICK QUIZ 7.26

Lookalikes: Hasty Generalization, False Cause, Slippery Slope

(A) Identify and explain which fallacy is committed in each of the following; and
(B) Explain how each might be confused with one of its lookalikes.

1. *Said in a campaign for Mayor:* "My opponent is opposed to increasing the number of police officers, yet there have been an increased number of crimes, especially crimes involving guns, this year in the city. If we don't put more police on the street, then the streets will degenerate into disorder and chaos with the thugs running everything. We don't want the criminals and thugs running this city. We have to put more police on the street."

2. We have proof that marijuana causes violent behaviour. In a murder trial in Alabama, the prosecution established that the defendant, previously a model young man, had been smoking marijuana. He became inflamed - nay, possessed - by overwhelming lust, and slew a rival for his girlfriend's affections. This is not the only case like this. In New York, several young children were smoking marijuana. They went on a rampage, smashing everything in their apartment. In San Francisco, an arsonist torched several buildings - this, after he became a regular marijuana user.

3. *A newspaper report of a scientific research study:* Psychologists have discovered that most male scientists make their major discoveries in their late twenties and thirties, which is also the period when their sexual interest is at its peak. Therefore, the psychologists concluded, male scientists strive to achieve to attract the attention of women. Scientific inquiry is driven by sexual desire.

Answers to the Quick Quizzes are available on the Premium Website at www.criticalthinking2e.nelson.com.

Module Summary

- Fallacies are patterns of false appeals and arguments that often are mistaken for good arguments.
- Fallacies violate one or more of the basic principles for a good argument or the constitutive rules of argumentation.
- Fallacies have various forms.
- Fallacies can be neutralized by identifying the pattern of reasoning for the argument, showing that the argument meets all of the criteria for a given fallacy, and explaining why that fallacy is a form of bad reasoning.
- Some fallacies commonly mistaken for one another (lookalikes) can be distinguished by noting what their similarities and differences are, and by paying close attention to the criteria for each of the lookalikes.
- Some arguments that appear to be fallacies may not be fallacies upon closer examination of the arguments, the criteria for the fallacy, and the context in which the arguments appear.

Argumentation Exercise: Neutralizing Fallacies in a Dialogue

Re-examine the A Dialogue on Copyright that begins this module. Rewrite the dialogue using the technique of neutralizing the fallacies for the various fallacies committed in the dialogue.

Writing Skills Exercise: Correcting Fallacies

Write a one-page essay with a thesis and defence of that thesis on a topic of your choice in which you commit as many fallacies as you can. Then critique and neutralize the fallacies and write a two-page critique of the fallacies committed in the original paper.

Analyzing and Assessing Extended Arguments

LEARNING OBJECTIVES

After completing this module you should be able to:

1. Analyze and portray the logical structure of an extended passage;
2. Clarify the meaning of key terms and phrases within an extended passage;
3. Assess the specific arguments within a passage for cogency and acceptability;
4. Assess the overall acceptability of a passage; and
5. Develop a written critique of your analysis of a passage.

A DIALOGUE ON COPYRIGHT AND PIRACY – CONTINUED

Peter: I came across an argument on copyright I want you to look at. I have a question about it.

Jean: Okay. Do you have it with you?

Peter: Here it is. What do you think the main argument is? Can you give me a brief synopsis and critique?

Jean: Sure. [Reads following passage]:

Pirates: I Don't Think So

Much of the concern about electronic copying and downloading of copyright materials has been misplaced. Although remix creators (those who take existing songs and sample them by using short clips) have occasionally been targets of the copyright wars, they are merely collateral damage. The targets have become every computer involved in file streaming of copyright material. Often the targets have been 13- and 14-year-old teens up to young adults. After a decade of trying to control file streaming, the law has neither slowed it down nor compensated artists. The ones benefitting from the anti-piracy laws and their enforcement are neither the artists nor their fans. The beneficiaries are the large multinational companies who own the rights to much of this material, but are themselves neither the writers nor the artists who make the art.

The multimedia giants have been trying to make the argument through their prosecutions of the 14-year-old "pirate" seated at her computer, that her copying means she is not buying, and not buying means she is inflicting a commercial loss on the multimedia giants. This is an intellectually dishonest argument. Copying does not mean the person will not buy the material. Many individuals download files to try out new singers and see if they like an album. If they do, they often then buy a licensed copy. Given that so much music is not played regularly, this is the only way a person can find out if she likes a new artist. File sharing is more like free advertising than theft. Not all advertising pays off in a sale.

More important, even if copying is depriving someone of a potential sale, there is no vested property right in potential sales. If there were, then my telling my friends that a new artist really sucks, with the result that they choose not to buy that artist's album, would deprive the artist of a potential sale. Should the artist, or more accurately, their multinational backer, be allowed to sue someone for costing them a sale? Playing an album for a friend who discovers he doesn't like it could amount to depriving the artist, and more likely the multinationals, of a potential sale and hence violate their vested property right. Hogwash.

If this were true, capitalism would simply not work. Capitalism is based on competition. But if my competitor builds a better product, it deprives me of a potential sale. If I have a vested property right in a potential sale, I should have a right to sue my competitor for building a better product. And that is absurd!

Piracy is not theft. Theft occurs when you take something that physically belongs to someone, and electronic files that are distributed over the Internet do not "belong" to anyone. If I downloaded something on which there is copyright and then sold that to someone else, I have deprived the owner of a legitimate sale. However, that is not what happens with much of the downloaded material. People download music and videos to try them out and see if they like them. Piracy is not theft: real pirates steal real things and deprive their owners of those things. Internet "pirates" make digital copies of electronic media. There is a difference.

(continued)

A "stolen" copy is not a lost sale. It is only a lost sale if the person would have bought it in the first place. If they never would have bought it in the first place, it is not a loss, only a trial. And a trial is not theft.

The multinationals (such as, Disney, Sony, and BMI) have been using the laws to protect their own interests by prosecuting individuals who they label as stealing from them. This can be seen by the fact that various multinationals (Disney being a leader in this) have sought to increase the term of copyright. When copyright was introduced in the United States in 1789, it lasted for 40 years. As a result of intensive lobbying, a copyright holder now holds copyright on their materials for life plus 110 years. Surely the original author needs no such protection. All this does is to serve the interests of the multinationals and their maintaining their profits for a much longer period of time. Interestingly, many European jurisdictions recognize a music short-time period for copyright; Britain's copyright on music is for 50 years from first publication. The result is that many works recorded in the late 1950s and early '60s are no longer covered by copyright in England, but will be for another 70 years in the United States. Canada's copyright protection is life of the author plus 50 years.

Corporations like the Motion Picture Association of America and the Recording Industry Association of America do not care about the artist. These laws are not for protecting the cartoonist whose designs were plagiarized and re-printed by some hack T-shirt company. These laws are to protect the vested interests of a multinational company that sued a 12-year-old girl for downloading music. These companies are making war on Gen-X and criminalizing them.

> Jean: Interesting argument. I am not going to try to give a synopsis and critique off the top of my head. I need to sit down and work my way through this.

> Peter: Okay, let's do that.

(to be continued)

8.1 Introduction

Peter has presented Jean with a longer passage that needs analysis. They are going to need some time to analyze this. Jean makes a good argumentation move by asking for time to think about and do the analysis. He is not going to be rushed into a quick answer when time is needed.

Many arguments are embedded in extended passages ranging from a paragraph to an entire book. Because we often encounter longer passages that we need to analyze and assess, instructors often ask students to write critical essays that require the analysis and evaluation of one or more texts, and because longer passages often involve multiple arguments and sub-arguments, we need a strategy for analyzing and critiquing them. The skills learned in identifying, structuring, and evaluating arguments in Modules 3 through 7 can be used to analyze such texts. This module integrates the material from those modules, provides an overall strategy for analyzing extended texts, and shows how to turn an extended argument analysis into a critical analysis essay.

8.2 Outline of the Model

The basic method of passage analysis consists of four main steps, some of which have several sub-steps. This is summarized in Table 8.1.

TABLE 8.1 A Model for Passage Analysis

Step	Name	Sub Step	Activity
1.	Read, annotate, and clarify the passage.	A	Skim for meaning, purpose, and conclusion.
		B	Read for detail and annotate the passage.
		C	Clarify key concepts and unclear claims and phrases.
2.	Portray the basic argument structure in the passage.	D	Identify the main and sub-arguments in the passage and supply missing premises.
		E	Test your analysis for clarity and accuracy.
3.	Assess the arguments.	F	Assess the specific arguments.
		G	Assess the overall argument.
4.	Present your analysis.	H	Put your analysis together into a form for presentation.

The remainder of the module elaborates and illustrates this model. We will use the following passage to illustrate the method.

8.3 Passage for Analysis

An Idea Whose Time Has Come

The government has no choice but to legalize the possession and sale of marijuana. First, individuals have a right to engage in whatever activities they choose, as long as they do not harm others. This is a basic assumption of our society. We allow people to ingest alcohol and nicotine, to eat unhealthy foods, and to engage in other risky behaviour (such as, hang-gliding and scuba diving). The use of marijuana puts no one but users at risk. Therefore, we should allow people to use marijuana.

Second, no one has conclusively established that marijuana is harmful.

Third, legalizing it will make money for the government through taxes and will curtail various evils (such as, the proliferation of grow-ops and the use of illegal marijuana profits to fund other criminal activities).

It might be argued that using marijuana can harm others. For example, it might be claimed people will use marijuana and then drive. However, drunk drivers kill people, yet we do not ban alcohol. Rather, we try to prevent people from driving while impaired.

Before continuing with this passage, the authors recommend you use the steps outlined in Table 8.1, above, to do your own analysis of this passage. Even better, take the steps one by one and do your own analysis before reading the section with the authors' analysis.

8.4 Step 1: Read, Annotate, and Clarify the Passage

A. Skim for Meaning, Purpose and Overall Conclusion

The goal of your first reading of a passage is to familiarize yourself with the purpose and main ideas in a passage, not to identify all the details. Read actively by asking questions of the text, thinking about it, and summarizing it. What is the passage about? What is the author trying to accomplish? What is the passage doing? What is the main conclusion? What is your hypothesis about the main reasons? Write a brief summary of your understanding of the argument of the passage. Identify any preliminary questions you have about the passage. Note that these are not challenges, but questions you need to probe further in order to understand the argument in the passage. (It is not uncommon to read the text differently on subsequent readings.)

An initial reading of the passage might give a relatively simple analysis:

> We should legalize marijuana because people have a right to do what they want and there is no proof it causes harm.

You might ask the following questions:

> Do people always have a right to do what they want?

> What harms do people allege marijuana causes and what is the evidence it show that it does not cause harm?

> What about possible harm to a fetus?

Your own analysis might differ from this in a number of ways. The first quick reading is to help you develop a hypothesis about the overall meaning of the passage and some questions you might raise about the argument in the passage. Formulate a brief summary of the main point and main reasons. You will test that when you do your more detailed analysis. The key point is not to become wedded to your initial hypothesis, but to treat it as an initial reading that needs to be tested. On second reading, we may discover that we have missed some important reasons or not have been as precise as we need to be. The initial formulation above missed the idea that legalizing marijuana will make money for the government through taxation.

For a longer text (such as, an article, a chapter of a book, a whole book) the basic principles still hold: skim for the core meaning, read actively by asking questions of the text (such as, how does this relate to that, how does the author support this, etc.), make a preliminary hypothesis about the main conclusion and main reasons. The following are some additional suggestions for reading a longer text:

- Read with a pen or pencil (not a highlighter) and annotate the text as you go. Use the margins of the text to make notes about the argument. Using a pen or pencil forces you to summarize and integrate the ideas and look for the relations.
- Start by skimming the text, noting titles and headings.
- Look at the introduction, conclusion, and section headings for cues to the main line of argument.
- Look for the *topic sentence* (the sentence containing the main point) in each paragraph. How does each relate to the overall topic?
- Make a list of questions about the argument in the text you wish to explore on further readings.
- Look for and circle **signposts** to the passage. These are both logical cue words and other indicators that authors use to identify the structure of the text (such as, "Three considerations for this proposal are ...", "It might be argued that ...", and "For example ...").
- Look for key concepts that are central to understanding the passage. Draw a box around these.
- Make summaries periodically of each section of the argument. It is often helpful to do this by identifying the main points, paragraph by paragraph, in the margins. After the first read, summarize the main conclusion and arguments of the entire text.

> **Signposts** are both logical cue words and other indicators that authors use to identify the structure of the text.

QUICK QUIZ 8.1

Read the Passage

Read the Passage "Pirates: I Don't Think So" in the dialogue that opens this module. That passage will be the basis for the Quick Quizzes in this module. It is reprinted on the Premium Website so you can do the analysis there. Read the passage and then answer the questions below.

1. Write a brief summary of the main point after the first reading (do not reread yet).
2. What is your hypothesis about the main point (or conclusion) of the passage? and
3. What questions do you have about the argument of the text?

Answers to the Quick Quizzes are available on the Premium Website at www.criticalthinking2e.nelson.com.

B. Read for Detail and Annotate the Passage

On your second and subsequent readings, study the passage more carefully, testing your initial hypothesis. Is there anything in the passage that will disconfirm your hypothesis about what the main arguments are? What questions do you have of the text that you hope to answer with a closer read?

Circle inference indicators, and box key concepts and unclear terms. Pay close attention to each sentence, and consider what it does in the overall context of the passage. (See Module 2, Section 2.4, for some functions of sentences in prose.) If the article is long, write in the margin a one-sentence summary that captures the main point of each paragraph. These can help in identifying the overall structure of the passage.

For a short passage, number and bracket all claims (remember that some sentences may have multiple claims). You can always eliminate redundant and irrelevant claims later.

Identify buried claims and write them as explicit claims. A **buried** or **implicit claim** is one that is contained within another assertion. For example, in the claim "The unfeasible idea that the government can fund all medical care and not go bankrupt should be dismissed," although the author appears to be making one claim, he or she is actually making two claims (the first is the claim "the idea that the government can fund all medical care and not go bankrupt should be dismissed" and the second is the claim "this idea is unfeasible").

Supply any obvious cue words, using square brackets to identify what you have supplied, whether words or implicit claims.

For longer texts you will likely need several additional readings. The first reading will be for the general meaning, as outlined previously. The second will be to get the basic structure of the text. In this reading you may simply want to identify the main point of each paragraph (write in the margins, rather than highlighting). When highlighting we tend to over-highlight. We also do not paraphrase, which is a more active reading process. As a result, highlighting a text tends to be more passive than forcing oneself to summarize in one's own words the main point in a paragraph.

Once you have identified the main point in each paragraph, you should try to see how the argument fits together as a whole. At that point you may need to examine specific paragraphs more closely for the fine details of the argument.

A sample annotation of the passage might be as follows:

An Idea Whose Time Has Come

1

[The government has no choice but to legalize the possession and sale of

2

marijuana.] First, [individuals have a right to engage in whatever activities

they choose as long as they don't harm others.] [This (the right of individuals

3

to engage in whatever activities they choose as long as they don't harm

others) is a basic assumption of our society.] [We allow people to ingest

4

alcohol and nicotine, to eat unhealthy foods, and to engage in risky behaviour

such as, hang-gliding and scuba diving as long as that behaviour harms no

5

one but themselves.] [The use of marijuana puts no one but users at risk.]

6

Therefore, [we should allow people to use marijuana.]

7

Second, [no one has conclusively established it is harmful.]

8

Third, [legalizing it will make money for the government through taxes] and

9

[legalizing it will curtail various evils, such as, the proliferation of grow-ops

and the use of illegal marijuana profits to fund other criminal activities.]

10

It might be argued that [using marijuana can harm others]. For example,

11

[it might be claimed that people will use marijuana and then drive.] However,

12

[drunk drivers kill people, yet we don't ban alcohol.] Rather, [we try to

13

prevent people from driving while impaired.]

In annotating this passage we have bracketed and numbered the individual claims.

If the passage were longer we could provide a brief one-sentence summary in the margin of the main point in each paragraph.

QUICK QUIZ 8.2

Annotate the Passage

Annotate the "Pirates: I Don't Think So" passage.

1. Circle all inference indicators;
2. Number and bracket all claims; and
3. Rewrite any fragments, referential indicators, and rhetorical questions.

Answers to the Quick Quizzes are available on the Premium Website at www.criticalthinking2e.nelson.com.

C. Clarify the Meaning of Key Concepts, Phrases, and Claims

Before trying to clarify anything, read the whole passage. Look up and, if necessary, replace unknown or unfamiliar terms by using a dictionary. Make sure the dictionary definition you choose fits the meaning of the term in context. (See Modules 2 and 9 for more on figuring out meaning in context.) If necessary, do a conceptual analysis (see Module 9), or look for materials within the passage (such as, examples or applications of the concept that will help you). If there are several possible ways to interpret the concept and the text does not make it clear which is intended, provide various paraphrases using the alternative meanings and consider the effects of each on the overall passage and the argument.

Write out any important unstated but clearly intended implications or suggestions of the reasons, conclusions, and argument as a whole. To do so, consider what the passage is trying to get across that is not actually stated explicitly.

Be careful not to confuse your assumptions about the argument or the issue with what the author is claiming. Ask yourself if you really understand how everything fits together, if you have a "feel" for the argument or passage as a whole (even if you do

ANALYZING AND ASSESSING EXTENDED ARGUMENTS **217**

not accept the claims made in it). Do not let any hostility you have for the position expressed mislead you into misrepresenting the argument (such as, by making it sound more stupid than you think it already is).

Not every vague, imprecise, unclear, or ambiguous term or phrase in a passage is necessarily central to the argument. One common error is to criticize as unclear a term or phrase that is inconsequential. Do not waste time criticizing what is not central to the argument.

If you do not know the meaning of the word "ingest," look it up. You may want to examine the concepts of "risky behaviour" and "harm to others." While these are reasonably clear from the passage, examining them more closely with a conceptual analysis might give you the basis for a deeper critique of the argument.

A clarification of this passage could include the following:

> The first is a qualification. All of the arguments address the recreational use of marijuana, not the medical uses. I would limit the scope of the argument to the former. Although the author does not specifically say that he is arguing for the recreational use of marijuana, all of his arguments support that and nothing is mentioned about possible medical justifications for the use of marijuana.
>
> Claim 2 puzzles me: It is an overly general claim that seems to have exceptions. I will need to qualify or limit this in some way. This will emerge in the argument analysis and through counterexamples.
>
> I am also a bit puzzled by what the author means by "conclusively established" in claim 7. If he means "establish beyond all reasonable doubt," then this may be stronger than is necessary and beyond what we would normally accept. We often restrict or limit potentially harmful drugs and food ingredients on lesser criteria. This may become a criticism on the grounds of being an overly strict criterion.
>
> Claim 7 presupposes that one of the major grounds for prohibiting something is its being harmful to either the user or others.

This last point may become significant if the author is implicitly assuming that the only major reason for prohibiting something is its potential harm. We may prohibit some things for other reasons. If the author is assuming that this is the only significant reason, then a challenge could be raised based on this.

QUICK QUIZ 8.3

Clarify Meaning of Concepts and Claims

1. Examine the text "Pirates: I Don't Think So" for clarity and precision of meaning. Is the meaning of any of the concepts unclear? Does a dictionary help in the clarification of the meaning? If not, can you paraphrase to clarify the meaning or come up with possible alternative meanings?
2. Are there any hidden implications in the premises? And,
3. Is each claim clearly stated?

Answers to the Quick Quizzes are available on the Premium Website at www.criticalthinking2e.nelson.com.

8.5 Step 2: Portray Argument Structure

A. Identify the Main and Sub-Arguments in the Passage

Formulate the Main Argument and Write a Synopsis

Start with the main conclusion. Using the key concepts, inference indicators, and the thesis sentence, *formulate the main argument in your own words.* If the argument hinges on the precise language used by the author, then use that. Otherwise, try to paraphrase the argument. Find, formulate, or paraphrase a sentence that as clearly as possible states what you take to be the argument's main conclusion.

Write a synopsis of the passage. Formulate what you see as the main point of the passage in one sentence by imagining you are writing a headline for the piece. Make it a substantive claim (such as, "Marijuana should be legalized") rather than a more general claim (such as, "The passage is about legalizing marijuana") that does not tell the reader what the passage is actually arguing. Check your formulation against the passage. Can most of the statements in the passage be seen as supporting that claim or in some way related to that claim? If not, consider an alternate paraphrase, unless much of the material is extraneous.

If your headline had read "People have a right to do what they want" it would not capture the main point of the passage, which is to argue for the legalization of marijuana. That captures a main reason, but not the main point of the whole passage.

Before portraying the structure of the argument, writing a synopsis of it can help you clarify exactly what is being argued. A **synopsis** is a brief characterization of the conclusion and the main line(s) of development of the argument, written in your own words. Once you have identified the main conclusion and the basic reasons, you can then try to fit in the other reasons that contribute to the argument.

> A **synopsis** is a brief characterization of the conclusion and the main line(s) of development of the argument, written in your own words.

In writing the synopsis, you may find that the rhetorical organization of the text is not a reliable guide to the logical structure of the argument. Repetition, extraneous material, irrelevant background information, digressions, and sloppy writing may obscure the logical structure. Note these, but do not include them in your standardization of the argument. They may be included in a critique of the argument; however, they should not appear in the synopsis because stylistic and rhetorical features are not relevant to the logic of the argument.

The following would be a good starting synopsis of the argument:

> The government should legalize the possession and sale of marijuana for recreational use for three reasons. First, a basic principle in our society is that people have a right to do what they want so long as they do not harm others. And no one has established that using marijuana is harmful to others. In addition, the legalizing of marijuana will make money for the government through taxes. Although it might be argued that marijuana can harm others, for example, through smoking and driving, it is not the use of marijuana but the driving while impaired that is the problem.

This passage has two arguments and a response to a challenge.

It is useful to lay out the full structure of both a shorter passage, such as this, as well as the full structure of longer passage, to understand all of the claims required for the passage.

The summary above does not capture that part of the argument that refers to the legalizing of marijuana as curtailing various evils. You would need to consider whether that is a significant argument that should be added, or an incidental comment. Since it does contribute to the author's case, we should include it.

QUICK QUIZ 8.4

Give a Synopsis of the Argument

1. Write a synopsis of the argument in "Pirates: I Don't Think So; and
2. Check your synopsis against the original text to see if you have captured everything.

Answers to the Quick Quizzes are available on the Premium Website at www.criticalthinking2e.nelson.com.

Develop the Sub-Arguments

An arrow diagram of a complex argument often has a tree structure, with the conclusion being like the trunk of the tree and the various lines of argument like the branches of the tree. An *argument tree* is an arrow diagram of a complex argument portraying the arguments and sub-arguments.

An **argument tree** is an arrow diagram of a complex argument portraying the arguments and sub-arguments.

Once you have identified the main lines of argument, *develop the sub-arguments*. Work systematically. Start from the main conclusion, the bottom of the argument tree, and work upward one line at a time into the sub-arguments and supporting arguments. If you get stuck, try to find a basic reason that supports a given line of argument and work down from there. Paraphrase each line of argument to get the gist of what each says.

Not all claims may fit into your initial analysis. Set aside the claims that do not fit. Once you have identified the main structure, see how the claims contribute to the passage. If they are extraneous material, ignore them.

Using the annotation of the passage above, we can give an arrow diagram of the passage:

$$11 + 12 + 13$$
$$\wr$$
$$3 \qquad 10$$
$$\downarrow \qquad \wr$$
$$2 + 5 \qquad 7 \qquad 8 \qquad 9$$
$$\searrow \qquad \searrow \swarrow \qquad \swarrow$$
$$1$$

Remember (as introduced in Section 3.9) that we diagram a challenge and a response to a challenge with wavy arrows "a" $\wr$ "b" – these are read as "'b' is false or should not be accepted because of 'a.'" In this diagram, 10 is a challenge to 5 (5 should not be accepted because of 10) and 11, 12, and 13 are responses to 10 (10 should not be accepted because of 11, 12, and 13).

We could also write this out in standard form.

This diagram shows three lines of argument. A *line of argument* is the set of arguments, supporting arguments and challenges and responses that make up one vertical column of argument in an arrow diagram.

A **line of argument** is the set of arguments, supporting arguments, and challenges and responses that make up one vertical column of argument in an arrow diagram.

Give Each Line of Argument a Name That Captures Its Main Reason

This helps you both to remember the line and to summarize the reasoning in that line. The three lines of argument in this passage could be called the "autonomy," the "no proof of harm," and the "tax benefits" lines of argument.

QUICK QUIZ 8.5

Portray Structure

1. Portray the structure of the argument in the passage: "Pirates: I Don't Think So."
2. How many lines of argument are there? And
3. What names would you give the lines of the argument?

Answers to the Quick Quizzes are available on the Premium Website at www.criticalthinking2e.nelson.com.

Longer Passages

For longer passages you will need to work systematically through the paragraphs. Start with the larger units (sections, paragraphs). Search the passage for reasons for each claim that acts as a conclusion. Ignore anything that does not contribute to the logical structure of the argument (such as, examples, repetitions of claims, rhetorical flourishes). Sometimes the argument of a long passage may be quite simple.

Using inference indicators and other cues, mechanically structure as much of the passage as you can. As you go through it note reasons and conclusions and then diagram them. Once you have done that consider the content of the claims to see whether any further logical connections can be identified.

Once you have identified the preliminary structure of the argument test your analysis against the passage by reading it claim by claim to make sure you have not left out anything crucial.

In some cases, we may have choices to make in the construction of the argument diagram. Generally we try to construct a diagram that reflects the logical structure and relations in the text, portrays the strongest argument of the alternative possibilities, and incorporates as many of the contributing statements and sub-arguments as possible. Sometimes it is not possible to succeed in all of these. A simpler formulation may omit substantial parts of the passage but still captures the core argument structure.

The structure of the argument may still be ambiguous or indeterminate after diagramming. To the extent that the intended inferences are unclear in the original text, the responsibility lies with the author and not with you.

One strategy when confronted with an unclear passage is to indicate that the passage is ambiguous and show why it is. Addressing this ambiguity may involve (a) selecting one interpretation of the passage and using that in your analysis, or (b) articulating the alternative possibilities and showing how each possibility fits into the larger argument. In choosing (a), select the strongest version of the argument and give reasons for your selection (for example, by demonstrating that it generates a better argument or is more consistent with other things that the author says either within the passage being analyzed or in other texts). In choosing (b), if in the course of identifying alternate possibilities for interpretation you create a better argument, you can argue for that one being the best interpretation, whether intended by the author or not.

Supply the Missing Reasons

We have outlined several ways of supplying missing reasons in Module 4. Use them to supply the missing reasons in the arguments. All that can legitimately be supplied to an argument as missing reasons are those claims that are being assumed by the argument and are necessary to make the argument work (i.e., to establish relevance and sufficiency, or validity). We can supply one of three types of possible missing reasons:

1. *The arguer's assumptions:* What the author consciously assumed or would accept as an assumption if asked – statements that are faithful to the author's beliefs and intentions, insofar as these are known. Often this requires background knowledge about the author and other texts the author has written.
2. *The minimal assumptions:* What is, logically speaking, necessary to establish criteria of relevance and sufficiency between the reasons and the conclusion.
3. *The optimal assumptions:* Claims that are both logically adequate and independently well supported – these are usually stronger than minimal assumptions and sometimes stronger than the author might accept. These assumptions help in constructing the best argument possible, given the materials you have to work with.

The basic rationale behind supplying missing reasons is to establish clearly the logical structure of the argument by filling in the assumptions the arguer is making. The types of missing reasons above may conflict in some cases. For example, adhering to the first option, the arguer's assumption may yield an invalid argument if the arguer has made a basic blunder in his or her argument or presentation of it. Adhering to options "2" or "3" may yield a good argument, but one that is inconsistent with the author's other statements or intentions. Which approach you adopt in such an instance will depend on your purposes in analyzing the text. If you are trying to determine what the arguer meant, the reconstruction of the argument should be as faithful to the author's beliefs and intentions as it can be. But if you are trying to determine how good a particular line of reasoning is, regardless of who authored it or what he or she had in mind, then the minimal and optimal assumptions are more important than fidelity to a particular author's intentions or text.

When analyzing an argument, always be careful to indicate where you have supplied missing reasons (or rewritten reasons), and why you have supplied them. (Just saying "because it was needed" is not enough – you need to be specific, explaining why what you have supplied is required by this particular argument.)

Test your argument analysis by comparing it to the text. Is there anything in the text that is not reflected in the argument diagram? Is your analysis true to the argument in the text?

This raises a question of interpretation. Is claim 7 to be treated as an independent line of argument or as part of the no-harm argument? Because both talk about harm, one might consider them part of the same argument. It also is a single claim with no sub-argument. A missing reason can easily be supplied. On the other hand, the issue of harm it raises is somewhat different from the "no harm to others" line of argument. Whereas the latter focuses on individual rights, this line focuses on the fact that no harm has been conclusively established. This raises an important issue: if something is believed to cause harm, but that harm has not been established (either conclusively or to a likely degree), then would we be justified in banning or restricting that activity on the mere suspicion of harm to self or others? This is a significant issue and may lead to a rich discussion. If you were interested in addressing that issue, then you would be justified in treating this as a separate line of argument.

Based on the version of the *principle of charity* where we try to identify the best argument the author is trying to give, treating this as a separate line of argument could give the author another line of argument for her or his case. It also raises the public policy issue of risk of harm when harm has not been established.

In the end, we have to make a choice based on our best judgment about the author's intent in giving the argument, and on our purpose for reconstructing and assessing her or his argument. And knowing the alternative constructions we should justify our reconstruction.

Test Your Understanding

Reread the passage and check your reconstruction against the text. Make sure that the central features of the original are captured in your paraphrase *and* that the paraphrase does not add additional materials *without justification*. If necessary, go back and reformulate and fine tune the reconstruction by asking yourself the following questions: Is everything you have supplied necessary for understanding the argument? Is there anything that is not clear? If so, is it because it is unclear in the passage, or because you have not captured some important information?

At this point, you should have an analysis of the argument in the passage. You can now move on to assessing the arguments. We will formulate, supply missing reasons, and assess the individual arguments in the next section.

8.6 Step 3: Assess the Arguments

Assess the Individual Arguments

An arguer is making a case for a position. That case consists of all of the lines of argument being advanced (whether one or many), together with the response to real or possible challenges. In determining whether an arguer has made his or her case, we need to examine each of the lines of argument the author presents. If the arguments are *deductive*, each line stands on its own. If the arguments are *inductive*, some of the lines may mutually support one another and some may be independent. As discussed in Module 3, a *convergent argument* is an argument that arrives at a common conclusion from at least two independent lines of reasoning. For example, when Darwin wrote *The Origin of Species,* he presented several lines of reasoning to establish his conclusion that evolution had occurred by natural selection: arguments from paleontology, geology, natural selection, and geographical distribution of species. In the twentieth century, additional independent lines of reasoning from genetics and DNA similarities of species and continental drift provided additional arguments to support his conclusion. By themselves, some of the lines (such as, the fossil remains) may not be conclusive. However, the convergence of multiple, independent lines of reasoning on a common conclusion can make the overall argument stronger than any single line taken in isolation. One can sometimes see this in a criminal case, where multiple independent lines of evidence converge on a common conclusion.

Assessing the argument follows the basic principles we have already encountered, with some additions. First, we assess the logical adequacy of each argument, then we assess the truth of the claims. Each line of argument must be assessed.

If we have diagrammed the argument with the conclusion at the bottom and the various independent arguments stemming from the conclusion, the argument structure will look like a tree. The main conclusion is its trunk and the main arguments and sub-arguments its branches. To assess a multi-line argument we start at the bottom of the *argument tree* and work up.

If the argument fails in a fundamental way at the bottom of the tree, then we do not have to go higher in the tree, unless we are interested in exploring the kinds of reasons that have been developed for this argument.

As you progress, evaluate each argument in the argument tree as to how sound or cogent it is. Then assess the claims, including presuppositions and corollaries, for adequacy. In most cases, adequate evaluation of the truth of the reasons requires some knowledge of the subject matter. There is no single set of rules or criteria and no test or procedure for deciding the truth or even the plausibility of reasons. However, the following guidelines can help in this task:

- Read each reason critically. Think about what it is claiming. Even if you think you agree with it, would the intended audience agree?
- Examine and evaluate the evidence for key claims. Where the claims are questionable, has evidence or one or more sub-arguments been provided? Examine those. Consider the different kinds of claims (empirical, conceptual, and normative) and the kinds of challenges that can be raised for each of those. Look for disconfirmations rather than confirmations.
- If there are general claims in the reasons, can they be challenged by counterexamples? Would limiting them in scope make them more defensible?
- Check for problematic presuppositions or corollaries.
- When offering a challenge or counterexample, consider possible responses the defender of the argument could give. Is it possible to limit the scope or qualify the claim to give the arguer a better argument?

Once you have supplied the missing reasons you can assess the individual arguments using the methods outlined in Modules 4, 5, and 6.

Assess the Specific Arguments for Logical Adequacy

Start the assessment with the main arguments, the ones that directly support the main conclusion. If those are good arguments, then move to the sub-arguments. Examine each of the lines of argument independently. Each line or sub-line that supports a conclusion needs to be examined. If there is a major problem at any level, then you do not need to examine the higher sub-arguments in that line of argument. (Review Modules 4 through 6 for the specific tools for argument assessment.)

Assess the Overall Argument

Once you have an analysis of the individual arguments you need to provide an overall assessment of the arguments made in the passage, including responses to challenges that the arguer has addressed. At the very least, your overall assessment is a summary of the acceptability of each main line of argument and whether or not the arguer has made a good case for his or her conclusion. It may also include suggestions as to how the argument could be improved, additional arguments that might help in developing the case, and any important insights that have emerged from the analysis.

We now need to integrate the assessment of the individual arguments into an overall assessment of the case that has been presented. Examine each line of argument to see if it is sound. If the arguer has one or more sound lines of argument supporting the conclusion, then the arguer has made his or her case. For the arguments that are not sound, consider how devastating the weaknesses are. Could someone who supports the position reasonably defend against the challenges by modifying the argument in minor ways? If so, develop those possible responses and consider what further challenges might be made. Consider ways that the argument might be improved.

Examine other relevant considerations. What we have developed thus far are arguments for a particular position. Are there other relevant arguments or considerations that could be brought to bear on this conclusion? (This leads us into issue analysis, discussed in Module 1.) Some of the questions you might want to ask yourself include:

1. Are there other arguments that support the same conclusion?
2. Are there other arguments that point to a different conclusion?
3. What are the implications of this argument and the basic reasons that have been given in related areas?

An argument may seem impeccable when considered by itself, but it may have implications that are inconsistent with other beliefs, ideas, or values.

Ask yourself what you can learn from the argument in the passage. Even when you do not accept an argument, you can often learn from it. Are there interesting or relevant considerations that are poorly developed and might be developed better? What can you suggest that might improve the arguments given?

Now go back to your criticisms and give an overall evaluation of the argument in this passage. Look at the strongest criticisms you have. Do they address all of the lines of argument or only some? Could some of your challenges be stronger if you had more information or evidence to support them? Does the argument in this passage make a very strong, moderate, inconsistent, or weak case for its conclusion?

Virtually every argument with an interesting and controversial conclusion is open to criticism. This does not mean that virtually every such argument is a poor argument. An argument may be strong even though it has flaws and even though we may have strong reasons for opposing its conclusion. A fair overall assessment involves identifying those strengths as well as the weaknesses.

Analyzing the argument, supplying missing reasons and assessing the marijuana passage produces the following analysis (note that missing reasons have been supplied using letters and square brackets and the numbering follows the number of the statements in the passage in Section 8.4 above.):

I. The Autonomy Argument:

2. Individuals have a right to engage in whatever activities they choose as long as they do not harm others.
5. The use of marijuana puts no one but users at risk.
A. [If someone has a right to something and the exercise of that right causes no harm to anyone other than the person whose right it is, then it should be legalized.]

∴ 1. Marijuana should be legalized.

Supplying "A" as a missing reason makes the argument valid (because it affirms the antecedent).

Claim 10, a potential challenge to 5, is answered by claims 11, 12, and 13. However, these do not constitute a good response. One particular example (such as, alcohol and driving) is identified, and then the argument is generalized to marijuana use and driving. What is needed is a more general defence of claim 5, specifically, what is objectionable is not marijuana *per se* but using it and then driving, which *could* cause harm to others. We should not ban either of these activities, which in themselves may be acceptable, but instead ban the combination of the two things. With this, that objection is handled and reason 5 is strong.

The main problem is with reason 2, not reason 5. The claim states that individuals have a right to engage in any activity they choose as long as it does not harm others. Although causing or potentially causing harm to others is grounds for curtailing an activity, the lack of harming others is not in itself grounds for allowing that activity and enshrining it as legally justified. I am prohibited from selling myself into slavery even though it would cause harm to no one but myself. Thus, reason 2 as stated is false, and the argument is not cogent.

II. The No Proof of Harm Argument:

7. No one has conclusively established that marijuana is harmful.

∴ 1. The government should legalize the possession and sale of marijuana.

This argument commits the fallacy of appeal to ignorance (as discussed in Module 7). As such, this line of reasoning is not acceptable. However, it might be possible to develop it by arguing more extensively about the conditions under which something (such as recreational drugs) should be legal. As given, it is a fallacy.

III. The Benefits Argument:

    8. Legalizing marijuana will make money for the government through taxes.

    9. Legalizing marijuana will curtail various evils (such as, other illegal activities).

    B. [If something will make money for the government and curtail other illegal activities, then it should be legalized.]

∴   1. The possession and sale of marijuana should be legalized.

This argument is valid (because it affirms the antecedent). We will grant reasons 8 and 9. The problem lies with the missing reason. Many things could produce benefits for the government – increasing the rates of taxation to usurious levels will make money, and executing anyone convicted of a serious crime might curtail other illegal activities. However, we do not do things merely because they benefit the government. Benefits must be weighed against costs, harms, and rights.

Although the argument is valid, it is not obviously cogent. More is needed to establish the missing reason; it also needs to be qualified and limited. Once that is done, the arguer would need to show that the benefits outweigh the harms and costs and do not infringe rights.

We could bring this together in the following overall assessment:

> The author has given three lines of argument. One is clearly a fallacy. Each of the other two, though valid, has questionable reasons that render each argument not cogent as presented. If the challenges to reason 2 could be addressed, this would be a much stronger argument. The benefits argument could be improved by identifying the benefits and harms of legalizing marijuana and showing that the benefits of legalizing marijuana outweigh the harms.

Assess Cogency

1. Supply missing premises for the arguments in the marijuana passage.
2. Using the topics model or the argument patterns, assess the arguments for validity.
3. Assess the arguments for cogency.
4. Explain and justify your assessments.

QUICK QUIZ 8.7

Give an Overall Assessment

Provide an overall assessment of the arguments in the passage "Pirates: I Don't Think So" using the criteria outlined in this section. What are the possible merits of the argument? Are there any considerations worth pursuing?

Answers to the Quick Quizzes are available on the Premium Website at www.criticalthinking2e.nelson.com.

8.7 Step 4: Present Your Assessment

Once you have developed your analysis of the passage, you still need to put it into a form for presentation, either to others or to yourself later on. In some cases, this will be as a paper or part of a paper you are submitting for a course (or an employer, friend, or an argument partner). In other cases, it may simply be for yourself. For example, if you are reading class materials (or even just some material you are interested in and may come back to later) that you want to remember, you should write a brief summary of the argument and your main critiques of it. Writing encourages you to articulate both your understanding and your critique of the argument.

The purpose of giving a critique is to identify the strengths and weaknesses of an argument so your reader can determine whether the argument should be accepted. In presenting your critique, you are making a case (or argument) about the argument in the passage. You need to do more than merely present your conclusions about the passage: you need to demonstrate your reasoning so the reader can make his or her own assessment of your assessment. This means that in developing a critique for an audience you need to focus your writing around the needs of your audience. In doing so, consider questions such as: What do they already know? What do they need to know in order to assess your conclusion? How can I present what they need to know in a way that they can easily understand?

To do this effectively you need to do the following:

I. *Identify the basic argument in the passage.* This tells the reader who has read the passage how you have reconstructed the passage. And it tells the reader who has not read the passage what the basic structure of the argument is.

II. *Give your overall assessment of the passage,* preferably in one sentence. In effect, this is your conclusion about the passage.

III. *Make your case to support that conclusion by:*
   i. *identifying clearly the structure of the argument you are critiquing.* The audience may not be familiar with the passage, but, even if they are, they may not reconstruct the argument as you have. In structuring the argument, pay attention to the specific parts you are going to critique. It helps to identify and label the separate lines of argument. Make the logic of the argument clear by using cue words and ordering the argument. If there is anything problematic in your reconstruction (such as, possible alternate reconstructions of the argument), indicate that and justify your preferred reconstruction. Identify supporting arguments, but provide details only if relevant to your critique.
   ii. *identifying the strengths and weaknesses of the arguments systematically.* Focus on the key strengths and weaknesses. If you critique a relatively minor point and ignore a major problem, the reader is likely to think you have not properly understood the argument. Order the critique in terms of severity of criticism and be as precise as possible. For example, state "The second premise has a false presupposition" rather than "There is a weakness in the argument." Simply saying there is a problem without identifying what exactly the problem is does not provide the reader with any way of determining how you are critiquing the argument.
   iii. *providing reasons to justify your analysis, which should include your strategic assessment of the main arguments in terms of cogency, soundness, and meaning.* Explain and give reasons for your assessment, such as, "The second reason

in this sub-argument is false because. . . ." If it is not obvious, explain how the deficiency affects the argument. The more explicit you can be in presenting and supporting your critique, the more likely the reader is to follow and accept your critique.

   iv. *indicating the significance of your critique* of the specific pieces on the overall argument.

IV. *Conclude by providing your overall assessment of the argument, possibly together with observations on how the argument could be improved.* Simply providing a laundry list of challenges does not provide an overall assessment of the argument. Is the line of reasoning completely flawed? Are there some insights but poor argument development? How might the argument be improved?

The following is a sample analysis of "An Idea Whose Time Has Come":

> The passage "An Idea Whose Time Has Come" presents three arguments for the conclusion that the government should legalize the sale and possession of marijuana.
>
> The "autonomy" argument asserts that individuals have a right to engage in activities as long as they do not harm others. Although this can be made valid, the missing reason (that we should not restrict autonomy unless it causes harm to others) is too general. It would allow selling oneself into slavery, which we do not permit. A more careful defence of this argument would give the author a stronger case.
>
> The "no proof of harm" argument asserts that since there is no proof of harm, we should legalize the possession and sale of marijuana. This is a fallacy of appeal to ignorance.
>
> The "benefits" argument asserts that since legalizing marijuana would produce benefits to the government through taxation and the curtailing of other evils, it should be legalized. Although this is a valid argument, the missing reason (that if something produces benefits it should be legalized) is false. Legalizing marijuana may also produce harms (such as, increased incidence of lung cancer). The argument needs to weigh the harms against the benefits.
>
> The author raises and addresses an objection that can be issued against the autonomy argument: that using marijuana can harm others. The author responds by drawing a parallel with drinking and driving. Neither, by itself, causes harm to others; however, put together, they can. We handle the problem of impaired driving by banning that, not the separate elements. Although this is a good response, it does not overcome the fact that the basic argument has a false reason and is not cogent.
>
> Overall, the author has not provided a single cogent argument to establish his or her conclusion. If the author could strengthen the autonomy argument by showing the conditions under which things should be legalized and when they should not be, and if he or she could improve the benefits argument by weighing the costs against the benefits, there would be a stronger case.

Module Summary

- Longer passages, more complex arguments, and extended passages with a lot of extraneous material or confused and muddy reasoning require more systematic analysis.
- We can use the skills arrow diagrams and paraphrase to analyze such passages.
- We can use the earlier skills of argument analysis for both deductive and non-deductive arguments to assess such passages.
- Our analysis should contain an assessment of the overall adequacy of the case made in the passage being analyzed. This module outlines ways of diagramming and assessing the arguments in complex passages in systematic ways, using both arrow diagrams and argument paraphrase.

Argumentation Exercise: Writing the Dialogue

Assume Peter and Jean have developed the analysis you have done in this module in the Quick Quizzes on the Copyright and Piracy Dialogue passage from the beginning of this module. Write the next two pages of their dialogue incorporating their analysis. Make sure they engage on one or more of the significant issues in this.

Analyze your dialogue to show what you have done in terms of the content of the discussion and the argumentation moves.

Writing Skills Exercise: Presenting Your Argument Critique as an Essay

Using your analytical skills developed in this module on the "Pirates: I Don't Think So" passage, develop a two-page essay in which you present your analysis and assessment of the argument and your overall assessment.

Conceptual Analysis

LEARNING OBJECTIVES

After completing this module you should be able to:

1. Explain what conceptual analysis is;
2. Identify a question of concept in a text;
3. Generate various kinds of cases (such as, paradigm, contrary, borderline, imaginary);
4. Use the techniques of reasoning by cases, similarities and differences, and conjectures and refutations to analyze the cases and develop the criteria for the meaning of the concept;
5. Use challenge cases to test and refine your analysis; and
6. Write and present a conceptual analysis.

A DIALOGUE ON COPYRIGHT AND PIRACY – CONTINUED

Peter: Thanks for your help in analyzing the passage "Pirates: I Don't Think So" (see dialogue in Module 8). I am puzzled about the notion of piracy as theft. The author seems to think that downloading electronic material is not theft. This seems odd to me. The author's argument is that downloading an electronic copy is not theft because it is more like a trial than outright theft and it does not deprive the holder of the copyright of a potential sale. I don't get it. The author owns the material. So isn't that theft?

Jean: I am not so sure. Consider the following case. Would you agree that taking a CD from a store is theft?

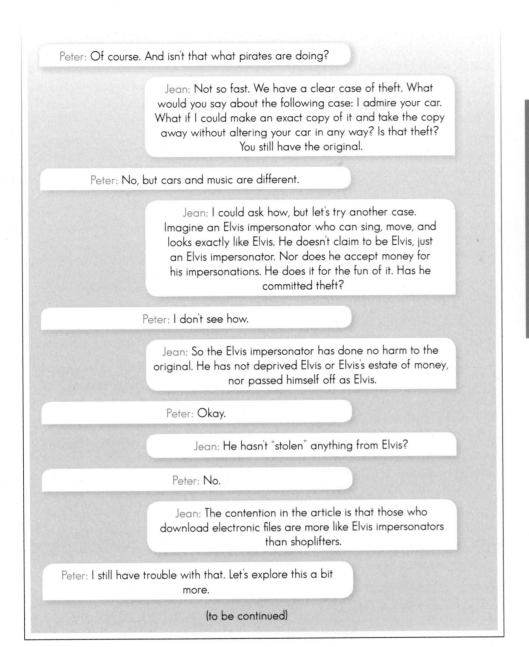

Peter: Of course. And isn't that what pirates are doing?

Jean: Not so fast. We have a clear case of theft. What would you say about the following case: I admire your car. What if I could make an exact copy of it and take the copy away without altering your car in any way? Is that theft? You still have the original.

Peter: No, but cars and music are different.

Jean: I could ask how, but let's try another case. Imagine an Elvis impersonator who can sing, move, and looks exactly like Elvis. He doesn't claim to be Elvis, just an Elvis impersonator. Nor does he accept money for his impersonations. He does it for the fun of it. Has he committed theft?

Peter: I don't see how.

Jean: So the Elvis impersonator has done no harm to the original. He has not deprived Elvis or Elvis's estate of money, nor passed himself off as Elvis.

Peter: Okay.

Jean: He hasn't "stolen" anything from Elvis?

Peter: No.

Jean: The contention in the article is that those who download electronic files are more like Elvis impersonators than shoplifters.

Peter: I still have trouble with that. Let's explore this a bit more.

(to be continued)

9.1 Introduction

In the dialogue Jean and Peter are using a technique called conceptual analysis to examine the meaning of the concept "theft." ***Conceptual analysis*** is a method of analyzing the meaning and use of concepts that uses various kinds of cases and tests of those cases to gain an understanding of concepts. It goes beyond dictionary definitions to provide an analysis of the way a concept is used in the language or in a given passage. It uses a form of reasoning (called "reasoning by cases") that is a central part of law, ethics, social policy, philosophy, nursing, and everyday reasoning, among other areas. *Reasoning by cases* involves analyzing cases that involve the use of the concept. A ***case*** is a concrete description of a complex situation that involves the use of the concept in question. Conceptual analysis relies on cases rather than examples, the difference being in how they are used. An *example* is used to illustrate

Conceptual analysis is a method of analyzing the meaning and use of concepts that uses various kinds of cases and tests of those cases to gain an understanding of concepts.

A **case** is a concrete description of a complex situation that involves the use of the concept in question.

something we already know, while a *case* is a description of a complex situation using the concept. It becomes the basis for analysis to discover something new. We use the case as a concrete referent and then extract the relevant criteria of meaning from it.

Conceptual analysis helps us analyze an author's use of a particular term as well as the meanings of complex ideas and concepts. In its latter use, it can be an excellent aid in working through an issue. This module identifies the basic techniques and uses of conceptual analysis as a tool for the clarification of meaning in everyday disputes and inquiries. We use conceptual analysis when the usual dictionary definitions are likely to be inadequate or when an author is using a term in a specific way.

Identifying Questions of Concept

Consider the following claim:

> Donor insemination (DI), or the fertilization of a woman's egg using the sperm of someone other than her husband is adultery, according to the Roman Catholic Church and some legal jurisdictions, though not in Canada.

This claim is likely to cause us some initial puzzlement, given that we do not normally consider DI adultery. The term "adultery" seems to be used in a non-standard way. That puzzlement could lead us to want to do a conceptual analysis of the term "adultery." What do we mean by "adultery"? Our response to the "what do you mean by 'adultery'?" is likely to be "that depends on what you mean by 'adultery'." When we encounter a claim that elicits such a response we are likely encountering a question of concept. A ***question of concept*** is a problem that hinges on the meaning of a concept, the relation of one concept to another, or the application of a concept to a specific situation. Other factors may influence our responses (such as, many consider there to be ethical issues about DI). However, before we can address any of the other issues we have to clarify the meaning of the central concept (in this case, adultery).

A **question of concept** is a problem that hinges on the meaning of a concept, the relation of one concept to another, or the application of a concept to a specific situation.

QUICK QUIZ 9.1

Identifying Questions of Concept

For each of the following:

(A) Identify the concept or question of concept that would need to be analyzed and that is not likely to be adequately explained by a dictionary; and

(B) Explain why it is a question of concept.

  1. Catherine MacKinnon claims that women in a patriarchal society are unable to consent to have sex with men.
  2. Can an androids be a moral agent? Could a chimpanzee be a moral agent?
  3. Some business ethicists claim bluffing is perfectly acceptable in business. Isn't bluffing a form of lying?
  4. Pornography objectifies and degrades women.
  5. Homosexuality, or any form of non-procreative sexual activity, is unnatural and therefore immoral.

A Case for Analysis

Let us consider a specific case:

> Robert Latimer had a twelve-year-old daughter, Tracy. She had Cerebral Palsy, was unable to talk, walk, or attend to her own bodily functions, and was in constant pain. One night, Latimer put Tracy in the cab of his truck, ran a hose to the cab from the exhaust, and killed her. He claimed he could no longer stand to see her suffer. Latimer claimed what he did was euthanasia. Although euthanasia is illegal, a substantial number of people consider it morally justified. His critics claimed he had murdered his daughter. Did Latimer "euthanize" or "murder" his daughter? Is there a difference? Are the concepts mutually exclusive?

The facts of the situation are not in doubt. What is in doubt is the meaning of the concept that characterizes it. What do we mean by "euthanasia" and what do we mean by "murder"? How are the two concepts related? And which applies in this particular case? These are three separate kinds of questions and they are all issues of concept:

1. What is the meaning of a concept?
2. How does the concept apply to other related concepts? and
3. How does the concept apply in this particular situation?

Although we can initially address a question of concept by looking up the word(s) in a dictionary, that is rarely satisfactory. The dictionary provides the following definition for euthanasia:

> euthanasia *n.* The act or practice of ending the life of an individual suffering from a terminal illness or an incurable condition. [Gk., a good death: *eu-, eu- + thanatos*, death.][1]

This does not help distinguish between euthanasia and murder. Nor does it help with the Latimer case. A dictionary definition often is just a report of how the word is commonly used in the language and does not cover new uses, unusual uses, or uses in specific contexts.

To summarize, we use conceptual analysis because:

- Dictionary definitions are sometimes inadequate;
- We want to analyze the meaning in context and the dictionary accounts are not precise enough to help us;
- Meanings vary and dictionaries do not always capture these variations;
- Some concepts are relatively new and their meanings are either not yet fixed or not yet recorded;

---

1 "Euthanasia." Def. ITP Nelson Canadian Dictionary of the English Language, 1997.

- We want to establish clear boundaries where there are not any yet for reasons of policy or ethics;
- The meanings of existing concepts are sometimes stretched and used in quite different ways from their main meanings and we need to be able to detect such shifts in meaning;
- We want to see how various concepts relate to one another; and /or
- It is a means of exploring an issue and helping us discover our reasons and thoughts on that issue.

In addition, using conceptual analysis can improve our reasoning skills in a variety of fields where it is used: ethics, law, policy, philosophy, most humanities and social sciences, and the developing of theory.

9.2 Doing Conceptual Analysis

The basic process of doing conceptual analysis involves generating cases that can be used both to develop and critique criteria for the meaning of the concept. We examine each case to identify the criteria that make it an example of the concept being analyzed. We suspend our understanding of prior definitions and see what there is about the case itself that makes it an instance of the concept. The aim is to *generate* a set of criteria, not confirm a pre-existing one. Usually, if we start with a prior set of criteria, we will tend to search for only those cases that confirm them and not be able to see the limitations of them.

Table 9.1 identifies the elements involved in doing conceptual analysis.

TABLE 9.1 Doing Conceptual Analysis

	Stage	Notes
1.	*Identify the concept and why it needs clarification.*	For an inquiry this can include the role the concept plays in the inquiry, or for a passage analysis the role the concept plays in the passage. In the Latimer case above, the concepts of euthanasia and murder need conceptual analysis to determine which concept his actions fall under. This can help us decide whether we hold Latimer morally accountable or excuse his actions.
2.	*Identify specific cases (concrete instances of the use of the concept.)*	Start with one or more cases involving a clear use of the concept other than the one being analyzed.
3.	*Analyze the cases for criteria of meaning/use.*	To develop the criteria of meaning/use that are inherent in the cases, we make conjectures about the possible criteria, challenge those criteria with new cases, and compare cases for similarities and differences.
4.	*Test and revise the criteria using additional cases.*	As we develop our criteria, we test them against new cases that can challenge or refute our criteria, and revise our criteria accordingly.

Table 9.2 identifies the basic reasoning strategies involved in dong conceptual analysis.

TABLE 9.2 Reasoning Strategies in Conceptual Analysis

	Reasoning Strategy	Explanation	Elaboration
1.	*The Principle of Similar Cases.*	Two things must be treated alike unless there is a relevant difference between them.	How are two cases alike? If we want to treat them differently, what is the relevant difference between them?
2.	*Counterexamples.*	These are cases designed to challenge a given set of criteria.	Typically these are variants of a case, or a new case, that challenge the criteria that have been developed.
3.	*Varying the criteria in a case.*	We systematically vary the various criteria by generating new cases in order to test criteria we have arrived at. Varying the criteria can be used to test the original criteria and to expand the proposed criteria.	How does varying the conditions of a case affect the meaning of the concept?
4.	*Examine how the concept is related to similar concepts.*	This may involve doing a parallel analysis of concepts related to the original.	How is *euthanasia* related to *murder, suicide,* and *suffering?*
5.	*Test the criteria.*	To see if they clarify the original situation. To see if they make sense in language.	The purpose of a conceptual analysis is to clarify the meaning of a concept. If the analysis does not clarify the meaning in the situation or results in our having to use the concept in a way dramatically at odds with ordinary usage, then we may need to consider another analysis.

9.3 Kinds of Cases

The core of conceptual analysis involves identifying and analyzing various kinds of cases. In the Latimer case described above we are faced with the following questions:

1. What do we mean by *euthanasia?*
2. What do we mean by *murder?*

3. How are the two concepts related? and
4. Does the concept of *euthanasia* apply in this particular case?

There are three different kinds of questions here: two about the meaning of concepts, one about the relation between concepts, and one about the application of the concept to a specific case.

Table 9.3 identifies the kinds of cases we can use for analysis.

TABLE 9.3 Kinds of Cases Used in Conceptual Analysis

	Name	Brief Explanation	Example: (Each Needs Developed into a Full Case)
1.	Paradigm or Model Case.	An ideal or perfect case of the concept being analyzed.	Clear case of euthanasia.
2.	Challenge Case.	A new case or modification of an existing case that challenges the existing criteria.	Involuntary euthanasia or euthanizing animals.
3.	Contrary or Opposite Case	A clear case of something that shares a key characteristic with the concept being analyzed but is contrary to the concept being analyzed.	A clear case of something that is not euthanasia but related to euthanasia (accidental death).
4.	Mixed or Mediant Case.	A case that fulfils only part of the criteria for the concept and often has features of several different concepts.	Suicide by someone with a terminal disease.
5.	Borderline Case.	A case that straddles the fuzzy boundary between one concept and another.	Assisted suicide.
6.	Invented Imaginary Case.	A made-up or imaginary situation that helps us clarify the logical criteria of a concept. This can be any of the other types (such as, paradigm, etc.).	An imaginary case of someone with Alzheimer's Disease.
7.	Science - Fiction Imaginary Case.	A made up or imaginary situation involving different realities. This can be any of the other types (such as, paradigm, etc.).	Can an android be euthanized?
8.	Related Concepts.	A concept that is connected to the concept under analysis, either as part of the explicit criteria for the concept being analyzed or as part of the vocabulary of related concepts.	Assisted suicide, death, and/ or consent.

The various kinds of cases provide different ways of exploring the meaning of a concept. We do not have to use every one in every case, nor use them sequentially. We use the kind that helps us understand the meaning of the concept in a specific situation. In learning them it is helpful to go through them sequentially to learn how each functions. Once we have done that we can use them in a more flexible way.

These will be developed and applied to the Latimer case below.

Model or Paradigm Cases

A *paradigm case* is an ideal, perfect, or model case of the concept being analyzed. It is a case no one would challenge as an instance of the concept, and it need not be real.

In analyzing the concept of euthanasia in order to address the Latimer case we would choose a clear example of euthanasia. (We cannot start with the Latimer case because it is the one in question. Since we are trying to gain clarity about it, starting with it is likely to result in a circular analysis.) To illustrate, let us use a modified version of a real case: the Sue Rodriguez case. If we did not know or have a real case available we could use an imaginary or hypothetical one.

Sue Rodriguez was a woman in her early forties who had contracted Lou Gehrig's disease (ALS), a wasting disease that slowly paralyzes various muscles until those necessary to keep the person alive (lungs and heart) fail. It is progressive and always kills. After a certain stage, death is fairly quick, but not painless. Sue Rodriguez had made various attempts to get the law changed to allow euthanasia. Although unsuccessful in this, as she began losing control of all her functions, she managed to get a doctor to help her die by injecting her with a lethal combination of drugs.

Virtually everyone would recognize this as a clear case of euthanasia. Indeed, it has become a textbook case of euthanasia. Now we need to analyze it. What is it that makes this a paradigm case of euthanasia? What criteria are we using that enable us to call this euthanasia? What is there about this case that is (a) typical and (b) essential of euthanasia?

Examining the case, we can extract the following possible criteria for the meaning of euthanasia:

Criteria for the Meaning of Euthanasia

1. The person being euthanized is suffering from a terminal illness;
2. The person is close to death;
3. The person wants to die; and
4. The person takes action to die.

This is our initial hypothesis about the criteria for the use of the concept. Are these four criteria sufficient? That is, if they are met, would we say the case is one of euthanasia? For example, if we can call something euthanasia without the person's having consented to it, then consent to being euthanized is not a necessary condition for the concept of euthanasia. Ideally, we want to identify the set of necessary and sufficient conditions for the use of a concept. (Review our discussion of necessary and sufficient conditions in Modules 2 and 4.)

The criteria we develop should clearly emerge from the cases and not go beyond them. Based on the Sue Rodriguez case, were we to propose a fifth criterion (say, the intention of the person who helped the person die is to ease her pain and suffering), we would be extending the criteria beyond the case's given characteristics. However, we could rewrite the case to include this. As we develop our cases and extract the criteria from them we elaborate and refine our criteria to meet our needs.

> A **paradigm case** is an ideal, perfect, or model case of the concept being analyzed.

CONCEPTUAL ANALYSIS **239**

The criteria above are not satisfactory because we can imagine a case that fits the stated criteria in which Sue Rodriguez, instead of having a physician help her, takes an overdose of sleeping pills, thus committing suicide. We need to distinguish between the two concepts by modifying criterion 4. This is one of the ways we develop criteria: imagining situations that would meet the existing criteria but would not be instances of the concept. This involves a use of a counterexample, what can be called in this context a *challenge case*, or a detailed case that challenges a specific set of criteria. Addressing the issue with criterion 4 we get the following:

Criteria for the Meaning of Euthanasia

1. The person being euthanized is suffering from a terminal illness;
2. The person is close to death;
3. The person wants to die; and
4. Another person assists the person to die.

We can continue with other paradigm cases and try to challenge these criteria, or we can move on to other kinds of cases and use those to test and extend our criteria for euthanasia. Normally, it is best to examine at least three cases of each kind to develop a final set of criteria. If we look at only one or two cases we may fix on one set of criteria that do not adequately characterize the concept. Furthermore, the greater the variety we introduce into our cases, the more likely we are to discover the necessary and sufficient conditions.

> **QUICK QUIZ 9.2**
>
> **Paradigm Cases**
>
> For the next series of Quick Quizzes we will use the following case for analysis:
>
> > I am talking with a friend and say that since I have been in the country for thirty years, I no longer feel like an immigrant and am going to apply for my citizenship papers. My friend says, "You will always be an immigrant. The only people who aren't are First Nations people."
>
> 1. What is the issue?
> 2. Identify the question(s) of concept in this passage; and
> 3. Generate three paradigm cases of each concept and identify the possible criteria that emerge from those cases.
>
> *Answers to the Quick Quizzes are available on the Premium Website at www.criticalthinking2e.nelson.com.*

Contrary or Opposite Cases

A *contrary* or *opposite case* is a clear case of something that shares a key characteristic with the concept being analyzed but is contrary to the concept being analyzed. A bank robber kills someone in the commission of a robbery. That is clearly not euthanasia. A person dies of natural causes. That is clearly not euthanasia. Both of these would

---

A **challenge case** is a detailed case that challenges a specific set of criteria.

A **contrary** or **opposite case** is a clear case of something that shares a key characteristic with the concept being analyzed but is contrary to the concept being analyzed.

be contrary cases. A person riding a bicycle is not a contrary case, nor is it a case of a similar type. Euthanasia has to do with dying. That is the general type. Only cases that share this characteristic are relevant contrary cases. Through this we have discovered another criteria of euthanasia: it is a form of death.

There are several conditions about the bank robbery and natural causes cases that clearly make them not examples of euthanasia:

1. In both cases there is a lack of consent. The individual did not consent to his or her death;
2. In neither case, as described, was the person suffering from a terminal illness; and
3. In neither case was it clear that the person wanted to die.

Comparing these with our original criteria, the contrary cases seem to confirm them as well as add to them. We now have the following:

Criteria for the Meaning of Euthanasia

1. The person being euthanized is suffering from a terminal illness;
2. The person is close to death;
3. The person wants to die;
4. The person consents to having someone help him or her die; and
5. Someone else takes direct action to assist the person to die.

Suppose the situation of the Rodriguez case were as described above, except that while she is nearing death she has not found a medical doctor to assist her. One night a burglar breaks into the house, she wakes, and is killed by the intruder. Would that be euthanasia? We would likely say "no." That is murder, not euthanasia. Even though she was terminally ill, was in a great deal of pain, was close to death, wanted to die, wanted to be euthanized, and someone else took action to kill her, she did not consent to this particular act by this person at this time and place. This is a clear contrary case.

To accommodate this we could modify the criteria as follows:

Criteria for the Meaning of Euthanasia

1. The person being euthanized is suffering from a terminal illness;
2. The person is close to death;
3. The person wants to die;
4. The person consents to having someone help him or her die; and
5. Someone else who has been designated takes direct action to assist the person to die.

We have modified criterion 5 to rule out murder. Sometimes it is useful to contrast paradigm cases and contrary cases to see what it is about the contrary cases that prevents them from being examples of the concept. What distinguishes the two cases in this situation is that the person did not consent to that particular person killing her, nor did she consent to the circumstances. Would it make a difference if the burglar knew she wanted to die and decided while there to do her a good deed by helping her to die? This is a variation on the previous contrary case. We would probably still say that it was murder. Even though the intent in this last variant of the case is different, killing her is not euthanasia.

Mediant or Mixed Cases

Not all cases are clear examples of the kind of thing we are trying to analyze. A **mediant** or **mixed case** fulfills only part of the criteria for the concept, and often includes features of several different concepts. Examining such cases can help us sharpen our criteria and determine what is essential for the concept and what is not.

Imagine a slightly different scenario: A doctor, knowing Sue Rodriguez wants to die but fearing repercussions, breaks into her home at night and gives her a lethal injection while she sleeps. Again, the specific consent is not there. What would we say now? Some might say it is euthanasia and others might say it is not. We tend to get hung up here on two competing issues: (1) whether the form of killing is euthanasia; and (2) whether it is morally justified. Sometimes we answer that the killing is not morally justified and, therefore, we want to say that it is not euthanasia. We must be careful not to conflate issues.

This is a difficult case. We have said euthanasia involves a person in specific circumstances consenting to a specific other person doing something to bring about the first person's death. Although Sue Rodriguez may have wanted to die and may even have asked this specific doctor to euthanize her, the doctor has done it in a way that is not clearly in accord with her wishes. For that reason, we might be hesitant to call it euthanasia.

Would it make a difference if the doctor, without Sue Rodriguez's knowledge, changed her medication in such a way that she would end up taking an overdose? Again, using the reasoning in the previous case, we might be hesitant to call it euthanasia. This is a mixed case because it meets some of the criteria but fails to meet others. On the basis of the reasoning we have given, the criteria it fails to meet are essential, and thus the mixed case, although having characteristics of euthanasia, is not euthanasia.

However, let us look at a parallel case. A nurse in a hospital deals with aged and chronically ill individuals. Some of them are near death and in considerable pain. Independently the nurse decides to give them lethal injections of morphine and potassium (which will stop their hearts). When caught, the nurse claims to simply have facilitated the patient's "peaceful death" (or euthanasia). Is this euthanasia or murder? While we are tempted to say murder, it may be both. If we agree to this, then we are saying the boundary between murder and euthanasia is not always a sharp one in some cases. There may be clear cases of murder, clear cases of euthanasia, and some mixed cases that may be both.

We have assumed that euthanasia must be voluntary (that is, something the patient requests and consents to). However, there is precedent for using the word "euthanasia" for involuntary euthanasia. We euthanize our pets when they are terminally ill, and they cannot consent. And in another vein entirely, the Nazis had a program they called "euthanasia" for the seriously ill and people with mental problems.

> A **mediant** or **mixed case** fulfills only part of the criteria for the concept and often includes features of several different concepts.

The problem is that involuntary euthanasia violates our basic ethical principles. We consider that in order to be ethically justified euthanasia must be voluntary. In the case we are examining, Latimer claims he did nothing ethically wrong because he was simply providing a peaceful death for his pain-racked daughter. That justification works for voluntary euthanasia, which is what most of us think of as euthanasia. Having discovered that we are analyzing voluntary (not involuntary) euthanasia we can adjust our criteria further:

Criteria for the Meaning of Voluntary Euthanasia

1. The person being euthanized is suffering from a terminal illness;
2. The person is close to death;
3. The person wants to die;
4. The person consents to having someone help him or her die;
5. Someone else who has been designated takes direct action to assist the person to die; and
6. In a time and place of his or her choosing.

QUICK QUIZ 9.4

Mediant or Mixed Cases

For the case in Quick Quiz 9.2 generate three mixed cases and identify their possible criteria. Compare these criteria with those developed in Quick Quizzes 9.2 and 9.3, and modify the criteria if necessary. Explain what makes these cases mixed cases.

Answers to the Quick Quizzes are available on the Premium Website at www.criticalthinking2e.nelson.com.

Borderline Cases

A *borderline case* is a case that straddles the fuzzy boundary between one concept and another. If we imagine there are a number of clear examples or instances of the concept and a number of clear examples or instances of things that are not the concept, then for many concepts there is a fuzzy boundary between the clear cases of x and the clear cases of *not x*. These are the borderline cases. By examining them and asking questions such as, "Why would it be included or not included?" and "How are we going to deal with the borderline case?," we can sharpen the criteria of what does and does not fit.

Consider another case (loosely based on a real case in Halifax): A man is dying of throat cancer. He will die sometime within the next four to twenty-four hours, during which time he will be in unbearable pain. Although not fully coherent, several times he cries out, "Stop the pain! I want it to end." However, he has not made a prior declaration that he wants to have increasing amounts of morphine even if it will stop his breathing. He has been given the maximum safe dosage of morphine, but it is not enough to relieve the pain. The attending physician gives him a combination of morphine and potassium, which stops his heart. Potassium has no other function than to stop the heart. Is this euthanasia? If so, is it voluntary or involuntary?

> A **borderline case** is a case that straddles the fuzzy boundary between one concept and another.

This is a difficult case. Our intuitions might differ from those of the former deputy coroner for Ontario, Dr. James Cairns. He believes this is murder, whereas some think it could be justified as euthanasia, although it is a borderline case. It has some of the characteristics of euthanasia but not others, and is on the boundary of the use of the concept. That Dr. Cairns and others do not agree may mean that they have different criteria for the meaning of "euthanasia," but it also may mean that they apply them differently in the borderline areas.

Part of the problem with this case is that the patient has given what can be taken as ambiguous consent. He has asked to have the pain stopped by saying, "I want it to end." Should that be interpreted as consent to euthanasia or simply a request for more of the painkiller? The maximum amount of morphine he can have without it stopping his heart is not working. He will die within hours and knows it.

Would the situation be different (or a variation of the case) if the attending physician had simply given increasing amounts of morphine to ease the pain, knowing it would bring about the patient's death? There are times when a physician will increase the amount of morphine to ease pain and it inadvertently stops the heart. Is that euthanasia? Whether one answers "yes" or "no" the critical feature is how the answer is defended. Some would suggest this is not euthanasia because the physician does not intend to end the life of the patient and the patient's death is an unintended but foreseeable possible consequence of the action. This means we are using the following as one of my criteria for euthanasia:

> The person performing the act that results in euthanasia intends the death of the other person.

The case of the attending physician administering potassium and morphine fits this condition. However, it is still clearly a borderline case. It ambiguously fits one of the other conditions: *The person being euthanized must consent to the act.* However, it is not clear from the situation that the person has consented. We have to make a decision about how to treat such a case. To understand the problems involved let us look at the next kind of case.

QUICK QUIZ 9.5

Borderline Cases

For the case in Quick Quiz 9.2 generate three borderline cases and identify their possible criteria. Compare these criteria with those developed in Quick Quizzes 9.2, 9.3, and 9.4, and modify the criteria if necessary. Explain what makes these cases borderline cases.

Answers to the Quick Quizzes are available on the Premium Website at www.criticalthinking2e.nelson.com.

| A **related concept** is a concept that is connected to the concept under analysis, either as part of the explicit criteria for the concept being analyzed or as part of the vocabulary of related concepts. |

Related Concepts

A ***related concept*** is a concept that is connected to the concept under analysis, either as part of the explicit criteria for the concept being analyzed or as part of the vocabulary of related concepts. Concepts partially get their meaning through their relation to other concepts in language. For example, the concept of rights is related to other concepts (such as, obligation, duty, responsibility) and to other kinds of rights (such as, human, civil). Examining related concepts helps us understand the concept in question.

One way of identifying related cases is simply by brainstorming other concepts associated with the one we are trying to clarify. Other concepts related to euthanasia include death, suicide, murder, and accidental death, as well as some of the concepts that appear in the criteria, such as, consent, terminal illness, pain, and suffering.

We might also consider phrases and statements that use the word and analyze those to see what light they shed on the concept. This can lead us to other possible concepts. For example, if we were clarifying "right" we might generate the following list of phrases and statements using the word:

My rights entitle me to ...
I have a right to ...
You have no right to ...
Animal rights ...
Smokers' rights ...

These might lead us to the related concepts of "having a right," "entitlement," holding rights in virtue of a characteristic one has (being a smoker, human, or animal), and possibly others. We might remember the phrase "a right, not a privilege" and contrast those two notions.

Let us look at a couple of other cases. The seven criteria work for the Sue Rodriguez case. However, instead of giving her a lethal injection, the physician provides her with a lethal drug cocktail and then leaves the premises. She takes the drug cocktail on her own. Is this euthanasia? I would say "no." Although the other person has facilitated her dying by providing the means, she is the one who actually undertakes the action that leads to her death. She has, in effect, committed suicide, although she has been assisted in that by someone else. In fact, we have a concept for this – assisted suicide, which involves a second party helping the ill person to die. Although assisted suicide is related to euthanasia, the two are not the same. The critical difference lies in whether the second person directly causes the death or simply provides the means for suicide. The border between these two concepts can sometimes be murky.

Some related concepts help us draw the boundaries between concepts (such as, murder versus assisted suicide), while others are necessary in elucidating the concept (such as, if euthanasia involves consent, then there are situations where we will need to know something about consent in order to determine whether a given case is an example of euthanasia).

We might also consider possible ways of qualifying the concept. The nurse example above gave us the related concept of involuntary euthanasia. In talking about euthanasia and consent, we have worked out that euthanasia with the patient's consent would be voluntary euthanasia. So the concept of euthanasia can be divided into voluntary and involuntary. The paradigm case of Sue Rodriguez would be an instance of voluntary euthanasia, the nurse case would be an instance of involuntary euthanasia, and the case of the patient with throat cancer would seem to straddle the borderline between the two.

Part of the reason we concern ourselves with clarifying the meaning of euthanasia is so we can determine whether it is morally justified or morally unjustified – two other related concepts. One of the clusters of meaning that euthanasia belongs to is that of moral discourse. We want to make distinctions in the assigning of moral responsibililty

A person who supplies the means for a suicide has, at worst, assisted in a person's dying, but he or she has not actually ended the person's life. The patient could still decide not to go through with the suicide. The person performing euthanasia is physically killing another person. The burglar is also physically killing another person. But the moral responsibility is different.

Another way of generating related concepts is by thinking of the various applications of the concept. Although we use "euthanasia" to apply to situations such as the Rodriguez case, we also apply it to our pets. This suggests a related use of the concept. When we have a veterinarian "put down" a beloved pet that is suffering and in pain, we call it "euthanasia" even though the pet has obviously not given consent. Alternatively, there are cases where people murder pets (such as, by putting out poison to kill the neighborhood cats). So we can draw a distinction between euthanasia and murder for pets as well as for humans.

Now for a difficult case: The Nazis developed a program to "euthanize" the seriously ill and those with mental problems, using some of the strategies they would later use in the mass extermination of Jews, gypsies, homosexuals, and others. Was this a proper use of the term "euthanasia," or is it an example of "concept stretching?" *Concept stretching* involves taking a concept with a reasonably well-agreed-upon use and extending the meaning far beyond its original use to validate something not normally justified by it. Concept stretching can occur when the boundaries of the term are not clearly defined, when the term is misunderstood, or when the boundaries of the concept are deliberately stretched for specific purposes. This often happens in heated controversies and political contexts. The concepts sexual harassment and pornography are two examples that have been stretched in the context of a controversy. For example, "pornography" originally meaning sexually explicit material, has been expanded to include portrayals that degrade or objectify women even if not sexually explicit.

The Nazi "euthanasia" program was, minimally, one of involuntary euthanasia since consent was neither sought nor given. However, we are reluctant to extend the word "euthanasia" to the Nazis' program for the following reason: in the context in which we use "euthanasia," the concept, whether voluntary or involuntary, applies to individual cases, not a state policy enforced on whole categories of people. Moreover, the point of the Nazi program was not to relieve patient pain and suffering but to rid the state of unwanted individuals. These differences are sufficient for us not to count this as euthanasia. Since the issues involved in each differ significantly we would rather not conflate them under one concept. For these reasons, we would not call the Nazi policy a legitimate use of the word "euthanasia." It is an example of concept stretching.

QUICK QUIZ 9.6

Related Concepts

For the case in Quick Quiz 9.2 generate three related concepts and identify their possible criteria. Compare these criteria with those developed in Quick Quizzes 9.2 through 9.5, and modify the criteria if necessary. Explain what makes these related concepts.

Answers to the Quick Quizzes are available on the Premium Website at www.criticalthinking2e.nelson.com.

Invented or Imaginary Cases

Invented or *imaginary cases* are hypothetical situations that help us clarify the logical criteria of a concept. There are two kinds of invented cases. One kind simply requires inventing a detailed case from features of the world we experience. The example of the nurse above is an invented case. Although the Rodriguez case is based on a real case, it did not have to be, and some of the variations (the burglar, for instance) were imaginary. We might better describe this kind of hypothetical case as an *invented situation.*

The second kind involves changing the features of the world in important ways and then asking what we would say about them. For example, if we have clarified the concept of person and understand it to mean "a bearer of rights" then we might construct an imaginary situation to test our criterion. A Martian lands on Earth. This Martian has desires, communicates with others of its species and with humans, reasons, feels pain, and has a host of other characteristics. Is it a person? Most people would probably say "yes." However, suppose now we discover this "person" is a well-crafted android, that is, it reproduces not through transmission of genetic material to offspring but through manufacturing processes. What would we say of it then? Alternatively, imagine we discover porpoises share all of the characteristics of this Martian. Would we say porpoises are persons? And what would this commit us to?

Let us apply this to our original situation. If we terminate the functioning of an android, have we killed it? If the android has been exposed to acids that will soon make it unable to function and it expresses a desire to have its functioning terminated, have we euthanized it? Is there a moral difference between terminating its functioning and terminating a human being who wishes to be euthanized?

In such cases we imagine fundamental changes in the reality we experience. If we know how to use the concept we are examining, we should know how to apply it to novel situations and cases, as well as know when we are puzzled by its application to novel cases. We use imaginary cases (in the above examples, they also happen to be borderline cases) to stretch and test our understanding of the original concept. They might also be looked upon as sophisticated ways of generating counterexamples to test our initial criteria. This second kind of invented case we can call science-fiction cases to differentiate them from invented situations based on real-world properties. A *science-fiction imaginary case* is one in which we imagine fundamental changes in the reality we experience. We use these to test our intuitions about the meaning of the concept.

The following is an example of a science-fiction case that applies to euthanasia: Imagine a situation in which Data on *Star Trek* has been exposed to a lethal pathogen that will kill all the members of the Starship Enterprise. The only way of stopping the infection is to atomize Data. Once atomized, he cannot be reassembled and thus will cease to exist. Because he is an android, his programming does not allow him to "kill" himself. He agrees to be atomized. Would we call this "euthanasia"? This case raises at least two interesting questions: (1) Can an android be euthanized? (2) Is it euthanasia if someone asks to be killed, not to prevent pain and suffering to himself or herself but to help others? Other conditions for euthanasia are met: it is done by another and there is consent. We can also consider a variation on this where the person infected with the pathogen was human, not an android. Is it euthanasia if a human consents to die to save others from pain and possibly death?

We might suggest this particular case is not euthanasia by calling the action "altruistic suicide." An essential feature of euthanasia seems to be that the person (in pain, suffering, and nearing death) seeks to die for him or herself, not to benefit another.

Consider a parallel case: A man is fatally ill but not suffering. His sister needs a heart transplant and his heart is a match. He offers to sacrifice himself so that his sister can have his heart. This does not meet the conditions for euthanasia, nor would we want to call it euthanasia. His intent is not to ease his own pain, but to use the opportunity to ease his sister's. Likewise, we can imagine a state of affairs where the members of a tribe on a distant planet sacrifice themselves so that siblings and other tribal members can have live organ transplants. We would not call this practice euthanasia. The intent of the person dying is not to ease his or her own pain and suffering but that of others. The context of the case is quite different.

To generate a science-fiction case we try to imagine a situation that is beyond the normal realm of experience. Imagining science-fiction situations, other possible societies, or variants in our reality is a way of generating such cases. Invented cases can be any of the other kinds: paradigm, contrary, borderline, mixed, or related.

Criteria for the Meaning of Euthanasia

1. The person being euthanized is suffering from a terminal illness;
2. The person is close to death;
3. The person wants to die;
4. The person consents to having someone help him or her die;
5. Someone else who has been designated takes direct action to assist the person to die;
6. In a time and place of his or her choosing;
7. The intent is to ease the pain and suffering of the dying person; and
8. The concept applies to individuals, not state policy aimed at groups or classes of people.

We now have a preliminary analysis of euthanasia. To address our initial question of whether euthanasia is murder, we should do the same kind of analysis with the concept of murder.

QUICK QUIZ 9.7

Invented or Imaginary Cases

For the case in Quick Quiz 9.2:

(A) Generate three imaginary cases, at least one of which is a science-fiction case;

(B) Identify the possible criteria found in those cases;

(C) Compare these criteria with those developed in Quick Quizzes 9.2 through 9.6, and modify the criteria if necessary; and

(D) Explain what makes these cases imaginary cases.

Answers to the Quick Quizzes are available on the Premium Website at www.criticalthinking2e.nelson.com.

9.4 Methods of Analysis

Generating cases is the starting point for conceptual analysis. Once they are generated, we must analyze the cases for the implicit criteria of their use. If we know how to use the concept, we know its meaning implicitly, even if we cannot necessarily articulate its meaning. This means we implicitly know the rules and criteria that govern the use of the concept. The point of generating cases is to provide us with clear examples (or referents) for the concept.

Conceptual analysis involves several discrete elements, outlined below. Some of the illustrations of these have been incorporated into the preceding section:

1. *Examine the cases, usually one by one to generate the criteria for the use of the concept.* This is why we want our cases to be as detailed as reasonable. What is there about the details of the situation that leads me to say that, for example, this is a paradigm use of the concept? What are the features found in this case that are general, and how do they apply to other cases? It is useful to analyze a few of each kind of case to help you abstract the concept. What are the similarities and differences among the cases? How do they affect the criteria?
2. *Synthesize the criteria.* Try to unify the criteria from the various cases. Reword and reformulate the criteria as precisely as possible.
3. *Critique your criteria.* (i) Compare the criteria against the existing cases to see whether they fit. (ii) Use counterexamples to challenge the criteria. Generate additional cases that fit the criteria but that may not be an instance of the concept. (iii) Generate additional cases that fit some of the criteria but not all, in order to test whether a given criterion or set of criteria are necessary and/or sufficient. Our discussion of euthanasia has used all of these methods of critiquing criteria.
4. *Revise your criteria and test again against the various cases.*

QUICK QUIZ 9.8

Synthesize and Critique the Criteria

(A) Examine the criteria developed in each of the cases for the analysis of the concept in Quick Quizzes 9.2 through 9.7, and synthesize them into one set of criteria;

(B) Identify possible challenges that might be made to the criteria you identified in Quick Quiz 9.8; and

(C) Develop those challenges, and then respond to them by modifying your criteria.

Answers to the Quick Quizzes are available on the Premium Website at www.criticalthinking2e.nelson.com.

By the time we have developed a variety of these cases and analyzed their criteria, we will have arrived at a set of criteria for the use of the concept, that is, we will have completed a conceptual analysis. We can continue to sharpen and refine our analysis with additional cases. However, we also need to know whether our analysis is useful. To determine this, we use the following steps:

I. Test Your Criteria Against the Original Context

What is the situation or context in which the problematic word and the need for a conceptual analysis arose? That is, what is the purpose of doing this conceptual analysis? We started with a question about whether or not the Latimer case was a case of euthanasia, and whether or not euthanasia is murder. We now take the criteria we have developed and apply them to the original situation. Do the criteria help us understand the situation better? Do they help us develop an answer to our original questions?

If you are confused by a particular concept, but your analysis makes no sense of the text, then you may not have analyzed the correct concept or your analysis may have somehow missed the point. For example, if you are puzzled about whether smokers have rights, but your analysis cannot be applied to smokers (as either having or not having rights), then you have not successfully analyzed the concept.

In the case of euthanasia we have produced a proposed set of criteria for the concept. Applying them systematically to the Latimer case, we find that they do not fit on several grounds:

TABLE 9.4 Testing the Euthanasia Criteria Against the Latimer Case

	Criteria for Euthanasia	Application to Latimer Case
1.	The person being euthanized is suffering from a terminal illness.	Although Tracy Latimer had a disease that would ultimately kill her, the disease was not likely to do that in the next few years.
2.	The person is close to death.	Tracy was not near death.
3.	The person wants to die.	From the facts of the situation we do not know this. Tracy was unable to speak and there is no evidence she had in any way indicated she wanted to die.
4.	The person consents to having someone help him or her die.	There is no indication she had given such consent and no one has contended that she did.
5.	Someone else who has been designated takes direct action to assist the person to die.	There is no indication she had designated anyone to take such action.
6.	In a time and place of his or her choosing.	Since there is no indication that Tracy chose to die, she could not have chosen a time or place.
7.	The intent is to ease the pain and suffering of the dying person.	This was the intent of Robert Latimer, but we do not know if it was the intent of Tracy Latimer, nor was she dying. In the absence of evidence we cannot assume this.
8.	The word applies to individuals, not state policy aimed at groups or classes of people.	This does apply to the Tracy Latimer case.

Based on these criteria and their application to the Tracy Latimer case, her death was not an instance of voluntary euthanasia. If 1 and 2 are essential for involuntary euthanasia (something we would have to establish through further analysis and argument), then it is also not a case of involuntary euthanasia.

There is a critical difference between analyzing the meanings of concepts and our beliefs about the concepts. The *meaning of the concept* is the set of common criteria for the use of the concept. They are what we presuppose when using the concept in the language. *Beliefs about a concept* are the specific beliefs we hold with respect to a given concept. These are not necessarily shared. Part of the meaning of the concept cat includes a furry, domesticated creature that purrs. Some of the beliefs about cats are that they are dirty, they are clean, they destroy flowerbeds by digging in them, and they chase mice. These are beliefs about cats, not part of the meaning of the concept. Some people believe that voluntary euthanasia is always morally wrong; others believe that it is often morally right. Some people believe that allowing it will lead to a wider use of euthanasia; others believe that it can be limited and strictly controlled. These are beliefs about the concept, not part of the meaning of the concept.

II. What Are the Practical Results of the Conceptual Analysis in the Language?

If we have clarified a concept and it requires a major rewriting of how the term is used in the language, that is, most claims once thought to be true using that concept would now be false, whereas many claims thought false would now be true, or most claims using the concept would now be meaningless, then we should reassess the analysis. If we are trying to clarify the concept as it is used in the language, then our results should not be drastically counterintuitive. For example, if our conceptual analysis results in a meaning for the concept euthanasia that negates most of the claims made about euthanasia, then we have not clarified the ordinary sense of the term. If our analysis conflates what are normally seen as distinct terms or applies only to a very few cases of what most people see as instances of that term or stretches the meaning of the concept to cover cases not normally thought of as instances of the word, then we have not clarified the ordinary concept of it as it is used in the language.

In some cases, we may want to argue for a technical or special use of a word (introduce a new concept). However, we should make this explicit and give the new concept a different name.

The above analysis of "euthanasia" seems to capture the way in which we use the word. It explains why the Nazis used the word (concept stretching), the euthanizing of pets (an extended use of the word), and the difference between voluntary and involuntary euthanasia.

In doing a conceptual analysis, we proceed only as far as necessary to clarify the concepts sufficiently for the purpose of the discussion or dispute we are involved in. Beyond that we may be trying to be overly precise. If we are simply engaged in clarifying the concept for our own understanding, then we can pursue it as far as necessary. After all, entire books have been written on the meaning of single concepts.

9.5 Presenting a Conceptual Analysis

Once we have completed a conceptual analysis we should at least summarize our criteria, apply them systematically and specifically to the conditions of the case or situation with which we began, and reach a conclusion.

Often we want to present our results to others, either as part of a paper in which we clarify the meaning of a concept before continuing to develop an argument based on it, or as an entire paper whose purpose is the presentation of the conceptual analysis.

The record of the process of inquiry, of arriving at our insights and ideas, is not usually the best format for presenting our ideas to an audience. This is true for virtually any material that we present. Offering the audience a blow-by-blow description of our reasoning process is likely to be counterproductive. So to move from generating an analysis to presenting that analysis, we need to make a case for our results.

The basic strategy for making a case involves identifying the issue for the reader, presenting our position about that issue, providing the relevant arguments, and leading the reader through the arguments. For a conceptual analysis presentation we must do a number of things outlined in Table 9.5.

TABLE 9.5 Presenting a Conceptual Analysis

	Steps	Meaning	Latimer Case Application
1.	Identify the issue or passage within which the issue arises.	Do not assume the reader knows the issue or the passage. Provide a brief synopsis.	Provide a brief synopsis of the Latimer case.
2.	Identify the issue of concept within the passage and explain why it is an issue of concept.	Why is this issue of concept important to the inquiry, dispute, position, or argument under consideration? How does the lack of clarity about the concept affect the discussion?	Explain how the lack of clarity about euthanasia and the problem of whether it is euthanasia or murder arises in the case.

3.	*Provide one or more cases that are central to the use of the concept being analyzed.*	Generate a range of cases (paradigm, contrary, mixed cases, etc.) and choose which to present to the reader.	The Sue Rodriguez case and the variants, including the burglar and the Halifax cases.
4.	*Identify the criteria for the use of the concept abstracted from the cases.*	Specify the separate criteria that emerge from the analysis. Make them as clear and precise as necessary for the analysis.	Criteria 1 through 8, from Table 9.4.
5.	*Show how the cases support the criteria.*	Give reasons why the various cases do or do not support the emerging criteria.	The Rodriguez burglar variant is not euthanasia because… .
6.	*Justify the criteria.*	Using the method of comparison and contrast as well as counterexamples to test our criteria can help us support the criteria. Use challenge cases to test the criteria. Show that our criteria cover the hard cases, handle the mixed cases, make important distinctions, fit the meaning of the context, and fit the language. Show either that these criteria for the use of the concept are those in use in the language or make an argument why these criteria should be adopted even though the criteria do not fit some of the uses of the concept in the language.	The homicidal physician who kills his patient without the patient's consent versus assisted suicide versus the original Rodriguez case. Arguing why each of these is or is not euthanasia helps establish the criteria.
7.	*Show how this clarification solves the issue of concept raised at the outset.*	Apply the criteria back to the original case and explain how this solves the initial question of concept.	Latimer committed murder, not euthanasia because… .

This pattern can be developed and expanded in a variety of ways. For example, steps 3, 4, 5, and 6 can be repeated a number of times before arriving at a final set of criteria. Step 3 can be developed and expanded using any of the types of cases we have identified. The central aim is to turn your detailed analysis into a presentation that the audience can follow and that they are likely to agree with on its merits.

You will likely have generated far more cases and variants of cases than you need to establish your conclusion. In developing your presentation, you need to select only the most salient cases and develop those. The android case and the altruistic suicide cases are not relevant to the Latimer case. One would not use the many variants of the Rodriguez case for a short presentation. Consider your audience and your purpose in writing in deciding which cases and analyses to use in your presentation.

9.6 Sample Conceptual Presentation: The Latimer Case

Was It Euthanasia?

Robert Latimer's twelve-year-old daughter, Tracy, suffered from severe Cerebral Palsy, was unable to talk or take care of basic bodily functions, and was in severe pain. Although the disease would eventually take her life, she was not likely to die for years. Robert Latimer killed his daughter by gassing her with carbon monoxide in the cab of his truck. He based his defence on the claim he had committed euthanasia to ease her pain and suffering. Critics claimed he had murdered his daughter. I will argue that what Latimer did was not euthanasia, in either the voluntary or involuntary sense, by examining the concept of euthanasia and showing it does not apply to this case.

A clear and widely acknowledged case of euthanasia is that of Sue Rodriguez. Ms. Rodriguez suffered from Lou Gehrig's disease. In the last stages of that disease, a person's breathing and heart muscles are paralyzed, and he or she dies a painful and horrible death. When Sue Rodriguez was near the end of the course of the disease, she arranged for a physician to give her a lethal injection that ended her life, since she was no longer able to do that for herself. She left a note saying this was what she wanted. This is a classic example of what we call euthanasia. The person euthanized, suffering from a fatal illness, is near death, is in pain, and is suffering. She asks for someone to help her to die. Based on this, we can suggest that the concept of euthanasia involves a person: (1) suffering from a terminal illness, (2) in the end stages of that illness, (3) who wishes to end her pain and suffering by dying, (4) seeks to die at a time and place of her choosing, and (5) is assisted in dying by someone of her choosing.

The first and simplest objection to the Tracy Latimer case being euthanasia might be that, while Sue Rodriguez had a physician assist her, Robert Latimer was not a physician. However, euthanasia does not require the assistance of a physician. We often hear of a husband assisting his wife to die, a child assisting a parent. As long as the other conditions are met, we still call this euthanasia.

Having someone assist in a person's death is an essential element of euthanasia. If I simply take an overdose of sleeping pills with all of the other conditions being met, I have not committed euthanasia; I have committed suicide. Even if someone has provided me the pills I use, it is suicide. We may call it assisted suicide, but not euthanasia. For it to be euthanasia the person who assists must take an active role in bringing about the death. While we could analyze what "active role" means, that is not at question in the Latimer case, and I will not address it in this essay.

Are all killings of people who are end-stage terminal and want to die euthanasia? I think not. The fact that someone wants to die under the conditions of euthanasia (1, 2, and 3, above) and does die under those conditions does not establish that it is euthanasia. Consider the following: Had someone broken into Sue Rodriguez's home the day before she had been euthanized, and, if while in the process of burglarizing the home, the intruder discovered her and killed her, we would not say that it was euthanasia, but that it was murder. Although most of the conditions for euthanasia would have been met, she had not given her consent to die at this time or in this way. Moreover, it would not have been the intent of the burglar to relieve her pain and suffering. Neither the consent condition nor intent condition would have been met.

However, let us consider a slightly different case. Sue Rodriguez has chosen the physician who will help her. She has specified the date and time of her death. However, the physician, unknown to the patient, gives her a lethal injection six months before she had intended to die. The physician believes her pain is becoming unbearable and acts to relieve her of it with a lethal injection. Is this euthanasia? It is clearly not voluntary euthanasia. Although she suffers from a terminal illness, is in the last stages of that illness, is in severe pain, is suffering, wants to be euthanized, and has given consent, she has not given consent for this time and under these conditions. The physician has acted independently. This case is closer to that of a caregiver who kills his elderly patients without their knowledge and consent because he believes that they are suffering. Even though there had been knowledge and consent in the case of Sue Rodriguez, the physician has acted independently and did not respect her wishes for a specific date of death. If anything, the physician has engaged in involuntary euthanasia. The intent condition is met but not the consent condition, which I consider a critical difference between voluntary and involuntary euthanasia.

Voluntary euthanasia occurs when an individual: (1) has a terminal disease, (2) is in the end stages of that disease, (3) is in severe pain and is suffering, (4) wants to die, (5) consents to have someone assist him or her to die, (6) does so on his or her own terms, and (7) when the intent of the death is to ease the pain and suffering of the person with the disease. Involuntary euthanasia occurs when conditions 1 through 3 are met and condition 7 is met by the person doing the euthanizing.

Based on these criteria, Robert Latimer did not engage in euthanasia when he killed his daughter. Although her disease was terminal (1), she was not in the last stages of that disease (not 2). She had severe pain and suffering (3), but there is no indication that she wanted to die (not 4), nor that she consented to die (not 5). Although Robert Latimer claimed, and I accept his claim, that he acted to ease her pain and suffering (7), there is no indication that Tracy Latimer was willing to die to ease that pain and suffering. This was Robert Latimer's choice and not his daughter's. The Latimer case clearly does not meet the conditions for voluntary euthanasia.

Nor does it meet the conditions for involuntary euthanasia. Although conditions 1, 3, and 7 (for Robert Latimer) are met for involuntary euthanasia, condition 2 is not. (If necessary, an argument could be developed about why condition 2 is necessary to distinguish euthanasia from murder.)

Notes on the Latimer Essay

The analysis presented in the sample essay above has been developed throughout the course of this module. In the essay, we have made a number of changes to the analysis. We did not use all of the cases nor all of the criteria. We selected the cases and criteria needed to address the issue, omitting those cases and criteria that did not directly address the immediate issue. We do not have to establish that our criteria fit the use of the concept in the language. The imaginary cases and the Nazi case do not advance the argument substantially, although they helped in developing an understanding of the concept. We have, therefore, dropped them. We also simplified and modified some of the cases and added new cases. As we developed our criteria and wrote the essay, we were able to see new cases and variants of cases that helped me advance and defend the criteria. We used those in writing the essay. Sometimes we develop cases that better illustrate the criteria once we have worked through the criteria.

This essay does not address the separate issue of whether Robert Latimer was morally justified in killing his daughter. We could claim that what he did was not euthanasia, as we have done, but was nonetheless, morally justified, which we have not argued. That is a separate issue and requires a separate argument. Many people were sympathetic to Robert Latimer's (and what they perceived to be Tracy's) plight and were willing to argue that he should not be held responsible because what he did was euthanasia. For them, euthanasia (the ending of terminal pain and suffering) would be sufficient grounds for excusing the action of killing his daughter (which everyone, including Robert Latimer) agreed he had done. Many others see his actions as horrific. This is a separate issue and needs to be argued separately.

QUICK QUIZ 9.10

Write Your Analysis

Briefly write a presentation of your conceptual analysis aimed at explaining it to other students who have not done this analysis. Follow the guidelines for presenting a conceptual analysis.

Answers to the Quick Quizzes are available on the Premium Website at www.criticalthinking2e.nelson.com.

Module Summary

- Conceptual analysis is a method of analyzing the meaning and use of concepts that goes beyond dictionary accounts and helps provide us with a deeper understanding of key concepts and issues.
- The method of conceptual analysis involves generating specific cases that we then analyze, using the method of reasoning by cases.
- We generate a variety of different kinds of cases (paradigm, contrary, mixed, borderline, and imaginary) as the basis for analysis.
- We analyze each case for the underlying criteria governing the use of the concept in that particular case.
- By analyzing multiple cases and different kinds of cases, we can develop a deeper understanding of the concept, its relation to other concepts, its possible applications, and its use in language.
- Through various techniques of analysis we can develop and test the criteria for the use of the concept. These criteria then help us understand the issue more fully and help us resolve potential questions about the meaning and application of the concept, both in the issue we are examining and in language in general.

Argumentation Exercise: Using Conceptual Analysis in a Dialogue

Review the article "Pirates: I Don't Think So" in the dialogue at the beginning of Module 8.

- Identify the uses of "theft" in that dialogue.
- Then read the dialogue in 9.1.
- Identify a number of cases that would help clarify the concept of theft.
- Develop the existing dialogue at the beginning of 9.1, incorporating those cases as challenge cases on the part of Jean and show how Peter could respond to them.

Writing Skills Exercise: Using Conceptual Analysis in an Essay

You have been asked to write an essay critiquing "Pirates: I Don't Think So." One part of the overall essay includes a conceptual analysis of key concepts. Select one key concept in the essay (one that an argument or conclusion hinges on), do a conceptual analysis of that concept and write a three-paragraph conceptual analysis argument using Table 9.5 to present that analysis. You are not writing the entire essay, only the part relating to the conceptual analysis of the concept. You may use "theft" or any other key concept in the passage. If you use theft, you may want to consider whether the concept is being used in the passage in the same way it is used in ordinary language.

Argumentation[1]

LEARNING OBJECTIVES

After completing this module you should be able to:

1. Explain the difference between argumentation, persuasion, rational persuasion, debate, and other forms of dialogue that use argument;
2. Explain the role of argument in each;
3. Identify the three main skills in argumentation and the components of those skills;
4. Use those skills in verbal argumentation;
5. Identify and use the two components of listening in argumentation; and
6. Engage effectively in an argument dialogue.

A DIALOGUE ON COPYRIGHT AND PIRACY – CONTINUED

Peter: So, you are saying that there is nothing wrong with downloading copyright material without paying the copyright holder because it does no harm.

Jean: Yes.

---

1 Jean would like to thank Professor Michael Gilbert, York University, whose work on the practical aspects of argumentation, as described in his book *How to Win an Argument* (2nd ed., Toronto: McGraw-Hill Ryerson, 1996.) and his *Effective Dispute Manual*, (unpublished, Toronto, 1981) has strongly influenced his ideas in this module.

Peter: So, if something does not cause harm, it is okay?

Jean: Yes.

Peter: So, if someone cheats on their partner and the partner never finds out about it that is okay?

Jean: But that is not the same thing!

Peter: You sound annoyed.

Jean: I am. It seems you are not addressing the issue.

Peter: Sorry, I was just trying to probe your assumption. How about this: someone steals $10 from his or her employer to buy a Tim's coffee and the employer never finds out. Is that okay?

Jean: Neither are the same. Both cause harm even if the partner or boss never knows.

Peter: How is the stealing case different from the downloading one? They both seem to be stealing to me.

Jean: In the case of the $10 you are depriving the employer of something that it is entitled to. You are not depriving the copyright holder of anything by downloading a copy of a song or movie.

Peter: Explain.

Jean: The copyright holder has a right to the physical materials he or she has produced. However, if I can make a copy without damaging the original, so long as I don't try to make money by selling it, I haven't harmed the original copyright holder. It's like my cloning your car or an Elvis impersonator. An Elvis impersonator doesn't harm Elvis' estate by giving a perfect impersonation.

Peter: Let's agree to that for the moment. Why do you say there is no harm to the original copyright holder?

Jean: Because the copyright holder has no right to potential sales. I haven't deprived her or him of a sale.

Peter: I want to disagree on that, but let's come back to that. First, though, I want to hear why you think that.

(to be continued)

10.1 Introduction

Peter and Jean have been engaged throughout this text in a process of argumentation. As initially defined, *argumentation* is the process of reasoning with reasoners – that is, of constructing arguments, presenting those arguments, challenging, and responding to those challenges in an ongoing dialogue. In this stage of the dialogue, they use a number of skills we will develop in this module, including clarifying, formulating, and challenging missing reasons, and various kinds of challenges and responses.

Although developing and challenging arguments are the core elements of argumentation, not all use of arguments in a discourse is argumentation. Arguments are used in a variety of other contexts, including such areas as persuasion, debate, and the law. Although the word "argumentation" is sometimes used to apply to all of these, there are some significant differences, the central ones being the aim or purpose of the discourse and the rules that govern that discourse.

Debate is an adversarial process in which opposing sides use arguments to defeat their opponents. The goal is not to reveal the truth about an issue as much as it is to establish who has given the better argument, thereby "winning." Debates often involve polarizing an issue and ignoring possibilities that would fall between the opposing viewpoints. A debater seeks out flaws in the opponent's position to show the weaknesses of that position and ultimately to defeat the opponent. To build a strong case the debater must maintain his or her original position. Usually governed by fairly strict rules of process and turn-taking, debates focus entirely on the issue and ignore the person. Courtroom law shares many of the characteristics of debate.

Persuasion is the process of trying to win someone over to a particular point of view or to motivate a person to perform a particular act. Persuasion that is based purely on reasons and argument is *rational persuasion,* which is a form of argumentation. However, most persuasion uses other methods (such as, appeals to emotion, desires, interests, threats of harm, or force). While arguments may be used toward these ends, they are simply a means to an end. Persuasion is allied with practices like marketing, rhetoric, and advertising. Typically, persuasion is one-sided because one person is trying to persuade another. The persuader does not expose his or her position to critique and normally does not expect to have his or her opinion changed.

Argumentation is a co-operative, reciprocal process in which both sides state their positions, challenge the positions of each other, and have their own positions challenged. Issues are addressed and positions adopted and abandoned solely in terms of reasons. The aim is to discover the truth about an issue. Both sides explore the complexities of their own position and that of the other. Either side may change its position and the reasons for it in numerous ways and may become rationally persuaded by an argument partner's position and reasons. Argumentation results in reflection on and a better understanding of one's own position as well as that of an argument partner's. Argumentation involves not simply providing justification for one's preexisting point of view but, rather, the examination, probing, and improving or modifying of it through reasoned discourse.

In practice, these and other modes of discourse involve the use of arguments (such as, in negotiation and legal proceedings), which often can and do overlap and intermingle. Argument is used in various ways and for varying purposes, as are many of the skills of argumentation. We may start out in an argumentation and end up in a debate or vice versa. Nonetheless, it is important to recognize the distinctions between the modes of discourse because both the aims and the rules of engagement in each are different. Although often not distinguished in our everyday experiences, understanding their differences can help us comprehend what is happening in any individual discourse and help us achieve our aims in it. It also helps us understand what pure argumentation can be like. The tools of argumentation are outlined in this module.

Argumentation is defined and distinguished from other forms of discourse both by its central aim and its constitutive rules. The central aim of argumentation is to find the truth about an issue through reasoned discourse. The *constitutive rules* (outlined in Module 1) define the practice of argumentation. Other forms of discourse (such as, debate, persuasion, legal argument, and advertising) have different aims and correspondingly different constitutive rules.

In much of the analysis and evaluation of argument in previous modules, we have viewed arguments as static texts. Even when dealing with written arguments that might be part of an ongoing discussion (such as, a series of articles, letters, or memos), we have treated them as containing a series of discrete and static arguments. Yet in our daily lives, most of us encounter arguments as fluid and dynamic. They are a part of ongoing discussions and dialogues and develop through interaction with one or more others. Sometimes they emerge from discussions. Sometimes they are embedded in texts and written responses to texts. In argumentation, more emphasis is placed on the challenges and responses to the challenges. This module examines the dynamic nature of argumentation and how to apply the skills developed in the preceding modules to it, with special emphasis on verbal argumentation.

10.2 The Dynamics of Argumentation

As outlined in Module 1, in an *argumentation encounter*, two or more *argument partners* engage in a *dialogue* in which one partner acts as an *advocate* for a position, while the other acts as a *challenger*. The *constitutive rules of argumentation* ideally govern the interaction between the argument partners. An argument over a given *issue* may continue over a number of encounters. Although our formulations are based on two arguers, argumentation can include more than two. A single individual can also take the role of both arguers (presenter and challenger) and conduct a dialogue with him or herself or with a text.

Although verbal argumentation is free flowing and dynamic, underlying the fluidity of the discussion, some core patterns help define the key features of an ideal argumentation encounter. How these manifest themselves in a discussion will vary considerably. To be effective in any argumentation, there are three core tasks that must be addressed:

1. Clarifying meaning;
2. Eliciting and identifying arguments; and
3. Evaluating arguments through challenging and responding to challenges.

Each task uses a specific set of skills. How we use them and in what order will vary between encounters. Take a look back at Figure 1.5 in Module 1 to refresh your memory.

Before Starting

Ideally, before engaging in argumentation we should answer for ourselves and our argument partner the question "What's the point?" Although we often fail to do this, thinking about the point of the encounter can help us clarify our desired outcome, which may be any of the following:

1. To explore an issue (yours or your argument partner's) to learn from it;
2. To present an argument and have your argument partner hear and understand it;

3. To present an argument and have your argument partner see that it is reasonable;
4. To present an argument and have your argument partner accept it; or
5. To refute an argument and have one's partner acknowledge it has been refuted.

The strategy adopted might vary depending on what outcome we want from the argumentation encounter. If we are simply exploring an issue with a friend and want to see what the respective positions commit each to, then we might adopt a different strategy than if we are trying to persuade.

Often we simply assume the point from the context and leave the possible outcomes unexplored. However, if our argument partner presumes a different possible outcome, the two arguers may miscommunicate. If that happens, we can simply step back and clarify the point of the encounter and what outcomes each person is looking for. If the outcomes are too discrepant, or the two parties have quite different and incompatible aims, then the encounter may have to end.

Active Listening and Feedback

Argumentation is a form of interactive communication based on listening and responding. Listening involves two components: active listening and feedback.

> Jean: Claim or argument
>
> Peter: So, you are saying that . . . (paraphrases X)

Active listening is paying attention to what the other person is saying, making sense of it, and separating it from any interpretations or responses we may have to it. Often when we are engaged in dialogue and we suspect we disagree with someone, we listen for flaws, for what we can challenge and refute in the other person's argument rather than to understand. Our listening is partial and selective. Giving our full attention and seeking to understand when we disagree is difficult. We naturally want to elaborate, challenge, add to, defend, attack an idea, or change the topic.

We often do not engage in active listening. Sometimes we are too busy thinking about our response and how we are going to challenge the other person. Sometimes we fear that if we focus our full attention on the other we will forget what we have to say. However, what often happens is that when we give full attention to what the other person is saying we gain a better understanding and, as a result, see stronger possible challenges. In argumentation, therefore, our first task is to understand what our argument partner is saying, and the nature of his or her commitment to that. Only when we understand our argument partner's position fully can we effectively engage with it.

Whenever we interact with another, we send messages on a number of levels: the *content level*, which is the substance of what we are discussing; and the *emotional* and *nonverbal level*, which is the way in which we express our thoughts. Active listening requires that we focus on both levels of communication. We often deprive ourselves of valuable information by focusing solely on the content (or spoken words), the reasons, conclusions, challenges, and responses, all while ignoring other aspects of communication. Listening to the emotional tone and nonverbal cues (such as, body language and tone of voice) that accompany the content can provide us with information about the person's meaning and his or her investment in the issue. The way someone says, "That is not an important reason" may tell us how significant the reason is. Said forcefully, it may mean the reason is in fact very important. Said diffidently, it may mean it really is not important. An argument partner's shaking of the head while another puts forward an argument may indicate disagreement, even though he or she does not say anything. When people become emotional it may mean the issue is particularly important to them. If reticent or hesitant, they may not be sure of what they are saying, or they may be disclosing something that is important but feel uncertain of how it will be taken. If reserved about what they are saying, they may be disengaged or simply be repeating what others have said, or may have no investment in the issue, and we are not hearing their reasons. Context and knowledge of the other person are both important factors in interpreting such cues.

Since communication is complex and we are sometimes not sure of what someone is saying, we need to give feedback about our understanding. This feedback is a hypothesis about what the person is meaning.

Providing feedback is paraphrasing for an argument partner our understanding of what he or she has said. In the paraphrase, we try to capture the core of the argument position, not simply repeat word for word what was said.

We have no way of knowing if our attempt to understand our argument partner is accurate unless we get feedback on our feedback. When giving feedback, we state our best hypothesis about what we think the other's argument is. Good feedback may reflect both the content and the emotional elements. If interpreting the emotional element, we do so by describing what we observe and then what we deduce the significance to be.

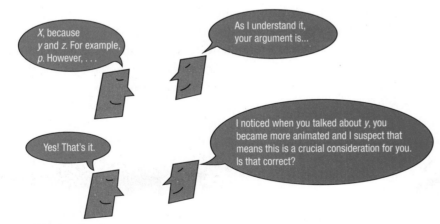

Figure 10.1 Feedback

We have to be careful to distinguish what we hear and observe from our interpretations. We confirm our interpretations with our argument partner, being careful not to anticipate his or her line of reasoning or add things to what he or she has said. If we train ourselves to reflect back the other's arguments before responding, we can accomplish two things. First, we make sure we have understood correctly before we raise our challenges. Second, we establish a certain amount of respect for our argument partner. We show we care enough to interpret his or her position correctly.

Listening actively and providing feedback has a further and equally important function. It slows down the attack–response cycle, which can lead to a destructive escalation of conflict. When we do not listen actively and provide feedback we tend to listen selectively for the criticisms of our own positions and the weaknesses of the other's, often failing to see the strong points in the other's position or to acknowledge the truly weak points in our own. By listening actively and representing the opposing arguments fairly and in their strongest light we establish that we are concerned with pursuing the truth and not simply scoring points at the other side's expense. This helps establish rapport with our argument partner.

Feedback is simply a hypothesis about what our argument partner intended; it is not necessarily accurate. Our goal in giving feedback is to identify clearly our argument partner's ideas, claims, or arguments. If an argument partner does not agree with the feedback, we should ask him or her to clarify. Some individuals may not pay close attention to what they themselves say and, therefore, may not realize what they have actually said. Rather than getting into a dispute about what was said, we grant them their intended meaning, using the *Principle of Charity* (as mentioned in Module 1).

Provide feedback every few minutes in the initial stages of developing the skill. Do not try to remember a half hour's conversation and then summarize it. Once you have developed the skill, use feedback at crucial points in the conversation to formulate the central line of argument or point of dispute, to clarify when you or your argument partner seem confused or off track, to summarize points of agreement, to reiterate a main argument or point, or to transition from one point to another in a conversation.

Ask your argument partner to give feedback of his or her understanding of what you have said as well. Listen to the feedback and check it for accuracy. Do not simply verify everything you hear. You can paraphrase to acknowledge what your argument partner has said, grant it for the time being until you have heard her or his argument, and then return to it for further examination. It is always possible that your message has not come across to your argument partner the way you intended it, or you may not be encoding your message in a way that can easily be understood. Rather than arguing over what you did or did not say, or getting sidetracked on the issue of who is or is not listening, correct your argument partner's interpretation and focus on the content of the message that you intended him or her to receive. Make sure the claims or arguments are as clear and precise as you want because you will have to defend them.

Often when we present arguments verbally, we have not thought through the issue completely. We construct our ideas and develop our arguments as we speak. Therefore, we may not express ourselves as correctly or precisely as we would like, searching for words and ideas concurrently. And sometimes our argument partners will not attend carefully to what they are saying. If both argument partners actively listen and paraphrase what they have heard, they can help each other formulate their arguments more accurately.

Eliciting Arguments

Eliciting the arguments in a discussion involves identifying what the issue is, the argument partners' positions on it, the reasons for their positions, and the structure of the argument. We do this by clarifying the issues and asking for reasons whenever our argument partner states a core position or a claim we want to examine. We use the components for identifying and portraying the structure of an argument developed in Module 2, and for identifying issues in Module 1.

Some of the questions we might use to elicit arguments include the following:

- "Why?"
- "What are your reasons for that?"
- "How would you support that?"
- "Can you give me another reason?"
- "What evidence do you have for your position?" and/or
- "Do you have any other reasons?"

To illustrate:

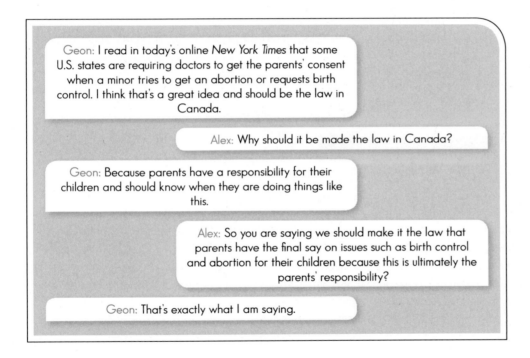

Geon: I read in today's online *New York Times* that some U.S. states are requiring doctors to get the parents' consent when a minor tries to get an abortion or requests birth control. I think that's a great idea and should be the law in Canada.

Alex: Why should it be made the law in Canada?

Geon: Because parents have a responsibility for their children and should know when they are doing things like this.

Alex: So you are saying we should make it the law that parents have the final say on issues such as birth control and abortion for their children because this is ultimately the parents' responsibility?

Geon: That's exactly what I am saying.

To help in this stage, paraphrase your understanding of the argument and ask for clarification and confirmation from your argument partner; for example:

"So what you are saying is that ... because ..."; or

"As I understand it your position is that ... and your reasons for that position are ...".

When structuring arguments verbally, use cue words to help identify reasons and conclusions. In the above dialogue, both Alex and Geon use cue words to help structure the argument.

When developing your understanding of the arguer's position, one good strategy is to continue probing and to identify the support for the reasons as illustrated in this dialogue. For example:

> **Alex:** Why is it ultimately the parents' responsibility?
>
> **Geon:** Because it's an issue of morals and it's the parents' responsibility to instil morals in their children. Besides, parents are financially responsible for their children.
>
> **Alex:** So you're saying that because the parents are responsible for the morals and the financial support of their children, they should have the final say in issues such as birth control and abortion?
>
> **Geon:** Yes.

Alex probes for further reasons. Geon introduces two reasons: morals and money. Alex could continue probing by asking the following questions: "Why do you think it is an issue of morals?" and "What does the financial issue have to do with whether or not parents should have a say in this?" This will give him a better understanding of Geon's position, and he can then choose where to probe further.

QUICK QUIZ 10.1

Probing Reasons

The Quick Quizzes in this module are designed to help develop your verbal argument skills, so they should be done reasonably quickly, without writing out various alternatives. After you have done them verbally, write them down. Then you can think about other possibilities.

For each of the brief arguments below, suggest three additional probes (questions) for reasons that B could use to find out more about A's argument. Do not challenge the argument.

1. A: I think we should have more bike lanes in the city because it will encourage more people to ride bikes and it will reduce traffic.
    B: i.
        ii.
        iii.
2. A: Downloading copyrighted music and videos from the Internet without paying for it should not be a crime. After all, it doesn't hurt anyone.
    B: i.
        ii.
        iii.
3. A: I do not think we should allow genetically modified foods to be sold and put into the food chain. After all, we do not know their long-term effects.
    B: i.
        ii.
        iii.

Answers to the Quick Quizzes are available on the Premium Website at www.criticalthinking2e.nelson.com.

Clarifying Meaning

The second task in argumentation is to clarify the meaning of terms and claims, including implications, presuppositions, and assumptions. Before we can develop a critique, we must know not only what our argument partner is saying, but also the intended meaning of his or her central claims and concepts. Some of the things we can do to clarify include:

- Ask for examples to illustrate concepts;
- Do a conceptual analysis on contentious and unclear concepts;
- Check the scope of claims (all, some, a few), especially if not specified;
- Ask our partner to clarify terms; and
- Test with implications of the use of the term.

Applying these to the parental consent dialogue above, we have the following:

Alex: What do you mean by "children"? People aged thirteen, sixteen, eighteen, twenty-one? (*Request for scope.*)

Geon: As long as someone is living in their parents' house, the parents should know and their approval should be sought. (*Clarifies the intended scope.*)

Alex: Even if they are old enough to vote or join the military? (*Testing the implication.*)

Geon: Yes, if they live at home. (*Accepting the implication.*)

Alex: What about if they legally move out at sixteen? (*A test of the application of the principle.*)

Geon: Yes, they are still minors. (*Acknowledges the application.*)

Alex: So you're saying that regardless of age, as long as a child is a minor or lives at home then parents should have the right to determine whether their child uses birth control or has an abortion? (*Restates the criteria.*)

Geon: Yes.

Alex: What if the "child" is twenty-five or even twenty-eight and hasn't left home because he or she is in school? (*Testing the implication.*)

Geon: I would put an upper age limit of twenty-one. (*Modifies and limits his claim.*)

Alex: Why then? (*Probing for a reason.*)

Alex could also probe the concept of "parents having responsibility for their children" and what that entails.

Thus far Alex is simply eliciting Geon's position and reasons. Had Alex started to challenge, issued a judgment (such as, "That's absurd!"), or counterargued, he would be arguing against a position he did not yet understand.

QUICK QUIZ 10.2

Clarifying Meaning

For each of the brief exchanges below, identify a concept or claim that might need to be clarified, and provide B with three questions that would probe for meaning of that concept.

1. A: I think pornography exploits women.
   Concept or claim:
   B: i.
      ii.
      iii.

(continued)

2. A: Some video games are sexist and encourage violence against women.
      Concept or claim:
   B: i.
      ii.
      iii.
3. A: Violent video games cause harm.
      Concept or claim:
   B: i.
      ii.
      iii.

Answers to the Quick Quizzes are available on the Premium Website at www.criticalthinking2e.nelson.com.

Evaluating

Evaluation includes testing and assessing both the truth of the claims and the logic of the argument. To evaluate, we address two basic questions:

1. Do the reasons adequately support the conclusion? and
2. Are the reasons true?

However, before evaluating the claims it is useful to identify the unstated and implicit assumptions. In dialogues, people often do not give full arguments, and the defender usually gives one reason or several independent reasons. As active listeners, we search for missing links that will make the arguments work, as indicated by Tali's probing in the following:

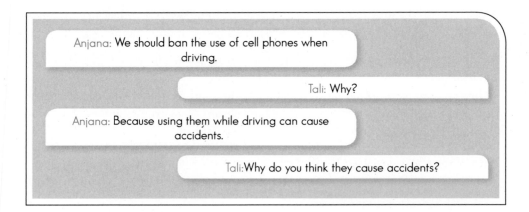

Anjana: We should ban the use of cell phones when driving.

Tali: Why?

Anjana: Because using them while driving can cause accidents.

Tali: Why do you think they cause accidents?

Often we are unaware of the implicit reason needed to make the argument valid. Someone skilled in argumentation can help with this through probing. Usually, as in this case, the reason given is the one considered the least contentious. People not trained in argument do not always realize they have omitted part of the argument on which their conclusion rests. If we want to be effective in helping our argument partners probe their arguments, we need to be able to supply the implicit reasons. Identifying the unstated reasons can give us more room for exploring and challenging an argument.

Identifying Unstated Reasons

What we want to be able to do in verbal argumentation is to think on our feet and to connect the stated reason to the conclusion. We can use one of four methods for doing this: the topics model; recognizing argument patterns, particularly conditions; a shortcut method; and the counterexample. Consider the above argument about cell phone use. We can supply the implicit reason:

> A. [We should ban anything that is likely to cause car accidents.]
>
> 1. Using cell phones while driving causes accidents.
>
> ---
>
> ∴ 2. Ban cell phone use while driving.

We can use one of these four models to generate the missing reason and from that the challenge to it.

Method I

The *topics model* (introduced in Module 4) involves asking two questions of the conclusion to find the missing reason:

1. Under what conditions? and
2. Does x meet those conditions?

The stated reason will answer one of these questions. By finding the answer to the other, which we can infer from the stated reason, we can supply the implicit reason. In the example above, the questions would be:

1. Under what conditions should we ban something? and
2. Does that apply to using cell phones while driving?

The answer to the first question is not given, but is implied by the answer to the second question, which is given (that using cell phones while driving causes accidents). This gives us the implicit reason: if something is likely to cause car accidents we should ban it. This is a general claim and we can challenge it with a counterexample.

Method II

The *conditional model* (introduced in Module 4) uses the stated reason and the conclusion. From them, we construct a conditional argument that affirms the antecedent. Once we have identified the conditional, we can generalize it.

For the above example, we can construct the following conditional claim:

> If using cell phones while driving causes car accidents, then we should ban their use.

We can generalize this to:

> If something causes car accidents, then we should ban it.
>
> Or
>
> Anything that causes car accidents should be banned.

We can then use a counterexample to challenge this.

Method III

The *shortcut method* builds on the implicit pattern in the two preceding methods. The argument can be stated as follows:

1. Using cell phones while driving causes accidents.

∴ 2. Ban cell phone use while driving.

The purposes of supplying an implicit reason are to help make the argument valid and to identify what assumptions someone is making in giving the argument. What both the preceding methods do is recognize that the terms in the conclusion must be reflected in the reasons and connected together. In this argument, the two terms in the conclusion are:

- *ban*
- cell phone use while driving.

The stated reason talks about:

- *using cell phones while driving*
- causing accidents

For the argument to work, we need a reason that connects the two unconnected terms. That is, we have to say something about banning things (the conditions under which we would ban something) and causing accidents:

We should ban things that cause car accidents.

In many arguments with one reason and a conclusion there will be a total of three terms used, one of which will be repeated. In this example, "cell phone use while driving" is the phrase that appears in both the reason and the conclusion. What we want to do is connect the two terms that are not yet connected, namely, things that should be banned and things that cause car accidents. That will give us an implicit reason. Consider the argument thus far, and identifying the topics by underlining and numbering them:

Using cell phones while driving causes accidents.

    1   2

∴ Ban the use of cell phones while driving.

    3   1

The numbering and underlining help us see the connections.

This identifise the common term (1) and connects it to the two remaining terms (2 and 3). We can now create the missing reason by connecting those two terms, as follows:

We should ban things that cause car accidents.

    3   2

While this does not work in all cases, and does not guarantee a valid argument in all cases, it often does provide a useful way of generating a hypothesis about the connection between the stated reason and the conclusion. By formulating this connection for ourselves about our argument partner's potential assumptions we can then formulate a counterexample to further probe his or her argument.

Method IV

The *method of counterexample* is an even simpler method. With this method we move straight to a counterexample from the argument without formulating the implicit reason. The argument is:

1. Using cell phones while driving causes accidents.

∴ 2. We should ban the use of cell phones while driving.

We identify the specific term or phrase that occurs in both the reason and the conclusion, substitute another term or phrase that might be relevant, and pose it as a counterexample to see if the person wants to ban that as well. The specific phrase that occurs in both the reason and the conclusion is "cell phones." What we want to do is find something done while driving that may cause accidents, but that the person would not want to ban (such as, eating, having kids in the car, and/or listening to the radio). In effect, we simply substitute another term or phrase for the one in the reason and pose that as a counterexample to our argument partner:

> Tali: So we should ban taking excited kids to hockey practice because they might distract the driver and cause accidents?

All counterexamples are based on the *principle of similar cases,* introduced in Module 6, which holds that all things that are alike should be treated alike, and when they are not we must justify the difference of treatment. This is basic to all reasoning. If an argument partner is going to reject the counterexample of driving excited kids to hockey practice as a cause of accidents, then he or she must provide a relevant reason for treating them differently.

Each of these methods provides a way of generating a missing reason and generating a challenge for the argument. Once we have generated the implicit reason, we can evaluate and challenge the argument.

QUICK QUIZ 10.3

Generating Counterexamples

For each of the brief exchanges below, without writing out the argument, generate a counterexample verbally.

1. A: I think we should have more bike lanes in the city because it will encourage more people to ride bikes and it will reduce traffic.

   B:

(continued)

2. A: Downloading copyrighted music and videos from the Internet without paying for it should not be a crime. After all, it does not hurt anyone.

   B:

3. A: I do not think we should allow genetically modified foods to be sold and put into the food chain. After all, we do not know their long-term effects.

   B:

Answers to the Quick Quizzes are available on the Premium Website at www.criticalthinking2e.nelson.com.

Argument Challenges and Responses

Once the responder has an understanding of the argument, he or she can try to determine what the person is committed to, whether the reasons support the conclusion, and whether the reasons are true. The primary way of doing this is through challenging our argument partner's arguments and then responding by developing further challenges. Some of the various kinds of challenges and responses that can be made are outlined in Table 10.1.

TABLE 10.1 Challenges and Responses

	Challenges	Responses
1.	To meaning. Asking for a clarification (what do you mean by …?). Requesting an example. Challenging a word's use. Pointing out the ambiguity of a word or claim. Challenging the scope of a claim (too broad or narrow).	Defining a word. Giving a paradigm example. Engaging in a conceptual analysis of a term (see Module 9). Limiting the scope of a word.
2.	To truth of claims. How do you know? Why is it true?	Provide evidence or additional reasons to support claim. Provide supporting arguments. If a reason is false, find a new one. If a claim cannot be defended, accept it "for the sake of argument" and explore the rest of the argument.
3.	Counterexamples.	Demonstrate that the counterexample does not apply. Embrace the consequences. Modify position. Modify argument.
4.	Implications.	Show it does not apply. Embrace the implication.

5.	Fallacies and Other Dirty Tricks.	If correctable, fix; if not, present a new argument. If a mistake, apologize.
6.	Other considerations: new factors to consider.	Discuss. Define. Elicit arguments.

Challenging Meaning

The following dialogue illustrates how we can challenge meaning:

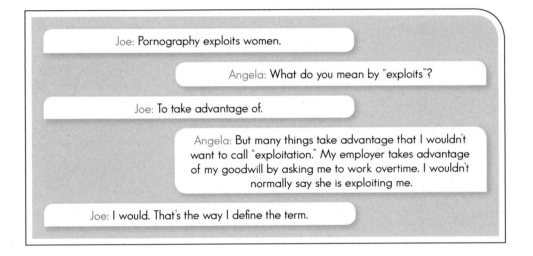

Joe: Pornography exploits women.

Angela: What do you mean by "exploits"?

Joe: To take advantage of.

Angela: But many things take advantage that I wouldn't want to call "exploitation." My employer takes advantage of my goodwill by asking me to work overtime. I wouldn't normally say she is exploiting me.

Joe: I would. That's the way I define the term.

Angela counterexamples Joe's definition of "exploits." Joe's response simply reasserts his definition of "exploits." Angela could either continue exploring the meaning of the term "exploit" and whether this is an adequate account of the meaning, or accept it "for the sake of argument" and probe in other directions. Alternatively, she could start a conceptual analysis on "exploits," or she could ask Joe for his evidence that pornography exploits women. The first probe focuses on the meaning, the second on the evidence.

QUICK QUIZ 10.4

Challenging Meaning

For each of the brief exchanges below, without writing out the argument, generate a challenge for the meaning and give an appropriate response. Use a different kind of challenge for each of the examples.

1. A: We should be allowed to use torture against terrorists to get them to inform us about future terrorist attacks.
   B: *Meaning challenge:*
   A: *Response to the challenge:*
      Kind of challenge:

(continued)

2. A: Downloading songs from the Net is not theft.
   B: *Meaning challenge:*
   A: *Response to the challenge:*
      Kind of challenge:
3. A: Sexual harassment is the misuse of power by a man against a woman.
   B: *Meaning challenge:*
   A: *Response to the challenge:*
      Kind of challenge:

Answers to the Quick Quizzes are available on the Premium Website at www.criticalthinking2e.nelson.com.

Challenging the Truth of Claims

One of the most obvious challenges to an argument is to show that a reason is false or likely false, as illustrated in the following exchange:

Jerry: Tommy Douglas was the greatest Canadian because he was one of the greatest Prime Ministers this country ever had.

Val: He was never Prime Minister; he was the Premier of Saskatchewan.

If we are defending a position and a basic reason is false, then we need a new argument. Perhaps Jerry has confused Douglas with someone who *was* Prime Minister. In some cases, even though a reason is false, we do not necessarily have to abandon the position because we may have other, more defensible reasons for the conclusion.

Challenges to the truth of claims include all challenges based on such questions as: "How do you know?" "What is your source?" "What is your evidence?" and the resulting discussions. A challenger does not have to show the claims are false but merely unsupported or inadequately supported. This is illustrated in the following interchange:

Chris: We need to take tougher measures against marijuana grow-houses. There are more and more of them all the time and they cause serious problems for those who live near them.

Kristen: Why do you think that? What is your evidence?

Chris: I heard on the news the other night that the number of grow-houses has increased by about 25 percent over the past two years.

Kristen: How did they arrive at that figure?

Chris is basing part of his claim for tougher measures on the increase in the number of grow-houses. Kristen challenges his source and then how they arrived at the number. She first challenges the source of his evidence, and then the adequacy of the evidence itself.

The material introduced in Module 4 on assessing various kinds of claims can be used to challenge the truth of a claim. If an argument partner is making a causal claim, we can examine whether all of the criteria for a causal claim have been met. If the person is advancing a normative claim, we can probe for the criteria being used to make the judgment and challenge whether those criteria are appropriate or the best available in this case. If the person is advancing a claim based on authority, we can use the criteria for an appropriate appeal to authority to determine whether the claim is acceptable.

Counterexamples

This text has introduced two kinds of counterexamples: one for claims and one for inferences. Both can be used in argumentation. Claim counterexamples are discussed more fully in Module 6. A *claim counterexample* is a *specific instance* that is designed to counter (show the limitations or falsity of) a claim or a generalization. An example is given in the following interchange:

Shari: We should ban drivers from using cell phones because cell phone use can cause accidents.

Roy: Cabdrivers and some truckers use cell phones instead of radios. Should we ban them from using them?

A claim counterexample has two components: a stem and an application. The *stem* is the term that shows up in the claim we are trying to counterexample and in the conclusion. The *application* is the specific case to which the stem is being applied, and usually shows up in the conclusion. In the above, the missing reason is "We should ban anything that can cause car accidents," the stem is "things we should ban," and the application in the original claim is "things that cause accidents."

The original example was applied to the specific case of cell phones. In generating a counterexample, we replace the specific application in the original argument with another application (or another example) and see if our argument partner would accept or reject the new claim. In this argument, the challenger replaces "all drivers" with a specific application: "cabdrivers and some truckers." Roy might have used "some police officers," or other possibilities. Roy could also go beyond various kinds of cell phone users, since the claim being challenged is "We should ban anything that causes car accidents." In other words, the counterexample retains the stem and substitutes another application to test whether or not the defender would accept the conclusion.

Original argument:

1. [Ban anything that causes accidents.]   *(implicit reason)*

2. Using cell phones while driving causes accidents.

∴ 3. We should ban the use of cell phones while driving.

In this argument, the implicit reason is a general claim, the stem is "things we should ban," and it is applied to the specific case of "drivers who use cell phones" to arrive at the consequence: ban drivers from using cell phones.

QUICK QUIZ 10.6

Stem and Application

In each of the following claims, identify the stem and the application. Provide an alternate application to generate a counterexample.

1. *The Adventures of Huckleberry Finn* is racist because it uses the n-word over 200 times. And anything that uses the n-word is racist.
   Stem:
   Application:
   New application:
   Counterexample:
2. It is legitimate to use torture on terrorists because they threaten national security. And it is legitimate to use torture on anyone who threatens national security.
   Stem:
   Application:
   New application:
   Counterexample:
3. UFOs exist. Many people have seen them.
   (This claim does not contain the general claim. That must be inferred.)
   Stem:
   Application:
   New application:
   Counterexample:

Answers to the Quick Quizzes are available on the Premium Website at www.criticalthinking2e.nelson.com.

To Roy's challenge that cabdrivers and truckers use cellphones and should we ban these, the arguer can respond in one of three possible ways: (1) by accepting the new application and embracing the consequences, (2) by rejecting the counterexample as irrelevant, or (3) by accepting the counterexample but rejecting the consequence. We will develop each one and provide an example to show the application. Roy challenges Shari:

> Roy: Cabdrivers and some truckers use cell phones instead of radios. Should we ban them from using cell phones?

Response I

The arguer can *accept the new application and embrace the consequences.* This involves accepting that the general principle applies to the new example and accepting the consequences.

> Shari: Sure, ban the cabdrivers' and truckers' use as well. They are some of the worst offenders.

Shari has accepted the counterexample as relevant and embraced its consequences. This tells the challenger Shari is committed to some of the consequences of her general claim. Roy could test with other counterexamples, both of types of cell phone users and of other kinds of things that can cause accidents.

> Roy: And you'd want to ban people from eating or drinking coffee while driving as well? They can cause accidents.

Roy has now provided counterexamples of other things that may cause accidents, but which Shari may or may not want to ban.

Response II

The arguer can reject the new counterexample as irrelevant. Since it is not the same kind of thing, the two cases can be treated differently.

> Roy: How about the police? They use both radios and cell phones while driving. And that can cause accidents.
> Shari: No, that's not what I am talking about. *(That is not the same kind of thing.)*
>
> Roy: Why not? *(Asking for a difference.)*
> Shari: They need cell phones for work, and using the cell phone while driving is part of their work. *(Supplies a relevant difference.)* I'm concerned about all of those people who don't need to use a cell phone while driving, those for whom it is a distraction from their driving. *(Expands on the difference and in so doing, qualifies her original reason.)*

In this case, Shari rejects the counterexample. When Shari does not give a reason, Roy asks the difference between the situation where the general claim applies and the one where it does not. Often, the response will open up new areas to probe. In this case, Shari supplies new information that qualifies the original argument: the conclusion is now not to ban all drivers from using cell phones but all drivers who *unnecessarily* use cell phones. This change requires a modification to the missing reason as well because it has to include this qualification. Roy could now use counterexamples to test other exceptions and to challenge the modified argument.

The challenger can also compare the stance taken with the original version of the argument and the later one. What is the difference between a cabdriver and a policeman? Why is Shari willing to ban one but not the other? Again, *the principle of similar cases* comes into play.

Response III

The argument partner can *accept the new application as relevant but not want to apply it to the stem*. The argument partner may acknowledge the counterexample's relevance, but not accept it in relation to the conclusion (that is, does not embrace the conclusion). In this case, the defender accepts the counterexample as relevant and accepts the consequences. In order to continue the argument, Shari must modify her original argument in some important way. Instead of the previous response, Shari could have given a different one:

> Roy: How about the police? They use both radios and cell phones while driving. And that can cause accidents.

> Shari: You're right. I guess we'd have to ban the police from using radios, but that would make their jobs much more difficult. And I don't want to do that.

Shari has accepted the counterexample as relevant and sees that it would lead her to a conclusion she does not want to accept. If she is going to sustain her argument, she is going to have to find some way of modifying either the reason or the conclusion so it will ban what she wants banned and not ban such things as police use of radios and cell phones. A specific counterexample or a set of counterexamples can lead Shari to realize that the position she has stated is untenable; however, that does not mean that the underlying consideration needs to be abandoned. Roy can help Shari develop her position by reformulating what she has said thus far:

> Roy: Let's reformulate. You want to cut down the number of accidents on the roads and highways. You see things that take a driver's attention from the road as contributing to accidents and many drivers' use of cell phones is a major thing that does this.

> Shari: Yes.

> Roy: So can we reformulate the argument to capture that? What is the difference between, say, the police and a regular citizen?

Roy has started the reformulation process to try to capture the core of what Shari was trying to get at. As Roy helps Shari reformulate, they can both gain a deeper understanding of how a good argument might work.

Inference counterexamples are used to challenge the inference in an argument by showing that the reasons do not support the conclusion. This is achieved by providing an argument counterexample (or a parallel argument that has the same structure with clearly acceptable reasons and a clearly false conclusion), thereby demonstrating that the structure of the original argument can lead to a false conclusion. Roy starts to reformulate Shari's argument by asking for her reasons in the following exchange:

> Roy: How do you know that using cell phones causes accidents?
>
> Shari: How do you know it doesn't?
>
> Roy: That's the same as arguing that because I don't know that the Earth is flat, it must be flat.

The inference is that if one does not know something then it must be true, which is the fallacy of appeal to ignorance (discussed in Module 7). The method that Roy uses to show it is unacceptable is an inference counterexample.

There are a number of possible responses each argument partner can make, depending on the circumstances. He or she can show there is not a parallel between the two argument forms, provide another reason, and/or in some other way modify the argument.

QUICK QUIZ 10.7

Challenging and Responding to Counterexamples

For each of the brief exchanges below, without writing out the argument, generate a counterexample (A) and give an appropriate response (B). Then identify the kind of counterexample (claim, inference) and the kind of response you would use.

1. A: Marijuana should be legalized for medical purposes because it is more effective than some other treatments.
   B:
   A:
   Kind of counterexample:
   Kind of response:

2. A: Astrology must be true because my friend claimed that it worked for her.
   B:
   A:
   Kind of counterexample:
   Kind of response:

3. A: You can't trust philosophers. My intro philosophy professor misled us on her grading scheme.
   B:
   A:
   Kind of counterexample:
   Kind of response:

Answers to the Quick Quizzes are available on the Premium Website at www.criticalthinking2e.nelson.com.

Implications

An implication is an unstated claim that follows from another (stated) claim in the argument. Usually, we draw implications from the conclusion and use those to show that accepting the conclusion commits the argument partner to something else, typically something untrue. However, implications can be drawn from any claim in the argument.

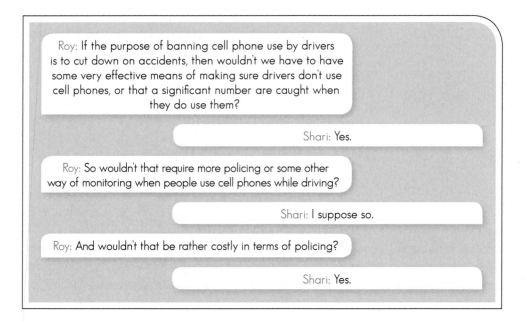

In the following exchange, Roy explores the implications of one of Shari's claims. By identifying a possible consequence of banning cell phone use while driving, Roy is trying to get Shari to commit to the fact that taking this action would require increased policing and increased costs. Roy is looking for an implication that Shari would not accept and that might lead Shari to change her argument.

The defender has a number of possible responses. The defender can:

1. *Embrace the implications* (as in the example above);
2. *Challenge the inference by taking the position* "That does not follow." In this case Shari will be asked to explain why not:

Shari: That does not follow. Police can enforce the law like they do with seat belts. That law didn't require more police, just more enforcement.

3. *Change the position.* In this case Shari could respond with:

Shari: I wonder if more education would work. That would be less costly than paying for more policing. Then maybe we could use police enforcement more judiciously.

3. A: If we require students to take a course in logic, then they will improve their reasoning, and that is a good thing. Therefore, we should require students to take logic.

B:

A:

Answers to the Quick Quizzes are available on the Premium Website at www.criticalthinking2e.nelson.com.

Unfair Tactics: Fallacies and Other Dirty Tricks

A *dirty trick* is any tactic in argumentation that gives an unfair advantage to one side. Dirty tricks typically give one side an unfair advantage in an exchange. However, they only work if just one side gets to use them. If both sides can misrepresent their data, no one has any basis on which to make a decision. If both sides can threaten the other, then all discussion breaks down. In order for argumentation to work, the rules of argumentation must be followed by the argument partner who is not using a dirty trick. If all sides in an argumentation use them, the aims of argumentation cannot be achieved.

If our argument partner uses a dirty trick, we often cannot be certain he or she intended to deceive or mislead. He or she simply could have made an error. The following strategy helps prevent escalation while correcting the error:

> A **dirty trick** is any tactic in an argumentation that gives an unfair advantage to one side.

TABLE 10.2 Countering Fallacies and Dirty Tricks in Argumentation

Step	Name	Explanation
1.	*Identify/recognize* the fallacy or dirty trick.	This depends on knowing the various fallacies and dirty tricks. It also relies on our monitoring the exchange and being aware if the exchange is not being fruitful and why.
2.	*Neutralize* the fallacy or dirty trick.	In some cases one can do this by simply recognizing what the argument partner is doing and not allowing it to interfere with addressing the issue (such as, by diverting the dialogue and bringing them back to the issue). One can also use the steps of neutralizing a fallacy with one's partner.
3.	*Raise the issue.*	If an argument partner persists in using fallacies and dirty tricks, you can simply let them know you are aware that a fallacy or dirty trick has been used without accusing them of an intentional wrongdoing (such as, by saying "the last three sets of data you have given me have had serious errors in them"). If the person is intentionally trying to gain an unfair advantage, this lets them know you are aware of the strategy.

(continued)

TABLE 10.2 Continued

Step	Name	Explanation
4.	*Confront and negotiate.*	If an argument partner persists in using unfair tricks, it may be that they simply do not know better and need to be educated, or it may mean they are engaged in an aim other than argumentation. You can confront them by: i. Identifying the tactics they are using; ii. Showing how they are unfair or block argumentation (by asking "what would happen if I gave you unreliable data? Could we reach an agreement?"); iii. Negotiating over how to proceed (by suggesting "how about if you have data, you double check it before you give it to me?"); and/or iv. If the argument partner continues to use unfair tactics, then we have the choice of continuing, knowing what our argument partner is doing or ending the interaction.

We can see how this operates in the following exchange between Shari and Roy:

Shari: Roy, everyone knows cell phone use while driving is dangerous.

Roy: (Suspecting Shari has committed an appeal to common belief fallacy (step 1), he could go with a counterexample or neutralize the fallacy; he decides to neutralize the fallacy.) Shari, are you aware you have used a similar argument several times in our discussion?

Shari: What argument?

Roy: You appeal to what everyone knows or believes (step 2).

Shari: And what's wrong with that?

Roy: It's a fallacy. That everyone knows something does not make it true (step 3).

Shari: Oh?

Roy: It doesn't. Everyone once "knew" the Earth was flat, but that didn't make it flat. A lot of science is based on challenging "what everybody knows." (Roy is using the techniques from neutralizing a fallacy.)

Later in their exchange, Shari commits another fallacy, and Roy is concerned she may be doing this intentionally, or at least that she is not being careful enough.

Roy: Shari, I really want to try to reach some kind of resolution on this issue. When you use fallacies, I get frustrated because they act as barriers to my understanding your position and to moving towards some kind of resolution. (Roy acknowledges the effect of fallacies on himself.) How would you like it if every time I gave an argument I engaged in reasoning that prevented you from understanding my real reasons?

Shari: I would be frustrated and probably get annoyed with you.

Roy: Right. And why would you be annoyed?

Shari: Because I would think you really don't want to argue, that we are not engaged in argumentation. Oh, I get it! Look, it's not that I intentionally try to commit fallacies to prevent understanding.

Roy: I know that.

Shari: It's just that I take a few shortcuts and end up using some responses that prevent good argumentation.

Roy: It happens. So how do we solve this?

Shari: (Laughing) How about when I do this you call me on it!

Roy: Deal.

Roy has confronted Shari about her use of dirty tricks and negotiated an agreement on how they can jointly address these. If Shari were trying to manipulate Roy by persisting in using dirty tricks, then he would have to make a decision about whether to continue the encounter or interaction.

A presenter can reply to a charge of fallacy by:

- Showing that although the argument may look like a fallacy it is not one;
- Fixing the fallacy if it can be fixed (a false cause fallacy or a faulty appeal to authority might be correctable under certain conditions);
- Modifying or changing the argument, including giving a new reason; and/or
- Acknowledging committing a fallacy.

In addition to the fallacies identified in Module 7, several other common dirty tricks and fallacies occur in verbal argument.

A common tactic is *labelling*. This happens when an argument partner dismisses an argument or position by providing a name or label rather than giving reasons for challenging the position. The following is an example of labelling:

> That's just a typical feminist (liberal, conservative) position.

Labels are commonly used to short-circuit the reasoning process. Defenders often end up responding to the label and arguing about the label rather than addressing the arguments. Labelling may fall under the category of the *ad hominem* or poisoning the well fallacy. However, sometimes it is best to recognize it simply as "labelling" and deal with it in that way. The easiest response is to refocus on the argument:

> I don't care what you want to call it. What specifically is wrong with the argument?

If an argument partner persists, we can raise the issue and, if that fails, confront him or her about the tactics used. We raise an issue by identifying what is occurring. For example:

> You are simply labelling my position, not giving a reasoned challenge.

Here we have verbalized what our argument partner is doing. In many cases, simply identifying what our argument partner has done will lead him or her to recognize it is not a legitimate move and to then modify the method of argumentation.

If an argument partner does not modify the method of argumentation and persists in using dirty tricks, we can directly confront him or her. We do this by identifying the move, pointing out the effect (such as, by showing how it violates the constitutive rules or thwarts the common aim in argumentation), and directly asking our argument partner if this is how he or she wants to interact. If we find our goals in the argumentation are not aligned, we have the option of walking away. The following responses illustrate how an argument partner might respond, using the model to confront someone who has used labels rather than reasons:

Speaker	Meaning
You continue to label my position without giving reasons. This does not address my argument. I could do the same and we would get nowhere in this discussion. We would simply call each other names.	Identifies the behaviour and shows the consequences if both engage in it.
Is this how you want to proceed?	Confronts the individual by suggesting a possible alternate rule for proceeding.
If so, then there is no chance of rational persuasion.	Identifies the common aim and the consequences of continuing with such tactics.
And if that is the case then I am not willing to continue.	Points out that you are willing to engage in argumentation and rational persuasion, but not other activities, especially when that activity puts you at a disadvantage. Your option is to walk away.

Disrupting, although not a fallacy, can interfere with argumentation. Disrupting occurs when an argument partner repeatedly interrupts what we are saying by interjecting or changing the topic. We can deal with a disrupter by leading him or her back to the main topic. If the person persists, we can raise and negotiate the issue, as outlined above. If necessary we can confront the disrupter.

QUICK QUIZ 10.9

Challenging and Responding to Dirty Tricks and Fallacies

In the following, Identify the dirty trick or fallacy if one is committed, and suggest a strategy for handling it (B).

1. Your argument partner says the following in response to your argument in defence of gay marriage:
   A: You're arguing for gay marriage? Are you homosexual or something?
   B:
2. Bhas quoted Rush Limbaugh's argument that executing Saddam Hussein was a mistake.
   A: You are using Rush Limbaugh as an authority. Don't you know he's just an apologist for a right-wing conservative viewpoint?
   B:
3. B has been arguing against teaching creationist theory in biology classes.
   A: That is what's wrong with society today. No one wants to take religion seriously.
   B:

4. B has given an argument for increasing the existing taxes and using the increase to pay down the national debt.
   A: Garbage!
   B:

Answers to the Quick Quizzes are available on the Premium Website at www.criticalthinking2e.nelson.com.

Other Considerations: New Factors to Consider

The raising of other considerations builds on the topics model and introduces into argumentation the broader aspects of issue analysis. In much argumentation the focus is on specific arguments. However, arguments are about issues. They are developed to help us in taking stands on issues. Focusing solely on arguments can blind us to the underlying issues and the concerns that give rise to those issues. Specific arguments (even good ones!) can sometimes miss the point of an issue or not adequately address an issue. And they may not address the relevant considerations of other positions on the issue. The raising of "other considerations" allows us to step back to see how the specific arguments fit into the overall context. It takes us away from the specific arguments to focus on the underlying issues and considerations. In so doing, it enables us to step back and examine what exactly is at issue and how best to approach it so that we can better formulate our arguments. It includes such tasks as:

I. Formulating or Reformulating the Issue

This can require stepping back from the specific argument, looking for the underlying considerations and motivations, and reframing the issue in terms of deeper, related, or other issues. Sometimes we start an argument without seeing the connections or broader issues, or recognizing the factors that motivate an individual to advance a particular argument. As we continue in the dialogue, we discover that we are not getting at the central issue or that there is something else going on. Formulating or reformulating the issue helps us reassess the issue as a whole. Reformulating the issue of copying copyright material as one of artist's rights, free advertising, or artistic freedom may each give us a different perspective and new lines of argument.

II. Framing and Reframing

Often we can gain a different understanding of an issue by framing or reframing it (such as, by putting it in a different context) or by expanding or contracting the scope or focus of the issue. Reframing the issue of copying copyright material as a form of "cloning" rather than "theft" gives us a different perspective on the issue.

III. Identifying Other Considerations

This includes asking an argument partner for additional considerations. This can involve looking for additional unstated reasons and possible objections and responses, including reasons that the argument partner does not advance. Some questions we can ask include:

- "What other reasons do you have for this?"
- "What are some of the common objections you have heard to this position?" and
- "How have others defended this position?"

IV. Comparing Other Perspectives and Positions

Identifying alternate perspectives and positions on the issue can give us further insight into the issue. Comparing similarities and differences with different perspectives and positions may give us insight into why our argument partner holds a particular position and why he or she appeals to certain considerations. Some questions we might ask include:

- "What might this issue look like from the perspective of the parents?" and
- "What kind of arguments do the teachers raise on this issue?"

V. Looking at Underlying Concerns

This includes looking at legitimate concerns expressed by our argument partner, elaborating on those concerns, and then exploring how the elaborations can be addressed. We might phrase this as follows:

- "It seems that your basic concern is ensuring that artists get proper credit for their work and sufficient income from it to continue engaging in creative work."

10.3 A Sample Argument Dialogue

Shari: Did you see that — there's another person driving and trying to talk on a cell phone! That shouldn't be allowed!

Roy: You sound really upset by that.

Roy reflects back Shari's feelings about the issue. She is listening to both his content and emotional level.

Shari: I am! Did you hear about that case in Fredericton where a driver on a cell phone crossed the line and crashed head-on into an oncoming car? It was a completely avoidable death. The driver died, along with two of her kids, and she killed the other driver. One family loses a mother, the other family loses a son.

Roy: That sounds horrible! You sound really upset about it.

Shari: I am.

Roy: So do you think we should ban cell phone use in cars?

Roy identifies a possible conclusion and suggests it to Shari.

Shari: Of course.

Roy: Why, exactly?

Shari agrees, and Roy probes for reasons.

Shari: Because it is unsafe. You can't do two things at once.

Roy: So you think that we should ban cell phone use for drivers because talking on them while driving is unsafe. And they are unsafe because you can't safely do two things at the same time?

Roy identifies and reflects back the argument. Note that it is a complex argument.

Shari: That's right.

Roy is now faced with which way to take the discussion:

1. He can probe the grounds for banning as follows:
    *   Why ban rather than do something else?
    *   How unsafe does something have to be to justify banning it?
2. He can probe the scope:
    *   All cell phones?
    *   Some kinds of cell phones – handheld vs. hands-free?
    *   Some users?
3. He can challenge the truth of the stated reason.
4. He can formulate and challenge the missing reason as follows.

Roy: But there are a lot of things that are unsafe, such as, having kids in the car and being distracted by their antics or taking a bunch of rowdy 10-year-olds to a hockey practice. Should we ban parents from taking their kids to hockey games?

Roy has formulated a missing reason (that we should ban anything that makes driving unsafe) and challenged that with a counterexample.

Shari: Of course not.
Roy: Why not? How are they different?

Shari rejects the counterexample and Roy asks for a reason using the *principle of similar cases.*

Shari: I don't know, maybe because you have to drive your kids around and you don't have to talk on a cell phone.
Roy: So let me get this straight. Your argument is that we should ban things that are unsafe to do when driving a car, so long as they are not necessary.

Shari responds and Roy probes her reasons:

Shari: Yes That's what I am saying.
Roy: How is driving kids to hockey practice necessary and talking on a cell phone not necessary?

Roy challenges Shari's response and asks for a relevant difference. Shari responds:

Shari: You know what I mean.
Roy: I'm not sure I do.

Shari: Well, kids have to get to hockey practice, but no one has to use a cell phone while driving.
Roy: But isn't a carful of unruly kids as distracting and as potentially dangerous as talking on a cell phone?

Shari: No, it's not.
Roy: Why not?
Shari: It just isn't.

Roy senses this is becoming unproductive. He has hit a point at which Shari does not have a reason or is not willing to give a reason. He could keep pushing but that might end the discussion, so he chooses another line of reasoning:

> Roy: Let's leave that for a moment. You said that using a cell phone while driving is unsafe. How do you know that?
>
> Shari: Well, it's just common sense. You have to dial and then focus on your conversation while driving. Your attention is split.
>
> Roy: A lot of things that seem to be common sense turn out to be wrong — it was once common sense that the Earth was flat. Have there been any studies?
>
> Shari: Yeah, I read a long article in a weekend newspaper awhile back that various academic studies and studies by insurance bureaus showed drivers who regularly used cell phones were four times as likely to be involved in injury-causing accidents than drivers who did not use cell phones.
>
> Roy: Sounds impressive. Do you know who did the studies?
>
> Shari: No, but they were reported in *The Globe and Mail*, so I assume they are reliable.
>
> Roy: I think I can accept that.
>
> Shari: So you see I'm right.
>
> Roy: Let's take this a bit further. You say that we should ban drivers from using cell phones while they are driving because cell phones are unsafe. And we agree that studies reported in *The Globe and Mail* have shown that they are unsafe.

Roy restates and summarizes the argument to this point. Shari agrees and Roy continues probing:

> Shari: That's what I said.
>
> Roy: But why ban all cell phone use in cars?
>
> Shari: Because it can lead to accidents.
>
> Roy: That's not quite what I mean. A lot of things can lead to accidents. Why is banning the best solution?

Roy returns to the missing reason:

> Shari: What else are we going to do?

Shari tries to turn the argument around by asking Roy to defend the alternative, a version of shifting the burden of proof.

> Roy: I'm not the one who wants to ban cell phones. You are. Why is banning them the appropriate response? Why not just fine those who are using cell phones and are involved in accidents?

Despite her attempt not to get drawn in, Shari does offer an alternative:

> Shari: That doesn't change people's behaviour and prevent the accidents in the first place. Look, you wouldn't want your son to be injured or killed by someone not paying attention because they were on a cell phone, would you?

Shari has not answered Roy's request for a reason. Rather than address that, she challenges the alternative. Shari introduces a personal consideration that could sidetrack the discussion.

Roy: No, I wouldn't want him to be hurt. However, I am not sure that banning all cell phones in cars is justified. Let me rephrase your argument. Rather than offer incentives for people not to use cell phones, you want to prevent the harm by punishing them after the fact. And this means banning cell phone use by drivers?

Roy paraphrases Shari's response as an argument. Shari accepts the paraphrase and elaborates:

Shari: Yes. Look. I see too many people driving, using cell phones, and not paying attention. The studies show that such people are far more likely to be involved in accidents than those who don't use cell phones while driving. I just want to stop some of the carnage on the roads. This seems reasonable and doesn't seriously infringe on anyone's rights or cause further harm. It just seems like the right thing to do.

Roy: You know, I do tend to agree with you on cutting the carnage. I'm just not sure that banning cell phones is the best way of doing that. Let's think about it and continue our talk at lunch tomorrow.

Shari: Sure.

This is a fairly typical example of an argumentation dialogue. Shari and Roy have probed issues and positions, considered some arguments, made some "mistakes," and learned about one another's positions. There is no one right way of pursuing an argumentation dialogue.

Now, let us explore the various things we can do that will undermine the goal of argumentation.

10.4 Escalation and De-escalation

Argumentation is an ongoing process. It involves not only the giving and challenging of arguments but the personal and interactive elements between people. As such, one of the things that can happen is *escalation*, or the intensification of the disagreement between two people. This occurs when what starts out as a disagreement over an issue is taken personally, emotions become heated, and there is an increase in hostility between the parties.

In the early stages of escalation, communication becomes more guarded and one or both parties become increasingly (and often unproductively) defensive. This results in distorted listening, where each side starts listening only for what supports his or her position and undermines the other's, ignoring positive information about the other's position. The argument may stray off the original issue and into other issues. The discussion tends to polarize around two opposing views, with the middle ground and alternatives overlooked. The ability to see the merits of the other side gets lost, often resulting in *cognitive rigidity* or the tendency to misinterpret the other side or to see only those things that support one's own position. Each side is likely to become increasingly anxious. A marked increase in hostility between the argument partners may lead to the two sides reaching the point where it is impossible to communicate with each other.

De-escalation is the reduction of tensions between the parties, which allows them to reestablish a relationship and return to the original issues.

If you find yourself engaged in a dialogue that is escalating, stop the process. Take a timeout to figure out what is going on. Make a decision about whether the discussion is worth continuing. Look for strengths in the other side's position and acknowledge the weaknesses in your own. If and when you resume, begin by reaffirming the process and the point of the discussion. Slow the process down. Try paraphrasing the other side's position with an emphasis on its strengths. This will help establish rapport. If heightened emotions were part of the escalation, acknowledge those and probe them. Identify commonalities at the start rather than differences.

Try reversing positions. Defend the other side's position and ask your argument partner to present your position as strongly as possible. If further signs of escalation present, stop the process and invite your argument partner to reflect on what is happening and how you can prevent a further recurrence of escalation.

Module Summary

- Argumentation is the process of reasoning, using the techniques of argument and issue analysis, in interaction with other argument partners.
- The dynamics of argumentation involve listening, eliciting arguments, clarifying meaning, evaluating arguments, and interacting with an argument partner through a process of probing, challenge, and response.
- Over time, the arguments develop, and individuals may be rationally persuaded to change their position as they become rationally persuaded of the weakness of their own position and the strength of an alternative.

Argumentation Exercise: Integrating Your Skills

Examine the Dialogues on Copyright in Modules 1 through 10.

1. Using the skills from this module, identify the various techniques used throughout the dialogues.
2. Acting as a coach to the two argument partners, suggest ways in which, from an argumentation standpoint, they could be more effective in the presentation, challenge and response to challenges.
3. Continue the dialogue for two more pages.

Writing Skills Exercise: Integrating Your Skills

Examine the dialogue between Shari and Roy on cell phone use in cars.

1. Briefly write one paragraph summarizing each of their arguments.
2. Critique each of their arguments and suggest how they could be improved.
3. Rewrite your one-paragraph summary, incorporating the insights from your critique.

Written Argumentation

LEARNING OBJECTIVES

After completing this module you should be able to:

1. Plan an essay, including analyzing the assignment, identifying the audience and purpose for writing, and generating ideas and arguments;
2. Develop and refine a thesis;
3. Develop an argument to support that thesis;
4. Decide whether to write an argument essay, make a case, or develop a balance of considerations argument, and develop that into an essay;
5. Construct a one-paragraph argument as a guide to writing the essay;
6. Transform an argument or a case into audience-based prose; and
7. Revise and edit for coherence and clarity.

A DIALOGUE ON COPYRIGHT AND PIRACY – CONTINUED

Jean: Guess what, Peter, my social studies instructor heard us talking yesterday and has asked me to write a five-page essay, outlining my arguments, but also addressing the various other positions in the issue. Since you have done these kinds of essays, can you give me some help in structuring the essay?

Peter: Sure. Let's start. What do you want to do in the essay?

Jean: I guess develop my arguments for my position.

Peter: Your instructor said she wanted you to consider other positions, didn't she?

Jean: Yes, but I'm not sure how to do that.

Peter: So, I guess we'll have to look at how to make a case and develop a balance of considerations argument. What about your arguments?

Jean: Well, I have some ideas about the ones I have developed with you, but not all of them were great.

Peter: You had some really good points, and a few clunkers. So we need to do some brainstorming. Some of the arguments we discussed were fairly clichéd. We need to do some brainstorming to see if we can come up with some new ideas, or at least a new slant on the existing ones.

Jean: Okay.

Peter: Once we have some more material to work with we can choose the best arguments and the ones best suited for your audience. Let's get started.

11.1 Introduction

Often we want or need to put our verbal argumentation into a written format. Although we can, and sometimes do, work systematically through an argument verbally, verbal argumentation is often much more dynamic and free-flowing. When we present our arguments in written form we have to be more systematic and linear in our presentation. We have to consider our audience, what they know, and what they need to know to understand and follow our arguments. The all-too-frequent strategies of simply sitting down and writing, or gathering a small bit of material and welding it together without a clear direction, usually result in poor arguments being made. In this module we will look at how to develop our argument ideas and sketches into interesting and effective essays.

We are often asked to produce an ***argument essay***, or an essay whose focus is the presenting and defending of one or more arguments for a position. For example, we might be required to write an essay for a humanities class on the role of education in Mary Shelley's novel *Frankenstein*. Simply developing a position and then producing an argument for that position is sufficient for this context.

Sometimes we are called on to produce an ***argumentation essay***, or one in which we are engaged with the positions and arguments of others on an issue. Although not a widely used term, *argumentation essay* identifies a type of essay that is broader than an argument essay. In an argumentation essay we not only present a position and arguments for that position, but we implicitly or explicitly engage with the positions and arguments of others on an issue. Our essay is part of an ongoing dialogue. This

An **argument essay** is an essay whose focus is the presenting and defending of one or more arguments for a position.

An **argumentation essay** is one in which we are engage with the positions and arguments of others on an issue.

is true whether or not the others in the dialogue read and respond. We write the argumentation essay with the intention of contributing to a discussion. This means that we try to build on the discussion as we understand it to this point. We represent the arguments of others fairly, challenge their arguments and positions, and anticipate and respond to their objections. We put ourselves into the place of a discussant in a dialogue as we compose and present the essay. Such essays can be found both inside and outside of the academic world. They are part of policy discussions, legal discussions, indeed, any discussion where we are expected to reflect our knowledge of the issue and address the various sides of an issue.

In both argument and argumentation essays we construct arguments with the intention of presenting them to an audience. To do this we use the basic skills of developing good arguments and responding to challenges. The central difference between argument and argumentation essays is that the argument essay tends to stand alone. It does not acknowledge other positions or arguments on the issue. The issue might even be unique to the essay. Sometimes the argument essay is the author's way of working through his or her own issue, and the audience is limited to whoever happens to be interested in that author's particular issue. By contrast, an argumentation essay is concerned, either implicitly or explicitly, with an issue on which other arguers have contributed and for which there is an audience. The author may explicitly mention and use other authors as foils in developing his or her own position, or may write on an issue of concern to others and address implicitly the positions and considerations of others, even though specific others may not be known. This is how the author addresses an ongoing dialogue, real or potential. An argumentation essay may initiate a dialogue by posing an issue of concern, taking a stand, and presenting a case on an issue. Whether others read and respond to it is not the point. It is framed as a contribution to a dialogue on a particular issue of concern to others.

Because of this difference, the demands on the two are different. Whereas the criteria for an argument essay to be good revolve around whether it has presented an argument that is sound, has sufficient supporting evidence, and so on, the demands of an argumentation essay are more stringent. Not only must it satisfy the criteria for a good argument essay, but it must also meet the conditions for good argumentation: it must engage with the issue and alternate positions on the issue, address challenges, and contribute something new to the ongoing dialogue. Being able to write a good argument essay is a prerequisite to engaging in written argumentation.

To write any essay we undertake two distinct processes: 1) composing ideas and 2) translating those ideas into audience-based prose. We sometimes move back and forth between these functions. The composing process consists of determining our purpose for writing, identifying our potential audience, generating ideas, developing those ideas into an argument, and making a case. Translating ideas into audience-based prose involves transforming the argument from a complex, multidimensional structure into a more linear presentation, which means organizing the argument to fit the structure of the essay and providing elements that will make it easier for a audience to follow the logic of the argument and understand the claims and arguments being made. It also includes the revising and editing process.

The primary purpose of this module is to help the essay-writer develop an argument and transform that into audience-based prose. This module focuses on argument essays because they are the basis on which argumentation essays are written and provide the skills that can be applied in the development of the more complex argumentation essay.

11.2 The Composing Process: Constructing an Argument

Composing an argument essay is a process of developing an idea and an argument, writing, evaluating, editing, and then rewriting, sometimes a number of times. Often we do not know precisely what we want to say until we have written and rewritten our ideas several times. Through writing, we can discover new ways of framing an issue, new positions, new considerations, and new ways of expanding arguments. Like any skill, writing and composing improves with practice and deteriorates with lack of use.

We begin an argument essay by identifying and refining a conclusion for which we will develop an argument. However, before we start, we need to know the essay's purpose and its intended audience.

What Is the Purpose?

To determine this we must ask the question "why are we writing this particular essay?" We can have different reasons for writing an essay (such as being part of an assignment, as a response to an article in the newspaper, to persuade someone of a position, to explore an issue, to present an alternate point of view, or to probe where a particular point of view leads). Different purposes can affect how thoroughly we pursue an issue, what we can assume, and what we need to develop. Even if we are simply constructing an essay for an assignment, we should seek personal reasons for writing the essay, or find something we can learn from the exercise. Often, if we have a personal interest, we create better arguments and write better essays.

Who Is the Audience?

All writing is for an audience. Different audiences have different requirements or different things that can be assumed, different things they need to know to be able to follow the argument, different reasons for reading the finished essay, and different assumptions, values, and attitudes toward the issue.

By identifying the audience we also identify the context in which we are writing. Writing an assignment for a course is different than writing for oneself to work out a position on an issue, and that is different from writing a letter to the Editor or writing a sketch of an argument for a friend. An informal communication with a colleague or friend usually does not require footnotes and citations, whereas an essay submitted for a course or publication does. In writing an essay for an instructor, the point might not be simply to generate a good argument for a position, but also to demonstrate certain skills and to work with certain materials. Such requirements set constraints and focus our purpose for writing the essay.

Analyzing an Assignment

When giving an assignment instructors often provide students with guidelines that offer direction for the finished essay.

Start by reading the entire assignment. Annotate it, identifying the requirements (the kind and purpose of the assignment) and constraints (the formatting, due date, length, submission criteria), and raising questions about what is being asked of you (the scope and formality). Make a list of what you need to do to complete the assignment successfully. Check this list frequently. You should consider the following:

1. *What is the point of this piece of writing?* Why are we constructing and presenting an argument on this topic? Obviously, one reason is that it is an assignment, and we need to complete it to pass the course. However, that does not get at why we are being asked to write about this particular subject. What are the various possible purposes the instructor has for assigning this essay? Not identifying the instructor's underlying purpose for the assignment (such as, demonstrating certain skills, using a particular mode of analysis) may prevent us from earning a good mark.

2. *Who is the audience?* Although the instructor is the one who will be evaluating the assignment, the audience may be presumed for the purpose of the assignment to be the other students in the class, other students who have not taken this class, or some other group. Since the instructor may have a certain audience in mind in giving the assignment, it is important to find this out.

3. *What is the context?* In the case of an assignment, one context is that of the course. Are you expected to demonstrate knowledge (concepts, categories, approaches) and skills learned in the course, or is there a wider context? If you are analyzing a contemporary controversy, how much of that controversy are you supposed to address?

4. *Are there any special considerations or constraints for the argument?* Ask yourself the following questions: *How long is the essay supposed to be? How much outside literature are we expected to cite? What is the format or style? How is the essay to be submitted?*

QUICK QUIZ 11.1

Analyzing an Assignment

Use the questions above to analyze the following assignments. Where the answers are not clear, identify the questions you would have to ask the instructor.

1. *One-page argument assignment for a first-year critical reasoning course:*
   Read the attached passage, "A Right to Die: The B.C. Supreme Court Changes the Law," and write a one page (one paragraph) argument on a central moral or policy issue arising from the case as it is presented here. You need to develop your own reasoning on this. Do not simply repeat the arguments in the passage. Your essay will be assessed on how well you frame an interesting and central issue, how well you develop and defend your argument, and how original your argument is. The use of outside materials is discouraged; however, if you use such material it must be cited appropriately.

   Do an argument analysis and critique of your own essay and submit that as an appendix.

   Since your essays will be marked and returned electronically and will be used for electronic peer review, you must use the following formatting conventions: The essay should be formatted in Microsoft Word or Rich Text Format (not WordPerfect), using an easy-to-read font (e.g., Arial) in 12-point type, black, and left justified.

   Due at midnight, Pacific Standard Time, March 26 *via* email.

2. *Assignment for a second year English literature course (the class has spent the past three weeks analyzing Mary Shelley's Frankenstein):*

   Write an essay on the role of education in Mary Shelley's *Frankenstein*. The essay should be ten pages and focus only on the primary source (the novel itself).

   The essay should use MLA format, cite all material appropriately, and include a bibliography of works consulted.

   The essay is due in class on October 1, at the beginning of class. Late essays will be marked down in accordance with the course policies.

3. *Assignment for a third year sociology course analyzing ethnicity and race:*
   Examine the Websites given for the Canadian, Irish, and Indian censuses. Find and identify their respective definitions of ethnicity and the questions used in the most recent census to measure ethnicity. Compare and contrast these definitions and relate them to the lectures on ethnicity. What conclusions can you draw about the categories used to identify ethnicity in the respective censuses? Relate to David's discussion of ethnicity.
   Length: 4 pages
   Due: In class of March 2, at the beginning of class.

Answers to the Quick Quizzes are available on the Premium Website at www.criticalthinking2e.nelson.com.

11.3 Generating Ideas

Having identified the purpose for writing, we next have to define the issue and start generating ideas about it. This may take a number of attempts. Producing an interesting thesis and argument worth defending may require some thought about the question, followed by analysis and research. Simply selecting the first or second idea that comes to mind is likely to result in a fairly trite position or one that half the class will adopt.

Our starting point will depend on the nature of the writing project. For a critical analysis we need to start by doing an extended analysis of the text or argument. If we are developing our own argument on an issue, we will usually start by trying to define clearly and precisely the issue we are investigating, exploring the alternate possible positions, the key concepts, and various ways of formulating the issue. A research project will involve gathering, organizing, and analyzing the appropriate information.

Whatever the kind of project, at some point we will need to generate the core position. The point of writing an argument essay is not simply to repeat what someone else has said, but to contribute something to the discussion or to find a point of view and support that with arguments. Even when using considerations that others have used we try to develop those considerations in an original or different way.

When research is involved, we do not simply read and report the materials unprocessed. We need to analyze, organize, and assess that information. To do this, ask yourself the following question: What positions have not been given? What other arguments are possible? Which arguments give the most support? Are there undeveloped considerations?

For some projects we can apply a particular method or mode of analysis (such as conceptual analysis, discussed in Module 9, or a model from a particular discipline to help generate ideas). This section introduces additional ways of producing and developing arguments.

Brainstorming and Free-writing

Brainstorming and free-writing are two common methods. **_Brainstorming_** involves trying to generate as much as we can on the topic in a given period of time without censoring, evaluating, or criticizing. **_Free-writing_** involves writing for a given period of time (such as, five, ten, fifteen minutes) on the topic without editing or constraining what we are saying. With both, once we have come up with some material, we then edit and analyze what we have produced to see if we can find something useful. The key to both techniques is for you to generate as many ideas within a given period of time as you can. When doing so do not worry about grammar or spelling. Just get the ideas down. You can correct the mechanics and work out the details later.

Brainteasers

Brainteasers[1] are specific techniques we can use to systematically generate ideas about a topic. They can help expand our thinking. For each brainteaser generate long lists of ideas and examples. To illustrate how they are used, we will imagine the following situation: The provincial government is proposing to raise tuition fees for university students. You have been assigned to write an argument essay on this. We can use the brainteasers below to help generate some ideas for the essay.

1. *Get beyond the obvious.* Go beyond your first (and second and third) idea. Original ideas are rarely the ones that initially enter our minds. Look for what is not obvious and do not censor yourself. Write down any idea you have. Even try the opposite of what comes to mind.

   For example, on the issue of a tuition increase, some of the first ideas you may have might be that raising tuition fees will put a greater burden on lower-income students, that some students might not be able to finish their programs, or that faculty and student–faculty contact hours might be increased. From these we can generate opposing considerations: Raising tuition fees might benefit lower-income students who can get grants, and disadvantage middle and upper-income students who cannot; it might encourage students to finish their programs sooner; or *not* raising fees might force universities and faculties to be more efficient in their delivery of programs.

2. *Good ideas are often complex.* Develop competing ideas that challenge your initial ones. Put your initial ideas on trial by examining alternatives to them. Working through competing ideas and testing each with details and possible support often leads to a more complex account. There may be both benefits and disadvantages to raising tuition fees. Explore them all. Which are likely to outweigh the others?

3. *Use your senses.* List sensory details about your topic. What does the topic look, sound, smell, taste, and feel like? Look for anything unusual or forgotten. Recall specific relative cases or scenarios that have sensory material to work from, and write down any ideas that emerge from this. Sensory details draw us into the

---

Brainstorming involves trying to generate as much as we can on the topic in a given period of time without censoring, evaluating, or criticizing.

Free-writing involves writing for a given period of time on the topic without editing or constraining what we are saying.

Brainteasers are specific techniques we can use to systematically generate ideas about a topic.

---

1 The idea of "brainteasers" was developed by and can be found in Bauman, M. Garrett, and Clifford M. Werier, *Ideas and Details: A Guide to Writing for Canadians.* Toronto: Harcourt Brace Canada, 1996. This text provides a more complete account of developing an essay, including material on research and on writing different kinds of essays from the argument essay covered here.

topic and provide sharper details. For example, you might conjure up images of students eating Kraft Dinner (already pushed to the limits), students driving expensive cars (because they can afford higher tuition), a student working long hours at a low-paying job (working to afford university), vacant arts classes and overfull economics and business classes (differences in student demand), or a small seminar room where students are questioning the instructor and one another (engaged students in a philosophy class).

4. *Examine the topic from alternate viewpoints.* Use different individual points of view, perspectives, disciplines, and positions. Look for the missing viewpoints. Probe each, trying to see the issue as others would. What truth would each reveal about the issue? This will often lead to more honest and sophisticated (or complex) ideas. Good ideas stand up to such examination, poor ones fade. Consider the "tuition increase" issue from the point of view of faculty, the administration, parents, and employers, as well as that of students. Consider it from the point of view of different disciplines or faculties and their particular perspectives. Consider it from the points of view of new Canadians, Aboriginal Canadians, taxpayers, business people, and others likely to be impacted by a tuition increase.

5. *Identify and challenge stereotypes, unquestioned ideas, and slogans.* These all prevent honest, imaginative thinking by encouraging us to think in accepted, ordinary patterns. List the "common truths" or obvious statements about your subject (such as, "students are generally opposed to tuition increases"). These are positions you will take if you want a substandard essay. Now find *exceptions* and *qualifications* to the items in this list. Generate as many as possible. After you have attacked the obvious, the unquestioned, the stereotypical, and the taken-for-granted, you can more honestly decide what you really think, and you will likely have plenty of material for an outline or draft. Attack stereotypes by looking at the range of variation within them. Challenge the stereotype that students are rich (or poor) by looking at the differences among students, that is, consider the different kinds of students there are, and how tuition increases might affect all of them in different ways.

6. *Develop classifications for your topic.* Classifying breaks a subject into categories and places individuals or things into each of the categories. Identify possible categories and subcategories for your topic. Look for interesting, vivid, and fresh classifications. Classifications help us see patterns and interconnections. Various classifications might produce different insights (such as, working students, nonworking students, full-time and part-time students, mature students, and direct-entry students, students in different programs, majors, and faculties).

7. *Develop comparisons and contrasts.* Compare this topic with another. Compare allocation of funding for higher education versus that for elementary and secondary education, education versus health funding, funding in private schools versus that in universities, and accountability in higher education versus that in secondary school.

8. *Create metaphors.* A metaphor is a special comparison between things in different categories. Metaphors stir the imagination and help in visualization. Find and explore the ideas behind metaphors. The metaphor can be the backbone of an essay, or simply help you create details that will add sparkle to the essay. For example, we can use the metaphor of students as sponges versus students as curious cats. For more on metaphors, see Module 2.

9. *List examples.* List all the specific examples you can think of. An example is a single, concrete instance, never a generality. For example, my friend Pia, a single mother, who is going to university and taking a liberal arts program; Ambreen in my anthropology class, who is working two jobs to afford school; Liam in the nursing program, a new Canadian and the first in his family to go to university. Analyze your examples.

10. *Make "bug" lists.* What really bugs me about *x* is [insert list of complaints]. This may help formulate a problem you can use as the basis for the essay. What bugs me about government is ...; about students is ...; about education is ... .

11. *Ask questions.* Ask all the hard questions you want answered. What is important to know about this topic? Ask the journalistic questions: who, what, when, where, why, and how? Then get beyond these. Try to answer the questions with all the ideas and details you can. Use some of the brainteasers above to help answer these questions.

   At various stages through the composing process, we should ask ourselves what we do not know and what we need to know to develop a better understanding of the issue, to be able to take a stand on the issue, to develop an argument, or to make a case. This is not just a matter of saying "I need more information," but of identifying the kind of material we need and how having it would advance our understanding of the project. Sometimes it is useful to identify, before undertaking a project, everything that we do not know about the topic. Taking a stand too soon on an issue can often lock us into a position and stop us from looking at other positions or challenges. The art of ignorance can leave us more flexible in considering alternatives. For our sample essay, some things we might not know and might need to answer before continuing include the following:

   i. What percentage of the cost of education is paid by tuition fees and what percentage by government grants?

   ii. What are the government's reasons for wanting to raise tuition fees?

   iii. What will the increased tuition fees be used for? and/or

   iv. If the fees are not raised, what effect will there be on students and on universities?

12. *Use humour and fantasy.* Think of all kinds of fantasy situations for your topic and look for the humorous side to them. For example, reverse the normal rules of reality (such as, tax employers to pay for upgrading the critical skills program), break a social, scientific, or mathematical law related to your topic and imagine the results (such as, treat higher education as being universally accessible as it is in some other countries), or create a new rule or law and imagine its results (such as, charging politicians for every bad decision they make that costs taxpayers money).

13. *Vary your thinking style* (verbal, visual, written). For example, if you normally think in words, try thinking in terms of images, diagrams, or sounds. What ideas does a triumphal march, a funeral dirge, or the Rolling Stones' "You Can't Always Get What You Want" bring to mind?

These are just examples of possible ways where you can use brainteasers to illuminate a topic. The more of these brainteasers you use the better prepared you will be for writing your essay. Your ideas will be better developed, more resistant to attack, and more original.

11.4 Developing the Argument

At some point we need to stop generating ideas and develop a thesis. This requires us to examine our various materials, formulate a central idea that we want to develop, and express that in a thesis statement. Completing the following sentences can help us start to develop a thesis:

- What I really want to say is ... .
- The most gripping part of my topic is ... .
- The key question about my topic a audience would want answered is ... .
- What interests me most about my topic is ... .

Before developing the argument we must develop a strong thesis and then reasons to support that thesis. If some of our reasons are weak we must provide support for them as well as address whatever possible challenges we can imagine.

What Is a Thesis?

A *thesis* is the conclusion of an argument. In an argument essay it is the main point being argued in the essay. Without a thesis, the essay is little more than a tangle of sentences and paragraphs. The thesis unifies the paragraphs and essay. Essential to both the development and evaluation of the arguments in an essay, the thesis provides the writer a focus for selecting material to support his or her argument. An unclear or nonexistent thesis makes it difficult for audiences to determine what the author is claiming and how the evidence supports the claim.

A good thesis should satisfy the following criteria:

1. It is a *substantive assertion or claim,* not a statement of a process or intent. That is, a thesis takes a stand on an issue. For example, "I am going to investigate the role of education in *Frankenstein*" is a statement of intent; it does not state a position. A substantive thesis would be "*Frankenstein* shows that technical knowledge without moral guidance and a connection to a social community is not really a product of education." This makes a claim, an assertion, about knowledge and education. It also needs to be defended, because it is not obvious.

> A **thesis** is the conclusion of an argument; in an argument essay it is the main point being argued in the essay.

2. It is *controversial, interesting,* and/or *original.* The thesis "*Frankenstein* shows that science can lead to disastrous consequences" is not particularly original. Get beneath the obviousness of that claim. What is it about science that can lead to this? Is it science or something else that can produce this outcome? That it is controversial means that it needs to be defended.

3. It is often *complex* or *complicated.* Good ideas are often complicated and/or qualified. The claim "*Frankenstein* shows that science can lead to disastrous consequences" is overly general. It suggests a very narrow or shallow way of seeing the topic and does not acknowledge the subtleties of the issue. This thesis "Although Mary Shelley appears to condemn scientific inquiry in *Frankenstein,* her main target is not scientific knowledge but human ambition" takes a deeper and more interesting slant on the topic.

4. It serves as the *central idea of a unified composition.* The thesis is the main point of the essay. It can be treated as the conclusion of an argument, with the body of the essay the support for that conclusion.

5. It is also *clear, precise,* and *adequately limited in scope for the space allotted.* This often means a topic is qualified or narrowed to an appropriate point. We cannot write a ten-page essay on everything in the novel *Frankenstein.* However, we can write quite a good essay of that length on the role of education in the novel.

QUICK QUIZ 11.3

Evaluating a Thesis

Examine the following proposed theses for a three-page argument essay on whether the government should crack down on street racing, and

(A) Identify how each does or does not fit the criteria of a good thesis.

(B) Suggest what could be done to improve the ones that do not fit the criteria.

(C) Are the theses as stated likely to be interesting to an audience of students who have been discussing the issue for two weeks? Explain.

1. Street racing is dangerous.
2. The government should ban street racing.
3. Anyone caught engaging in street racing should have his or her car confiscated and face a minimum of two years in jail.
4. Although street racing can sometimes be dangerous, it would be futile to attempt a ban on all street racing.
5. A more effective approach to dealing with street racing than further banning an already illegal activity would be educating and imposing curfews on young drivers.

Answers to the Quick Quizzes are available on the Premium Website at www.criticalthinking2e.nelson.com.

Developing and Refining a Thesis

Make an assertion about your topic and write it down. Use the criteria on page 301 to 302 to start refining your thesis. There are two parts to refine a thesis: (1) developing clarity and precision, and (2) identifying the ideas that need to be supported.

In developing clarity and precision, examine your proposed thesis. What exactly does it say? Look at each term you have used. Does the statement capture exactly what you mean, what you want to say? Could it be phrased more precisely? Consider this thesis from an essay on Mary Shelley's *Frankenstein:*

Mary Shelley believed that education was detrimental to human kind.

To refine the thesis, isolate each term in the statement (every noun, adjective, and adverb) and make it more precise by asking who, what, when, where, why, and how, as well as how much/many, how do we know this, and so on. The sample thesis above contains a number of terms (such as *Shelley, believed, education, detrimental, human kind).* By applying the questions to each of the terms and phrases in this statement, we get the following:

TABLE 11.1 Making a Claim More Precise

Term	Making it more precise
Shelley:	Presumably the audience knows who Mary Shelley is. If not, we can explain. Is there something about her personal circumstances that is relevant here? What were her views on education and science? How did those affect her writing of the book?
Believed:	Did she actually believe this or is this something that she simply expresses as one of the themes in her novel? How do we know what Shelley's real beliefs are? Perhaps this needs to be better phrased.
Education:	All education, some education, certain types of education? Is it the education, or how that education is used, that is the problem? What kind of education and what aspect of education are we referring to here? "Education" is a big topic. Do we really want to say *all* education? Qualifying terms, phrases, and claims often leads to a more defendable thesis.
Detrimental:	How is it detrimental? Detrimental is an abstract term. Is there a more precise word that could be used here? Is "detriment" inherent in education? If so, how? Or is it somehow an accidental feature? To make this into a more defensible thesis we would minimally need to qualify what Shelley means by "education," how it is "detrimental," and whether it is detrimental in the same way to everyone.
To mankind:	To all human kind? Some? Only a few? To make this into a more defensible thesis, we would minimally need to specify the scope and how it is detrimental to mankind.

For example, the government is considering raising tuition fees next year. Consider the following as a thesis for a two-page argument essay, or an opinion piece for the student news paper:

Tuition fees should not be raised.

As a thesis for a two-page argument essay, this has several problems. It uses the passive rather than active voice. A better thesis would specify the agent (or who is raising the fees), making the sentence active. In most provinces, the government sets the range of permissible increases and the individual universities and colleges work within that. Further, this does not specify which tuition fees are in question (it could be fees for universities, colleges, College of General and Professional Educations in Quebec, undergraduate programs, or graduate and professional programs). Nor does it specify the time frame (it could be next year, the next three years, or indefinitely).

A better thesis would be the following:

> The provincial government should not raise undergraduate and graduate tuition fees in the province for the next three years.

The more qualified or limited in scope a claim is the easier it is to defend. For example, we can more easily defend the claim that some rock music that is crude and offensive and should be censored than the claim that all rock music should be censored. Although it is always best not to bite off more than you can chew, you should not make your claim so narrow as to make it trivial.

QUICK QUIZ 11.4

Refining a Thesis

For each of the following possible theses, identify what needs to be established. Where possible, make it a better thesis by using the information in Section 11.4. Where it already is a good thesis, show how it meets the criteria for a good thesis.

The assignment is to write a two-page argument essay that is to be used as the basis for further discussion of the issue. The students have been studying the specific topic for three weeks.

1. For a first-year sociology course: Criminal behaviour is more a product of the individual's specific interactions with his or her peer group than of general social norms.
2. For a second-year urban planning course: We should ban cars in the city.
3. For a first-year course on genetics and society: Although the knowledge gained from genetics promises major gains in agriculture, medicine, and forensics, it also poses serious threats to individual privacy and well-being.
4. For a second-year computer ethics course: Maintaining the privacy of individuals is an important concern for those delivering computer services, and every company should have and follow a privacy policy.

Answers to the Quick Quizzes are available on the Premium Website at www.criticalthinking2e.nelson.com.

Developing the Argument

We now need to develop the reasons to support the thesis. We can do this by using the brainteasers (in Section 11.4 above) and formulating reasons from those by using the issues model (outlined in Module 1) to develop considerations and turn them into reasons, or by using the topics model (outlined in Module 4) to identify the topics in the conclusion and then develop reasons to support those topics by generating answers to the topics questions.

The following uses the topics model on the tuition example in the preceding section to illustrate the process. We can identify three topics for the revised tuition thesis:

1. The provincial government;
2. Should not raise undergraduate and graduate tuition fees; and
3. For the next three years.

We can generate the following questions:

Q1: Under what conditions should someone not raise undergraduate and graduate tuition fees?

Q2: Does this apply to the government?

Q3: Why three years?

Using the brainstorming method we can generate possible answers for each of the three questions:

Q1:

1. Raising tuition fees makes it more difficult for existing students to complete their degrees.
2. It makes it more costly for incoming students.
3. It may prevent future students, especially students from low-income families, from going to university.
4. It may mean that more students take on more debt to complete their degrees.
5. It may mean that students move away from the liberal arts and toward "more practical" degrees, such as science, economics, and business.

Q2:

1. The provincial government has an obligation to encourage students to complete their degrees.
2. It is in the government's and province's economic interest for students to complete their degrees.
3. The government has both social policy (social justice) and economic interests in encouraging more students to attend university.
4. The government has a social policy interest in encouraging more students from lower-income families to attend university.
5. Both the government and society have an interest in minimizing the debt students take on as a result of university education.
6. A greater focus on "more practical" degrees will likely mean less development of some of the core critical skills and attitudes that we expect students to attain in university.

Q3:

1. Three years allows time to do a better assessment of university funding.

Once we have a set of reasons we need to select the ones that are most important or interesting and most relevant to our intended audience. Reasons 1 through 4 in Question 1 are commonly given when governments suggest raising tuition fees. The audience is likely to know these. Unless we have something new or interesting to add to the argument, we are likely to rehash old considerations. Reason 5 is more interesting and not as familiar. Although we can mention the other reasons if there is space, developing reason 5 would likely lead to new considerations on the argument. Reasons 1 through 6 under Question 2 might also shed new light on the issue, thus developing the other part of the argument. Or to develop a more original approach to the argument we could select one of reasons 1 through 4 in Question 1 and then work on developing the reasons in Q2.

We could have used other methods for generating the reasons. What is important is that we generate a sufficient number to be able to select from them that are best for our purposes in the essay we are writing.

Next, we should make the argument as strong as possible. If it is a deductive argument, we try to make it sound; if inductive, we try to make it cogent. Using reason 5 from Question 1, we get the following argument:

1. The government's raising tuition fees will likely result in students moving away from the liberal arts and toward "more practical" degrees (such as, science, economics, and business).
2. This is undesirable.

∴ 3. The government should not raise tuition fees.

Reason 1 could be turned into a conditional, in which case the argument is valid (because it affirms the antecedent). Once we know the conclusion is adequately supported by the reasons we should check each reason to see if it is acceptable. If any is likely to be challenged or not obvious, we should either provide support for that reason through sub-arguments or rewrite the reason to make it more defensible.

The first reason in the argument seems plausible, although we may want to develop a sub-argument to support it. Reason 2 in this argument is weak because it does not say why reason 1 is undesirable. To strengthen it there are two possible reasons we could include:

4. Having fewer students taking liberal arts courses would weaken the liberal arts programs and leave undeveloped the core critical skills they are designed to teach. Fewer students mean fewer faculty members and fewer courses. As a result there would be less opportunity for all students to gain the skills taught in liberal arts courses.
5. Professional programs have extensive course requirements that allow for few electives outside their major requirements. As a result, students will have less opportunity to gain the skills taught in liberal arts courses.

We could develop each of these into a sub-argument to support reason 2. We examine each to see if either is obvious and likely to be accepted by the audience, or if they need further defence. (Since we are illustrating the basic strategy for writing an essay, rather than developing the details of the essay, we will not do that here.)

Before writing up the argument we should consider possible challenges and responses to it. The following two objections could be raised to reasons 4 and 5 above. Both presuppose that the liberal arts currently provide critical skills. The following objections could be raised:

6. The liberal arts do not provide these skills now.
7. Liberal arts courses are not the only or best place to acquire these skills.

These objections would then need to be elaborated upon and responded to.

In dealing with objections and challenges it is important to note that we often do not have conclusive responses. From both argumentation and psychological points of view, it is better to acknowledge a legitimate objection and admit that we do not have a conclusive response than to ignore it or try to present a partial or inconclusive response. From an argumentation point of view, if we are trying to arrive at the truth about an issue, presenting an argument as though it is stronger than it actually is defeats the basic purpose. Psychologically, presenting a weak response, or an argument as strong when it is not, undermines our credibility as an arguer in the eyes of our argument partner.

A Sketch of the "No Tuition Increase" Argument

Using the numbers from above, the arrow diagram of our argument would look like this:

$$6 \qquad 7$$
$$\downarrow \qquad \downarrow$$
$$\underline{4 + 5}$$
$$\downarrow$$
$$\underline{1 + 2}$$
$$\downarrow$$
$$3$$

The One-Paragraph Argument

Having developed a thesis, we need to organize the argument. One way to do this is by developing an outline. However, outlines can be sketchy and more topic-oriented than argument-oriented. We end up with a set of sub-topics, but the connections between them may not be clear.

An alternative method is to develop a one-paragraph argument. A ***one-paragraph argument*** is a paragraph in which we develop the basic logical structure of our case. It is like the abstract of a essay, and should contain the thesis and all of the key reasons that will be developed. It is usually less than one page.

In writing a one-paragraph argument for our essay, we start with our thesis statement, which we develop into a paragraph outlining the main points of the argument we are going to make in the essay. Every claim in the paragraph must support the thesis. This paragraph then serves as the basis for the outline of the essay. Each of the sentences can, in turn, act as a topic sentence for one or more paragraphs in the essay.

Using the sample thesis and the questions we formulated above, a one-paragraph argument might look something like this:

> The provincial government should not raise undergraduate and graduate tuition fees in the province for the next three years. Increased tuition fees will likely result in students moving away from the liberal arts and toward "more practical" degrees, such as, science, economics, and business. This is undesirable because it would weaken the liberal arts programs and leave undeveloped the core critical skills, such as, critical reading, reasoning, and writing, that all programs, including professional ones, rely on. To the objection that liberal arts courses are not the only or best options for acquiring such skills, I respond that liberal arts programs are currently the only ones systematically developing such skills, whereas other programs have no incentives to teach such skills systematically.

> A **one-paragraph argument** is a paragraph in which we develop the basic logical structure of our case.

Ideally, the thesis should be the first sentence of the paragraph. We can then identify what minimally needs to be shown to establish our thesis, and reassess each statement in the one-paragraph argument to determine whether it actually contributes to the argument. If we find a claim that does not contribute to clarifying, defending, or supporting the thesis, then we drop that statement. If we find a gap (or something that needs to be established to support the thesis and that is not established in the one paragraph argument) then we need to add to the argument. The goal is to produce, in one paragraph, a conclusion (or thesis) and the basic reasons that support that conclusion. Developing our paragraph from a properly constructed argument structure ensures that the one-paragraph argument contains all that is necessary and only what is necessary.

Once we have a good one-paragraph argument, we can develop it into an outline for the essay. The paragraph's remaining sentences become the topic sentences for the body of the essay. We can use the same method to develop the rest of the essay's paragraphs.

The advantage of this method is that it forces the writer to develop an argument and test that argument early on. The one-paragraph argument serves as an abstract of the logic of the essay and enables the writer to develop an overall view of it early in the writing process.

QUICK QUIZ 11.5

The One-Paragraph Argument

In each of the following one-paragraph arguments, identify the thesis and then determine which claims are relevant and which are not relevant to establishing it. Rewrite the passage to organize the claims while eliminating the irrelevant claims.

1. Although marijuana can be used for some medical conditions it should not be legalized either for medical or recreational use. Marijuana has been used to relieve the nausea that accompanies chemotherapy, for example. It should not be used for medical use because there are other, more effective treatments. Many people claim marijuana helps them relax and that it is not harmful. But marijuana has proven harmful effects. Moreover, it is an addictive drug. Legalizing it for medical purposes would be allowing the use of a dangerous drug when more effective drugs are available. For similar reasons, it should not be legalized for recreational purposes. It has harmful effects and is addictive.

2. University courses should consist of fewer lectures and make available the information delivered in lectures through materials (such as iPod videocasts). Most students have iPods, and video iPods are not expensive. Downloading iPod videos is easy. Many students can't attend class regularly because they have jobs and other commitments. One survey says that over half of all students work at least fifteen hours a week. Some have family commitments as well. Many lecturers are boring. One professor I had simply read from the assigned text. Lectures being available in video format would help ESL students who often need to hear a lecture several times to get its full meaning. Many students are ESL students.

Answers to the Quick Quizzes are available on the Premium Website at www.criticalthinking2e.nelson.com.

11.5 Making a Case

The preceding sections help us develop an argument on an issue. However, an argument, even a good one, is not necessarily sufficient to establish a position. An argument presents one set of related reasons for a position we are defending. A *case* for a position is a set of arguments and sub-arguments, and the responses to the main challenges, structured to show that the position being argued is superior to other positions. For example, a lawyer can make an argument on a particular issue in a trial; however, to win the case, the lawyer must show that his or her arguments outweigh those presented by the other side. While both lawyers may have some good individual arguments, their goals are to try to show that they have made a better *case*, that is, that their collection of evidence and arguments as a whole is superior to those of the other side.

Thus far, we have made an *argument* for not increasing tuition, but we have not yet made a *case*. To turn our argument into a case we would have to introduce further reasons for our position, challenge the other side's main strong points, and show that the considerations for our position outweigh those for the other side. Normally there will be strong reasons for the various positions taken on an issue. In order to weigh and balance the various arguments for the alternative positions we need to use a balance of considerations argument.

> A **case** for a position is a set of arguments and sub-arguments, and the responses to the main challenges, structured to show that the position is superior to other positions.

The Balance of Considerations Argument

A *balance of considerations argument* is an argument that examines the relevant considerations for the alternative positions on an issue and argues that one is better. We use it when there are good reasons for several sides of an issue. A balance of considerations argument acknowledges and addresses the various legitimate considerations on both sides of the argument. Additionally, it shows that, given these various considerations, one side is better than the other. In rare cases it may argue that the two are relatively evenly matched. In such cases we must argue that point.

Imagine a couple discussing where to go for a winter vacation. They engage in the following discussion:

> A **balance of considerations argument** is an argument that examines the relevant considerations for the alternative positions on an issue and argues that one is better.

Pat: I think we should take our winter vacation in Jamaica. I need to go somewhere quiet and would really like some good food.

Chris: I would really like to go someplace where I can do some shopping, and the shopping is not that great in Jamaica.

Pat: I agree, but I do like the food there.

Chris: The last time we were there, it wasn't all that quiet. How about St. Maarten? It's quiet. There are wonderful secluded beaches. The food is great — French and Dutch. And I can go shopping.

Pat: Sounds better than Jamaica. Let's look into it.

Pat makes the argument for taking a winter vacation in Jamaica. Chris partially counters that argument and makes a case for St. Maarten that challenges one of Pat's reasons for going to Jamaica and incorporates his other concerns.

Using a balance of considerations argument on the issue of whether the government should raise tuition would require us not just to provide reasons for not raising tuition, but also to address the reasons the government has for raising it. Then we would need to argue that even though there are some strong arguments for the government's position, the considerations against it outweigh those for it. Having explored considerations *against* raising tuition, we will now explore some *for* raising tuition:

- Universities could hire more faculty or not cut existing members.
- Universities could maintain or lower faculty–student ratios, thereby improving teaching quality.
- Universities could increase facilities, including access to libraries and computers.
- Universities need such increases simply to maintain existing staff and services.

These are good and relevant considerations. To show why the "no tuition increase" considerations outweigh these, we could explain how these goals could be achieved without a tuition increase, or argue that the underlying interests behind the "no tuition increase" arguments outweigh the considerations for the other position.

Many essays written for an academic audience call for a balance of considerations argument. Whether we were analyzing human origins, the role of genes versus environment in explaining behaviour, the causes of the increase in school violence, whether Pluto should be classified as a planet, or almost any academic issue, there are competing considerations and theories that we would need to address. The same is true for social, ethical, and policy issues, where competing values and principles are invoked.

Whether we give an argument, make a case, or give a balance of considerations argument will depend on the context, our audience, and what we are trying to accomplish.

QUICK QUIZ 11.6

The Balance of Considerations Argument

For each of the following issues, identify the alternate positions and competing considerations. Identify possible overriding considerations that would weigh the argument toward one side or the other.

1. Should parents be allowed to spank their children?
2. Should the government ban cell phone use while driving?

Answers to the Quick Quizzes are available on the Premium Website at www.criticalthinking2e.nelson.com.

11.6 Developing Audience-Based Prose

Knowing the Audience

Once we have developed an argument or a case, we need to turn it into audience-based prose, which means we will have to accomplish two things: (1) address the audience and their interests; and (2) present the arguments clearly and with signposts so that the audience can follow.

Although in developing an argument we ideally start out thinking of the potential audience, we often lose sight of that. In turning our arguments into audience-based prose, we should review our purposes and the audience and refine our arguments accordingly.

To successfully address the audience we must identify the audience's knowledge (including both concepts and facts), attitudes, viewpoints, interests, and needs regarding the issue, as well as our purpose in addressing the audience in this essay. If the audience is not likely to know certain concepts or have certain information, then we have to introduce and explain those concepts and provide the relevant information with supporting documentation. If we are presenting the argument on tuition developed above to a general audience, we may need to explain the skills taught in liberal arts courses and why they are not likely to be taught in professional courses. If our audience is composed primarily of university faculty, we need not explain that.

We should also make a reasonable assessment of the audience's attitudes and viewpoints. This does not mean we simply write so that our argument agrees with them, but that we consider the audience's viewpoints when constructing and presenting our arguments. For instance, in a secular context we would not use religious-based arguments. If arguments are going to seriously challenge an audience's perspective, it is best to look for and start with areas of agreement before moving to the more controversial areas.

In presenting the "no tuition increase" argument to members of the government who are in favour of raising tuition fees, we would likely start with points on which we agree (such as, that developing certain skills found in the liberal arts is an important part of a university education and needed for developing good citizens). Then we would move to the more contentious part of the argument. Having agreed on the basic points thus far, the audience is more likely to hear us out on the other reasons.

Turning Arguments into Audience-Based Prose

Prose is simply ordinary speech or writing. It can be contrasted with poetry and visuals (such as, argument diagrams). The challenge of putting arguments into prose is in transforming our complex, multifaceted, and sometimes visual representations of arguments into a linear form. Arguments contain many different parts, some are more important than others (such as, reasons, main conclusions, intermediate conclusions, objections, responses, issues, definitions, and examples). In prose we can only present one idea at a time. Part of our challenge is to identify what needs to be presented in what order for the audience to be able to follow the argument.

If we were to transcribe a simple argument as it is given, we would likely end up with some fairly inert prose. The argument:

1. If the government raises tuition fees, students will likely study for "more practical" degrees (such as, science, economics, and business).

2. Having students take "more practical" degrees (such as, science, economics, and business) is undesirable.

∴ 3. The government should not raise tuition fees.

becomes the following:

If the government raises tuition fees, students will likely take "more practical" degrees (such as, science, economics, and business). Students taking "more practical" degrees (such as, science, economics, and business) is undesirable. Therefore, the government should not raise tuition fees.

This contains redundancies and is not very fluid. To turn the argument into more fluid prose, we often have to reorder the claims, supply cue words, and eliminate redundancies. Doing this gives us the following:

> The government should not raise tuition fees. If it does, students will likely choose to study toward "more practical" degrees (such as, science, economics, and business). This would be undesirable because it would undermine the liberal arts programs and would result in many students not learning the critical skills that the liberal arts teach.

QUICK QUIZ 11.7

Turning a Simple Argument into Prose

Rewrite each of the following arguments into a fluid prose paragraph that clearly displays the structure of the argument:

I. Background: Tara has submitted an expense form for reimbursement for attending a conference and entertaining a dozen clients and co-worker Eli at an expensive dinner.

1. Eli claims he was not at the dinner.
2. Eli claims that he did not see Tara at any of the sessions at the conference, including the plenary session.
3. Eli did see her at the reception and the evening banquet.
4. Eli claims that at the time of the dinner for which Tara is claiming expenses, he was with another company client.
5. He has offered to supply the name of the client to his manager.
6. Eli is trustworthy.

∴ 7. Tara has falsified her expense account.
8. If someone has falsified expenses, he or she has stolen from the company.

∴ 9. Tara has stolen from the company.
10. If someone steals from the company, he or she should be fired.

∴ 11. Tara should be fired.

II. Background: The ACME company has just gone through a reorganization.

1. If a reorganization results in an increase in morale, greater productivity, and more profits, with no serious detrimental effects, then it is a success.
2. The reorganization of the ACME bolt company resulted in an increase in morale.
3. The reorganization of the ACME bolt company resulted in greater productivity.
4. The reorganization of the ACME bolt company had no serious detrimental effects.

Turning Complex Arguments into Prose

We can use the same techniques (reordering claims, supplying cue words, and eliminating redundancies) to transform more complex arguments with multiple lines of argument into prose. We then have to develop the connections and flow between the lines of argument. This will be discussed next.

The Structure of the Essay

Argument essays typically have three components, each with a different function: (1) an introduction, (2) a body, and (3) a conclusion.

The *body* of the essay builds the argument for the thesis by developing each of the lines of reasoning. The order of presentation of the arguments should allow the audience to move through the essay fluidly, following the logic of the arguments.

The body should contain only material that either directly supports the thesis or illustrates and clarifies it. Unless background material, historical origins of the issue, discussion of various authors, or parallel issues are directly related to the argument, they should be omitted.

Start with your strongest argument. Generally, audiences notice and best remember what comes first and what comes last. This is true for the overall essay and for paragraphs within the essay. Putting the weakest argument first draws attention to it and makes the audience expect more weak arguments. Burying the strongest argument in the middle of the essay is likely to result in it being ignored. As mentioned earlier, the argument we start

---

2 Supporters of intelligent design are individuals who believe that evolution cannot explain the observed complexity of nature; that the complexity of nature must be explained by appeal to the theory that nature was intelligently designed; and that this can be determined through scientific means.

with should be one that the audience is likely to agree with, thereby establishing a climate of agreement. We then move to the more contentious and controversial arguments.

The *conclusion* not only provides a summary of the argument but takes the audience back to the broader issues and their implications. The introduction framed and established a broader context for the issue and the essay has added something to the discussion of it. The conclusion should identify what the essay has contributed and suggest where one could go from there, perhaps stating the limits of the discussion, specific research or arguments that could be pursued, or possible further lines of inquiry based on the arguments of the essay. These should be specific and not simply state "More research needs to be done."

Placing Definitions and Objections

Where definitions and objections are placed within the essay depends on how they function in an argument. If a definition is central to understanding the issue, then we may put an abbreviated form of it in the introduction of the essay or in the first paragraph of the body of the essay, depending on how that affects the flow of the essay. If the term being defined comes later in the argument, the definition normally follows the first use of the term. If it is placed before it, the audience will not know why the term is being defined and likely will not remember the term's meaning by the time it needs to be applied.

Objections and responses to objections are normally placed after the argument or reason that is being objected to. In exceptional cases, we might start with an objection to a position or argument, address the objection, and then develop our own argument. As with most rules of writing, if there are good reasons for breaking them, they can and should be broken.

Making Connections: Paragraphs

In addition to its overall structure the essay should have an internal logic or structure. This internal structure is built on the paragraphs and transitions between paragraphs.

Each paragraph within the body of the essay develops one argument or one objection and response (or in longer essays one reason within an argument). If the essay is quite long and the argument is quite involved, an argument may require two or more paragraphs.

Paragraphs have an internal structure. Each develops one point, which should be stated as a single claim either at the beginning or end of the paragraph. This helps the reader who would skim through the essay, and makes it easier for the careful reader to follow the logic of the argument. In an argument essay, if the paragraph contains an entire argument, its topic sentence will be the conclusion and the rest of the paragraph will develop that argument and support the key claim.

One way of testing the coherence of a paragraph is to identify the topic sentence and then examine each sentence to see how it relates to the topic sentence. If it does not support it or provide an illustration, the statement is probably irrelevant and should be removed. (See "Turning Arguments into Audience-Based Prose" above for more about topic sentences.)

Use signposts to guide your audience through the essay. These are transition devices that let the audience know the flow of the essay. For example, if an argument structure has three sub-arguments, we might start the second sub-argument with "My second argument is …". Alternatively, if we have named the arguments, we can say something like "The main conclusion of the 'harm to children' argument is …" or "This is supported by … ." Other signposts might include "An objection to this position is …" or "In response to this…".

11.7 Revising and Editing

Revising focuses on the big issues: the logic, coherence, clarity, and flow of the essay. Editing focuses on making sentence-level changes: correcting spelling and grammar, altering word choice, and sentence flow. Good writers revise and edit in two separate steps.

Revising for Coherence: Paragraphs and Whole Texts

After writing an essay, set it aside and focus on something else for a while before revising. Distancing yourself somewhat from your work allows you to come at it with fresh eyes.

If possible, have a peer review the essay. Peer reviewers provide concrete feedback about what works and what does not work. Also, offer to be a peer reviewer for others. Critically examining the work of others helps sharpen your own perceptions and writing.

Read the essay aloud at least once, noting where it sounds stilted or does not flow. If possible, tape your reading and listen to it or have another person read the essay while you listen. This exercise often helps you identify awkwardness, slips of logic, and gaps in the essay.

- Look at the whole text for coherence. Construct an outline, *précis*, or one-paragraph argument of the essay. Start with the thesis statement. Then go through the text paragraph by paragraph, selecting the topic sentence (or main point) in each. Examine the argument using the suggestions for constructing a one-paragraph essay in Section 11.5. See if the argument flows clearly from one point to the next. If not, reorder and rewrite the paragraphs, or if possible, introduce transitions. If there are sentences that do not contribute to the argument, re-examine them and revise so they do contribute, or cut them.

Examine the overall essay to see if you have included enough signposts for the audience. Not simply logical cue words, signposts signal to the audience where he or she is in an essay and where major changes of direction occur. They are also used to clearly indicate when you are presenting your own position and when you are presenting an alternate position or a challenge to the position you are defending.

Now look at each paragraph individually, starting with its topic sentence. Examine each sentence in the paragraph in the same way you examined the sentences of the one-paragraph argument. How does each relate to the topic sentence? What does it contribute to the overall argument? If it does not contribute to the argument or serve to illustrate a point in the argument, rewrite it so it does or remove it.

Revising for Clarity and Style: The Sentence Level

Both when writing and revising the essay, we should strive to make the text (each sentence, transitions, and the overall organization) as clear as possible. A clearer style requires using the active voice (rather than the passive) voice, using concrete nouns and descriptive verbs (rather than prepositional phrases, adjectives, and adverbs), and eliminating unnecessary words and redundancies. Pat Lanham in *Revising Prose* (5th ed. Englewood Cliffs, N.J.: Prentice Hall, 2006.) has proposed a "paramedic method" for turning sick and weak prose into more robust prose. The following expands on his method:

- *Identify and circle the prepositions in a passage.* Extensive use of prepositional phrases takes attention away from the subject and verb and deadens prose. Prepositions include *after, before, in, on, at, to, apart from, above, from, by, beside, over, among, through, around,* and *between.* One prepositional phrase is fine. Sometimes two in a row is unavoidable. More than that suggests that the sentence lacks focus. Replace prepositions or prepositional phrases with stronger verbs and nouns:

Initial: After considering the objections in light of the relevant information and for the purposes mentioned we conclude that additional research is needed for the purpose of resolving the issue.

- The prepositional phrases make the text sluggish. Rewriting to eliminate them and using an active voice in place of *is needed,* we get the following:

Revised: We need further research to respond to the relevant objections and resolve the issue.

- *Circle forms of the verb to be (is, are, was, were, will be, seems to be, etc.).* Forms of "to be" often signal the passive voice and, even when the sentence is not passive, they are weak verbs. Note, however, that "be" verbs help form the progressive tense (e.g., are writing) and are necessary in this construction.

Initial: There are some situations in which arguments are not persuasive.

Revised: Sometimes arguments do not persuade.

In the initial sentence, the main action falls in the subordinate clause ("in which ..."), not in the main clause. Not only is the revision shorter, but it focuses the audience's attention on the action.

- *In each sentence identify what action is occurring.* Often the action has been turned into a prepositional phrase with no agent in sight. Who (or what) is acting? (See the preceding example.)
- *Put the action into a simple, active verb form, preferably with a human subject.* This technique helps when you find your prose confusing or hard to follow. It is based on the principle that the actor in a sentence should serve as the subject of a sentence and the action should be in the sentence's verbs. The following examples illustrate this:

Initial: A situation has arisen in which the raising of tuition has been proposed by the province and to which students and parents are opposed.
Revised: The province has proposed raising tuition fees. Students and their parents are opposed.
Initial: This essay is in need of a stronger thesis.
Revised: This essay needs a stronger thesis. *(Eliminating three words — two prepositions — results in a stronger statement.)*
Initial: There is much discussion among students about the proposed tuition increase.

This sentence uses a "to be" verb, relies on an abstract term (*discussion*) that hides the action, and buries the subject of the action (students) in a prepositional phrase.

Revised: Students are discussing the proposed tuition increase.

The rewrite replaces the passive voice, in which we do not know who the actor is, with the active voice and changes the weak *is* to a stronger verb.

Initial: In this essay I show why tuition increases should not be implemented by the provincial government.

Revised: This essay examines why the provincial government should not implement tuition increases.

- *Rewrite nominalizations as verbs or adjectives.* A *nominalization* is a noun that replaces a verb or adjective. For example, instead of "organization" use "organize," which forces you to identify the actor. When nominalizations are used, actors are often hidden in prepositional phrases. Fewer nominalizations make our language clearer. For example:

Initial: The intention of the province is to proceed with the implementation of the proposal with the utmost haste. *(eighteen words)*

Revised: The province intends to implement the proposal quickly. *(eight words)*

The revision turns nominalizations into actions and eliminates unnecessary prepositional phrases.

- *Use simpler, more concrete terms rather than abstract ones.* Using plain language makes your writing clearer and easier to read. In each of the following, the first term is a nominalization, the second a somewhat abstract verb, and the third a plainer and more concrete verb, as seen in Table 11.2.

TABLE 11.2 Abstract and Concrete Terms

Nominalization	Abstract Verb	More Concrete Verb
Assertion	Assert	Say
Am cognizant of	Have knowledge of	Know
Demonstration of	Demonstrate	Show
Discourse, conversation	Converse	Talk
Initiative	Initiate	Start
Modification	Modify	Change

- *Eliminate needless introductory words.* We often start sentences with preambles that contribute little to the content. The following are some common examples of unnecessary wordiness:

    The question as to whether …
    The reason why is that …
    Owing to the fact that …
    On the basis of …
    In regard to …
    It is the opinion of the author that …
    The point of this is that …

These can often be rewritten or eliminated altogether:

Initial: The question as to whether the province should raise tuition fees is not easy to answer.

Revised: Whether the province should raise tuition fees is not an easy question to answer.

Sometimes other words within a sentence do little work and can be eliminated.

QUICK QUIZ 11.8

Making Prose Clearer

Revise each of the following sentences to make the statements clearer and more forceful:

1. The issue of importance noted by this writer is the extent of control that groups of parents should have over what is being taught in the schools. (From a student essay on the *Huck Finn* dialogue, used with permission.)
2. According to this writer, it is imperative that in light of the issue that we are considering, it should be given further thought.
3. There has been a modification to the expectation about the release date of the proposed new edition of the software.
4. In this essay, the reasons why tuition increases by the provincial government should not be implemented will be examined.
5. The crossing of the blue line is an action engaged in by a player acting in the capacity of a forward.

Answers to the Quick Quizzes are available on the Premium Website at www.criticalthinking2e.nelson.com.

Editing

Finally, edit the essay for grammar, spelling, subject–verb agreement, correct use of words (such as, *there, their*), and formatting.

Title Your Essay

A well-chosen title helps frame the essay and tells the audience what it is about. "The Tuition Essay," "Project #1," or "Tuition in University" tells the audience little about the content or position of the essay. Use your imagination to devise a title. Your title, thesis, and opening paragraph convey to the audience your basic argument. Weakness in any or all of these undermines the effort that you put into your essay. More descriptive titles might be "No to Tuition Increase," "Tuition: A Loss of Critical Skills," or "More Tuition, Less Liberal Arts." These tell more precisely what the essay is about.

Module Summary

- Writing an argument essay involves not just putting an argument into written form, but doing so while attending to our purpose for writing, the audience and the context of presentation, and the other arguers on the issue.
- Although we are not directly talking with these arguers in our essay, we are addressing them and the intended audience.
- We need to present opponents' arguments fairly while contributing to the ongoing discussion with our essay.
- The two processes central to writing an argument essay are composing (which includes developing an argument) and turning that argument into audience-based prose.
- In composing we develop a position and the considerations that support that position, then turn those into reasons.
- We can develop reasons by using the issues model, the topics model, brainstorming and editing, or doing research.
- We have to make arguments as strong as possible and are expected to contribute something new to the ongoing dialogue.
- Sometimes we have to make a case rather than simply develop an argument for a position.
- With complicated issues we often need to develop a balance of considerations argument.
- The challenge of presenting complex, nonlinear arguments in a sequential form that the audience can understand and follow is the main task of producing audience-based prose.
- For simple arguments we work from the formal structure of the arguments we have produced, eliminate the redundancies, order the claims, and provide cue words.
- For complex, multilinear arguments, on the essay level we connect the various arguments, provide signposts, and develop a coherent, integrated structure; on the paragraph level we write a coherent paragraph in which all of the claims support the topic sentence; and on the sentence level we write clear sentences.
- Once we have produced an essay, we need to revise for logic, coherence, clarity, and flow, edit for grammar, spelling, agreement, and word choice, and provide a good descriptive title for the essay.

Argumentation Exercise: Developing Arguments, Objections, and Responses on a Position in a Dialogue

Examine a blog in which the contributors present reasons for and against a position. Good sources are the editorial and opinion pages of major newspapers (such as, *The Globe and Mail,* the *New York Times,* or *The Washington Post).* Other sources can be found online—try Googling "Canadian political blogs." What will make for a good source for this exercise is a blog with a diversity of positions on an issue and some good reasons for the different positions. Identify a number of the positions and reasons found in the blog. You cannot do everything; focus on a few typical positions and reasons and explore those.

Write a dialogue in which each of the two argument partners develop and defend their positions, raise objections to their argument partner's positions and arguments, and respond to the objections to their own.

Writing Skills Exercise: Essay Critique and Rewrite

Select an essay you have written for a course other than this one and

1. Construct an argument analysis and assessment of the essay;
2. Critique the argument (see Module 8);
3. Using your analysis, rewrite the essay to make the argument and essay stronger;
4. How could the materials from this module have helped you write a stronger essay originally? What were your major improvements (conceptualization, stylistics, argumentation)?

EPILOGUE

Argumentation in Academic, Public, and Personal Life: Tolerance and Engagement

Argument and argumentation enter into our lives in many ways. They are tools for exploring what we believe and what we should do, for assessing the evidence and reasoning for our beliefs, and for the decisions we make about what to do. We use these in a variety of contexts, in our academic, public, and personal lives.

Much of academic inquiry revolves around controversies and disputes or inquiry. Inquiry is often undertaken to resolve controversy and disputes: *How old is the Earth? Is light composed of particles or fields of force? Did Shakespeare write Macbeth? What is the best form of corporate governance?*

Such academic inquiries and controversies are carried out in the context of a community of inquirers and against a background of shared knowledge and expectations. The members of that community of inquirers (whether in English literature, philosophy, biology, women's studies, sociology, or any other academic discipline) are expected to be familiar with the background or context of the controversy or inquiry. That is, they are expected to know and address the relevant evidence, arguments, positions, and issues within that controversy, including the relevant contributions and challenges within it (and sometimes the surrounding materials and fields). Part of what is involved in establishing competence within a field is learning the issues, controversies, and state of knowledge within that discipline. As a student, you are in the process of learning the topography of the field you are studying.

An academic issue, then, is set against a background context of claims, arguments, evidence, other related issues, and an ongoing discussion about these by the community of inquirers. A key defining feature of academic discourse is the commonly shared goal of the pursuit of truth. This acts as a guideline and constraining factor on the discourse. Academics do not knowingly introduce claims and evidence that are faulty, false, or shoddy. Doing so would mislead and take away from the pursuit of truth and lead to being discredited within the field. In this, academic discourse shares a common feature with argumentation.

The situation is somewhat different with personal and public discourse. Some personal argumentation involves a specific, immediate issue. "Should we have Thai or Indian for supper?" That specific issue has reasons relevant to it but, as it is given, is not a complex issue. I am simply trying to find out what I should do. There may be no broader implications or issues. The focus of the discussion in personal discourse may involve questions such as "What should I do?" "What should I believe?" "What should I major in?" "What do I believe about abortion?" and so on. My personal values and goals are an integral part of my reasoning about these issues.[1]

On the other hand, some of the personal issues we take positions on (such as, "Should gay marriage be legalized?" "Should the state relax privacy laws?" "Should *The Adventures of Huckleberry Finn* be banned?" "Is abortion immoral?" Should I download copyright materials?") are a combination of public issues and personal ones. We are wondering what we believe and/or should personally do about such issues. But they are also public issues: it is not just a matter of our personal preferences. Our reasoning has gone beyond the personal to a public forum, intersecting with the reasoning, the argumentation, going on within a community of inquirers. To enter into that, we need to address the issues and considerations being raised by that community of inquirers. Our focus is no longer what we believe, what we should do, but how do we contribute to this ongoing discussion.

Although our personal beliefs and values come into play in helping us determine what position we will take, these issues that are being debated in a public forum are similar in structure to academic ones. A community of people is engaging in discourse about them. However, there is often a more loosely defined set of positions, arguments, considerations, and evidence on these issues. Unlike the situation in the academic world, no one has to demonstrate competence or show an understanding of the background arguments in order to participate in the discussion. Sometimes the argument partners engaging in the controversy have additional agendas (social, political, economic, or personal). In some cases, individual participants may be committed neither to discovering the truth about the issues nor to the rules of argumentation but may have instead a different aim in their discourse. As individuals, we have to wade through all of this extraneous material to identify and assess the issues, arguments, and positions, and, eventually, to take our own stand.

If our goal is to engage in argumentation, then we seek the truth about the issue, with the idea that it will guide us in our beliefs and our actions. Ideally, we want to base our beliefs and actions on the best available reasoning, argument, and evidence. If we want to know what treatment we should undertake for cancer, we do not simply select the first claim that comes along or the first piece of reasoning that strikes our fancy. Rather,

---

1 We are not claiming personal decisions and reasoning is, should be, or can only be "merely" personal or subjective. We are claiming that often in engaging in such reasoning, we take into account our basic values and preferences. That does not mean that we do not consider the various arguments and considerations available in the broader public sphere. Part of becoming a skilled critical thinker is going beyond personal opinion and developing our positions and arguments in light of the broader reasoning on an issue. For some issues (such as, "Which restaurant should I go to?") there may be no broader controversy. For others (such as, "What do I believe about abortion?") there will be a broader discourse and our reasoning will need to take that into consideration.

we examine the various alternatives and the evidence for them, and make our decision based on our assessment of the evidence. Insofar as we want to base our beliefs and decisions on the best available evidence, we will use the principles of argumentation to develop our own beliefs and positions on issues. And that will involve using some of the features of academic argumentation, such as, looking for the best available arguments and evidence, critically examining the arguments of others, presenting our arguments for critical evaluation by others, responding to critical evaluation, and holding our beliefs provisionally.

But why should we do this? Why should we be rational? Why should we not, as many do, simply use arguments to defend and state our positions and ignore the principles of argumentation? Ultimately, this is a choice we make about who we are and who we will become, and how we engage with others and the world—to base our choices and beliefs on evidence based on the best available reasoning rather than simply letting our surroundings condition us.

Who we are and what we will become are influenced very strongly by what we do and what we believe. When we simply respond unreflectively to the beliefs of those around us, we are allowing our past and present experience to condition our present and future. Reflecting on and thinking about our ideas and actions, challenging, probing, looking for reasons, and examining the basis of our reasons and choices will enable us to make choices about how we should live our lives and how we should relate to others. In so doing, we become more autonomous and get outside of the little island that is our self and, by engaging with others and the world, develop who we are. We take control of who we are and will become.

But there is a stronger reason. We live in a world of plurality and difference. A central issue in our lives is how we, as individuals and as members of a community and a society. should deal with the diversity within and outside of our own groups and between groups. Mere tolerance is not enough, for tolerance simply recognizes differences without seeking to engage or bridge those differences. It gives us little or no common ground. Argumentation is a way of bridging differences, of understanding, and of possibly effecting rational persuasion. Argumentation and critical thinking in general are ways of becoming, of engaging with the world and with others, of sharing, of recognizing, of respecting and probing differences and similarities, of discovery and inquiry, and of commitment. Reason will not always help us bridge differences, but it will give us a better understanding of those differences. And with that, we can make more informed decisions about how to address them.

Let us reason together and create better selves and a better world.

GLOSSARY

Abusive *ad hominem* fallacy: involves making a personal attack on another person's expertise, character, intelligence, good faith, or other personal characteristic to demonstrate that the person's argument or position should not be considered. (page 172)

Active listening: paying attention to what the other person is saying, making sense of it, and separating it from any interpretations or responses we may have to it. (page 262)

***Ad hominem* fallacy:** involves attacking the individual, rather than the individual's arguments, as a way of dismissing the individual's arguments. (page 172)

Advocate: someone who takes the role of defending a position in an argument. (page 16)

Aesthetic claim: a normative claim concerned with issues of art and beauty. (page 152)

Ambiguity: occurs when a term, phrase, or sentence has two or more distinct meanings, and when both make sense in the given context, so it is not clear which one is specifically intended. (page 41)

Ambiguous position: refers to a statement that can have more than one identifiable meaning in a given context. (page 19)

Analogy: draws an explicit comparison between two different things and on the basis of some similarities suggests that other uncompared elements are also similar. (pages 45, 126)

Antecedent: the claim after the "if" in a conditional statement. (page 92)

Argue: give reasons for a conclusion. (page 13)

Argument: consists of a set of at least two related claims, one of which is offered as justification, evidence, or support for another. (page 12)

Argumentation: a form of discourse in which we use arguments to understand and assess an issue more fully. (page 15)

Argumentation essay: one in which we engage with the positions and arguments of others on an issue. (page 293)

Argument essay: an essay focused on presenting and defending one or more arguments for a position. (page 293)

Argument from analogy: an argument that draws a parallel from a better known or less controversial case to a less well known or more controversial case, and concludes from a known trait of the first to something controversial or unknown about the second. (page 126)

Argument paraphrase: seeks to capture the core argument in the original text or dialogue. (page 66)

Argument partner: someone who is either defending or critiquing an argument (or sometimes both). (page 15)

Argument tree: an arrow diagram of a complex argument portraying the arguments, and sub-arguments. (page 220)

Arrow diagram: displays the structure of an argument using arrows to identify the reasons in relation to each other and to the conclusion. (page 69)

Assertion: a claim; it may be supported or unsupported. (page 59)

Assumed or missing reason: a claim that is required by the argument to establish relevance or sufficiency or both between the reasons and the conclusion. (page 109)

Balance of considerations argument: an argument that examines the relevant considerations for the alternative positions on an issue and argues that one is better. (page 309)

Basic reason: a claim that is a starting point of an argument for which no further justification is given. (page 73)

Biased sample: one that skews its representativeness in some way so that not all of the variability and frequency among the items have an equal chance of being in the sample. (page 121)

Borderline case: a case that straddles the fuzzy boundary between one concept and another. (page 243)

Brainstorming: involves trying to generate as much as we can on the topic in a given period of time without censoring, evaluating, or criticizing. (page 298)

Brainteasers: specific techniques we can use to systematically generate ideas about a topic. (page 298)

Buried or implicit claim: one that is contained within another assertion. (page 216)

Case for a position: a set of arguments and sub-arguments, and the responses to the main challenges, structured to show that the position is superior to other positions. (page 309)

Case in conceptual analysis: a concrete description of a complex situation that involves the use of the concept in question. (page 233)

Categorical claim: relates categories of things to one another. (page 89)

Causal inference: involves drawing a connection between two states of affairs and inferring that one causes the other. (page 123)

Challenge case: a detailed case that challenges a specific set of criteria. (page 240)

Challenge to a claim: to deny or challenge the acceptability of a claim. (page 79)

Challenger: someone who takes the role of critiquing a position or argument. (page 16)

Circumstantial *ad hominem* fallacy: involves trying to show that an individual's argument should be rejected because of the individual's personal circumstances and relationship with the subject of the argument. (page 172)

Claim: a statement that can be true or false. (page 9)

Clear: being clear means we can easily and accurately understand or express what is being said. (page 31)

Code words: involve a kind of ambiguity in which the context of an audience determines the meaning. (page 43)

Cogent: a non-deductive argument is cogent if the reasons are true and strongly support the conclusion. (page 119)

Components of argument: the reasons and conclusion. (page 58)

Concepts: ideas we have of things. (page 33)

Conceptual analysis: a method of analyzing the meaning and use of concepts that uses various kinds of cases and tests of those cases to gain an understanding of concepts. (page 233)

Conceptual claim: a claim about the meanings of words and expressions. (page 147)

Conclusion: the claim that is being supported, and for which reasons are given. (page 12)

Conditional argument: an argument that contains at least one conditional (if ..., then ...) statement. (page 93)

Conditional chain argument: an argument that reasons from one set of conditional claims to another set of conditional claims. (page 98)

Conditional statement: a single claim that asserts that one state of affairs is conditional upon another. (page 92)

Confirmation bias: occurs when we look for evidence to support our claims rather than for the possible evidence that might disconfirm or challenge our claims. (page 114)

Conjunct: one of the claims in a conjunction. (page 100)

Conjunction: a claim of the logical form *a* and *b*, where *a* and *b* are both themselves claims. (page 100)

Conjunctive argument: an argument involving a conjunction as a main reason or as a conclusion. (page 100)

Connotation: the subjective and emotional associations we make with a concept or word. (page 35)

Consensus within the field: occurs within a body of knowledge when the vast majority of experts agree on the relevant basic claims. (page 131)

Consequence: a causal effect of the state of affairs described in a claim. (page 161)

Consequent: the claim after the "then" in a conditional statement. (page 92)

Constitutive rules: those key rules or principles that define an activity. (page 20)

Content: includes the substance of what is being argued: the issues, claims, positions, and conclusions produced through the practice of arguing. (page 15)

Contrary or opposite case: a clear case of something that shares a key characteristic with the concept being analyzed, but is contrary to the concept being analyzed. (page 240)

Convergent argument: one in which each reason stands entirely on its own, that is, it constitutes an independent reason for the conclusion, and each of the reasons offers independent support for the conclusion. (page 70)

Core human value: one based on the kinds of beings we are and the kinds of things that enhance human well-being. (page 154)

Corollary: a claim that follows from an explicit statement. (page 161)

Correlation: a claim that two things vary together. (page 124)

Counterarguments: arguments given against a position or the reasons for a position. (page 21)

Counterexample: a specific example that shows either a general claim is false or unacceptable or that an argument pattern leads from true premises to a false conclusion. (page 107)

Countervailing cause: one that inhibits the action of another cause. (page 124)

Criterial claim: one based on some general criterion or criteria for evaluation. (page 149)

Critical reasoning: thinking systematically and reflecting on our reasoning by analyzing and evaluating it according to standards and assessing the standards we use. (page 5)

Deductive argument: one in which accepting the reasons logically requires that we accept the conclusion or we contradict ourselves. (page 83)

Definition: gives a word meaning by establishing a common understanding of a concept. (page 46)

Description: a statement (or set of statements) that provides an account or report of the facts, details, or particulars of a situation, event, or topic. (page 60)

Direct correlation: one in which the two variables either increase or decrease together. (page 124)

Direct observation report: a report based on the direct observation of someone. (page 146)

Dirty trick: any tactic in an argumentation that gives an unfair advantage to one side. (page 281)

Disanalogy: a significant dissimilarity that challenges the conclusion of an analogical argument. (page 128)

Disjunct: one of the alternatives in a disjunction. (page 99)

Disjunction: a claim of the logical form "either a or b." (page 98)

Doublespeak: involves using an abstract or imprecise word (or phrase) in place of a concrete or precise one with the intent of concealing what is being said. (page 42)

Elliptical: an elliptical use of language involves the use of a simpler or condensed statement for a more complex one. (page 44)

Emotive force: identifies the emotional nature (positive or negative) within the connotation. (page 37)

Empirical claim: one whose truth is ultimately established by observation and/or the inferences we make based on those observations. (page 144)

Essential definition: seeks to identify the necessary and sufficient conditions for the use of a concept. (page 48)

Ethical claim: a normative claim concerned with issues of right and wrong behaviour, fairness, equity, duty, obligation, and justice. (page 152)

Ethical principle: a normative claim that identifies a core human value and enshrines it in a general claim. (page 152)

Ethical rule: a rule of behaviour or judgment that identifies a specific kind of action as right or wrong. (page 153)

Ethics: (in this text) refers to the systematic and rational examination of the moral rules and principles of individuals and groups, as well as to the developing of a system of conduct based on rational grounds. (page 152)

Euphemism: involves using a neutral or vague term to refer to something unpleasant or offensive. (page 42)

Evaluative: means using criteria to evaluate or judge different alternatives. (page 149)

Evidential claim: a claim for which we can give reasons that refer to things in the world independent of subjective beliefs. (page 10)

Exclusive disjunction: disjunction in which only one of the disjuncts can be true. (page 99)

Expert: someone who knows a body of knowledge. (page 131)

Explanation: a statement (or set of statements) identifying the causes, context, consequences, factors influencing, or motivations of an object, process, state of affairs, or behaviour. (page 60)

Fallacy: a pattern of reasoning that is fundamentally erroneous. (page 166)

Fallacy of appeal to force or the threat of force: occurs when, instead of offering rational grounds for a position, the arguer uses or threatens to use coercion to get another to do something or to accept an idea. (page 175)

Fallacy of appeal to ignorance: uses an opponent's inability to prove something as evidence for the truth of the arguer's own conclusion. (page 186)

Fallacy of appeal to popularity, common belief, or common practice: rests on making the claim that something is true and should be accepted because it is widely believed, accepted, or done. (page 197)

Fallacy of appealing to emotion: involves appealing to emotions (such as pity, shame, flattery, disgust, sympathy, or some other emotion) instead of reasons as a way of persuading someone to believe or to do something. (page 176)

Fallacy of begging the question (circular argument): occurs when someone assumes what he or she has set out to prove. (page 189)

Fallacy of equivocation: is committed when an arguer uses one word or phrase that has two different meanings, and the different meanings are used in the argument. (page 191)

Fallacy of false cause: committed when the arguer fails to establish all of the conditions for a causal connection. (page 202)

Fallacy of false dichotomy (also called false dilemma or false alternative): occurs when the arguer presents only two alternatives, as though they exhaust the range of possibilities, when there are actually other alternatives, and then forces a choice between the two. (page 205)

Fallacy of faulty analogy: occurs when an arguer draws an inappropriate comparison between two things. (page 206)

Fallacy of faulty appeal to authority: occurs when there has been a significant breach of one or more of the conditions for a legitimate appeal to authority. (page 200)

Fallacy of hasty generalization: committed when an arguer violates the criteria for a good generalization. (page 202)

Fallacy of loaded presupposition: involves making a claim or asking a question that has a contentious presupposition buried in it, and not independently defending the presupposition. (page 188)

Fallacy of poisoning the well: involves attempting to put an opponent in such a position that anything he or she says will be dismissed prior to the opponent being heard. (page 174)

Fallacy of self-evident truth: involves the arguer presenting a contentious position in need of defence as being self-evident and not in need of defence. (page 186)

Fallacy of shifting the burden of proof: occurs when the arguer defending the position shifts the burden of proof to the critic. (page 185)

Field or body of knowledge: an area of inquiry in which there is widespread consensus on the basic claims, evidence, and theories, based on evidence available to anyone, and this consensus is recognized by others as authoritative. (page 131)

Final conclusion: the last conclusion of a serial argument. (page 73)

Free-writing: involves writing for a given period of time on the topic without editing or constraining what we are saying. (page 298)

Frequency: refers to how often the relevant characteristics occur within the population. (page 120)

General claim: a claim about a group or class. (page 120)

Generalization: the result of a process of reasoning from a limited number of cases to a broader range of cases. (page 119)

Genetic fallacy: attempts to show that a claim or idea is false or should be discounted because of its origins. (page 195)

Hostile climate variant of the poisoning the well fallacy: involves establishing a climate where anything said by the target group is dismissed as not being worthy of consideration. (page 179)

Hypostatization: (also called reification: literally, making a thing of a concept) involves ascribing existence to abstract or conceptual entities and treating them as though they are concrete entities with the properties of agents. (page 43)

Illustration: a statement that provides an example for another claim. (page 60)

Imperfect correlation: one in which only some instances are associated with one another and vary together. (page 124)

Implication: a symbolic effect that follows from a claim. (page 161)

Imprecise: being imprecise involves being less exact than the context requires or allows. (page 31)

Inclusive disjunction: one in which both disjuncts may be true. (page 99)

Inference indicator: a word or phrase that indicates there is a logical relationship between one claim (or set of claims) and another claim (or set of claims), and indicates their functions as reasons or a conclusion in an argument, and is more reliable than using position and function. (page 63)

Inference to the best explanation: a non-deductive argument in which the conclusion is offered as an explanation for the facts cited in the reasons. (page 135)

Informed opinion: the opinion of an individual who is knowledgeable about a particular subject. (page 134)

Interdependence form of begging the question: occurs when the reasons are acceptable only if we have already accepted the conclusion or some important aspect of the conclusion. (page 190)

Intermediate conclusion: a claim that serves as a conclusion of at least one reason as well as a reason for yet another argument. (page 73)

Invalid: a deductive argument is invalid if we can affirm the reasons and deny the conclusion. (page 86)

Invented or imaginary cases: hypothetical situations that help us clarify the logical criteria of a concept. (page 247)

Inverse correlation: one in which the two variables vary inversely to one another. (page 124)

Issue: a point of contention within a given context and between at least two points of view that elicits disagreement about the truth of the issue. (page 17)

Limitation of scope: refers to limiting the population about which we are generalizing. (page 122)

Line of argument: the set of arguments, supporting arguments, and challenges and responses that make up one vertical column of argument in an arrow diagram. (page 220)

Linked argument: has two or more reasons related to one another that must be considered part of the same argument. (page 70)

Linked reasons: ones that need to be considered together. (page 70)

Logical equivalence (or definitional) form of begging the question: occurs when the reasons and conclusion say the same thing but in different words. (page 189)

Logical structure: (or logical form) of an argument is the logical relationship between the terms or claims of an argument. (page 89)

Logical terms: terms that show the logical relationship between claims or terms within an argument. (page 89)

Lookalikes: fallacies that have similar characteristics and are commonly mistaken for one another. (page 169)

Main issue: the issue we are trying to resolve or understand. (page 18)

Meaning or sense of a concept: the rules of use for a concept, often captured in a definition. It is derived from a set of shared expectations or rules of use that members of a language community have about a given concept. (page 34)

Mediant or mixed case: fulfills only part of the criteria for the concept and often has features of several different concepts. (page 242)

Metaphor: a literary device in which a phrase that refers to one thing is applied to a different kind of thing. (page 45)

Missing or unstated conclusion: a conclusion that follows from the stated reasons in an argument but is not explicitly stated by the author. (page 109)

Mixed claims: claims whose criteria for acceptability depend upon some combination of empirical, conceptual, and normative criteria. (page 155)

Morals and morality: (in this text) refers to the specific principles, rules, and behaviours of individuals and groups. (page 152)

Narrative: a descriptive account that tells a story. (page 60)

Necessary condition: a condition that must be present for the resultant condition to occur, but by itself is not sufficient to produce the resultant condition. (pages 48, 91)

Neutral claim: a claim with little or no emotional connotation. (page 37)

Neutralize a fallacy: to render the fallacy ineffective by showing what is wrong with it. (page 182)

Non-deductive argument: one in which the reasons, if accepted, provide plausible or probable grounds for accepting the conclusion. (page 83)

Normative claim: one that expresses or prescribes a value. (page 148)

Occam's Razor: a principle for evaluating alternate hypotheses which states that, given two alternatives, so long as there are no differences in the observed consequences, we should prefer the one with the fewest principles or assumptions. (page 137)

One-paragraph argument: a paragraph in which we develop the basic logical structure of our case. (page 307)

Operational definition: defines a concept by prescribing a procedure or operation required to determine if something is the case or is occurring. The result of the procedure or operation is the concept being defined. (page 47)

Opinion: an unsupported belief. (page 9)

Ostensive definition: defines a concept by providing examples of it rather than outlining criteria for its use. (page 47)

Paradigm case: an ideal, perfect, or model case of the concept being analyzed. (page 239)

Paraphrase: involves restating in one's own words the core meaning of a passage or text. (page 65)

Perfect correlation: one in which in every instance whenever one of the correlated items varies the other also varies. (page 124)

Persuasive definition: uses evaluative language in an attempt to convince people to take a particular view. (page 51)

Plausible claim: a claim is plausible if, given a background set of information, the claim could be true, is supported by independent evidence, and is likely or worth considering. (page 137)

Population: the group of things we are drawing a conclusion about. (page 120)

Portraying the structure of an argument: involves identifying the component parts of argument and their relationship to one another in that particular argument and then displaying them in either standard form or arrow diagram. (page 67)

Position: a stand taken on an issue. (page 19)

Practical claim: a normative claim concerned with decisions about appropriate courses of action. (page 152)

Precise: being precise involves being as exact as the context requires or allows. (page 31)

Preference claim: one based on a personal expression of preference. (page 149)

Presupposition: a claim that logically precedes another claim and must be true in order for the claim it presupposes to be true. (page 158)

Principle of Significant Difference: holds that if we propose to treat two things differently that appear to be the same, we must provide some reason for doing so. (page 157)

Principle of Similar Cases: holds that all things that are alike should be treated alike. (page 157)

Process: how the people in an argument relate to each other. (page 16)

Propositional claim: relates claims to one another. (page 89)

Qualifier: a word that restricts a claim by limiting the kinds of things the claim applies to. (page 40)

Quantifier: a word that indicates how many members of a group a claim applies to. (page 40)

Question of concept: a problem that hinges on the meaning of a concept, the relation of one concept to another, or the application of a concept to a specific situation. (page 234)

Rational inquiry: the rational pursuit of truth about an issue through reasoned discussion, using arguments and the rational appreciation of different perspectives. (page 16)

Reason: a claim that provides support, evidence, or justification for the conclusion. (sometimes called a premise) (page 12)

Reasoned opinion: a belief for which explicit reasons are provided. (page 10)

Reasoning: the process of connecting and assessing ideas. (page 4)

Red herring fallacy: involves introducing an irrelevant issue into an argument to confuse or sidetrack discussion of the issue. (page 192)

Referent: the object (thing, process, activity) that a concept or word refers to. (page 34)

Related concept: concept that is connected to the concept under analysis, either as part of the explicit criteria for the concept being analyzed or as part of the vocabulary of related concepts. (page 244)

Reliable generalization: one which meets the basis conditions for reliability. (page 121)

Reportive definition: defines the meaning of a term by reporting how it is used within a language community. (page 48)

Representative sample: a sample is representative if it accurately represents the variability in the population and frequency of that variability. (page 120)

Response to a challenge: the denial of a challenge claim. (page 79)

Sample: the group of things actually observed before arriving at a generalization. (page 120)

Science-fiction imaginary case: one in which we imagine fundamental changes in the reality we experience. (page 247)

Scope of a claim: the range of instances that a claim applies to. (page 158)

Scope of a definition: the range of cases that a definition applies to appropriately. (page 52)

Serial argument: an argument within an argument, where the conclusion of one argument serves as the reason for another argument. (page 73)

Signposts: are both logical cue words and other indicators that authors use to identify the structure of the text. (page 215)

Simple opinion: a belief for which no explicit reasons are provided. (page 9)

Slippery slope fallacy: occurs when the arguer suggests one action sets off a sequence of others that will lead to an inevitable end result, which is usually seen as undesirable. (page 204)

Sound argument: a deductive argument is sound if it is valid and has true reasons. (page 86)

Standard form of an argument: a way of displaying the structure of an argument with each claim on a separate numbered line with the reasons above and the conclusion below a line. The conclusion is also indicated by three equilateral dots. (page 67)

Stipulative definition: specifies a meaning for a word in a particular context. (page 50)

Straw person (originally "straw man") fallacy: occurs when a simpler or distorted argument is attacked instead of a stronger one. (page 193)

Sufficient condition: one whose occurrence is sufficient to produce or indicate the presence of another. (pages 49, 91)

Summary: involves restating in one's own words the order of ideas as they are presented in the passage, text, or discussion, without necessarily capturing the logical connections among the claims. (pages 66, 119)

Supported claim: a claim for which support, justification, or evidence is given. (page 9)

Synopsis: a brief characterization of the conclusion and the main line(s) of development of the argument written in your own words. (page 219)

Thesis: the conclusion of an argument; in an argument essay it is the main point being argued in the essay. (page 301)

Topic: a subject for discussion, a term in an argument. (page 103)

Topics model: a method for determining validity by connecting the topics in the conclusion with the topics in the reasons. (page 103)

Vague: a concept or claim is vague when its meaning or application is unclear, fuzzy, or inexact in the context of the purposes for which it is being used. (page 38)

Valid: a deductive argument is valid if accepting the reasons logically requires us to accept the conclusion. (page 86)

Variability: the range of difference or variation within the population. (page 120)

Weighting criteria: involves giving priority to some criteria over others. (page 150)

Words: linguistic entities that convey a meaning. (page 33)

INDEX

Note: Boldface terms are defined in the Glossary.

abstract terms, 317
abusive *ad hominem* fallacy, 172
academic discourse, 322–323
active listening, 262–264
ad hominem fallacy, 168, 169, 172–173, 178–182
advocates, 16
aesthetic claims, 152
affirming claims, 58, 94
ambiguity, 41–42, 221–222
ambiguous positions, 19
analogies, 45, 126–129
analogues, 206
analysis of arguments. *See also* argument structure; passage
    analysis model
    argument identification, 59–62
    claim identification, 58–59
    components of the argument, 58
    conclusion identification, 62–67
    defined, 5
    inference indicators, 63–64
    mixed prose passages, 76–78
    order of reasons and conclusions, 65–67
    reason identification, 62–67
annotation, 215–217
antecedents, 92, 168
appealing to emotion fallacy, 176–177, 181
appeals to authority or experts, 130–134
appeals to ignorance fallacy, 186
appeal to force or threat of force fallacy, 175–176, 180–181
appeal to popularity, common belief, or common practice,
    197–199
applications, 275–278
argue, 13
argument. *See also* analysis of arguments; **deductive
    arguments; non-deductive arguments**
    assessment of, 223–227
    components of, 58
    critical analysis of, 14
    defined, 12, 59
    fallacies compared, 166–167
    identification of, 59–62
    overview, 12–13
argumentation
    challenges and responses, generally, 272–273
    clarification of meaning, 267
    components of, 15–16

constitutive rules of, 20–23
counterexamples, 275–279
defined, 20, 25, 259–260
dirty tricks during, 281–284
dynamics of, 24–25
eliciting arguments in, 264–266
escalation and de-escalation, 289–290
evaluation, 268
implications, 279–280
issue analysis, 285–286
issues and, 17
meaning challenges, 273
outcome sought and, 261–262
overview, 15, 259–260
purposes of, 324
for rational inquiry, 16–17
sample dialogue for, 286–289
truth of claim challenges, 274–275
unstated reason identification, 269–271
argumentation essays, 293–294
argument essays
    argument development, 304–308
    audience-based prose in, 310–314
    composing process for, 295–296
    idea generation, 297–300
    making cases, 309–310
    overview, 293–294
    revising and editing, 315–318
    thesis for, 301–304
argument paraphrases, 66
argument partners, 15–16, 21
argument patterns, 89–90, 110–111
argument principle, 21, 23
arguments from analogy, 126–129
argument structure
    arrow diagrams, 69–71
    challenges to a claim, 79–80
    complex arguments, 71–76
    standard form, 67–69
argument trees, 220
arrow diagrams, 69–71, 220
assertions, 59
assignment analysis, 295–296
assumed reasons and conclusions, 109–113
audiences, 295, 310–314
authorities, appeals to, 130–134